ANNUAL EDITIONS

Global Issues 10/11

Twenty-Sixth Edition

EDITOR

Robert M. Jackson
California State University, Chico

Robert M. Jackson is a professor emeritus of political science and past dean of the School of Graduate, International and Sponsored Programs at California State University, Chico. In addition to teaching courses on third-world politics and globalization, he has published articles on the international political economy, international relations simulations, and political behavior. Dr. Jackson has been responsible for numerous international training programs for professionals from throughout the world. International educational exchanges and study-abroad programs also have been an area of special interest. His research and professional travels include China, Japan, Hong Kong, Taiwan, Singapore, Malaysia, Spain, Portugal, Morocco, Belgium, Germany, the Czech Republic, the Netherlands, Italy, Russia, Mexico, Guatemala, Honduras, Costa Rica, El Salvador, Brazil, Chile, and Argentina.

McGraw Hill

Connect
Learn
Succeed™

Mc Graw Hill

Connect
Learn
Succeed™

ANNUAL EDITIONS: GLOBAL ISSUES, TWENTY-SIXTH EDITION

Published by McGraw-Hill, a business unit of The McGraw-Hill Companies, Inc., 1221 Avenue of the Americas, New York, NY 10020. Copyright © 2011 by The McGraw-Hill Companies, Inc.

Some ancillaries, including electronic and print components, may not be available to customers outside the United States.

Annual Editions is published by the **Contemporary Learning Series** group within The McGraw-Hill Higher Education division.

1 2 3 4 5 6 7 8 9 0 WDQ/WDQ 1 0 9 8 7 6 5 4 3 2 1 0

ISBN 978–0–07–805058–9
MHID 0–07–805058–8
ISSN 1093–278X

Managing Editor: *Larry Loeppke*
Developmental Editor: *Debra A. Henricks*
Editorial Coordinator: *Mary Foust*
Editorial Assistant: *Cindy Hedley*
Production Service Assistant: *Rita Hingtgen*
Permissions Coordinator: *DeAnna Dausner*
Senior Marketing Manager: *Julie Keck*
Senior Marketing Communications Specialist: *Mary Klein*
Marketing Coordinator: *Alice Link*
Director Specialized Production: *Faye Schilling*
Senior Project Manager: *Joyce Watters*
Design Specialist: *Margarite Reynolds*
Production Supervisor: *Sue Culbertson*
Cover Graphics: *Kristine Jubeck*

Compositor: Laserwords Private Limited
Cover Images: The McGraw-Hill Companies, Inc./Jill Braaten (inset); © Getty Images/RF (background)

Library in Congress Cataloging-in-Publication Data
Main entry under title: Annual Editions: Global Issues. 2010/2011.
  1. Global Issues—Periodicals by Jackson, Robert M., *comp.* II. Title: Global Issues
658'.05

www.mhhe.com

Editors/Academic Advisory Board

Members of the Academic Advisory Board are instrumental in the final selection of articles for each edition of ANNUAL EDITIONS. Their review of articles for content, level, and appropriateness provides critical direction to the editors and staff. We think that you will find their careful consideration well reflected in this volume.

ANNUAL EDITIONS: Global Issues 10/11
26th Edition

EDITOR

Robert M. Jackson
California State University, Chico

ACADEMIC ADVISORY BOARD MEMBERS

Preface

The beginning of the new millennium was celebrated with considerable fanfare. The prevailing mood in much of the world was that there was a great deal for which we could congratulate ourselves. The very act of sequentially watching on television live celebrations from one time zone to the next was proclaimed as a testimonial to globalization and the benefits of modern technology. The tragic events of September 11, 2001, however, were a stark reminder of the intense emotions and methods of destruction available to those determined to challenge the status quo. The subsequent wars in Afghanistan and Iraq along with continuing acts of terror have dampened the optimism that was expressed at the outset of the twenty-first century.

As the second decade of the twenty-first century begins, new challenges are rising to the top of the political agenda. Global climate change, growing pressures on oil's supply and demand equation, and the problem of nuclear proliferation are among those most frequently discussed.

While the mass media may focus on the latest crisis for a few weeks or months, the broad forces that are shaping the world are seldom given the in-depth analysis that they warrant. Scholarly research about these historic forces of change can be found in a wide variety of publications, but these are not readily accessible. In addition, students just beginning to study global issues can be discouraged by the terminology and abstract concepts that characterize much of the scholarly literature. In selecting and organizing the materials for this book, we have been mindful of the needs of beginning students and have, thus, selected articles that invite the student into the subject matter.

Each unit begins with an introductory article(s) providing a broad overview of the subject area to be studied. The following articles examine in more detail specific case studies that often identify the positive steps being taken to remedy problems. Recent events are a continual reminder that the world faces many serious challenges, the magnitude of which would discourage even the most stouthearted individual. While identifying problems is easier than solving them, it is encouraging to know that many are being addressed.

Perhaps the most striking feature of the study of contemporary global issues is the absence of any single, widely held theory that explains what is taking place. As a result, we have made a conscious effort to present a wide variety of points of view. The most important consideration has been to present global issues from an international perspective, rather than from a purely U.S. or Western point of view. By encompassing materials originally published in different countries and written by authors of various nationalities, the anthology represents the great diversity of opinions that people hold. Two writers examining the same phenomenon may reach very different conclusions. It is not just a question of who is right or wrong, but rather understanding that people from different vantage points can have differing perspectives on an issue.

Another major consideration when organizing these materials was to explore the complex interrelationship of factors that produce social problems such as poverty. Too often, discussions of this problem (and others like it) are reduced to arguments about the fallacies of not following the correct economic policy or not having the correct form of government. As a result, many people overlook the interplay of historic, cultural, environmental, economic, and political factors that form complex webs that bring about many different problems. Every effort has been made to select materials that illustrate this complex interaction of factors, stimulating the beginning student to consider realistic rather than overly simplistic approaches to the pressing problems that threaten the existence of civilization.

In addition to an annotated table of contents and a topic guide, included in this edition of *Annual Editions: Global Issues* are Internet references that can be used to further explore topics addressed in the articles.

This is the twentieth-sixth edition of *Annual Editions: Global Issues.* When looking back over more than two decades of work, a great deal has taken place in world affairs, and the contents and organization of the book reflect these changes. Nonetheless, there is one underlying constant. It is my continuing goal to work with the editors and staff at McGraw-Hill Contemporary Learning Series to provide materials that encourage the readers of this book to develop a life-long appreciation of the complex and rapidly changing world in which we live. This collection of articles is an invitation to further explore the global issues of the twenty-first century and become personally involved in the great issues of our time.

I want to thank Jennifer Emick for her outstanding assistance on all phases of the development of this latest edition.

Finally, materials in this book were selected for both their intellectual insights and readability. Timely and well-written materials should stimulate good classroom lectures and discussions. I hope that students and teachers will enjoy using this book. Readers can have input into the next edition by completing and returning the postage-paid article rating form in the back of the book.

Robert M. Jackson
Editor

Contents

UNIT 1
Global Issues in the Twenty-First Century: An Overview

The concepts in bold italics are developed in the article. For further expansion, please refer to the Topic Guide.

UNIT 2
Population and Food Production

UNIT 3
The Global Environment and Natural Resources Utilization

The concepts in bold italics are developed in the article. For further expansion, please refer to the Topic Guide.

UNIT 4
Political Economy

The concepts in bold italics are developed in the article. For further expansion, please refer to the Topic Guide.

UNIT 5
Conflict

The concepts in bold italics are developed in the article. For further expansion, please refer to the Topic Guide.

UNIT 6
Cooperation

The concepts in bold italics are developed in the article. For further expansion, please refer to the Topic Guide.

UNIT 7
Values and Visions

The concepts in bold italics are developed in the article. For further expansion, please refer to the Topic Guide.

Correlation Guide

The *Annual Editions* series provides students with convenient, inexpensive access to current, carefully selected articles from the public press. **Annual Editions: Global Issues 10/11** is an easy-to-use reader that presents articles on important topics such as *population, environment, political economy,* and many more. For more information on *Annual Editions* and other *McGraw-Hill Contemporary Learning Series* titles, visit www.mhhe.com/cls.

This convenient guide matches the units in **Annual Editions: Global Issues 10/11** with the corresponding chapters in two of our best-selling McGraw-Hill Political Science textbooks by Rourke and Boyer.

Annual Editions: Global Issues 10/11	International Politics on the World Stage, Brief, 8/e by Rourke/Boyer	International Politics on the World Stage, 12/e by Rourke
Unit 1: Global Issues in the Twenty-First Century: An Overview	**Chapter 1:** Thinking and Caring about World Politics **Chapter 2:** The Evolution of World Politics **Chapter 5:** Globalization: The Alternative Orientation	**Chapter 1:** Thinking and Caring about World Politics **Chapter 2:** The Evolution of World Politics **Chapter 5:** Globalism: The Alternative Orientation
Unit 2: Population and Food Production	**Chapter 8:** International Law and Human Rights	**Chapter 14:** Preserving and Enhancing Human Rights and Dignity
Unit 3: The Global Environment and Natural Resources Utilization	**Chapter 12:** Preserving and Enhancing the Biosphere	**Chapter 15:** Preserving and Enhancing the Biosphere
Unit 4: Political Economy	**Chapter 6:** Power, Statecraft, and the National State: The Traditional Structure **Chapter 7:** Intergovernmental Organizations: Alternative Governance **Chapter 10:** National Economic Competition: The Traditional Road **Chapter 11:** International Economics: The Alternative Road	**Chapter 7:** Intergovernmental Organization: Alternative Governance **Chapter 8:** National Power and Statecraft: The Traditional Approach **Chapter 12:** National Economic Competition: The Traditional Road
Unit 5: Conflict	**Chapter 6:** Power, Statecraft, and the National States: The Traditional Structure **Chapter 9:** Pursuing Security	**Chapter 8:** National Power and Statecraft: The Traditional Approach **Chapter 10:** National Security: The Traditional Road **Chapter 11:** International Security: The Alternative Road
Unit 6: Cooperation	**Chapter 8:** International Law and Human Rights **Chapter 11:** International Economics: The Alternative Road	**Chapter 9:** International Law and Justice: An Alternative Approach **Chapter 13:** International Economic Cooperation: The Alternative Road
Unit 7: Values and Visions	**Chapter 3:** Levels of Analysis and Foreign Policy **Chapter 8:** International Law and Human Rights	**Chapter 3:** Levels of Analysis and Foreign Policy **Chapter 14:** Preserving and Enhancing Human Rights and Dignity

Topic Guide

This topic guide suggests how the selections in this book relate to the subjects covered in your course. You may want to use the topics listed on these pages to search the Web more easily.

On the following pages a number of websites have been gathered specifically for this book. They are arranged to reflect the units of this Annual Editions reader. You can link to these sites by going to *http://www.mhhe.com/cls*.

All the articles that relate to each topic are listed below the bold-faced term.

Agriculture
1. Global Trends 2025: A Transformed World: Executive Summary
2. Could Food Shortages Bring Down Civilization?
6. Get Smart
11. The Next Breadbasket?: How Africa Could Save the World—and Itself
14. Water of Life in Peril
21. Can Extreme Poverty Be Eliminated?
22. The Ideology of Development
26. Promises and Poverty

Communication
19. It's a Flat World, after All
20. Why the World Isn't Flat
35. Tehran's Take: Understanding Iran's U.S. Policy

Conservation
2. Could Food Shortages Bring Down Civilization?
3. Navigating the Energy Transition
14. Water of Life in Peril
15. Troubled Waters
16. Acacia Avenue: How to Save Indonesia's Dwindling Rainforests
17. Cry of the Wild

Cultural customs and values
4. The Rise of the Rest
5. Feminists and Fundamentalists
7. The Century Ahead
8. Population & Sustainability
9. Why Migration Matters
18. Globalization and Its Contents
19. It's a Flat World, after All
20. Why the World Isn't Flat
21. Can Extreme Poverty Be Eliminated?
22. The Ideology of Development
24. The Case against the West: America and Europe in the Asian Century
34. Lifting the Veil: Understanding the Roots of Islamic Militancy
38. Geneva Conventions
39. Is Bigger Better?
40. A World Enslaved
42. Humanity's Common Values: Seeking a Positive Future
43. Life, Religion and Everything
44. Don't Blame the Caveman: Why Do We Rape, Kill and Sleep Around?

Demographics
1. Global Trends 2025: A Transformed World: Executive Summary
7. The Century Ahead
8. Population & Sustainability
9. Why Migration Matters
10. Pandemic Pandemonium

Dependencies, international
4. The Rise of the Rest
9. Why Migration Matters

11. The Next Breadbasket?: How Africa Could Save the World—and Itself
18. Globalization and Its Contents
19. It's a Flat World, after All
20. Why the World Isn't Flat
24. The Case against the West: America and Europe in the Asian Century
25. "Chimerica" Is Headed for a Divorce
26. Promises and Poverty
28. It's Still the One

Development, economic
1. Global Trends 2025: A Transformed World: Executive Summary
2. Could Food Shortages Bring Down Civilization?
4. The Rise of the Rest
5. Feminists and Fundamentalists
10. Pandemic Pandemonium
11. The Next Breadbasket?: How Africa Could Save the World—and Itself
18. Globalization and Its Contents
19. It's a Flat World, after All
20. Why the World Isn't Flat
24. The Case against the West: America and Europe in the Asian Century
26. Promises and Poverty
27. Not Your Father's Latin America
39. Is Bigger Better?

Development, social
5. Feminists and Fundamentalists
11. The Next Breadbasket?: How Africa Could Save the World—and Itself
21. Can Extreme Poverty Be Eliminated?
22. The Ideology of Development
24. The Case against the West: America and Europe in the Asian Century
26. Promises and Poverty
31. The Real War in Mexico: How Democracy Can Defeat the Drug Cartels
38. Geneva Conventions
39. Is Bigger Better?
41. Chile Starts Early
42. Humanity's Common Values: Seeking a Positive Future
43. Life, Religion and Everything
44. Don't Blame the Caveman: Why Do We Rape, Kill and Sleep Around?

Ecology
3. Navigating the Energy Transition
6. Get Smart
8. Population & Sustainability
12. Climate Change
14. Water of Life in Peril
15. Troubled Waters
16. Acacia Avenue: How to Save Indonesia's Dwindling Rainforests
17. Cry of the Wild
19. It's a Flat World, after All
21. Can Extreme Poverty Be Eliminated?
43. Life, Religion and Everything

Internet References

The following Internet sites have been selected to support the articles found in this reader. These sites were available at the time of publication. However, because websites often change their structure and content, the information listed may no longer be available. We invite you to visit http://www.mhhe.com/cls for easy access to these sites.

Annual Editions: Global Issues 10/11

General Sources

U.S. Information Agency (USIA)
http://www.america.gov

USIA's home page provides definitions, related documentation, and discussions of topics of concern to students of global issues. The site addresses today's Hot Topics as well as ongoing issues that form the foundation of the field.

World Wide Web Virtual Library: International Affairs Resources
http://www.etown.edu/vl

Surf this site and its extensive links to learn about specific countries and regions, to research various think tanks and international organizations, and to study such vital topics as international law, development, the international economy, human rights, and peacekeeping.

UNIT 1: Global Issues in the Twenty-First Century: An Overview

The Henry L. Stimson Center
http://www.stimson.org

The Stimson Center, a nonpartisan organization, focuses on issues where policy, technology, and politics intersect. Use this site to find varying assessments of U.S. foreign policy in the post–cold war world and to research other topics.

The Heritage Foundation
http://www.heritage.org

This page offers discussion about and links to many sites having to do with foreign policy and foreign affairs, including news and commentary, policy review, events, and a resource bank.

The North-South Institute
http://www.nsi-ins.ca/ensi/index.htm

Searching this site of the North-South Institute, which works to strengthen international development cooperation and enhance gender and social equity, will help you find information and debates on a variety of global issues.

UNIT 2: Population and Food Production

The Hunger Project
http://www.thp.org

Browse through this nonprofit organization's site, whose goal is the sustainable end to global hunger through leadership at all levels of society. The Hunger Project contends that the persistence of hunger is at the heart of the major security issues threatening our planet.

Penn Library: Resources by Subject
http://www.library.upenn.edu/cgi-bin/res/sr.cgi

This vast site is rich in links to information about subjects of interest to students of global issues. Its extensive population and demography resources address such concerns as migration, family planning, and health and nutrition in various world regions.

World Health Organization
http://www.who.int

This home page of the World Health Organization will provide you with links to a wealth of statistical and analytical information about health and the environment in the developing world.

WWW Virtual Library: Demography & Population Studies
http://demography.anu.edu.au/VirtualLibrary

A definitive guide to demography and population studies can be found at this site. It contains a multitude of important links to information about global poverty and hunger.

UNIT 3: The Global Environment and Natural Resources Utilization

National Geographic Society
http://www.nationalgeographic.com

This site provides links to material related to the atmosphere, the oceans, and other environmental topics.

National Oceanic and Atmospheric Administration (NOAA)
http://www.noaa.gov

Through this home page of NOAA, part of the U.S. Department of Commerce, you can find information about coastal issues, fisheries, climate, and more. The site provides many links to research materials and to other Web resources.

SocioSite: Sociological Subject Areas
http://www.pscw.uva.nl/sociosite/TOPICS

This huge site provides many references of interest to those interested in global issues, such as links to information on ecology and the impact of consumerism.

United Nations Environment Programme (UNEP)
http://www.unep.ch

Consult this home page of UNEP for links to critical topics of concern to students of global issues, including desertification, migratory species, and the impact of trade on the environment.

UNIT 4: Political Economy

Belfer Center for Science and International Affairs (BCSIA)
http://ksgwww.harvard.edu/csia

BCSIA is the hub of Harvard University's John F. Kennedy School of Government's research, teaching, and training in international affairs related to security, environment, and technology.

U.S. Agency for International Development
http://www.usaid.gov

Broad and overlapping issues such as democracy, population and health, economic growth, and development are covered on this website. It provides specific information about different regions and countries.

Internet References

The World Bank Group

http://www.worldbank.org

News, press releases, summaries of new projects, speeches, publications, and coverage of numerous topics regarding development, countries, and regions are provided at this World Bank site. It also contains links to other important global financial organizations.

UNIT 5: Conflict

DefenseLINK

http://www.defenselink.mil

Learn about security news and research-related publications at this U.S. Department of Defense site. Links to related sites of interest are provided. The information systems BosniaLINK and GulfLINK can also be found here. Use the search function to investigate such issues as land mines.

Federation of American Scientists (FAS)

http://www.fas.org

FAS, a nonprofit policy organization, maintains this site to provide coverage of and links to such topics as global security, peace, and governance in the post–cold war world. It notes a variety of resources of value to students of global issues.

ISN International Relations and Security Network

http://www.isn.ethz.ch

This site, maintained by the Center for Security Studies and Conflict Research, is a clearinghouse for information on international relations and security policy. Topics are listed by category (Traditional Dimensions of Security, New Dimensions of Security, and Related Fields) and by major world region.

The NATO Integrated Data Service (NIDS)

http://www.nato.int/structur/nids/nids.htm

NIDS was created to bring information on security-related matters to within easy reach of the widest possible audience. Check out this website to review North Atlantic Treaty Organization documentation of all kinds, to read *NATO Review,* and to explore key issues in the field of European security and transatlantic cooperation.

UNIT 6: Cooperation

Carnegie Endowment for International Peace

http://www.ceip.org

An important goal of this organization is to stimulate discussion and learning among both experts and the public at large on a wide range of international issues. The site provides links to *Foreign Policy,* to the Moscow Center, to descriptions of various programs, and much more.

OECD/FDI Statistics

http://www.oecd.org/statistics

Explore world trade and investment trends and statistics on this site from the Organization for Economic Cooperation and Development. It provides links to many related topics and addresses the issues on a country-by-country basis.

U.S. Institute of Peace

http://www.usip.org

USIP, which was created by the U.S. Congress to promote peaceful resolution of international conflicts, seeks to educate people and to disseminate information on how to achieve peace. Click on Highlights, Publications, Events, Research Areas, and Library and Links.

UNIT 7: Values and Visions

Human Rights Web

http://www.hrweb.org

The history of the human rights movement, text on seminal figures, landmark legal and political documents, and ideas on how individuals can get involved in helping to protect human rights around the world can be found in this valuable site.

InterAction

http://www.interaction.org

InterAction encourages grassroots action and engages government policymakers on advocacy issues. The organization's Advocacy Committee provides this site to inform people on its initiatives to expand international humanitarian relief, refugee, and development-assistance programs.

World Map

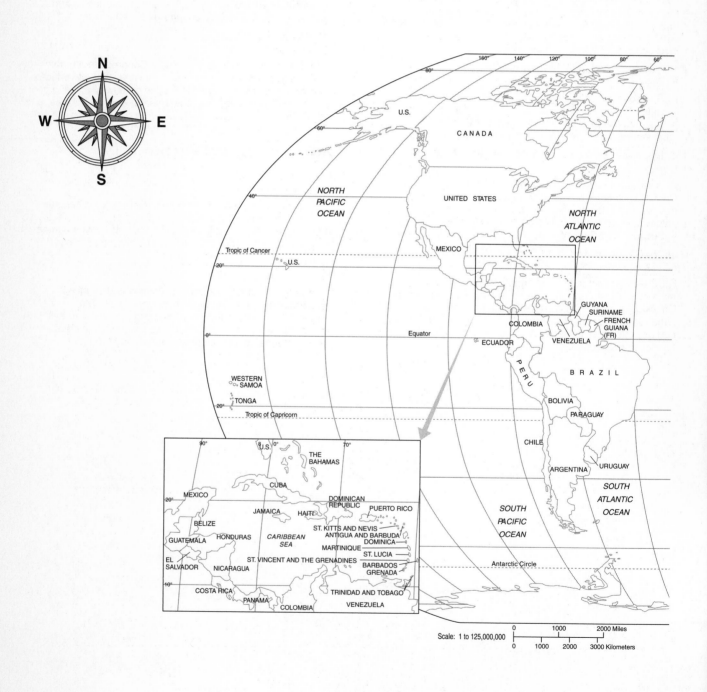

N
W E
S

160° 140° 120° 100° 80° 60°
80°

U.S.
CANADA
60°
UNITED STATES
40°
NORTH
PACIFIC
OCEAN
MEXICO
Tropic of Cancer
20°
U.S.

NORTH
ATLANTIC
OCEAN

GUYANA
SURINAME
FRENCH
GUIANA
(FR)
COLOMBIA
VENEZUELA
Equator 0°
ECUADOR

P E R U
B R A Z I L

WESTERN
SAMOA
BOLIVIA
TONGA
PARAGUAY
20°
Tropic of Capricorn

CHILE
SOUTH
ATLANTIC
OCEAN

ARGENTINA URUGUAY

SOUTH
PACIFIC
OCEAN

Antarctic Circle

90° 0° U.S. 0° 70°
THE
BAHAMAS
MEXICO CUBA
20° DOMINICAN
REPUBLIC PUERTO RICO
JAMAICA HAITI
BELIZE ST. KITTS AND NEVIS
ANTIGUA AND BARBUDA
GUATEMALA HONDURAS CARIBBEAN DOMINICA
SEA MARTINIQUE ST. LUCIA
EL ST. VINCENT AND THE GRENADINES
SALVADOR NICARAGUA BARBADOS
GRENADA
10°
COSTA RICA TRINIDAD AND TOBAGO
PANAMA
COLOMBIA VENEZUELA

Scale: 1 to 125,000,000

0 1000 2000 Miles
0 1000 2000 3000 Kilometers

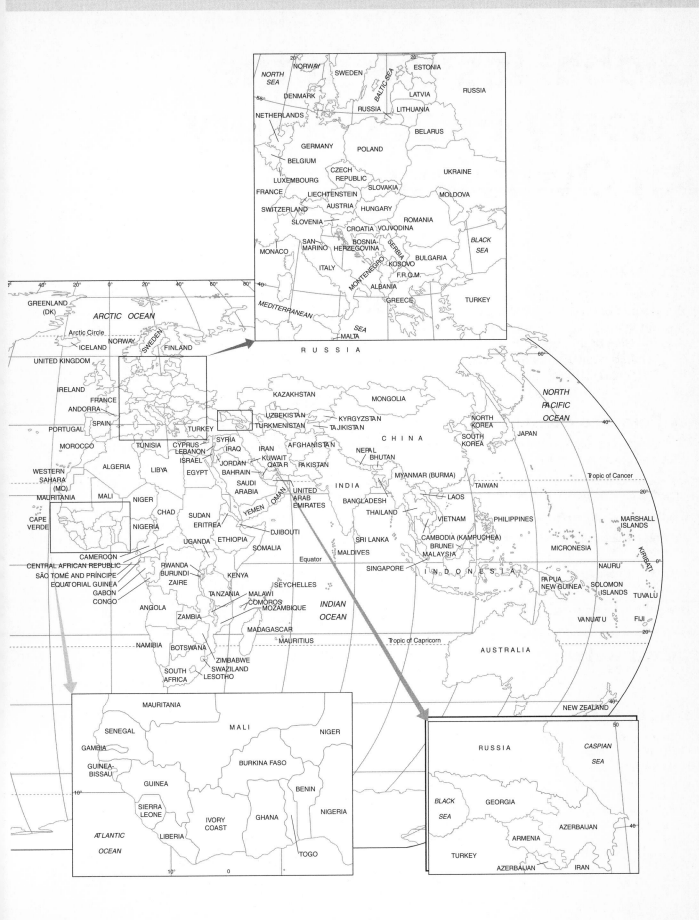

UNIT 1

Global Issues in the Twenty-First Century: An Overview

Unit Selections

Key Points to Consider

• Do the analyses of any of the authors in this section employ the assumptions implicit in the allegory of the balloon? If so, how? If not, how are the assumptions of the authors different?

• All the authors point to interactions among different factors. What are some of the relationships that they cite? How do the authors differ in terms of the relationships they emphasize?

• What assets that did not exist 100 years ago do people now have to solve problems?

• What events during the past 65 years have had the greatest impact on shaping the realities of contemporary international affairs?

• What do you consider to be the five most pressing global problems of today? How do your answers compare to those of your family, friends, and classmates?

• Describe how international affairs might differ in the year 2050. Why do you think these differences will come about?

Student Website

www.mhhe.com/cls

Internet References

The Henry L. Stimson Center
http://www.stimson.org

The Heritage Foundation
http://www.heritage.org

The North-South Institute
http://www.nsi-ins.ca/ensi/index.htm

Imagine yellow paint being brushed onto an inflated, clear balloon. The yellow color, for purposes of this allegory, represents "people." In many ways the study of global issues is first and foremost the study of people. Today, there are more human beings occupying Earth than ever before. In addition, we are in the midst of a period of unprecedented population growth. Not only are there many countries where the majority of people are under age 16, but also due to improved health care, there are a greater number of older people alive today than ever before. The effect of a growing global population, however, goes beyond sheer numbers, for this trend has unprecedented impacts on natural resources and social services. An examination of population trends and the related topic of food production is a good place to begin an in-depth study of global issues.

Imagine that our fictional artist next dips the brush into a container of blue paint to represent "nature." The natural world plays an important role in setting the international agenda. Shortages of raw materials, climate change, regional droughts, and pollution of waterways are just a few examples of how natural resources can have global implications.

Adding blue paint to the balloon reveals one of the most important underlying concepts found in this book. Although the balloon originally was covered by both yellow and blue paint (people and nature as separate conceptual entities), the two combined produce an entirely different color: green. Talking about nature as a separate entity or people as though they were somehow removed from the forces of the natural world is a serious intellectual error. The people–nature relationship is one of the keys to understanding many of today's most important global issues.

The third color to be added to the balloon is red. This color represents "social structures." Factors falling into this category include whether a society is urban or rural, industrial or agrarian, and consumer-oriented or dedicated to the needs of the state. The relationship between this component and the others is extremely important. The impact of political decisions on the environment, for example, is one of the most significant features of the contemporary world. Will the whales or bald eagles survive? Historically, the forces of nature determined which species survived or perished. Today, survival depends on political decisions or indecision. Understanding the complex relationship between social structure and nature (known as ecopolitics) is central to the study of global issues.

Added to the three primary colors is the fourth and final color of white. It represents the "meta" component (i.e., those qualities that make human beings different from other life forms). These include new ideas and inventions, culture and values, religion and spirituality, and art and literature. The addition of the white paint immediately changes the intensity and shade of the mixture of colors, again emphasizing the relationship among all four factors.

If the painter continues to ply the paintbrush over the miniature globe, a marbling effect becomes evident. From one area to the next, the shading varies because one element is more dominant than another. Further, the miniature system appears dynamic. Nothing is static; relationships are continually

© MedioImages/Getty/Images

changing. This leads to a number of important insights: (1) There are no such things as separate elements, only connections or relationships; (2) changes in one area (such as the climate) will result in changes in all other areas; and (3) complex and dynamic relationships make it difficult to predict events accurately, so observers and policymakers are often surprised by unexpected events.

This book is organized along the basic lines of the balloon allegory. The first unit provides a broad overview of a variety of perspectives on the major forces that are shaping the world of the twenty-first century. From this "big picture" perspective more in-depth analyses follow. Unit 2, for example, focuses on population, disease, and hunger. Unit 3 examines the environment and related natural resource issues. The next three units look at different aspects of the world's social structures. They explore issues of economics, national security, conflict, and international cooperation. In the final unit, a number of "meta" factors are presented.

The reader should keep in mind that, just as it was impossible to keep the individual colors from blending into new colors on the balloon, it is also impossible to separate global issues into discrete chapters in a book. Any discussion of agriculture, for example, must take into account the impact of a growing population on soil and water resources, as well as new scientific breakthroughs in food production. Therefore, the organization of this book focuses attention on issue areas; it does not mean to imply that these factors are somehow separate.

With the collapse of the Soviet empire and the end of the cold war, the outlines of a new global agenda have emerged. Rather than being based on the ideology and interests of the two superpowers, new political, economic, environmental, cultural, and security issues are interacting in an unprecedented fashion. Rapid population growth, environmental decline, uneven economic progress, and global terrorist networks are all parts of a complex state of affairs for which there is no historic parallel. As we enter the second decade of the twenty-first century, signs abound that we are entering a new era. In the words of Abraham Lincoln, "As our case is new, so we must think anew."

Compounding this situation, however, is a whole series of old problems such as ethnic and religious rivalries.

The authors in this first unit provide a variety of perspectives on the trends that they believe are the most important to understanding the historic changes at work at the global level. This discussion is then pursued in greater detail in the following units.

Although the authors look at the same world, they often come to different conclusions. This raises an important issue of values and beliefs, for it can be argued that there really is no objective reality, only differing perspectives. In short, the study of global issues will challenge each thoughtful reader to examine her or his own values and beliefs.

Global Trends 2025: A Transformed World
Executive Summary

U.S. NATIONAL INTELLIGENCE COUNCIL

The **international system**—as constructed following the Second World War—will be almost unrecognizable by 2025 owing to the rise of emerging powers, a globalizing economy, a historic transfer of relative wealth and economic power from West to East, and the growing influence of nonstate actors. By 2025, the international system will be a **global multipolar one** with gaps in national power[1] continuing to narrow between developed and developing countries. Concurrent with the shift in power among nation-states, the relative power of various nonstate actors—including businesses, tribes, religious organizations, and criminal networks—is increasing. The players are changing, but so too are the scope and breadth of transnational issues important for continued global prosperity. Aging populations in the developed world; growing energy, food, and water constraints; and worries about climate change will limit and diminish what will still be an historically unprecedented age of prosperity.

Historically, emerging multipolar systems have been more unstable than bipolar or unipolar ones. Despite the recent financial volatility—which could end up accelerating many ongoing trends—we do not believe that we are headed toward a complete breakdown of the international system, as occurred in 1914–1918 when an earlier phase of globalization came to a halt. However, the next 20 years of transition to a new system are fraught with risks. Strategic rivalries are most likely to revolve around trade, investments, and technological innovation and acquisition, but we cannot rule out a 19th century-like scenario of arms races, territorial expansion, and military rivalries.

This is a story with **no clear outcome,** as illustrated by a series of vignettes we use to map out divergent futures. Although the United States is likely to remain the single most powerful actor, the United States' relative strength—even in the military realm—will decline and U.S. leverage will become more constrained. At the same time, the extent to which other actors—both state and nonstate—will be willing or able to shoulder increased burdens is unclear. Policymakers and publics will have to cope with a growing demand for multilateral cooperation when the international system will be stressed by the incomplete transition from the old to a still-forming new order.

Economic Growth Fueling Rise of Emerging Players

In terms of size, speed, and directional flow, the transfer of **global wealth and economic power** now under way—roughly from West to East—is without precedent in modern history. This shift derives from two sources. First, increases in oil and commodity prices have generated windfall profits for the Gulf states and Russia. Second, lower costs combined with government policies have shifted the locus of manufacturing and some service industries to Asia.

Growth projections for Brazil, Russia, India, and China (the BRICs) indicate they will collectively match the original G-7's share of global GDP by 2040–2050. **China** is poised to have more impact on the world over the next 20 years than any other country. If current trends persist, by 2025 China will have the world's second largest economy and will be a leading military power. It also could be the largest importer of natural resources and the biggest polluter. **India** probably will continue to enjoy relatively rapid economic growth and will strive for a multipolar world in which New Delhi is one of the poles. China and India must decide the extent to which they are willing and capable of playing increasing global roles and how each will relate to the other. **Russia** has the potential to be richer, more powerful, and more self-assured in 2025 if it invests in human capital, expands and diversifies its economy, and integrates with global markets. On the other hand, Russia could experience a significant decline if it fails to take these steps and oil and gas prices remain in the $50–70 per barrel range. No other countries are projected to rise to the level of China, India, or Russia, and none is likely to match their individual global clout. We expect, however, to see the political and economic power of other countries—such as Indonesia, Iran, and Turkey—increase.

For the most part, China, India, and Russia are not following the Western liberal model for self-development but instead are using a different model, "**state capitalism.**" State capitalism is a loose term used to describe a system of economic management that gives a prominent role to the state. Other rising powers—South Korea, Taiwan, and Singapore—also used state capitalism to develop their economies. However, the impact of Russia, and particularly China, following this path is potentially much greater owing to their size and approach to "democratization." We remain optimistic about the *long-term* prospects for **greater democratization,** even though advances are likely to be slow and globalization is subjecting many recently democratized countries to increasing social and economic pressures with the potential to undermine liberal institutions.

Many other countries will fall further behind economically. **Sub-Saharan Africa** will remain the region most vulnerable to economic disruption, population stresses, civil conflict, and political instability. Despite increased global demand for commodities for which Sub-Saharan Africa will be a major supplier, local populations are unlikely to experience significant economic gain. Windfall profits arising from sustained increases in commodity prices might further entrench corrupt or otherwise ill-equipped governments in several regions, diminishing the prospects for democratic and market-based reforms. Although many of **Latin America's** major countries will have become middle income powers by 2025, others, particularly those such as Venezuela and Bolivia that have embraced populist policies for a protracted period, will lag behind—and some, such as Haiti, will have become even poorer and less governable. Overall, Latin America will continue to lag behind Asia and other fast-growing areas in terms of economic competitiveness.

Asia, Africa, and Latin America will account for virtually all **population growth** over the next 20 years; less than 3 percent of the growth will occur in the West. Europe and Japan will continue to far outdistance the emerging powers of China and India in per capita wealth, but they will struggle to maintain robust growth rates because the size of their working-age populations will decrease. The US will be a partial exception to the aging of populations in the developed world because it will experience higher birth rates and more immigration. The number of migrants seeking to move from disadvantaged to relatively privileged countries is likely to increase.

The number of countries with youthful age structures in the current "arc of instability" is projected to decline by as much as 40 percent. Three of every four youth-bulge countries that remain will be located in Sub-Saharan Africa; nearly all of the remainder will be located in the core of the Middle East, scattered through southern and central Asia, and in the Pacific Islands.

New Transnational Agenda

Resource issues will gain prominence on the international agenda. Unprecedented global economic growth—positive in so many other regards—will continue to put pressure on a number of **highly strategic resources,** including energy, food, and water, and demand is projected to outstrip easily available supplies over the next decade or so. For example, non-OPEC liquid hydrocarbon production—crude oil, natural gas liquids, and unconventionals such as tar sands—will not grow commensurate with demand. Oil and gas production of many traditional energy producers already is declining. Elsewhere—in China, India, and Mexico—production has flattened. Countries

capable of significantly expanding production will dwindle; oil and gas production will be concentrated in unstable areas. As a result of this and other factors, the world will be in the midst of a fundamental energy transition away from oil toward natural gas, coal and other alternatives.

The World Bank estimates that **demand for food** will rise by 50 percent by 2030, as a result of growing world population, rising affluence, and the shift to Western dietary preferences by a larger middle class. Lack of access to stable supplies of water is reaching critical proportions, particularly for agricultural purposes, and the problem will worsen because of rapid urbanization worldwide and the roughly 1.2 billion persons to be added over the next 20 years. Today, experts consider 21 countries, with a combined population of about 600 million, to be either cropland or freshwater scarce. Owing to continuing population growth, 36 countries, with about 1.4 billion people, are projected to fall into this category by 2025.

Climate change is expected to exacerbate resource scarcities. Although the impact of climate change will vary by region, a number of regions will begin to suffer harmful effects, particularly water scarcity and loss of agricultural production. Regional differences in agricultural production are likely to become more pronounced over time with declines disproportionately concentrated in developing countries, particularly those in Sub-Saharan Africa. Agricultural losses are expected to mount with substantial impacts forecast by most economists by late this century. For many developing countries, decreased agricultural output will be devastating because agriculture accounts for a large share of their economies and many of their citizens live close to subsistence levels.

New technologies could again provide solutions, such as viable alternatives to fossil fuels or means to overcome food and water constraints. However, all current technologies are inadequate for replacing the traditional energy architecture on the scale needed, and new energy technologies probably will not be commercially viable and widespread by 2025. The pace of technological innovation will be key. Even with a favorable policy and funding environment for biofuels, clean coal, or hydrogen, the transition to new fuels will be slow. Major technologies historically have had an "adoption lag." In the energy sector, a recent study found that it takes an average of 25 years for a new production technology to become widely adopted.

Despite what are seen as long odds now, we cannot rule out the possibility of an **energy transition** by 2025 that would avoid the costs of an energy infrastructure overhaul. The greatest possibility for a relatively quick and inexpensive transition during the period comes from better renewable generation sources (photovoltaic and wind) and improvements in battery technology. With many of these technologies, the infrastructure cost hurdle for individual projects would be lower, enabling many small economic actors to develop their own energy transformation projects that directly serve their interests—e.g., stationary fuel cells powering homes and offices, recharging plug-in hybrid autos, and selling energy back to the grid. Also, energy conversion schemes—such as plans to generate hydrogen for automotive fuel cells from electricity in the homeowner's garage—could avoid the need to develop complex hydrogen transportation infrastructure.

Prospects for Terrorism, Conflict, and Proliferation

Terrorism, proliferation, and conflict will remain key concerns even as resource issues move up on the international agenda. Terrorism is unlikely to disappear by 2025, but its appeal could diminish if economic growth continues and youth unemployment is mitigated in the Middle East. Economic opportunities for youth and greater political pluralism probably would dissuade some from joining terrorists' ranks, but others—motivated by a variety of factors, such as a desire for revenge or to become "martyrs"—will continue to turn to violence to pursue their objectives.

In the absence of employment opportunities and legal means for political expression, conditions will be ripe for disaffection, growing radicalism, and possible recruitment of youths into **terrorist groups.** Terrorist groups in 2025 will likely be a combination of descendants of long-established groups—that inherit organizational structures, command and control processes, and training procedures necessary to conduct sophisticated attacks—and newly emergent collections of the angry and disenfranchised that become self-radicalized. For those terrorist groups that are active in 2025, the diffusion of technologies and scientific knowledge will place some of the world's most dangerous capabilities within their reach. One of our greatest concerns continues to be that terrorist or other malevolent groups might acquire and employ biological agents, or less likely, a nuclear device, to create mass casualties.

Although **Iran's** acquisition of nuclear weapons is not inevitable, other countries' worries about a nuclear-armed Iran could lead states in the region to develop new security arrangements with external powers, acquire additional weapons, and consider pursuing their own nuclear ambitions. It is not clear that the type of stable deterrent relationship that existed between the great powers for most of the Cold War would emerge naturally in the Middle East with a nuclear-weapons capable Iran. Episodes of low-intensity conflict taking place under a nuclear umbrella could lead to an unintended escalation and broader conflict if clear red lines between those states involved are not well established.

We believe **ideological conflicts** akin to the Cold War are unlikely to take root in a world in which most states will be preoccupied with the pragmatic challenges of globalization and shifting global power alignments. The force of ideology is likely to be strongest in the Muslim world—particularly the Arab core. In those countries that are likely to struggle with youth bulges and weak economic underpinnings—such as Pakistan, Afghanistan, Nigeria, and Yemen—the radical Salafi trend of Islam is likely to gain traction.

Types of **conflict** we have not seen for awhile—such as over resources—could reemerge. Perceptions of energy scarcity will drive countries to take actions to assure their future access to energy supplies. In the worst case, this could result in interstate conflicts if government leaders deem assured access to energy resources, for example, to be essential for maintaining domestic stability and the survival of their regimes. However, even actions short of war will have important geopolitical consequences. Maritime security concerns are providing a rationale for naval buildups and modernization efforts, such as China's and India's development of blue-water naval capabilities. The buildup of regional naval capabilities could lead to increased tensions, rivalries, and counterbalancing moves but it also will create opportunities for multinational cooperation in protecting critical sea lanes. With water becoming more scarce in Asia and the Middle East, cooperation to manage changing water resources is likely to become more difficult within and between states.

The risk of **nuclear weapon use** over the next 20 years, although remaining very low, is likely to be greater than it is today as a result of several converging trends. The spread of nuclear technologies and expertise is generating concerns about the potential emergence of new nuclear weapon states and the acquisition of nuclear materials by terrorist groups. Ongoing low-intensity clashes between India and Pakistan continue to raise the specter that such events could escalate to a broader conflict between those nuclear powers. The possibility of a future disruptive regime change or collapse occurring in a nuclear weapon state such as North Korea also continues to raise questions regarding the ability of weak states to control and secure their nuclear arsenals.

If nuclear weapons are used in the next 15–20 years, the international system will be shocked as it experiences immediate humanitarian, economic, and political-military repercussions. A future use of nuclear weapons probably would bring about significant geopolitical changes as some states would seek to establish or reinforce security alliances with existing nuclear powers and others would push for global nuclear disarmament.

A More Complex International System

The trend toward greater diffusion of authority and power that has been occurring for a couple decades is likely to accelerate because of the emergence of new global players, the worsening institutional deficit, potential expansion of regional blocs, and enhanced strength of nonstate actors and networks. The **multiplicity of actors** on the international scene could add strength—in terms of filling gaps left by aging post-World War II institutions—or further fragment the international system and incapacitate international cooperation. The diversity in type of actor raises the likelihood of fragmentation occurring over the next two decades, particularly given the wide array of transnational challenges facing the international community.

The rising BRIC powers are unlikely to challenge the international system as did Germany and Japan in the 19th and 20th centuries, but because of their growing geopolitical and economic clout, they will have a high degree of freedom to customize their political and economic policies rather than fully adopting Western norms. They also are likely to want to preserve their policy freedom to maneuver, allowing others to carry the primary burden for dealing with such issues as terrorism, climate change, proliferation, and energy security.

Existing multilateral institutions—which are large and cumbersome and were designed for a different geopolitical order—will have difficulty adapting quickly to undertake new missions, accommodate changing memberships, and augment their resources.

Nongovernmental organizations (NGOs)—concentrating on specific issues—increasingly will be a part of the landscape, but NGO networks are likely to be limited in their ability to effect change in the absence of concerted efforts by multilateral institutions or governments. Efforts at greater inclusiveness—to reflect the emergence of the newer powers—may make it harder for international organizations to tackle transnational challenges. Respect for the dissenting views of member nations will continue to shape the agenda of organizations and limit the kinds of solutions that can be attempted.

Greater **Asian regionalism**—possible by 2025—would have global implications, sparking or reinforcing a trend toward three trade and financial clusters that could become quasi-blocs: North America, Europe, and East Asia. Establishment of such quasi-blocs would have implications for the ability to achieve future global World Trade Organization (WTO) agreements. Regional clusters could compete in setting trans-regional product standards for information technology, biotechnology, nanotechnology, intellectual property rights, and other aspects of the "new economy." On the other hand, an absence of regional cooperation in Asia could help spur competition among China, India, and Japan over resources such as energy.

Intrinsic to the growing complexity of the overlapping roles of states, institutions, and nonstate actors is the **proliferation of political identities,** which is leading to establishment of new networks and rediscovered communities. No one political identity is likely to be dominant in most societies by 2025. Religion-based networks may be quintessential issue networks and overall may play a more powerful role on many transnational issues such as the environment and inequalities than secular groupings.

The United States: Less Dominant Power

By 2025 the US will find itself as one of a number of important actors on the world stage, albeit still the most powerful one. Even in the military realm, where the US will continue to possess considerable advantages in 2025, advances by others in science and technology, expanded adoption of irregular warfare tactics by both state and nonstate actors, proliferation of long-range precision weapons, and growing use of cyber warfare attacks increasingly will constrict US freedom of action. A more constrained US role has implications for others and the likelihood of new agenda issues being tackled effectively. Despite the recent rise in anti-Americanism, the US probably will continue to be seen as a much-needed regional balancer in the Middle East and Asia. The US will continue to be expected to play a significant role in using its military power to counter global terrorism. On newer security issues like climate change,

US leadership will be widely perceived as critical to leveraging competing and divisive views to find solutions. At the same time, the multiplicity of influential actors and distrust of vast power means less room for the US to call the shots without the support of strong partnerships. Developments in the rest of the world, including internal developments in a number of key states—particularly China and Russia—are also likely to be crucial determinants of US policy.

2025—What Kind of Future?

The above trends suggest major **discontinuities,** shocks, and surprises, which we highlight throughout the text. Examples include nuclear weapons use or a pandemic. In some cases, the surprise element is only a matter of **timing:** an energy transition, for example, is inevitable; the only questions are when and how abruptly or smoothly such a transition occurs. An energy transition from one type of fuel (fossil fuels) to another (alternative) is an event that historically has only happened once a century at most with momentous consequences. The transition from wood to coal helped trigger industrialization. In this case, a transition—particularly an abrupt one—out of fossil fuels would have major repercussions for energy producers in the Middle East and Eurasia, potentially causing permanent decline of some states as global and regional powers.

Other discontinuities are less predictable. They are likely to result from an interaction of several trends and depend on the quality of leadership. We put uncertainties such as whether China or Russia becomes a democracy in this category. China's growing middle class increases the chances but does not make such a development inevitable. Political pluralism seems less likely in Russia in the absence of economic diversification. Pressure from below may force the issue, or a leader might begin or enhance the democratization process to sustain the economy or spur economic growth. A sustained plunge in the price of oil and gas would alter the outlook and increase prospects for greater political and economic liberalization in Russia. If either country were to democratize, it would represent another wave of democratization with wide significance for many other developing states.

Also **uncertain** are the outcomes of demographic challenges facing Europe, Japan, and even Russia. In none of these cases does demography have to spell destiny with less regional and global power an inevitable outcome. Technology, the role of immigration, public health improvements, and laws encouraging greater female participation in the economy are some of the measures that could change the trajectory of current trends pointing toward less economic growth, increased social tensions, and possible decline.

Whether global institutions adapt and revive—another key uncertainty—also is a function of leadership. Current trends suggest a dispersion of power and authority will create a global governance deficit. Reversing those trend lines would require strong leadership in the international community by a number of powers, including the emerging ones.

Some uncertainties would have greater consequences—should they occur—than would others. In this work, we emphasize the overall potential for greater conflict—some forms of which could threaten globalization. We put WMD terrorism and a Middle East nuclear arms race in this category. In the four fictionalized scenarios, we have highlighted new challenges that could emerge as a result of the ongoing global transformation. They present new situations, dilemmas, or predicaments that represent departures from recent developments. As a set, they do not cover all possible futures. ***None of these is inevitable or even necessarily likely;*** but, as with many other uncertainties, the scenarios are potential game-changers.

- In *A World Without the West,* the new powers supplant the West as the leaders on the world stage.
- *October Surprise* illustrates the impact of inattention to global climate change; unexpected major impacts narrow the world's range of options.

- In *BRICs' Bust-Up,* disputes over vital resources emerge as a source of conflict between major powers—in this case two emerging heavyweights—India and China.
- In *Politics Is Not Always Local,* nonstate networks emerge to set the international agenda on the environment, eclipsing governments.

Note

1. National power scores, computed by the International Futures computer model, are the product of an index combining the weighted factors of GDP, defense spending, population, and technology.

From *Atlantic Council,* November 2008, pp. vi–xiii.

Could Food Shortages Bring Down Civilization?

Lester R. Brown

One of the toughest things for people to do is to anticipate sudden change. Typically we project the future by extrapolating from trends in the past. Much of the time this approach works well. But sometimes it fails spectacularly, and people are simply blindsided by events such as today's economic crisis.

For most of us, the idea that civilization itself could disintegrate probably seems preposterous. Who would not find it hard to think seriously about such a complete departure from what we expect of ordinary life? What evidence could make us heed a warning so dire—and how would we go about responding to it? We are so inured to a long list of highly unlikely catastrophes that we are virtually programmed to dismiss them all with a wave of the hand: Sure, our civilization might devolve into chaos—and Earth might collide with an asteroid, too!

For many years I have studied global agricultural, population, environmental, and economic trends and their interactions. The combined effects of those trends and the political tensions they generate point to the breakdown of governments and societies. Yet I, too, have resisted the idea that food shortages could bring down not only individual governments but also our global civilization.

I can no longer ignore that risk. Our continuing failure to deal with the environmental declines that are undermining the world food economy—most important, falling water tables, eroding soils, and rising temperatures—forces me to conclude that such a collapse is possible.

The Problem of Failed States

Even a cursory look at the vital signs of our current world order lends unwelcome support to my conclusion. And those of us in the environmental field are well into our third decade of charting trends of environmental decline without seeing any significant effort to reverse a single one.

In six of the past nine years world grain production has fallen short of consumption, forcing a steady drawdown in stocks. When the 2008 harvest began, world carryover stocks of grain (the amount in the bin when the new harvest begins) were at 62 days of consumption, a near record low. In response, world grain prices in the spring and summer of last year climbed to the highest level ever.

As demand for food rises faster than supplies are growing, the resulting food-price inflation puts severe stress on the governments of countries already teetering on the edge of chaos. Unable to buy grain or grow their own, hungry people take to the streets. Indeed, even before the steep climb in grain prices in 2008, the number of failing states was expanding. Many of their problems stem from a failure to slow the growth of their populations. But if the food situation continues to deteriorate, entire nations will break down at an ever increasing rate. We have entered a new era in geopolitics. In the 20th century the main threat to international security was superpower conflict; today it is failing states. It is not the concentration of power but its absence that puts us at risk.

States fail when national governments can no longer provide personal security, food security, and basic social services such as education and health care. They often lose control of part or all of their territory. When governments lose their monopoly on power, law and order begin to disintegrate. After a point, countries can become so dangerous that food relief workers are no longer safe and their programs are halted; in Somalia and Afghanistan, deteriorating conditions have already put such programs in jeopardy.

Failing states are of international concern because they are a source of terrorists, drugs, weapons, and refugees, threatening political stability everywhere. Somalia, number one on the 2008 list of failing states, has become a base for piracy. Iraq, number five, is a hotbed for terrorist training. Afghanistan, number seven, is the world's leading supplier of heroin. Following the massive genocide of 1994 in Rwanda, refugees from that troubled state, thousands of armed soldiers among them, helped to destabilize neighboring Democratic Republic of the Congo (number six).

Our global civilization depends on a functioning network of politically healthy nation-states to control the spread of infectious disease, to manage the international monetary system, to control international terrorism and to reach scores of other common goals. If the system for controlling infectious diseases—such as polio, SARS, or avian flu—breaks down, humanity will be in trouble. Once states fail, no one assumes responsibility for their debt to outside lenders. If enough states disintegrate, their fall will threaten the stability of global civilization itself.

A New Kind of Food Shortage

The surge in world grain prices in 2007 and 2008—and the threat they pose to food security—has a different, more troubling quality than the increases of the past. During the second half of the 20th century, grain prices rose dramatically several times. In 1972, for instance, the Soviets, recognizing their poor harvest early, quietly cornered the world wheat market. As a result, wheat prices elsewhere more than doubled, pulling rice and corn prices up with them. But this and other price shocks were event-driven—drought in the Soviet Union, a monsoon failure in India, crop-shrinking heat in the U.S. Corn Belt. And the rises were short-lived: Prices typically returned to normal with the next harvest.

In contrast, the recent surge in world grain prices is trend-driven, making it unlikely to reverse without a reversal in the trends themselves. On the demand side, those trends include the ongoing addition of more than 70 million people a year; a growing number of people wanting to move up the food chain to consume highly grain-intensive livestock products [see "The Greenhouse Hamburger," by Nathan Fiala; *Scientific American,* February 2009]; and the massive diversion of U.S. grain to ethanol-fuel distilleries.

The extra demand for grain associated with rising affluence varies widely among countries. People in low-income countries where grain supplies 60 percent of calories, such as India, directly consume a bit more than a pound of grain a day. In affluent countries such as the U.S. and Canada, grain consumption per person is nearly four times that much, though perhaps 90 percent of it is consumed indirectly as meat, milk, and eggs from grain-fed animals.

The potential for further grain consumption as incomes rise among low-income consumers is huge. But that potential pales beside the insatiable demand for crop-based automotive fuels. A fourth of this year's U.S. grain harvest—enough to feed 125 million Americans or half a billion Indians at current consumption levels—will go to fuel cars. Yet even if the entire U.S. grain harvest were diverted into making ethanol, it would meet at most 18 percent of U.S. automotive fuel needs. The grain required to fill a 25-gallon SUV tank with ethanol could feed one person for a year.

The recent merging of the food and energy economies implies that if the food value of grain is less than its fuel value, the market will move the grain into the energy economy. That double demand is leading to an epic competition between cars and people for the grain supply and to a political and moral issue of unprecedented dimensions. The U.S., in a misguided effort to reduce its dependence on foreign oil by substituting grain-based fuels, is generating global food insecurity on a scale not seen before.

Water Shortages Mean Food Shortages

What about supply? The three environmental trends I mentioned earlier—the shortage of freshwater, the loss of topsoil, and the rising temperatures (and other effects) of global warming—are making it increasingly hard to expand the world's grain supply fast enough to keep up with demand. Of all those trends, however, the spread of water shortages poses the most immediate threat. The biggest challenge here is irrigation, which consumes 70 percent of the world's freshwater. Millions of irrigation wells in many countries are now pumping water out of underground sources faster than rainfall can recharge them. The result is falling water tables in countries populated by half the world's people, including the three big grain producers—China, India, and the U.S.

Usually aquifers are replenishable, but some of the most important ones are not: The "fossil" aquifers, so called because they store ancient water and are not recharged by precipitation. For these—including the vast Ogallala Aquifer that underlies the U.S. Great Plains, the Saudi aquifer and the deep aquifer under the North China Plain—depletion would spell the end of pumping. In arid regions such a loss could also bring an end to agriculture altogether.

In China the water table under the North China Plain, an area that produces more than half of the country's wheat and a third of its corn, is falling fast. Overpumping has used up most of the water in a shallow aquifer there, forcing well drillers to turn to the region's deep aquifer, which is not replenishable. A report by the World Bank foresees "catastrophic consequences for future generations" unless water use and supply can quickly be brought back into balance.

As water tables have fallen and irrigation wells have gone dry, China's wheat crop, the world's largest, has declined by 8 percent since it peaked at 123 million tons in 1997. In that same period China's rice production dropped 4 percent. The world's most populous nation may soon be importing massive quantities of grain.

But water shortages are even more worrying in India. There the margin between food consumption and survival is more precarious. Millions of irrigation wells have dropped water tables in almost every state. As Fred Pearce reported in New Scientist:

> Half of India's traditional hand-dug wells and millions of shallower tube wells have already dried up, bringing a spate of suicides among those who rely on them. Electricity blackouts are reaching epidemic proportions in states where half of the electricity is used to pump water from depths of up to a kilometer [3,300 feet].

A World Bank study reports that 15 percent of India's food supply is produced by mining groundwater. Stated otherwise, 175 million Indians consume grain produced with water from irrigation wells that will soon be exhausted. The continued shrinking of water supplies could lead to unmanageable food shortages and social conflict.

Less Soil, More Hunger

The scope of the second worrisome trend—the loss of topsoil—is also startling. Topsoil is eroding faster than new soil forms on perhaps a third of the world's cropland. This thin layer of essential plant nutrients, the very foundation of civilization, took long stretches of geologic time to build up, yet it is typically only about six inches deep. Its loss from wind and water erosion doomed earlier civilizations.

In 2002 a U.N. team assessed the food situation in Lesotho, the small, landlocked home of two million people embedded within South Africa. The team's finding was straightforward: "Agriculture in Lesotho faces a catastrophic future; crop production is declining and could cease altogether over large tracts of the country if steps are not taken to reverse soil erosion, degradation and the decline in soil fertility."

In the Western Hemisphere, Haiti—one of the first states to be recognized as failing—was largely self-sufficient in grain 40 years ago. In the years since, though, it has lost nearly all its forests and much of its topsoil, forcing the country to import more than half of its grain.

The third and perhaps most pervasive environmental threat to food security—rising surface temperature—can affect crop yields everywhere. In many countries crops are grown at or near their thermal optimum, so even a minor temperature rise during the growing season can shrink the harvest. A study published by the U.S. National Academy of Sciences has confirmed a rule of thumb among crop ecologists: For every rise of one degree Celsius (1.8 degrees Fahrenheit) above the norm, wheat, rice, and corn yields fall by 10 percent.

In the past, most famously when the innovations in the use of fertilizer, irrigation, and high-yield varieties of wheat and rice created the "green revolution" of the 1960s and 1970s, the response to the growing demand for food was the successful application of scientific agriculture: the technological fix. This time, regrettably, many of the most productive advances in agricultural technology have already been put into practice, and so the long-term rise in land productivity is slowing down. Between 1950 and 1990 the world's farmers increased the grain yield per acre by more than 2 percent a year, exceeding the growth of population. But since then, the annual growth in yield has slowed to slightly more than 1 percent. In some countries the yields appear to be near their practical limits, including rice yields in Japan and China.

Some commentators point to genetically modified crop strains as a way out of our predicament. Unfortunately, however, no genetically modified crops have led to dramatically higher yields, comparable to the doubling or tripling of wheat and rice yields that took place during the green revolution. Nor do they seem likely to do so, simply because conventional plant-breeding techniques have already tapped most of the potential for raising crop yields.

Jockeying for Food

As the world's food security unravels, a dangerous politics of food scarcity is coming into play: Individual countries acting in their narrowly defined self-interest are actually worsening the plight of the many. The trend began in 2007, when leading wheat-exporting countries such as Russia and Argentina limited or banned their exports, in hopes of increasing locally available food supplies and thereby bringing down food prices domestically. Vietnam, the world's second-biggest rice exporter after Thailand, banned its exports for several months for the same reason. Such moves may reassure those living in the exporting countries, but they are creating panic in importing countries that must rely on what is then left of the world's exportable grain.

In response to those restrictions, grain importers are trying to nail down long-term bilateral trade agreements that would lock up future grain supplies. The Phillippines, no longer able to count on getting rice from the world market, recently negotiated a three-year deal with Vietnam for a guaranteed 1.5 million tons of rice each year. Food-import anxiety is even spawning entirely new efforts by food-importing countries to buy or lease farmland in other countries.

In spite of such stopgap measures, soaring food prices and spreading hunger in many other countries are beginning to break down the social order. In several provinces of Thailand the predations of "rice rustlers" have forced villagers to guard their rice fields at night with loaded shotguns. In Pakistan an armed soldier escorts each grain truck. During the first half of 2008, 83 trucks carrying grain in Sudan were hijacked before reaching the Darfur relief camps.

No country is immune to the effects of tightening food supplies, not even the U.S., the world's breadbasket. If China turns to the world market for massive quantities of grain, as it has recently done for soybeans, it will have to buy from the U.S. For U.S. consumers, that would mean competing for the U.S. grain harvest with 1.3 billion Chinese consumers with fast-rising incomes—a nightmare scenario. In such circumstances, it would be tempting for the U.S. to restrict exports, as it did, for instance, with grain and soybeans in the 1970s when domestic prices soared. But that is not an option with China. Chinese investors now hold well over a trillion U.S. dollars, and they have often been the leading international buyers of U.S. Treasury securities issued to finance the fiscal deficit. Like it or not, U.S. consumers will share their grain with Chinese consumers, no matter how high food prices rise.

Plan B: Our Only Option

Since the current world food shortage is trend-driven, the environmental trends that cause it must be reversed. To do so requires extraordinarily demanding measures, a monumental shift away from business as usual—what we at the Earth Policy Institute call Plan A—to a civilization-saving Plan B. [see "Plan B 3.0: Mobilizing to Save Civilization," at www.earthpolicy.org/Books/PB3/]

Similar in scale and urgency to the U.S. mobilization for World War II, Plan B has four components: a massive effort to cut carbon emissions by 80 percent from their 2006 levels by 2020; the stabilization of the world's population at eight billion by 2040; the eradication of poverty; and the restoration of forests, soils, and aquifers.

Net carbon dioxide emissions can be cut by systematically raising energy efficiency and investing massively in the development of renewable sources of energy. We must also ban deforestation worldwide, as several countries already have done, and plant billions of trees to sequester carbon. The transition from fossil fuels to renewable forms of energy can be driven by imposing a tax on carbon, while offsetting it with a reduction in income taxes.

Stabilizing population and eradicating poverty go hand in hand. In fact, the key to accelerating the shift to smaller families is eradicating poverty—and vice versa. One way is to ensure at least a primary school education for all children, girls as well as boys. Another is to provide rudimentary, village-level health care, so that people can be confident that their children will survive to adulthood. Women everywhere need access to reproductive health care and family-planning services.

The fourth component, restoring the earth's natural systems and resources, incorporates a worldwide initiative to arrest the fall in water tables by raising water productivity: the useful activity that can be wrung from each drop. That implies shifting to more efficient irrigation systems and to more water-efficient crops. In some countries, it implies growing (and eating) more wheat and less rice, a water-intensive crop. And for industries and cities, it implies doing what some are doing already, namely, continuously recycling water.

At the same time, we must launch a worldwide effort to conserve soil, similar to the U.S. response to the Dust Bowl of the 1930s. Terracing the ground, planting trees as shelterbelts against windblown soil erosion, and practicing minimum tillage—in which the soil is not plowed and crop residues are left on the field—are among the most important soil-conservation measures.

There is nothing new about our four interrelated objectives. They have been discussed individually for years. Indeed, we have created entire institutions intended to tackle some of them, such as the World Bank to alleviate poverty. And we have made substantial progress in some parts of the world on at least one of them—the distribution of family-planning services and the associated shift to smaller families that brings population stability.

For many in the development community, the four objectives of Plan B were seen as positive, promoting development as long as they did not cost too much. Others saw them as humanitarian goals—politically correct and morally appropriate. Now a third and far more momentous rationale presents itself: Meeting these goals may be necessary to prevent the collapse of our civilization. Yet the cost we project for saving civilization would amount to less than $200 billion a year, a sixth of current global military spending. In effect, Plan B is the new security budget.

Time: Our Scarcest Resource

Our challenge is not only to implement Plan B but also to do it quickly. The world is in a race between political tipping points and natural ones. Can we close coal-fired power plants fast enough to prevent the Greenland ice sheet from slipping into the sea and inundating our coastlines? Can we cut carbon emissions fast enough to save the mountain glaciers of Asia? During the dry season their meltwaters sustain the major rivers of India and China—and by extension, hundreds of millions of people. Can we stabilize population before countries such as India, Pakistan, and Yemen are overwhelmed by shortages of the water they need to irrigate their crops?

It is hard to overstate the urgency of our predicament. [For the most thorough and authoritative scientific assessment of global climate change, see "Climate Change 2007. Fourth Assessment Report of the Intergovernmental Panel on Climate Change," available at www.ipcc.ch] Every day counts. Unfortunately, we do not know how long we can light our cities with coal, for instance, before Greenland's ice sheet can no longer be saved. Nature sets the deadlines; nature is the timekeeper. But we human beings cannot see the clock.

We desperately need a new way of thinking, a new mind-set. The thinking that got us into this bind will not get us out. When Elizabeth Kolbert, a writer for the *New Yorker*, asked energy guru Amory Lovins about thinking outside the box, Lovins responded: "There is no box."

There is no box. That is the mind-set we need if civilization is to survive.

From *Scientific American*, May 2009. Copyright © 2009 by Lester R. Brown. Reprinted by permission of the author.

Navigating the Energy Transition

Michael T. Klare

Between now and 2050 or so, the world will undergo a great social, economic, and technological transition. In place of the fossil fuels—oil, coal, and natural gas—that now satisfy most of our energy needs and define key aspects of contemporary civilization, a new class of renewable energy sources will come to dominate the industrial landscape. Huge arrays of wind turbines and solar panels will replace the smokestacks and refineries that now surround major cities. In place of gasoline, filling stations will provide advanced biofuels or hydrogen to supply fuel cells. High-speed rail lines will connect major cities, while light rail will snake through large and small cities and their suburbs. Our homes, schools, factories, and offices will be designed to use as little energy as possible for heating, cooling, and illumination.

From our vantage point today, we can readily envision the world of 2050, and picture how the development of alternative sources of energy will alter our lives and those of our descendants. What is *less* clear is how we will get from here to there. At the conclusion of the process, the global economy and its myriad transportation systems will have been reconstructed along new lines, and the human population will have learned to live in new and more environmentally sensitive ways. But the transition from our current energy system to one based largely on renewables will be fraught with danger and crisis, as the supply of existing fuels dwindles and that of alternative fuels proves inadequate to make up the difference. Navigating this great transition could well prove the most difficult challenge facing the human community in the twenty-first century—and it is a challenge that has already forced itself upon us.

Why will this prove such a great challenge, and why is it upon us now? Let us begin with the obvious: An abundant supply of affordable energy is essential for the effective functioning of the world economy. Without such a supply, the global economy slows and suffers all sorts of disorders and trauma. We saw ample evidence of this in the spring and summer of 2008, when oil prices reached record levels, causing intense misery for the automotive, airline, and tourism industries, as well as for farmers, truckers, and commuters. High oil prices were not the direct cause of the financial meltdown of late 2008, but they were a significant factor in the subprime mortgage crisis that ultimately triggered the meltdown, in that they boosted the monthly costs faced by hard-pressed homebuyers in remote exurbs (the epicenter of the subprime pandemic). The price of gasoline only dropped when the economic crisis suppressed international demand, and it will stay low only so long as the crisis persists. As soon as economic activity rebounds, oil prices will climb again.

Energy is tied to another critical concern of the emerging era: global climate change. The largest single constituent of the greenhouse gases that are deemed responsible for planetary warming is carbon dioxide (CO_2), and the principal source of the CO_2 now accumulating in the outer atmosphere is the burning of fossil fuels to generate electricity or power motor vehicles. The more we rely on fossil fuels for these purposes, the greater will be the emissions of CO_2 and the faster the warming of the planet. The obvious solution to this peril is to reduce consumption of oil, coal, and natural gas. But this will require accelerating the development of climate-friendly alternatives, and this will take time and a great infusion of capital. Meanwhile, we still need abundant supplies of energy—affordable energy—and this puts a premium on the increased output of fossil fuels.

The intensified pursuit of fossil fuels to satisfy vital economic requirements will also bear on yet another key aspect of the current epoch: growing geopolitical rivalry among the major powers. In a world in which every nation must endeavor to satisfy its requirement for an adequate supply of energy, the competition for access to the world's remaining reserves of oil and natural gas is destined to become increasingly fierce. This has led the major consuming nations to employ every means at their disposal—including military means—to gain advantage in the competitive struggle over diminishing stocks of energy. In some cases, this has led to an influx of arms into areas of instability, as in Africa and Central Asia; in others, to the permanent deployment of military forces, as in the Persian Gulf and Caspian Sea basin. As the competition for fossil fuels increases, these geopolitical rivalries are likely to gain further momentum.

So the three greatest concerns of the moment—the global economy, the environment, and geopolitical competition—are directly tied to the nature of the world's existing energy mix. And this is where the problem lies. The types of energy on which we currently rely to satisfy most of our needs are not likely to prove adequate to meet future requirements—yet the harder we work to increase their availability, the more we doom the planet to catastrophic climate disorder and recurring geopolitical crisis.

Things as They Are

To grasp better these underlying realities, it is essential to examine the world's existing energy balance. At present, most of the world's energy is derived from fossil fuels. According to the US Department of Energy (DOE), fully 86 percent of total world energy consumption was satisfied in 2005, the most recent year for which comprehensive figures are available, by such fuels—36.7 percent by oil, 26.5 percent by coal, and 23.2 percent by natural gas. An additional 7.7 percent was provided by hydropower and renewable sources of energy, and 5.9 percent by nuclear power (see the table World Energy Consumption by Source).

It is the relative abundance of fossil fuels that has largely propelled the great economic expansion of the past 65 years, enabling not only the reconstruction of Europe and Japan after World War II but also the industrialization of Brazil, China, India, South Korea, Taiwan, and other rapidly growing economies. Over the course of this remarkable epoch, the industrialized nations erected a global civilization based on easy access to affordable fuels and electricity to power a vast array of motor vehicles, aircraft, computers, and other power-hungry devices. All this has been made possible because the international energy industry has—until now—largely succeeded in continually expanding the global output of oil, coal, and natural gas. Clearly, if this civilization is to continue to thrive in the years ahead and be extended to even more countries in the developing world, this extraordinary feat of energy-supply expansion will have to be repeated again and again.

Indeed, the DOE projected in the summer of 2008 that worldwide energy demand would grow by 50 percent between 2005 and 2030, from 462 to 695 quadrillion British thermal units (BTUs). This represents an enormous increase—the 233 quadrillion BTUs that must be added over the next quarter century is the equivalent of current energy consumption by the United States, Europe, and Japan combined. Most of this added energy, the DOE assumes, will have to be supplied by the most common and well-developed fuels: oil, coal, and natural gas. According to DOE projections, these three fuels will provide approximately the same share of world energy in 2030—85.8 percent—as they did in 2005.

Only a radical increase in the tempo of change can ensure that alternative sources of energy will be available in 2025.

If the energy industry were capable of supplying all this added fossil-fuel energy in 2030, that would be good news for the global economy, in that the older industrialized nations could maintain their high levels of consumption while the developing world experienced fast consumption growth. But it is extremely unlikely that the industry will be capable of meeting this objective. Although the net supply of fossil fuels may continue to increase, the global availability of oil will probably go into decline well before the end of this period. Natural gas supplies are likely to remain stagnant. This leaves only coal—the most CO_2-intensive of the three fossil fuels—as a rising source of energy. The bottom line: insufficient energy supplies combined with rising greenhouse-gas emissions.

The most troubling aspect of this equation involves oil. Although the DOE and many oil industry officials claim that global petroleum supplies will be sufficient to satisfy international requirements between now and 2030, many experts doubt that this will prove to be the case. In its *World Energy Outlook* released on November 12, 2008, the International Energy Agency (IEA), a Paris-based organization affiliated with the Organization for Economic Cooperation and Development, warned that global oil supplies may not be adequate to meet global needs in the years ahead. The agency gave three reasons that this might be so. First, existing fields are running out of oil at a faster rate than previously thought. Second, most newly developed oil fields are smaller and less productive than those currently in operation. And third, investors are shying away from costly and complex projects in "frontier" oil regions like the deep waters of the Gulf of Mexico, the Gulf of Guinea, Siberia, and the Caspian Sea.

Of the three reasons, perhaps the most startling was the revelation concerning the rapid depletion of existing fields. Although the world possesses tens of thousands of operating wells, most of our oil is drawn from several hundred giant reservoirs that

World Energy Consumption by Source—2005 (Actual) and 2030 (Projected)

Energy Source	2005 (Actual)		2030 (Projected)	
	Consumption Quad BTUs	Percent of World Total	Consumption Quad BTUs	Percent of World Total
Oil and biofuels	169.4	36.7	229.3	33.0
Natural gas	107.4	23.2	164.7	23.7
Coal	122.5	26.5	202.2	29.1
Nuclear	27.5	5.9	39.4	5.7
Hydropower, Renewables, others	35.5	7.7	59.0	8.5
Total, world	462.2	100.0	694.7	100.0

Source: US Department of Energy, *International Energy Outlook 2008* (Washington, DC: 2008), Table A2, p. 97.

produce hundreds of thousands of barrels per day. Almost all of these fields were discovered a quarter of a century or more ago, and many have already passed their peak level of daily output and are now experiencing a steady rate of decline. Previously, energy analysts assumed that this rate of decline was, on average, about 4 to 5 percent per year across the board—a conceivably manageable rate assuming sufficient investment in new oil field development by the major oil companies. But after conducting a survey of the world's 800 top-producing oil fields, the IEA concluded that the natural decline rate of these reservoirs is closer to 9 percent per year, a wholly unexpected and troubling outcome that tells us we are moving far more rapidly toward the end of the Petroleum Age than was previously assumed.

Replacing 4 percent of the world's oil supply every year is one thing; replacing 9 percent is a vastly greater challenge, given the huge cost and difficulty of developing new fields. Although the oil companies are spending greater amounts every year to locate and develop promising deposits, they are finding fewer and smaller fields. And the reservoirs they do manage to bring on line tend to empty out much faster than the giants discovered earlier, in the golden years of discovery following World War II. For example, the two major discoveries of the 1960s, the North Slope of Alaska and the North Sea, are already experiencing rapid rates of output decline. Only two large discoveries have been made since then—the Kashagan field in the Caspian Sea and the Tupi field in Atlantic waters off Rio de Janeiro—and both pose extraordinary technical challenges to the companies hoping to bring them into production.

The only way to ensure adequate supplies of oil in the years ahead is for the world's oil companies to make mammoth investments in drilling rigs, pipelines, and other infrastructure to bring new reservoirs into production. According to the IEA, satisfying anticipated world demand in 2030 will require a minimum of $350 billion per year (in 2007 dollars) in such investments *every year* between now and then. But much of this money will have to be spent on facilities in the hurricane-prone waters of the Gulf of Mexico and the Atlantic, or in conflict-prone areas of Africa, the Middle East, and Central Asia—which gives pause to investors.

Even before the onset of the world's current economic crisis, many investors were deterred by the rising cost of such ventures and, in the case of projects in Africa, the Middle East, and the former Soviet Union, by the potential for big losses as a result of conflict, sabotage, corruption, or governmental intervention. Since the economic crisis erupted, investors have become even more skittish, proving extremely reluctant to commit large sums to any projects that entail risks of this sort. Thus, even though oil resources could prove abundant in some of these areas, it is questionable whether they will be brought on line in time to satisfy global needs. As noted by the IEA in its November 12 report: "It cannot be taken for granted" that the major private oil companies and government-owned oil firms like Saudi Aramco will allocate sufficient funds "to keep up the necessary pace of investment."

What this means, in sum, is that the worldwide supply of petroleum is likely to fall short of projected global requirements in the decades to come. To put this in further perspective, the most recent edition of the DOE's *International Energy Outlook* projects that world oil supply will rise from 83.6 million barrels per day in 2005 to 95.7 million barrels in 2015, 101.3 million in 2020, and 112.5 million in 2030. (This includes conventional oil plus "nonconventional" supplies such as shale oil, Canadian tar sands, and biofuels.) But many experts, drawing on the sort of analysis presented above, now believe that world production will reach a peak in output well before 2030, probably between 2010 and 2015, at a level of about 95 million barrels per day. They believe output will remain at about that level for several years and then commence an irreversible decline—dropping far below the DOE's estimate of 112 million barrels for 2030. This means that, by 2030 or so, the world could be looking at a short-fall of anywhere from 25 to 30 million barrels of oil per day—a huge plunge in the global supply of energy.

More Carbon Needed

Clearly, any effort to satisfy world fuel requirements in the years after 2015 will require a significant increase in the production of *other* sources of energy. In the first instance, this will lead to greater dependence on the two other fossil fuels, natural gas and coal. Many experts believe that the output of gas and coal can be substantially augmented to compensate for the declining availability of oil. But this, too, could prove problematic.

Without going into great detail, any increase in the global output of natural gas will confront many of the same sorts of hurdles encountered in the case of petroleum. Like petroleum, gas is a finite substance produced by natural phenomena over many millions of years and is often found in similar geological formations. Just as the global output of oil is expected to reach a maximum or peak level in the not-too-distant future, so too will natural gas attain a peak in the third or fourth decade of the century.

Competition for access to the world's remaining reserves of oil and natural gas is destined to become increasingly fierce.

Also as in the case of oil, many of the world's largest reservoirs of gas have already been located and exploited, suggesting that less-attractive fields—those in remote locations like northern Alaska, eastern Siberia, and the Arctic Ocean—are all that remain for future development. Some additional gas is trapped in coal beds, shale rock, and other distinctive geological formations that can be mined with appropriate technologies. Industry experts believe it will be possible to exploit all these remote and "nonconventional" sources of gas. However, the cost will be high, and it is doubtful that these sources will ever prove sufficient to replace more than a tiny share of the energy now provided by oil.

Any increase in the consumption of natural gas will also entail significant geopolitical risks. No less than 56 percent of the world's known gas reserves are held by just three countries—Russia, Iran, and Qatar—and these three have recently taken steps to solidify their control over the fuel's future utilization by creating the nucleus of a "natural gas OPEC." Several other leading gas producers, including Algeria, Libya, Saudi Arabia, and the Central Asian states, have also expressed interest in forming such a cartel, suggesting the likelihood of future constraints on natural gas's global availability. This is precisely the sort of environment in which conflict could arise over access to sources of natural gas, much as has been the case in past years over access to sources of petroleum.

Coal presents a rather different set of problems. Coal is expected to remain relatively abundant well into the middle of the century (after which it, too, will reach a peak in production and go into decline). Moreover, large deposits of it are located in major energy-consuming nations like China, India, Russia, and the United States. With existing technology, coal is the cheapest fuel available for producing electricity, so its use is growing in many developing countries as well as in the United States. According to the DOE, China's coal consumption will grow by 120 percent between 2005 and 2030; in India it will grow by 80 percent, and in the United States by 31 percent. Coal can also be used as a feedstock for synthetic gas and diesel fuel, making it an attractive substitute for natural gas and oil as these materials become increasingly scarce.

However, any increase in coal consumption using existing combustion technologies will result in a speed-up of global warming and an onslaught of climatic disasters. This is so because coal releases more carbon dioxide per unit of energy generated than do the other two fossil fuels. Scientists and engineers are working on a technique to separate the carbon from the coal and bury it before combustion occurs—so-called carbon capture and storage (CCS) technology. But plants using this technique are expected to be far more costly than existing ones, and at this point no commercial facility employs this method. As the impacts of global warming grow more severe, power companies will come under greater pressure to use this technology, but it is unlikely that it will have achieved widespread adoption by 2030. What is more likely, at that point, is an increase in conventional coal technology, producing a heightened risk of catastrophic climate change.

Alternating Current

Obviously, the best hope for all of us on the planet (and for our descendents) is for the energy industry—and the world's major governments—to invest in a massive, rapid expansion of alternative sources of energy, especially renewables like solar, wind, geothermal, and advanced (non-edible) biofuels. These sources are not derived from finite materials like oil, natural gas, and coal but are infinitely replaceable, and release very little or no carbon in their operation. Eventually, when the great energy transition is completed, most of the world's energy supply is likely to be derived from these sources. But increasing the amount of energy supplied by these sources will prove an uphill and expensive struggle—and until that process is completed, we could be in for very difficult times.

At present, renewables and hydropower supply only 7.7 percent of the world's energy. According to the latest projections from the DOE, this figure will only rise to 8.5 percent by 2030, not including biofuels; with the addition of bio-fuels, it would rise by another percentage point or two. (Nuclear power provides another 5.9 percent of world supply currently. Although nuclear power is likely to continue playing a small but significant role in satisfying world energy needs, it poses so many safety, non-proliferation, and waste disposal challenges, as well as legal and financial challenges to investors, that it is unlikely to exceed single digits in its net contribution to the global supply.) Even if we assume these figures are overly pessimistic, this is hardly enough to compensate for the decline in oil or our perilous reliance on coal. Only a tripling or quadrupling in the share of energy provided by renewables and advanced biofuels by 2030 can put us far along the path of a successful transition.

Several factors account for the slow pace of renewable energy's development. To begin with, major utilities and their government backers have long been accustomed to relying on oil, coal, gas, and nuclear power, so they have been reluctant to make major investments in alternative sources of power. According to the IEA, three-quarters of the world's projected output of electricity in 2020 (and more than half in 2030) will come from generation facilities that are already in operation today—almost all of them powered by fossil fuels or nuclear energy. Furthermore, most of the new plants under construction—especially in China and India, where the demand for added electricity is greatest—are of this type. It will be very hard, under these circumstances, to increase the share of energy provided by alternative sources.

In addition, wind, solar, biofuels, and other, more advanced sources of energy face many obstacles that must be overcome before they can replace fossil fuels on a very large scale. Wind and solar power pose a common set of problems. Both collect energy intermittently, and so are off line for considerable periods of time. Also, both achieve their maximum effectiveness in remote areas like the American Southwest (in the case of solar power) or high plains (for wind) that are far removed from areas of greatest demand, and so lack adequate connectivity to the electrical grid. Biofuels pose different problems. Most ethanol in the United States is manufactured from corn ears, a valuable source of food for humans and animals; the very process of making it, moreover, entails a large and wasteful input of energy.

To overcome these various obstacles, huge sums must be spent—on developing new storage batteries so that energy collected from wind and the sun can be harvested when the supply is great and later dispersed when it is not; on an expanded (and more efficient) electrical grid connecting vast solar arrays and wind farms to major population centers; and on advanced biofuels using nonfood plant matter as a feedstock, and chemical rather than thermal means of manufacturing ethanol. Additional investment is also needed to develop other promising but as-yet unproven technologies, including hydrogen fuel cells, wave energy, and fusion reactors.

But even with a huge increase in spending on energy alternatives, such as President-elect Barack Obama and his supporters in Congress have proposed, it is highly unlikely that renewables, advanced biofuels, and climate-safe (that is, CCS) coal will be available on a large enough scale in 2030 to make up for what is likely to be an inadequate supply of oil and natural gas. Increased efforts at conservation will help, as will greater reliance on public transportation. But it is hard to escape the conclusion that in the middle stages of the great transition, from roughly 2020 to 2040, global energy supplies—except for climate-threatening coal—will be insufficient to meet global needs.

Competition Heats Up

In a world constrained by inadequate stockpiles of energy, we can expect intense geopolitical competition for whatever supplies *are* available at any given time. As the US National Intelligence Council (NIC) suggested in its November 2008 assessment of the likely strategic environment in 2025: "The rising energy demands of growing populations and economies may bring into question the availability, reliability, and affordability of energy supplies. Such a situation would heighten tensions between states competing for limited resources, especially if accompanied by increased political turbulence in the Middle East and a general loss of confidence in the ability of the marketplace to satisfy rising demands."

The NIC report, *Global Trends 2025: A Transformed World*, is particularly illuminating because it focuses on the same period discussed in this article: the midpoint in the great transition from fossil fuels to a post-petroleum economy. The report suggests, as well, that the world of 2025 will be well on its way toward the adoption of alternative forms of energy, yet will still be highly dependent on fossil fuels to satisfy most day-to-day requirements. At the same time, according to the report, significant problems will have arisen in boosting output of oil and gas to match rising worldwide demand. The result, it predicts, is an environment of perceived scarcity. In such an environment, political leaders will see no option but to employ any means at their disposal to maximize their own country's supplies—even at the risk of conflict with equally desperate competitors.

Most of our oil is drawn from several hundred giant reservoirs and many have already passed their peak.

"In the worst case," observes the NIC report, "this could lead to interstate conflicts if government leaders deem assured access to energy resources to be essential to maintaining domestic stability and the survival of their regime." Even in the absence of war, competition for energy will have important geopolitical implications as states undertake strategies to hedge against the possibility that existing energy supplies will not meet rising demands. For example, "energy-deficient states may employ transfers of arms and sensitive technologies and the promise of a political and military alliance as inducements to establish strategic relationships with energy-producing states."

Read deeper into the NIC report, and you find numerous portrayals of a world torn apart by relentless struggle over precarious supplies of oil and natural gas. Central Asia comes in for particular attention as a site of potential conflict among the United States, Russia, and China for control over that region's hydrocarbon reserves. Africa, a growing source of oil for the United States and China, is also seen as a potential site of geopolitical rivalry. Even the Arctic—increasingly open to oil and gas drilling as a result of global warming—is deemed a possible locale for conflict.

These kinds of rivalries are doubly dangerous. Not only do they risk full-scale war among the major powers, with all the destructive effects that would entail, but they would also consume mammoth sums of money that could otherwise be devoted to the development of energy alternatives, thereby slowing the transition to a post-petroleum industrial system. In fact, a world of recurring energy wars could make a successful transition impossible, or delay it until such time as the world economy had contracted substantially and global warming had advanced much further than it might have otherwise.

It is painfully evident, then, that the current pace of transition is far too slow to achieve the intended results in time to avert global catastrophe. Only a radical increase in the tempo of change can ensure that alternative sources of energy will be available in 2025 and beyond to compensate for the decline in oil and prevent increased dependence on unsafe coal. This will require vastly greater expenditures on efforts to realize the full potential of wind power, solar, geothermal, advanced biofuels, hydrogen, and climate-safe coal, along with increased investment in public transportation. The world of 2050 can be a bright, livable environment in which renewable energy sources power prosperity—but only if we take steps now to accelerate the transition from our current energy system to its unavoidable replacement.

MICHAEL T. KLARE, a *Current History* contributing editor, is a professor at Hampshire College and author of *Rising Powers, Shrinking Planet: The New Geopolitics of Energy* (Metropolitan Books, 2008).

From *Current History*, January 2009, pp. 26–32. Copyright © 2009 by Current History, Inc. Reprinted by permission.

The Rise of the Rest

It's true China is booming, Russia is growing more assertive, terrorism is a threat. But if America is losing the ability to dictate to this new world, it has not lost the ability to lead.

FAREED ZAKARIA

Americans are glum at the moment. No, I mean really glum. In April, a new poll revealed that 81 percent of the American people believe that the country is on the "wrong track." In the 25 years that pollsters have asked this question, last month's response was by far the most negative. Other polls, asking similar questions, found levels of gloom that were even more alarming, often at 30- and 40-year highs. There are reasons to be pessimistic—a financial panic and looming recession, a seemingly endless war in Iraq, and the ongoing threat of terrorism. But the facts on the ground—unemployment numbers, foreclosure rates, deaths from terror attacks—are simply not dire enough to explain the present atmosphere of malaise.

American anxiety springs from something much deeper, a sense that large and disruptive forces are coursing through the world. In almost every industry, in every aspect of life, it feels like the patterns of the past are being scrambled. "Whirl is king, having driven out Zeus," wrote Aristophanes 2,400 years ago. And—for the first time in living memory—the United States does not seem to be leading the charge. Americans see that a new world is coming into being, but fear it is one being shaped in distant lands and by foreign people.

Look around. The world's tallest building is in Taipei, and will soon be in Dubai. Its largest publicly traded company is in Beijing. Its biggest refinery is being constructed in India. Its largest passenger airplane is built in Europe. The largest investment fund on the planet is in Abu Dhabi; the biggest movie industry is Bollywood, not Hollywood. Once quintessentially American icons have been usurped by the natives. The largest Ferris wheel is in Singapore. The largest casino is in Macao, which overtook Las Vegas in gambling revenues last year. America no longer dominates even its favorite sport, shopping. The Mall of America in Minnesota once boasted that it was the largest shopping mall in the world. Today it wouldn't make the top ten. In the most recent rankings, only two of the world's ten richest people are American. These lists are arbitrary and a bit silly, but consider that only ten years ago, the United States would have serenely topped almost every one of these categories.

These factoids reflect a seismic shift in power and attitudes. It is one that I sense when I travel around the world. In America, we are still debating the nature and extent of anti-Americanism. One side says that the problem is real and worrying and that we must woo the world back. The other says this is the inevitable price of power and that many of these countries are envious—and vaguely French—so we can safely ignore their griping. But while we argue over why they hate us, "they" have moved on, and are now far more interested in other, more dynamic parts of the globe. The world has shifted from anti-Americanism to *post*-Americanism.

I. The End of Pax Americana

During the 1980s, when I would visit India—where I grew up—most Indians were fascinated by the United States. Their interest, I have to confess, was not in the important power players in Washington or the great intellectuals in Cambridge.

People would often ask me about . . . Donald Trump. He was the very symbol of the United States—brassy, rich, and modern. He symbolized the feeling that if you wanted to find the biggest and largest anything, you had to look to America. Today, outside of entertainment figures, there is no comparable interest in American personalities. If you wonder why, read India's newspapers or watch its television. There are dozens of Indian businessmen who are now wealthier than the Donald. Indians are obsessed by their own vulgar real estate billionaires. And that newfound interest in *their own* story is being replicated across much of the world.

How much? Well, consider this fact. In 2006 and 2007, 124 countries grew their economies at over 4 percent a year. That includes more than 30 countries in Africa. Over the last two decades, lands outside the industrialized West have been growing at rates that were once unthinkable. While there have been booms and busts, the overall trend has been unambiguously upward. Antoine van Agtmael, the fund manager who coined the term "emerging markets," has identified the 25 companies most likely to be the world's next great multinationals. His list includes four companies each from Brazil, Mexico, South Korea, and Taiwan; three from India, two from China, and one each from Argentina, Chile, Malaysia, and South Africa. This is something much broader than the much-ballyhooed rise of China or even Asia. It is the rise of the rest—the rest of the world.

We are living through the third great power shift in modern history. The first was the rise of the Western world, around the 15th century. It produced the world as we know it now—science and technology, commerce and capitalism, the industrial and agricultural revolutions. It also led to the prolonged political dominance of the nations of the Western world. The second shift, which took place in the closing years of the 19th century, was the rise of the United States. Once it industrialized, it soon became the most powerful nation in the world, stronger than any likely combination of other nations. For the last 20 years, America's superpower status in every realm has been largely unchallenged—something that's never happened before in history, at least since the Roman Empire dominated the known world 2,000 years ago. During this Pax Americana, the global economy has accelerated dramatically. And that expansion is the driver behind the third great power shift of the modern age—the rise of the rest.

At the military and political level, we still live in a unipolar world. But along every other dimension—industrial, financial, social, cultural—the distribution of power is shifting, moving away from American dominance. In terms of war and peace, economics and business, ideas and art, this will produce a landscape that is quite different from the one we have lived in until now—one defined and directed from many places and by many peoples.

The post-American world is naturally an unsettling prospect for Americans, but it should not be. This will not be a world defined by the decline of America but rather the rise of everyone else. It is the result of a series of positive trends that have been progressing over the last 20 years, trends that have created an international climate of unprecedented peace and prosperity.

I know. That's not the world that people perceive. We are told that we live in dark, dangerous times. Terrorism, rogue states, nuclear proliferation, financial panics, recession, outsourcing, and illegal immigrants all loom large in the national discourse. Al Qaeda, Iran, North Korea, China, Russia are all threats in some way or another. But just how violent is today's world, really?

A team of scholars at the University of Maryland has been tracking deaths caused by organized violence. Their data show that wars of all kinds have been declining since the mid-1980s and that we are now at the lowest levels of global violence since the 1950s. Deaths from terrorism are reported to have risen in recent years. But on closer examination, 80 percent of those casualties come from Afghanistan and Iraq, which are really war zones with ongoing insurgencies—and the overall numbers remain small. Looking at the evidence, Harvard's polymath professor Steven Pinker has ventured to speculate that we are probably living "in the most peaceful time of our species' existence."

Why does it not feel that way? Why do we think we live in scary times? Part of the problem is that as violence has been ebbing, information has been exploding. The last 20 years have produced an information revolution that brings us news and, most crucially, images from around the world all the time. The immediacy of the images and the intensity of the 24-hour news cycle combine to produce constant hype. Every weather disturbance is the "storm of the decade." Every bomb that explodes is BREAKING NEWS. Because the information revolution is so new, we—reporters, writers, readers, viewers—are all just now figuring out how to put everything in context.

We didn't watch daily footage of the two million people who died in Indochina in the 1970s, or the million who perished in the sands of the Iran-Iraq war ten years later. We saw little of the civil war in the Congo in the 1990s, where millions died. But today any bomb that goes off, any rocket that is fired, any death that results, is documented by someone, somewhere and ricochets instantly across the world. Add to this terrorist attacks, which are random and brutal. "That could have been me," you think. Actually, your chances of being killed in a terrorist attack are tiny—for an American, smaller than drowning in your bathtub. But it doesn't feel like that.

The threats we face are real. Islamic jihadists are a nasty bunch—they do want to attack civilians everywhere. But it is increasingly clear that militants and suicide bombers make up a tiny portion of the world's 1.3 billion Muslims. They can do real damage, especially if they get their hands on nuclear weapons. But the combined efforts of the world's governments have effectively put them on the run and continue to track them and their money. Jihad persists, but the jihadists have had to scatter, work in small local cells, and use simple and undetectable weapons. They have not been able to hit big, symbolic targets, especially ones involving Americans. So they blow up bombs in cafés, marketplaces, and subway stations. The problem is that in doing so, they kill locals and alienate ordinary Muslims. Look at the polls. Support for violence of any kind has dropped dramatically over the last five years in all Muslim countries.

Militant groups have reconstituted in certain areas where they exploit a particular local issue or have support from a local ethnic group or sect, most worryingly in Pakistan and Afghanistan where Islamic radicalism has become associated with Pashtun identity politics. But as a result, these groups are becoming more local and less global. Al Qaeda in Iraq, for example, has turned into a group that is more anti-Shiite than anti-American. The bottom line is this: since 9/11, Al Qaeda Central, the gang run by Osama bin Laden, has not been able to launch a single major terror attack in the West or any Arab country—its original targets. They used to do terrorism, now they make videotapes. Of course one day they will get lucky again, but that they have been stymied for almost seven years points out that in this battle between governments and terror groups, the former need not despair.

Some point to the dangers posed by countries like Iran. These rogue states present real problems, but look at them in context. The American economy is 68 times the size of Iran's. Its military budget is 110 times that of the mullahs. Were Iran to attain a nuclear capacity, it would complicate the geopolitics of the Middle East. But none of the problems we face compare with the dangers posed by a rising Germany in the first half of the 20th century or an expansionist Soviet Union in the second half. Those were great global powers bent on world domination. If this is 1938, as some neoconservatives tell us, then Iran is Romania, not Germany.

Others paint a dark picture of a world in which dictators are on the march. China and Russia and assorted other oil potentates are surging. We must draw the battle lines now, they warn, and engage in a great Manichean struggle that will define the next century. Some of John McCain's rhetoric has suggested that he adheres to this dire, dyspeptic view. But before we all sign on for a new Cold War, let's take a deep breath and gain some perspective. Today's rising great powers are relatively benign by historical measure. In the past, when countries grew rich they've wanted to become great military powers, overturn the existing order, and create their own empires or spheres of influence. But since the rise of Japan and Germany in the 1960s and 1970s, none have done this, choosing instead to get rich within the existing international order. China and India are clearly moving in this direction. Even Russia, the most aggressive and revanchist great power today, has done little that compares with past aggressors. The fact that for the first time in history, the United States can contest Russian influence in Ukraine—a country 4,800 miles away from Washington that Russia has dominated or ruled for 350 years—tells us something about the balance of power between the West and Russia.

Compare Russia and China with where they were 35 years ago. At the time both (particularly Russia) were great power threats, actively conspiring against the United States, arming guerrilla movement across the globe, funding insurgencies and civil wars, blocking every American plan in the United Nations. Now they are more integrated into the global economy and society than at any point in at least 100 years. They occupy an uncomfortable gray zone, neither friends nor foes, cooperating with the United States and the West on some issues, obstructing others. But how large is their potential for trouble? Russia's military spending is $35 billion, or 1/20th of the Pentagon's. China has about 20 nuclear missiles that

can reach the United States. We have 830 missiles, most with multiple warheads, that can reach China. Who should be worried about whom? Other rising autocracies like Saudi Arabia and the Gulf states are close U.S. allies that shelter under America's military protection, buy its weapons, invest in its companies, and follow many of its diktats. With Iran's ambitions growing in the region, these countries are likely to become even closer allies, unless America gratuitously alienates them.

II. The Good News

In July 2006, I spoke with a senior member of the Israeli government, a few days after Israel's war with Hezbollah had ended. He was genuinely worried about his country's physical security. Hezbollah's rockets had reached farther into Israel than people had believed possible. The military response had clearly been ineffectual: Hezbollah launched as many rockets on the last day of the war as on the first. Then I asked him about the economy—the area in which he worked. His response was striking. "That's puzzled all of us," he said. "The stock market was higher on the last day of the war than on the first! The same with the shekel."

The government was spooked, but the market wasn't.

Or consider the Iraq War, which has produced deep, lasting chaos and dysfunction in that country. Over two million refugees have crowded into neighboring lands. That would seem to be the kind of political crisis guaranteed to spill over. But as I've traveled in the Middle East over the last few years, I've been struck by how little Iraq's troubles have destabilized the region. Everywhere you go, people angrily denounce American foreign policy. But most Middle Eastern countries are booming. Iraq's neighbors—Turkey, Jordan, and Saudi Arabia—are enjoying unprecedented prosperity. The Gulf states are busy modernizing their economies and societies, asking the Louvre, New York University, and Cornell Medical School to set up remote branches in the desert. There's little evidence of chaos, instability, and rampant Islamic fundamentalism.

The underlying reality across the globe is of enormous vitality. For the first time ever, most countries around the world are practicing sensible economics. Consider inflation. Over the past 20 years hyperinflation, a problem that used to bedevil large swaths of the world from Turkey to Brazil to Indonesia, has largely vanished, tamed by successful fiscal and monetary policies. The results are clear and stunning. The share of people living on $1 a day has plummeted from 40 percent in 1981 to 18 percent in 2004 and is estimated to drop to 12 percent by 2015. Poverty is falling in countries that house 80 percent of the world's population. There remains real poverty in the world—most worryingly in 50 basket-case countries that contain 1 billion people—but the overall trend has never been more encouraging. The global economy has more than doubled in size over the last 15 years and is now approaching $54 trillion! Global trade has grown by 133 percent in the same period. The expansion of the global economic pie has been so large, with so many countries participating, that it has become the dominating force of the current era. Wars, terrorism, and civil strife cause disruptions temporarily but eventually they are overwhelmed by the waves of globalization. These circumstances may not last, but it is worth understanding what the world has looked like for the past few decades.

III. A New Nationalism

Of course, global growth is also responsible for some of the biggest problems in the world right now. It has produced tons of money—what businesspeople call liquidity—that moves around the world. The combination of low inflation and lots of cash has meant low interest rates, which in turn have made people act greedily and/or stupidly. So we have witnessed over the last two decades a series of bubbles—in East Asian countries, technology stocks, housing, subprime mortgages, and emerging market equities. Growth also explains one of the signature events of our times—soaring commodity prices. $100 oil is just the tip of the barrel. Almost all commodities are at 200-year highs. Food, only a few decades ago in danger of price collapse, is now in the midst of a scary rise. None of this is due to dramatic fall-offs in supply. It is demand, growing global demand, that is fueling these prices. The effect of more and more people eating, drinking, washing, driving, and consuming will have seismic effects on the global system. These may be high-quality problems, but they are deep problems nonetheless.

The most immediate effect of global growth is the appearance of new economic powerhouses on the scene. It is an accident of history that for the last several centuries, the richest countries in the world have all been very small in terms of population. Denmark has 5.5 million people, the Netherlands has 16.6 million. The United States is the biggest of the bunch and has dominated the advanced industrial world. But the real giants—China, India, Brazil—have been sleeping, unable or unwilling to join the world of functioning economies. Now they are on the move and naturally, given their size, they will have a large footprint on the map of the future. Even if people in these countries remain relatively poor, as nations their total wealth will be massive. Or to put it another way, any number, no matter how small, when multiplied by 2.5 billion becomes a very big number. (2.5 billion is the population of China plus India.)

The rise of China and India is really just the most obvious manifestation of a rising world. In dozens of big countries, one can see the same set of forces at work—a growing economy, a resurgent society, a vibrant culture, and a rising sense of national pride. That pride can morph into something uglier. For me, this was vividly illustrated a few years ago when I was chatting with a young Chinese executive in an Internet café in Shanghai. He wore Western clothes, spoke fluent English, and was immersed in global pop culture.

He was a product of globalization and spoke its language of bridge building and cosmopolitan values. At least, he did so until we began talking about Taiwan, Japan, and even the United States. (We did not discuss Tibet, but I'm sure had we done so, I could have added it to this list.) His responses were filled with passion, bellicosity, and intolerance. I felt as if I were in Germany in 1910, speaking to a young German professional, who would have been equally modern and yet also a staunch nationalist.

As economic fortunes rise, so inevitably does nationalism. Imagine that your country has been poor and marginal for centuries. Finally, things turn around and it becomes a symbol of economic progress and success. You would be proud, and anxious that your people win recognition and respect throughout the world.

In many countries such nationalism arises from a pent-up frustration over having to accept an entirely Western, or American, narrative of world history—one in which they are miscast or remain bit players. Russians have long chafed over the manner in which Western countries remember World War II. The American narrative is one in which the United States and Britain heroically defeat the forces of fascism. The Normandy landings are the climactic highpoint of the war—the beginning of the end. The Russians point out, however, that in fact the entire Western front was a sideshow. Three quarters of all German forces were engaged on the Eastern front fighting Russian troops, and Germany suffered 70 percent of its casualties there. The Eastern front involved more land combat than all other theaters of World War II put together.

Such divergent national perspectives always existed. But today, thanks to the information revolution, they are amplified, echoed, and disseminated. Where once there were only the narratives laid out by *The New York Times, Time, Newsweek,* the BBC, and CNN, there are now dozens of indigenous networks and channels—from Al Jazeera to New Delhi's NDTV to Latin America's Telesur. The result is that the "rest" are now dissecting the assumptions and narratives of the West and providing alternative views. A young Chinese diplomat told me in 2006, "When you tell us that we support a dictatorship in Sudan to have access to its oil, what I want to say is, 'And how is that different from your support of a medieval monarchy in Saudi Arabia?' We see the hypocrisy, we just don't say anything—yet."

The fact that newly rising nations are more strongly asserting their ideas and interests is inevitable in a post-American world. This raises a conundrum—how to get a world of many actors to work together. The traditional mechanisms of international cooperation are fraying. The U.N. Security Council has as its permanent members the victors of a war that ended more than 60 years ago. The G8 does not include China, India or Brazil—the three fastest-growing large economies in the world—and yet claims to represent the movers and shakers of the world economy. By tradition, the IMF is always headed by a European and the World Bank by an American. This "tradition," like the segregated customs of an old country club, might be charming to an insider. But to the majority who live outside the West, it seems bigoted. Our challenge is this: Whether the problem is a trade dispute or a human rights tragedy like Darfur or climate change, the only solutions that will work are those involving many nations. But arriving at solutions when more countries and more non-governmental players are feeling empowered will be harder than ever.

IV. The Next American Century

Many look at the vitality of this emerging world and conclude that the United States has had its day. "Globalization is striking back," Gabor Steingart, an editor at Germany's leading news magazine, Der Spiegel, writes in a best-selling book. As others prosper, he argues, the United States has lost key industries, its people have stopped saving money, and its government has become increasingly indebted to Asian central banks. The current financial crisis has only given greater force to such fears.

But take a step back. Over the last 20 years, globalization has been gaining depth and breadth. America has benefited massively from these trends. It has enjoyed unusually robust growth, low unemployment and inflation, and received hundreds of billions of dollars in investment. These are not signs of economic collapse. Its companies have entered new countries and industries with great success, using global supply chains and technology to stay in the vanguard of efficiency. U.S. exports and manufacturing have actually held their ground and services have boomed.

The United States is currently ranked as the globe's most competitive economy by the World Economic Forum. It remains dominant in many industries of the future like nanotechnology, biotechnology, and dozens of smaller high-tech fields. Its universities are the finest in the world, making up 8 of the top ten and 37 of the top fifty, according to a prominent ranking produced by Shanghai Jiao Tong University. A few years ago the National Science Foundation put out a scary and much-discussed statistic. In 2004, the group said, 950,000 engineers graduated from China and India, while only 70,000 graduated from the United States. But those numbers are wildly off the mark. If you exclude the care mechanics and repairmen—who are all counted as engineers in Chinese and Indian statistics—the numbers look quite different. Per capita, it turns out, the United States trains more engineers than either of the Asian giants.

But America's hidden secret is that most of these engineers are immigrants. Foreign students and immigrants account for almost 50 percent of all science researchers in the country. In 2006 they received 40 percent of all PhDs. By 2010, 75 percent of all science PhDs in this country will be awarded to foreign students. When these graduates settle in the country, they create economic opportunity. Half of all Silicon Valley start-ups have one founder who is an immigrant or first generation American. The potential for a new burst of

American productivity depends not on our education system or R&D spending, but on our immigration policies. If these people are allowed and encouraged to stay, then innovation will happen here. If they leave, they'll take it with them.

More broadly, this is America's great—and potentially insurmountable—strength. It remains the most open, flexible society in the world, able to absorb other people, cultures, ideas, goods, and services. The country thrives on the hunger and energy of poor immigrants. Faced with the new technologies of foreign companies, or growing markets overseas, it adapts and adjusts. When you compare this dynamism with the closed and hierarchical nations that were once superpowers, you sense that the United States is different and may not fall into the trap of becoming rich, and fat, and lazy.

American society can adapt to this new world. But can the American government? Washington has gotten used to a world in which all roads led to its doorstep. America has rarely had to worry about benchmarking to the rest of the world—it was always so far ahead. But the natives have gotten good at capitalism and the gap is narrowing. Look at the rise of London. It's now the world's leading financial center—less because of things that the United States did badly than those London did well, like improving regulation and becoming friendlier to foreign capital. Or take the U.S. health care system, which has become a huge liability for American companies. U.S. carmakers now employ more people in Ontario, Canada, than Michigan because in Canada their health care costs are lower. Twenty years ago, the United States had the lowest corporate taxes in the world. Today they are the second-highest. It's not that ours went up. Those of others went down.

American parochialism is particularly evident in foreign policy. Economically, as other countries grow, for the most part the pie expands and everyone wins. But geopolitics is a struggle for influence: as other nations become more active internationally, they will seek greater freedom of action. This necessarily means that America's unimpeded influence will decline. But if the world that's being created has more power centers, nearly all are invested in order, stability and progress. Rather than narrowly obsessing about our own short-term interests and interest groups, our chief priority should be to bring these rising forces into the global system, to integrate them so that they in turn broaden and deepen global economic, political, and cultural ties. If China, India, Russia, Brazil all feel that they have a stake in the existing global order, there will be less danger of war, depression, panics, and breakdowns. There will be lots of problems, crisis, and tensions, but they will occur against a backdrop of systemic stability. This benefits them but also us. It's the ultimate win-win.

To bring others into this world, the United States needs to make its own commitment to the system clear. So far, America has been able to have it both ways. It is the global rule-maker but doesn't always play by the rules. And forget about standards created by others. Only three countries in the world don't use the metric system—Liberia, Myanmar, and the United States. For America to continue to lead the world, we will have to first joint it.

Americans—particularly the American government—have not really understood the rise of the rest. This is one of the most thrilling stories in history. Billions of people are escaping from abject poverty. The world will be enriched and ennobled as they become consumers, producers, inventors, thinkers, dreamers, and doers. This is all happening because of American ideas and actions. For 60 years, the United States has pushed countries to open their markets, free up their politics, and embrace trade and technology. American diplomats, businessmen, and intellectuals have urged people in distant lands to be unafraid of change, to join the advanced world, to learn the secrets of our success. Yet just as they

are beginning to do so, we are losing faith in such ideas. We have become suspicious of trade, openness, immigration, and investment because now it's not Americans going abroad but foreigners coming to America. Just as the world is opening up, we are closing down.

Generations from now, when historians write about these times, they might note that by the turn of the 21st century, the United States had succeeded in its great, historical mission—globalizing the world. We don't want them to write that along the way, we forgot to globalize ourselves.

Adapted from The Post-American World by **FAREED ZAKARIA.** © 2008 by **FAREED ZAKARIA.** With permission of the publisher, W.W. Norton & Company, Inc.

Feminists and Fundamentalists

Reassertions of an idealized past and a restored 'women's place' are occurring, from Kabul to Cambridge, at a time when the international community has concurred that women's rights are a global good.

Kavita Ramdas

The women's movement, as we refer to it now, was one of the most successful movements of the past century. It has been successful in many ways. Perhaps the most tangible evidence is that women's rights have become a desirable commodity, something that in the company of civilized nations people are proud to hold up as a model of what they have achieved, much in the way that democracy has become a global good.

In 1995, 189 countries signed a pact accepting the Beijing Declaration and Platform for Action as an expression of their goals. The platform called itself "an agenda for women's empowerment. It aims at removing obstacles to women's active participation in all spheres of public and private life, through a full and equal share in economic, social, cultural, and political decision making. This means the principle of shared power and responsibility should be established at home, in the workplace, and in wider national and international communities. Equality between women and men is a matter of human rights and a condition for social justice. It is also a necessary and fundamental prerequisite for equality, development, and peace."

These are, indeed, the ideals to which we as an international community should aspire. And in achieving this recognition of women's rights as a global good, we have arguably accomplished one of the most essential outcomes for any social movement: a broad and diverse constituency now concurs that it shares certain values and that we should all collectively promote them.

The women's movement has also been successful, maybe a little less so, with respect to a narrower definition of accomplishment: legal progress in a variety of areas. Today we see—and we sometimes take it for granted—that women are admitted to educational institutions where years ago they were not accepted; that women enjoy opportunities to pursue careers in fields formerly closed to them; that they have inheritance rights, the right to open their own bank accounts, and so forth.

Of course, women still have a long way to go in achieving the narrower legal definition of equality, even in America. Something that seems fairly basic—equal pay for equal work—has not been and probably will not be approved. The Equal Rights Amendment languishes still in the halls of the US Congress. And the United States remains one of the few countries that has not signed the Convention on the Elimination of All Forms of Discrimination against Women.

It does seem, however, that most of the world's nations have accepted women's rights as a global good. And yet the question arises: Is this achievement permanent? Is there some development that might threaten this and future advances of the women's movement?

Social Insecurity

While many of us have arrived at an apparent consensus about the good sense of making women's rights central to our enterprise as forward-looking communities, we are also seeing that the world is coping with unprecedented and unbelievably rapid change—change in science and technology, in social structures, in the movement of people and ideas across borders. As a consequence, all kinds of relationships that once were given are today up for grabs: relationships between individuals and communities, between citizens and states, between parents and children, between husbands and wives. Because of this, millions of people at some fundamental level feel less secure.

Now, the world as we know it has been run to this point by men. Therefore, today's pervasive insecurity is also challenging the prevailing structures in which men set the rules, including the rules of public discourse and political engagement. So what we are seeing is a reaction. The world has mostly agreed that women's rights are a good thing. But, at the same time, this frightening sense of change is condensing into one particular evidence of that change. And that evidence is the transformed position of women in our societies.

The result is a variety of efforts to reassert idealized notions of the past. Islamic fundamentalism is one example that attracts considerable attention. But the assertion of an idealized past is happening across the world, across cultures, within different religious traditions, in different countries and languages, and at all levels of society.

Sistani and Summers

Consider the cases of Iraq's Ali al-Sistani and America's Lawrence Summers. Obviously, these are very different men. They do not share a similar worldview, and they come from very different contexts. Grand Ayatollah Sistani, who wants to impose fundamentalist Islamic constraints on Iraqi women, lives in a rapidly transforming postcolonial society. His is a Muslim country, where the past is alive. Summers—the president of Harvard University who infamously wondered aloud whether women have the same innate abilities in math and science as men—lives in a highly developed capitalist society.

Yet America is also a society in which women increasingly challenge academia and male privilege within academia. Both Iraq and the United States are attempting to respond to where women are located within their social structures. I would argue that both Sistani and Summers are trying, at some level, to place boundaries around what women's roles ought to be.

They are doing so because these roles are up for grabs, and because the aspirations of women pose a widespread dilemma. Having more or less signed on in general to the global good of women's rights, many people around the world feel insecure about what women's advances might mean for their own lives, for their own relationships, for decision making in their own institutions.

This is the global threat: the feeling that somehow, if we let women just take off with this idea about women's rights, who knows where it could go? The last US presidential election highlighted a classic example of this fear, with a number of state ballot referendums drawing voters determined to defend the institution of marriage against perceived erosion.

Indeed, for some the very relevance of men to the reproductive process seems under assault. State governments in America continue to impose restrictions on abortion. But what significance do male partners retain if, outside of marriage between "man and wife," a woman can go to a sperm bank and make an independent choice to have a child? And what does this mean for society? And how do you begin to control this?

The Way We Were

It is not an accident that mass rapes became a symbol of the Bosnian war during the 1990s. An estimated 20,000 to 50,000 Bosnian women were raped during that genocidal conflict. Indeed, mass rape has become a feature of modern warfare—a strange phenomenon, when you consider that warfare has also become so highly technologically developed. We have all these amazing smart bombs, yet we also witness one of the most medieval forms of exerting power. What does this represent, in a society, more broadly?

And how do we think about this reassertion of an idealized past, these "fundamentalisms?" They are certainly not unique to one religion; I have watched Hindu fundamentalists in India spend the past eight years eulogizing one male god in a society that has long prided itself on worshipping numerous goddesses as well as gods.

Predictably, the idealized tradition, the fundamentalist challenge, is borne everywhere on the backs of women, and there is widespread reluctance to oppose it. This is what we found in Afghanistan under the Taliban, a brutal form of gender apartheid that was allowed to exist until the United States invaded in the aftermath of 9-11. Even today, we hear many arguments for why we should not impose human rights on societies that have other cultural traditions—why, if women are treated badly, we ought to be careful about making demands because that may be how things are done in those societies.

The kind of violence that women and girls experience on a day-to-day basis around the world, the kind of entrenched discrimination they face—if this behavior were applied against almost any ethnic or national minority, there would be loud and persistent calls for intervention. After the US invasion of Afghanistan, some rhetoric was heard about the liberation of that country's women. But, as Afghan women would point out, that liberation did not happen until two edifices, two towers, were attacked in the United States.

The variety of fundamentalisms notwithstanding, the one thread they share is the attempt to control women's bodies, the ability of women to move freely, and their ability to speak with any kind of free voice within their societies. It is ironic but telling that these reassertions of an idealized past and a restored "women's place" are occurring, from Kabul to Cambridge, at a time when the international community has concurred that women's rights are a global good. They are occurring at a time when every major international foundation and financial institution has agreed that no development goals—whether in economics, political development, or social development—can be achieved without investing in girls' education and the full and equal participation of women.

The Feminist Vanguard

Fortunately, while there is a threat, there is also hope. The hope is that the women's movement and the advancement of women's rights will be the vanguard in the international community's struggle to overcome fundamentalisms.

You can see this hope in the dilemma the US government is struggling with right now. The Bush administration is caught in a tricky contradiction. Because we have all agreed that women's rights are a global good, the administration cannot say that women's rights do not matter. Yet it is deeply beholden to a Christian fundamentalist movement within the United States that truly believes we must return to an idealized notion of the past.

The Southern Baptist Church, for example, has decided to put the word "obey" back in marriage vows; a woman should obey her husband (it is not in the man's vows). Promise Keepers is another movement that harkens back to eighteenth- and nineteenth-century definitions of husbands as hunter-gatherers and women as loyal wives who stay at home and raise the family. President Bush himself has made a number of speeches that evoke idealized images of a time when, as my husband would say, "men were men, and women were women."

The harkening back to a more constrictive order for women continues while the United States claims to be liberating women overseas from uncivilized nations that do not support women's equality. Human rights are held up as a global good even as they are undermined in the everyday lives of women. At the level of implementation, what you actually see are increasing restrictions on the freedom and control that women have—over their reproductive choices and access to contraception, for example—along with cutbacks in spending on health and education that harm women the most.

> **This is the global threat: the feeling that somehow, if we let women just take off with this idea about women's rights, who knows where it could go?**

Some think Title IX has gone too far and want to turn it back. When many hear the term "Title IX," they think it has to do with women in sports. In fact, it has everything to do with President Summers' comments about women in the sciences. Title IX of the 1972 Education Amendments to the 1964 Civil Rights Act required fair access to a wide variety of educational resources—from soccer playing fields to science laboratories.

There are many levels at which, in the face of rhetorical acceptance of women's rights, policies and proposals are being pursued that would undermine achievements that took decades to accomplish. The women's movement has a vital role in resisting rollbacks.

Changing Culture

I work in the international arena, and people often ask me, "Why do other cultures not value women's rights?" And I like to remind them that there is nothing unique about cultures, and that there is no culture I can think of that intrinsically values women's rights.

Reformers in the United States fought for a very long time for women to be recognized as more than just the property of men, just as they struggled for the rights of black people to be recognized as human beings. Cultures are not static. There is nothing that says Western culture is inherently thoughtful and considerate and inclusive of women, minorities, or anyone else.

Why have some cultures evolved to a place where equal rights are regarded as desirable? Because those who have been most oppressed within these cultures have chosen to fight for the right to be treated with equality and dignity. And this is the same thing that is happening today in most of the world. In India, in Afghanistan, in Iraq, in Peru, in the indigenous communities of Mexico, people are struggling to have their culture evolve as a living, breathing thing, and to have women and girls who have not traditionally had voice in those cultures to now have voice.

There is hope in this—in women's rights as a fulcrum on which societies can tip toward modernity, not in the narrowly defined sense of Westernization, but true modernity, in terms of imagining a different conception of how the world can be organized. Women's movements struggle precisely at this fulcrum between modernity and the fundamentalist pressures to regress, and here there is promise.

In my work I have seen women in the most oppressive and closed societies take extraordinary risks and truly challenge the status quo. I have seen them find ways to make their culture more inclusive, more accepting, and more fundamentally equal for all people within their societies.

My organization, the Global Fund for Women, worked with Afghan women's groups during the Taliban's rule, both in refugee camps in Pakistan and in secret schools for girls—and for boys, I might add, inside Afghanistan. (One of the things people often do not think about is that the success of the women's movement accrues to both women and men. When the Taliban pulled women out of schools in Afghanistan, 65 percent of primary school teachers in the country were women. The government's action jeopardized the education of a whole generation of Afghan boys, who then had no alternative but to go to Islamic religious schools.)

What we found in our work over those years with a number of Afghan women's groups is that they are incredibly strategic about building alliances with male allies within their communities. They do not see their fight as a struggle against men. They see it as a struggle against the patriarchal system. They have been extraordinarily creative about choosing their priorities.

I was in Afghanistan in 2003 after the Taliban had been toppled. Like everyone else, I had seen the pictures of women throwing off their burqas, which everyone in the United States was very excited about (but which most women in Afghanistan, in fact, have not done; while in Iraq many more women have put them back on). To me, far more a sign of liberation in Afghanistan was a scene I witnessed in a small classroom in Kabul, where three women taught a class of 45 male teachers—village school teachers from different provinces around Afghanistan.

These three women, their heads covered in scarves, were discussing the pedagogy of successful education. Amid building blocks made out of recycled cigarette cartons, they were talking to the male teachers about how educators need to make learning joyful and pleasurable, something that children can be enthused about.

When it was time for questions and answers, I asked, "What does it feel like to be sitting in a classroom and listening to three women teachers teaching you?" One man raised his hand and said, "I'm a professor of mathematics and science, and for 25 years, Afghan schoolchildren are boys who have learned how to hold an AK-47 before they learned how to do basic math. I haven't been in a school that has had a science laboratory for 25 years." He said, "During these 25 years, it was women who kept education alive in our country, and I think it's time we should be learning from the women." It was an extraordinary statement, and to me, more powerful than any picture of a woman pulling off her burqa.

"Equal to What?"

Across much of the world the leadership of the women's movement has shifted from the kinds of experiences that Western feminists underwent in the 1960s and 1970s, which were very important and in many ways necessary, but which were very much filled with conflict. There is a willingness now in the developing world to be more inclusive, an approach born out of necessity and also from a sense that this is a struggle we have to be in together.

Women's groups in different parts of the world are showing an increasing ability to build on the notion that their states and the international institutions have all signed onto—this idea that women's rights are a global good—while at the same time finding a way to make it real in their own communities, finding a way to say, "Well, so what happens when the old traditions die?"

In Ethiopia, for example, over 90 percent of women go through female genital mutilation (FGM) as a rite of passage, and women's organizations are challenging the practice. But they are not challenging it from the perspective of "this is an evil, ancient, tribal tradition." Rather, they are looking to the root causes of the tradition.

As I heard an Ethiopian mother explain it, "If you know that the only economic security for your daughter is to ensure that she gets married, and if you know that no one will marry her unless she has gone through the process of FGM, because you cannot assure her purity otherwise, then you have no choice as a mother but to make your daughter go through it, even though you don't have to explain to us how painful it is and what the health consequences are, because each of us has lived those experiences."

If, however, we create an environment in which girls can go to school and stay in school longer, and women have opportunities to earn an income and contribute to their families, then girls will not have to depend for their economic prospects on being married off at age 12 or 13. And if we look at the status of widows in Ethiopia and attend to their security, we can also make a difference, because it turns out that it is the widows who get paid for performing the circumcision ceremony. They depend on this ritual as a means of support because people abandon them at the edges of villages.

The environment fostered by educational and microenterprise initiatives is one that emphasizes joint efforts among men and women within a community. It is not one that says men are the problem. Indeed, women often are just as much the perpetrators of traditional values and practices as men are. What has come through clearly for women's organizations in the rest of the world is that we are struggling against a system, and this system oppresses both women and men who are caught within it.

In the 1960s and 1970s, feminists in the United States were saying, "We want to be equal to you, we want to play on your playing fields, we want to play the same game." Today the women's movement internationally is saying something very different. It is asking the question: "Equal to what?" What do we want to be equal to? And what is the game we should be playing together, men and women, to ensure a freer, more just world that offers more opportunities for all of us?

KAVITA RAMDAS is president and CEO of the Global Fund for Women.

Get Smart

Pandemics. Global Warming. Food shortages. No more fossil fuels. What are humans to do? The same thing the species has done before: evolve to meet the challenge. But this time we don't have to rely on natural evolution to make us smart enough to survive. We can do it ourselves, right now, by harnessing technology and pharmacology to boost our intelligence. Is Google actually making us smarter?

JAMAIS CASCIO

Seventy-four thousand years ago, humanity nearly went extinct. A super-volcano at what's now Lake Toba, in Sumatra, erupted with a strength more than a thousand times that of Mount St. Helens in 1980. Some 800 cubic kilometers of ash filled the skies of the Northern Hemisphere, lowering global temperatures and pushing a climate already on the verge of an ice age over the edge. Some scientists speculate that as the Earth went into a deep freeze, the population of *Homo sapiens* may have dropped to as low as a few thousand families.

The Mount Toba incident, although unprecedented in magnitude, was part of a broad pattern. For a period of 2 million years, ending with the last ice age around 10,000 B.C., the Earth experienced a series of convulsive glacial events. This rapid-fire climate change meant that humans couldn't rely on consistent patterns to know which animals to hunt, which plants to gather, or even which predators might be waiting around the corner.

How did we cope? By getting smarter. The neurophysiologist William Calvin argues persuasively that modern human cognition—including sophisticated language and the capacity to plan ahead—evolved in response to the demands of this long age of turbulence. According to Calvin, the reason we survived is that our brains changed to meet the challenge: we transformed the ability to target a moving animal with a thrown rock into a capability for foresight and long-term planning. In the process, we may have developed syntax and formal structure from our simple language.

Our present century may not be quite as perilous for the human race as an ice age in the aftermath of a super-volcano eruption, but the next few decades will pose enormous hurdles that go beyond the climate crisis. The end of the fossil-fuel era, the fragility of the global food web, growing population density, and the spread of pandemics, as well as the emergence of radically transformative bio- and nanotechnologies—each of these threatens us with broad disruption or even devastation. And as good as our brains have become at planning ahead, we're still biased toward looking for near-term, simple threats. Subtle, long-term risks, particularly those involving complex, global processes, remain devilishly hard for us to manage.

But here's an optimistic scenario for you: if the next several decades are as bad as some of us fear they could be, we can respond, and survive, the way our species has done time and again: by getting smarter. But this time, we don't have to rely solely on natural evolutionary processes to boost our intelligence. We can do it ourselves.

Most people don't realize that this process is already under way. In fact, it's happening all around us, across the full spectrum of how we understand intelligence. It's visible in the hive mind of the Internet, in the powerful tools for simulation and visualization that are jump-starting new scientific disciplines, and in the development of drugs that some people (myself included) have discovered let them study harder, focus better, and stay awake longer with full clarity. So far, these augmentations have largely been outside of our bodies, but they're very much part of who we are today: they're physically separate from us, but we and they are becoming cognitively inseparable. And advances over the next few decades, driven by breakthroughs in genetic engineering and artificial intelligence, will make today's technologies seem primitive. The nascent jargon of the field describes this as "intelligence augmentation." I prefer to think of it as "You + ."

Scientists refer to the 12,000 years or so since the last ice age as the Holocene epoch. It encompasses the rise of human civilization and our co-evolution with tools and technologies that allow us to grapple with our physical environment. But if intelligence augmentation has the kind of impact I expect, we may soon have to start thinking of ourselves as living in an entirely new era. The focus of our technological evolution would be less on how we manage and adapt to our physical world, and more on how we manage and adapt to the immense amount of knowledge we've created. We can call it the Nöocene epoch, from Pierre Teilhard de Chardin's concept of the Nöosphere, a collective consciousness created by the deepening interaction of human minds. As that epoch draws closer, the world is becoming a very different place.

Of course, we've been augmenting our ability to think for millennia. When we developed written language, we significantly increased our functional memory and our ability to share insights and knowledge across time and space. The same thing happened with the invention of the printing press, the telegraph, and the radio. The rise of urbanization allowed a fraction of the populace to focus on more-cerebral tasks—a fraction that grew inexorably as more-complex economic and social practices demanded more knowledge work, and industrial technology reduced the demand for manual labor. And caffeine and nicotine, of course, are both classic cognitive-enhancement drugs, primitive though they may be.

With every technological step forward, though, has come anxiety about the possibility that technology harms our natural ability to think. These anxieties were given eloquent expression in these pages by Nicholas Carr, whose essay "Is Google Making Us Stupid?" (July/August 2008 *Atlantic*) argued that the information-dense, hyperlink-rich, spastically churning Internet medium is effectively rewiring our brains, making it harder for us to engage in deep, relaxed contemplation.

Carr's fears about the impact of wall-to-wall connectivity on the human intellect echo cyber-theorist Linda Stone's description of "continuous partial attention," the modern phenomenon of having multiple activities and connections under way simultaneously. We're becoming so accustomed to interruption that we're starting to find focusing difficult, even when we've achieved a bit of quiet. It's an induced form of ADD—a "continuous partial attention-deficit disorder," if you will.

There's also just more information out there—because unlike with previous information media, with the Internet, creating material is nearly as easy as consuming it. And it's easy to mistake more voices for more noise. In reality, though, the proliferation of diverse voices may actually improve our overall ability to think. In *Everything Bad Is Good for you,* Steven Johnson argues that the increasing complexity and range of media we engage with have, over the past century, made us smarter, rather than dumber, by providing a form of cognitive calisthenics. Even pulp-television shows and video games have become extraordinarily dense with detail, filled with subtle references to broader subjects, and more open to interactive engagement. They reward the capacity to make connections and to see patterns—precisely the kinds of skills we need for managing an information glut.

Scientists describe these skills as our "fluid intelligence"—the ability to find meaning in confusion and to solve new problems, independent of acquired knowledge. Fluid intelligence doesn't look much like the capacity to memorize and recite facts, the skills that people have traditionally associated with brainpower. But building it up may improve the capacity to think deeply that Carr and others fear we're losing for good. And we shouldn't let the stresses associated with a transition to a new era blind us to that era's astonishing potential. We swim in an ocean of data, accessible from nearly anywhere, generated by billions of devices. We're only beginning to explore what we can do with this knowledge-at-a-touch.

Moreover, the technology-induced ADD that's associated with this new world may be a short-term problem. The trouble isn't that we have too much information at our fingertips, but that our tools for managing it are still in their infancy. Worries about "information overload" predate the rise of the Web (Alvin Toffler coined the phrase in 1970), and many of the technologies that Carr worries about were developed precisely to help us get some control over a flood of data and ideas. Google isn't the problem; it's the beginning of a solution.

The trouble isn't that we have too much information at our fingertips, but that our tools for managing it are still in their infancy.

In any case, there's no going back. The information sea isn't going to dry up, and relying on cognitive habits evolved and perfected in an era of limited information flow—and limited information access—is futile. Strengthening our fluid intelligence is the only viable approach to navigating the age of constant connectivity.

When people hear the phrase *intelligence augmentation,* they tend to envision people with computer chips plugged into their brains, or a genetically engineered race of post-human super-geniuses. Neither of these visions is likely to be realized, for reasons familiar to any Best Buy shopper. In a world of ongoing technological acceleration, today's cutting-edge brain implant would be tomorrow's obsolete junk—and good luck if the protocols change or you're on the wrong side of a "format war" (anyone want a Betamax implant?). And then there's the question of stability: Would you want a chip in your head made by the same folks that made your cell phone, or your PC?

Likewise, the safe modification of human genetics is still years away. And even after genetic modification of adult neurobiology becomes possible, the science will remain in flux; our understanding of how augmentation works, and what kinds of genetic modifications are possible, would still change rapidly. As with digital implants, the brain modification you might undergo one week could become obsolete the next. Who would want a 2025-vintage brain when you're competing against hotshots with Model 2026?

Yet in one sense, the age of the cyborg and the super-genius has already arrived. It just involves external information and communication devices instead of implants and genetic modification. The bioethicist James Hughes of Trinity College refers to all of this as "exocortical technology," but you can just think of it as "stuff you already own." Increasingly, we buttress our cognitive functions with our computing systems, no matter that the connections are mediated by simple typing and pointing. These tools enable our brains to do things that would once have been almost unimaginable:

- powerful simulations and massive data sets allow physicists to visualize, understand, and debate models of an 11-dimension universe;

- real-time data from satellites, global environmental databases, and high-resolution models allow geophysicists to recognize the subtle signs of long-term changes to the planer;
- cross-connected scheduling systems allow anyone to assemble, with a few clicks, a complex, multimodal travel itinerary that would have taken a human travel agent days to create.

If that last example sounds prosaic, it simply reflects how embedded these kinds of augmentation have become. Not much more than a decade ago, such a tool was outrageously impressive—and it destroyed the travel-agent industry.

That industry won't be the last one to go. Any occupation requiring pattern-matching and the ability to find obscure connections will quickly morph from the domain of experts to that of ordinary people whose intelligence has been augmented by cheap digital tools. Humans won't be taken out of the loop—in fact, many, many *more* humans will have the capacity to do something that was once limited to a hermetic priesthood. Intelligence augmentation decreases the need for specialization and increases participatory complexity.

As the digital systems we rely upon become faster, more sophisticated, and (with the usual hiccups) more capable, we're becoming more sophisticated and capable too. It's a form of co-evolution: we learn to adapt our thinking and expectations to these digital systems, even as the system designs become more complex and powerful to meet more of our needs—and eventually come to adapt to us.

Consider the Twitter phenomenon, which went from nearly invisible to nearly ubiquitous (at least among the online crowd) in early 2007. During busy periods, the user can easily be overwhelmed by the volume of incoming messages, most of which are of only passing interest. But there is a tiny minority of truly valuable posts. (Sometimes they have extreme value, as they did during the October 2007 wildfires in California and the November 2008 terrorist attacks in Mumbai.) At present, however, finding the most-useful bits requires wading through messages like "My kitty sneezed!" and "I hate this taco!"

But imagine if social tools like Twitter had a way to learn what kinds of messages you pay attention to, and which ones you discard. Over time, the messages that you don't really care about might start to fade in the display, while the ones that you do want to see could get brighter. Such attention filters—or focus assistants—are likely to become important parts of how we handle our daily lives. We'll move from a world of "continuous partial attention" to one we might call "continuous augmented awareness."

As processor power increases, tools like Twitter may be able to draw on the complex simulations and massive data sets that have unleashed a revolution in science. They could become individualized systems that augment our capacity for planning and foresight, letting us play "what-if" with our life choices: where to live, what to study, maybe even where to go for dinner. Initially crude and clumsy, such a system would get better with more data and more experience; just as important, we'd get better at asking questions. These systems, perhaps linked to the cameras and microphones in our mobile devices, would eventually be able to pay attention to what we're doing, and to our habits and language quirks, and learn to interpret our sometimes ambiguous desires. With enough time and complexity, they would be able to make useful suggestions without explicit prompting.

And such systems won't be working for us alone. Intelligence has a strong social component; for example, we already provide crude cooperative information-filtering for each other. In time, our interactions through the use of such intimate technologies could dovetail with our use of collaborative knowledge systems (such as Wikipedia), to help us not just to build better data sets, but to filter them with greater precision. As our capacity to provide that filter gets faster and richer, it increasingly becomes something akin to collaborative intuition—in which everyone is effectively augmenting everyone else.

In pharmacology, too, the future is already here. One of the most prominent examples is a drug called modafinil. Developed in the 1970s, modafinil—sold in the U.S. under the brand name Provigil—appeared on the cultural radar in the late 1990s, when the American military began to test it for long-haul pilots. Extended use of modafinil can keep a person awake and alert for well over 32 hours on end, with only a full night's sleep required to get back to a normal schedule.

While it is FDA-approved only for a few sleep disorders, like narcolepsy and sleep apnea, doctors increasingly prescribe it to those suffering from depression, to "shift workers" fighting fatigue, and to frequent business travelers dealing with time-zone shifts. I'm part of the latter group: like more and more professionals, I have a prescription for modafinil in order to help me overcome jet lag when I travel internationally. When I started taking the drug, I expected it to keep me awake; I didn't expect it to make me feel smarter, but that's exactly what happened. The change was subtle but clear, once I recognized it: within an hour of taking a standard 200-mg tablet, I was much more alert, and thinking with considerably more clarity and focus than usual. This isn't just a subjective conclusion. A University of Cambridge study, published in 2003, concluded that modafinil confers a measurable cognitive-enhancement effect across a variety of mental tasks, including pattern recognition and spatial planning, and sharpens focus and alertness.

I'm not the only one who has taken advantage of this effect. The Silicon Valley insider webzine *Tech Crunch* reported in July 2008 that some entrepreneurs now see modafinil as an important competitive tool. The tone of the piece was judgmental, but the implication was clear: everybody's doing it, and if you're not, you're probably falling behind.

This is one way a world of intelligence augmentation emerges. Little by little, people who don't know about drugs like modafinil or don't want to use them will face stiffer competition from the people who do. From the perspective of a culture immersed in athletic doping wars, the use of such drugs may seem like cheating. From the perspective of those who find that they're much more productive using this form of enhancement, it's no more cheating than getting a faster computer or a better education.

Modafinil isn't the only example; on college campuses, the use of ADD drugs (such as Ritalin and Adderall) as study aids has become almost ubiquitous. But these enhancements are primitive. As the science improves, we could see other kinds of cognitive-modification drugs that boost recall, brain plasticity, even empathy and emotional intelligence. They would start as therapeutic treatments, but end up being used to make us "better than normal." Eventually, some of these may become over-the-counter products at your local pharmacy, or in the juice and snack aisles at the supermarket. Spam e-mail would be full of offers to make your brain bigger, and your idea production more powerful.

Such a future would bear little resemblance to *Brave New World* or similar narcomantic nightmares; we may fear the idea of a population kept doped and placated, but we're more likely to see a populace stuck in overdrive, searching out the last bits of competitive advantage, business insight, and radical innovation. No small amount of that innovation would be directed toward inventing the next, more powerful cognitive-enhancement technology.

This would be a different kind of nightmare, perhaps, and cause waves of moral panic and legislative restriction. Safety would be a huge issue. But as we've found with athletic doping, if there's a technique for beating out rivals (no matter how risky), shutting it down is nearly impossible. This would be yet another pharmacological arms race—and in this case, the competitors on one side would just keep getting smarter.

The most radical form of superhuman intelligence, of course, wouldn't be a mind augmented by drugs or exocortical technology; it would be a mind that isn't human at all. Here we move from the realm of extrapolation to the realm of speculation, since solid predictions about artificial intelligence are notoriously hard: our understanding of how the brain creates the mind remains far from good enough to tell us how to construct a mind in a machine.

But while the concept remains controversial, I see no good argument for why a mind running on a machine platform instead of a biological platform will forever be impossible; whether one might appear in five years or 50 or 500, however, is uncertain. I lean toward 50, myself. That's enough time to develop computing hardware able to run a high-speed neural network as sophisticated as that of a human brain, and enough time for the kids who will have grown up surrounded by virtual-world software and household robots—that is, the people who see this stuff not as "Technology," but as everyday tools—to come to dominate the field.

Many proponents of developing an artificial mind are sure that such a breakthrough will be the biggest change in human history. They believe that a machine mind would soon modify itself to get smarter—and with its new intelligence, then figure out how to make itself smarter still. They refer to this intelligence explosion as "the Singularity," a term applied by the computer scientist and science-fiction author Vernor Vinge. "Within thirty years, we will have the technological means to create superhuman intelligence," Vinge wrote in 1993. "Shortly after, the human era will be ended." The Singularity concept is a secular echo of Teilhard de Chardin's "Omega Point," the

culmination of the Nöosphere at the end of history. Many believers in Singularity—which one wag has dubbed "the Rapture for nerds"—think that building the first real AI will be the last thing humans do. Some imagine this moment with terror, others with a bit of glee.

My own suspicion is that a stand-alone artificial mind will be more a tool of narrow utility than something especially apocalyptic. I don't think the theory of an explosively self-improving AI is convincing—it's based on too many assumptions about behavior and the nature of the mind. Moreover, AI researchers, after years of talking about this prospect, are already ultra-conscious of the risk of runaway systems.

More important, though, is that the same advances in processor and process that would produce a machine mind would also increase the power of our own cognitive-enhancement technologies. As intelligence augmentation allows us to make *ourselves* smarter, and then smarter still, AI may turn out to be just a sideshow: we could always be a step ahead.

So what's life like in a world of brain doping, intuition networks, and the occasional artificial mind?

Banal.

Not from our present perspective, of course. For us, now, looking a generation ahead might seem surreal and dizzying. But remember: people living in, say, 2030 will have lived every moment from now until then—we won't jump into the future. For someone going from 2009 to 2030 day by day, most of these changes wouldn't be jarring; instead, they'd be incremental, almost overdetermined, and the occasional surprises would quickly blend into the flow of inevitability.

By 2030, then, we'll likely have grown accustomed to (and perhaps even complacent about) a world where sophisticated foresight, detailed analysis and insight, and augmented awareness are commonplace. We'll have developed a better capacity to manage both partial attention and laser-like focus, and be able to slip between the two with ease—perhaps by popping the right pill, or eating the right snack. Sometimes, our augmentation assistants will handle basic interactions on our behalf; that's okay, though, because we'll increasingly see those assistants as extensions of ourselves.

The amount of data we'll have at our fingertips will be staggering, but we'll finally have gotten over the notion that accumulated information alone is a hallmark of intelligence. The power of all of this knowledge will come from its ability to inform difficult decisions, and to support complex analysis. Most professions will likely use simulation and modeling in their day-to-day work, from political decisions to hairstyle options. In a world of augmented intelligence, we will have a far greater appreciation of the consequences of our actions.

This doesn't mean we'll all come to the same conclusions. We'll still clash with each other's emotions, desires, and beliefs. If anything, our arguments will be more intense, buttressed not just by strongly held opinions but by intricate reasoning. People in 2030 will look back aghast at how ridiculously unsubtle the political and cultural disputes of our present were, just as we might today snicker at simplistic advertising from a generation ago.

Conversely, the debates of the 2030s would be remarkable for us to behold. Nuance and multiple layers will characterize even casual disputes; our digital assistants will be there to catch any references we might miss. And all of this will be everyday, banal reality. Today, it sounds mind-boggling; by then, it won't even merit comment.

What happens if such a complex system collapses? Disaster, of course. But don't forget that we already depend upon enormously complex systems that we no longer even think of as technological. Urbanization, agriculture, and trade were at one time huge innovations. Their collapse (and all of them are now at risk, in different ways, as we have seen in recent months) would be an even greater catastrophe than the collapse of our growing webs of interconnected intelligence.

A less apocalyptic but more likely danger derives from the observation made by the science-fiction author William Gibson: "The future is already here, it's just unevenly distributed." The rich, whether nations or individuals, will inevitably gain access to many augmentations before anyone else. We know from history, though, that a world of limited access wouldn't last forever, even as the technology improved: those who sought to impose limits would eventually face angry opponents with newer, better systems.

Even as competition provides access to these kinds of technologies, though, development paths won't be identical. Some societies may be especially welcoming to biotech boosts; others may prefer to use digital tools. Some may readily adopt collaborative approaches; others may focus on individual enhancement. And around the world, many societies will reject the use of intelligence-enhancement technology entirely, or adopt a cautious wait-and-see posture.

The bad news is that these divergent paths may exacerbate cultural divides created by already divergent languages and beliefs. National rivalries often emphasize cultural differences, but for now we're all still standard human beings. What happens when different groups quite literally think in very, very different ways?

The good news, though, is that this diversity of thought can also be a strength. Coping with the various world-historical dangers we face will require the greatest possible insight, creativity, and innovation. Our ability to build the future that we want—not just a future we can survive—depends on our capacity to understand the complex relationships of the world's systems, to take advantage of the diversity of knowledge and experience our civilization embodies, and to fully appreciate the implications of our choices. Such an ability is increasingly within our grasp. The Nöocene awaits.

JAMAIS CASCIO is an affiliate at the Institute for the Future and a senior fellow at the Institute for Ethics and Emerging Technologies.

UNIT 2

Population and Food Production

Unit Selections

Key Points to Consider

- What are the basic characteristics and trends of the world's population? How many people are there? How long do people typically live?

- How fast is the world's population growing? What are the reasons for this growth? Describe the variations in the demographic transition from one region to the next.

- In many regions of the world, the graying of the population is an important trend. What are some of the political implications of this trend?

- Is it possible to reverse population growth without requiring population control?

- How does rapid population growth affect the quality of the environment, social structures, and the ways in which humanity views itself?

- In an era of global interdependence, how much impact can individual governments have on demographic changes?

- What are the causes of hunger in the world? Are agricultural resources sufficient to feed a growing population?

- What are some of the infectious diseases that threaten the human population? Are organizational resources, both national and international, sufficient to meet this timeless challenge?

- How can economic and social policies be changed in order to reduce the impact of population growth on environmental quality?

Student Website

www.mhhe.com/cls

Internet References

The Hunger Project
   http://www.thp.org
Penn Library: Resources by Subject
   http://www.library.upenn.edu/cgi-bin/res/sr.cgi
World Health Organization
   http://www.who.int
WWW Virtual Library: Demography & Population Studies
   http://demography.anu.edu.au/VirtualLibrary

After World War II, the world's population reached an estimated 2 billion people. It had taken 250 years to triple to that level. In the six decades following World War II, the population tripled again to 6 billion. When the typical reader of this book reaches the age of 50, demographers estimate that the global population will have reached 8 1/2 billion! By 2050, or about 100 years after World War II, some experts forecast that 10 to 12 billion people may populate the world. A person born in 1946 (a so-called baby boomer) who lives to be 100 could see a six-fold increase in population.

Nothing like this has ever occurred before. To state this in a different way: In the next 50 years there will have to be twice as much food grown, twice as many schools and hospitals available, and twice as much of everything else just to maintain the current and rather uneven standard of living. We live in an unprecedented time in human history.

One of the most interesting aspects of this population growth is that there is little agreement about whether this situation is good or bad. The government of China, for example, has a policy that encourages couples to have only one child. In contrast, there are a few governments that use various financial incentives to promote large families.

In the second decade of the new millennium, there are many population issues that transcend simple numeric or economic considerations. The disappearance of indigenous cultures is a good example of the pressures of population growth on people who live on the margins of modern society. Finally, while demographers develop various scenarios forecasting population growth, it is important to remember that there are circumstances that could lead not to growth but to a significant decline in global population. The spread of AIDS and other infectious diseases reveals that confidence in modern medicine's ability to control these scourges may be premature. Nature has its own checks and balances to the population dynamic. This factor is often overlooked in an age of technological optimism.

The lead article in this section provides an overview of general demographic trends, with a special focus on issues related to aging. In the second article, the often-overlooked issue of

© Photlick—Image and Click/Alamy Images

reversing the increase in human population as a strategy for achieving long-term balance with the environment is described. The third article examines the politically important issue of global patterns in migration.

There are, of course, no greater checks on population growth than the availability of an adequate food supply and control of the spread of infectious diseases. Some experts question whether current agricultural technologies are sustainable over the long run. How much food are we going to need, and how are farmers and fishermen going to provide it? Will markets deliver food to those in greatest need? Finally, the continuous threat of the spread of disease and the ability of national and international public health organizations to contain it are issues directly related to population issues.

Making predictions about the future of the world's population is a complicated task, for there are a variety of forces at work and considerable variation from region to region. The danger of oversimplification must be overcome if governments and international organizations are going to respond with meaningful policies. Perhaps one could say that there is not a global population problem but rather many population challenges that vary from country to country and region to region.

The Century Ahead

CHRIS WILSON

The twentieth century was, above all else, a century of population growth; the twenty-first century will be a century of aging. Between 1900 and 2000 the world's population quadrupled, from around 1.5 billion to over 6 billion. Most of this increase occurred after World War II. At present, it seems unlikely that the population will grow by more than about a further 50 percent. The most plausible forecasts see a population numbering between 9 and 10 billion by about 2050, with stability or decline in total population thereafter.

However, the population at older ages will increase far more quickly in the coming century than in the last. Indeed, the end of population growth and its replacement by aging are logically related. All rapidly growing populations are young. If each birth cohort is larger than the one before, there will always be plenty of young people.

Population growth was so characteristic of the recent past that we tend to regard it as the norm. However, for most of human history the long-run rate of population growth has been very close to zero. From the biblical Adam and Eve, it would have taken only thirty-two doublings of the population to reach over 8 billion. At the rate of population growth seen in the 1960s and early 1970s—over 2 percent a year, implying a doubling time of around thirty years—and given that the gap between generations is also usually about thirty years, such an increase could have taken place inside a millennium. Even James Ussher's 1650 estimate of October 23, 4004 B.C. as the date of creation implies we have been around much longer than that. And since *Homo sapiens* actually emerged one hundred and fifty thousand or so years ago, the rate of growth has obviously been close to zero.

Similarly, extrapolating the growth rates of the recent past into the future soon yields logically impossible figures. Ansley Coale once calculated that a growth rate of 2 percent a year sustained for five thousand years would lead to the sheer volume of human beings exceeding that of the solar system.

The absence of growth is a necessary but not sufficient condition for aging; we also need long life expectancy. In populations before the modern medical era, relatively few people survived to reach three score years and ten. Thus, population aging is a novelty requiring both long lives and a low growth rate (i.e., low fertility). Though rare in the past, these conditions are now becoming the norm around the world.

When demographers try to understand the determinants of aging, they use one of social science's great generalizing models: the demographic transition. When a population modernizes, it undergoes, along with many other aspects of development, a set of interconnected changes called the demographic transition. According to this model, every population at some point has high fertility (mostly between four and six children per woman) and low life expectancy (mostly between twenty-five and forty years). With the spread of modern medicine and public health, mortality improves; as family planning and contraceptive use become the norm, fertility falls. Usually life expectancy rises first, with a delay before fertility declines. This difference in timing leads to substantial population growth before the two processes come back into balance.

This process of transition began in the late eighteenth and nineteenth centuries in Europe, the United States, and the other neo-Europes; it became a global phenomenon after World War II. Today, more than half of the world's people live in places where fertility is at or below the level needed for long-run intergenerational replacement (about 2.1 children per woman), and global life expectancy is approaching seventy years.

Trends in mortality can be followed in considerable detail for many European countries from the mid-nineteenth century, and for a few especially well-documented cases, as far back as the late 1700s. For Japan and the United States detailed information dates back to the early twentieth century. What these statistics reveal is both simple and striking. There has been an enormous reduction in mortality, with life expectancy for the two sexes combined now approaching, or even exceeding, eighty in most developed countries. Even more remarkably, this progress has been very regular for many decades. Jim Oeppen and James Vaupel have shown, for example, that the trend in "best-practice" life expectancy (i.e., the country with the longest life expectancy in each year) has been linear for more than 150 years.[1] In each decade the "state of the art" has increased about 2.5 years. Moreover, although there has been some variation at the national level, most developed countries have demonstrated strongly linear trends in life expectancy for the whole of the twentieth century.

Paradoxically, although this trend has been evident in mortality statistics for many decades, it is only in the last few years that it has been recognized. Demographers, actuaries, and others concerned with forecasting mortality had always hitherto assumed that life expectancy was approaching some asymptotic limit and would thus level off in the near future. But if there is some biological limit to extending longevity, there is no sign of it yet. As Oeppen and Vaupel point out, estimates of the maximum possible life expectancy made throughout the twentieth century were, on average, surpassed within five years of being made. This consistent error is of more than purely academic interest—pension- and health-care systems have been funded on the basis of large underestimates of the number of elderly people in the future.

The linearity of the upward climb in life expectancy has occurred in spite of the fact that very different age groups and causes of death have been involved in different eras. Before World War II, almost all progress took place in reducing infectious diseases, with the biggest impact for infants and children. In contrast, today much of the improvement is concentrated at old ages. Perhaps the best analogy for these remarkable changes is to be found in models of economic growth. Just as modern theory hypothesizes the existence of an endogenous rate of growth that is in some sense built into our economic system, so too there may be an endogenous rate of improvement in health, as measured by life expectancy. In any event, we have every reason to expect that continued increases in the average length of life will augment population aging.

There are, of course, exceptions to this optimistic picture. In the Soviet Union and its client states in Eastern and Central Europe, life expectancy stagnated from the 1960s until the end of Communism. It then worsened still further in many cases, in the immediate aftermath of the revolution. In Russia and many of the post-Soviet states it remains low, especially for men. Male life expectancy in Russia today is roughly the same as it was in 1950: about sixty years. To put this stagnation into perspective, the equivalent figure for the United States has increased since 1950 by almost ten years from sixty-six to seventy-six.

In the post-Communist countries further west, however, the last decade has seen rapid improvements; life expectancy there will likely converge to levels seen in Western Europe within a few decades. The origins of the health crisis under Communism and its persistence in Russia, Ukraine, and the other post-Soviet states is a matter of heated debate in both the scientific and general literature. Whatever the cause, the crisis serves as a warning against unqualified Panglossian optimism. Likewise, the emergence of HIV/AIDS and the associated reemergence of tuberculosis make clear that all future estimates of improvement in public health must take into account the potential for severe reversals.

Overall, however, the last half-century has seen unprecedented convergence in mortality patterns around the world. While rich countries still lead in life expectancy, the gap between these leaders and most developing countries has shrunk substantially. In fact, there has been more convergence in demography than in any other aspect of modernization. For example, consider Latin America as a whole, where the United Nations estimates current life expectancy is seventy-two years, and GDP per head (adjusted for inflation and other factors) is below $4,000, according to the Organization for Economic Cooperation and Development. Now consider the United States. Life expectancy in the United States was seventy-two years as recently as the early 1970s. In contrast, the U.S. GDP per head exceeded $4,000 by 1900. Latin America is a century behind the United States in income growth, but only thirty to thirty-five years behind in life expectancy. We can make similar comparisons for most developing countries. And though the gaps in educational attainment or urbanization are somewhat smaller than in GDP per head, none of the other conventional quantitative indices of development has converged as rapidly as demography.

In recent decades there has also been a striking convergence in fertility, which has declined rapidly in most countries. More than half of the world's population now lives in countries or regions in which fertility is below the level needed for intergenerational replacement.[2] In most of Southern Europe (including Italy and Spain) and in most of Central and Eastern Europe, the total fertility rate (the number of children born per woman) is below 1.3. Similar values are now seen in Japan, South Korea, and many of the more developed parts of China. Even some countries that might seem unlikely candidates have experienced rapid fertility decline. In Iran, for example, fertility fell from over six children per woman to just over two between the mid-1980s and mid-1990s. In contrast, fertility in the United States has seemed to defy gravity, staying close to or even above the replacement level for the last two decades. Among the developing countries in which fertility is now lower than in the United States are China, Brazil, Thailand, and Tunisia. If the trends of the last twenty-five years continue for another decade or so, the U.S. fertility level will be well above the median for the human population as a whole.

The very speed of fertility decline in many countries will produce an exaggerated form of aging. While aging is an inevitable and global phenomenon, countries in which fertility has fallen rapidly will experience a form of 'super aging' in the middle decades of this century. The baby boom cohorts of Southern Europe or the pretransition cohorts in China are very large compared to those that followed, and their getting old will greatly exacerbate any problems that aging generates.

There is also a sense in which aging can be 'locked in' as part of a country's demographic regime through a form of negative momentum. For example, in Southern Europe, the large number of baby boomers moving through the childbearing ages has disguised the very low fertility rate of recent decades. The largest age groups at present are those ages 25 to 39. In the coming decades, however, the much smaller cohorts born since the mid-1980s will be in the reproductive ages. Unless these cohorts (currently ages 0 to 19) have much higher fertility than their parents, the number of births in countries such as Italy and Spain will shrink even more rapidly in the future than it has so far. In contrast, the United States and other countries in which fertility has stabilized at close to the replacement level (in Europe, they include France and the Nordic countries) will face much less severe challenges from demographic disruption.

The future is always uncertain to some degree, but when trends have been so clear and so consistent for decades, they form a solid basis for prediction. It is very close to certain that aging will be one of the defining global phenomena in the twenty-first century. The ways in which societies choose to adapt to this new reality will test the old adage that "demography is destiny." Fatalism, however, is uncalled for—to a substantial degree we can still choose our future. However, demography does impose strong constraints on the range of feasible options. Taking these constraints into account is the basis for informed reactions to the challenges posed by aging.

Notes

1. Jim Oeppen and James W. Vaupel, "Broken Limits to Life Expectancy," *Science 296* (2002): 1030–1031.

2. Chris Wilson, "Fertility Below Replacement Level," *Science 304* (2004): 207–209.

CHRIS WILSON is a staff member of the World Population Program at the International Institute for Applied Systems Analysis in Laxenberg, Austria. One of Europe's most widely cited demographers, he is currently researching the causes and consequences of global demographic convergence.

Population & Sustainability

Reversing the rise in human numbers is the most overlooked and essential strategy for achieving long-term balance with the environment. Contrary to widespread opinion, it does not require "population control"

ROBERT ENGELMAN

In an era of changing climate and sinking economies, Malthusian limits to growth are back—and squeezing us painfully. Whereas *more people* once meant more ingenuity, more talent, and more innovation, today it just seems to mean *less for each*. Less water for every cattle herder in the Horn of Africa. (The United Nations projects there will be more than four billion people living in nations defined as water-scarce or water-stressed by 2050, up from half a billion in 1995.) Less land for every farmer already tilling slopes so steep they risk killing themselves by falling off their fields. (At a bit less than six tenths of an acre, global per capita cropland today is little more than half of what it was in 1961, and more than 900 million people are hungry.) Less capacity in the atmosphere to accept the heat-trapping gases that could fry the planet for centuries to come. Scarcer and higher-priced energy and food. And if the world's economy does not bounce back to its glory days, less credit and fewer jobs.

It's not surprising that this kind of predicament brings back an old sore topic: human population and whether to do anything about it. Let's concede up front that nothing short of a catastrophic population crash (think of the film *Children of Men,* set in a world without children) would make much difference to climate change, water scarcity or land shortages over the next decade or so. There are 6.8 billion of us today, and more are on the way. To make a dent in these problems in the short term without throwing anyone overboard, we will need to radically reduce individuals' footprint on the environment through improvements in technology and possibly wrenching changes in lifestyle.

But until the world's population stops growing, there will be no end to the need to squeeze individuals' consumption of fossil fuels and other natural resources. A close look at this problem is sobering: short of catastrophic leaps in the death rate or unwanted crashes in fertility, the world's population is all but certain to grow by at least one billion to two billion people. The low-consuming billions of the developing world would love to consume as Americans do, with similar disregard for the environment—and they have as much of a right to do so. These facts suggest that the coming ecological impact will be of a scale that we will simply have to manage and adapt to as best we can.

Population growth constantly pushes the consequences of any level of individual consumption to a higher plateau, and reductions in individual consumption can always be overwhelmed by increases in population. The simple reality is that acting on both, consistently and simultaneously, is the key to long-term environmental sustainability. The sustainability benefits of level or falling human numbers are too powerful to ignore for long.

In the U.S., this discussion remains muted all the same. Population concerns may lurk within the public anger over illegal immigration or over the unwed California mother of octuplets earlier this year. But to the extent that the news media address domestic population growth at all, it is through euphemisms such as "sprawl" (the theoretical culprit in pollution of the Chesapeake Bay, for example) or the economy (the theoretical driver of increased greenhouse gas emissions). You are more likely to read about population growth in a letter to the editor than in a news story or editorial.

When President-elect Barack Obama pledged in late 2008 to bring U.S. carbon dioxide emissions to their 1990 levels by 2020, environmentalists struggled to swallow their dismay. The European Union, after all, had committed itself to 20 percent *reductions* from 1990 levels. But on a per capita basis, President Obama's pledge was somewhat *more* ambitious than the E.U.'s was. Because of much more rapid population growth than in the E.U., Americans would be cutting their individual emissions by 26 percent under his plan and Europeans by 25 percent under theirs. Any pledges to lower emissions by a uniform percentage among industrial countries will be much harder for the U.S. to achieve, simply because it is gaining people so fast through immigration and a birthrate that is higher than average for a developed nation.

The bitterness of the immigration debate has helped keep U.S. population growth off-limits in the national conversation. In industrial countries outside of North America, however, population is creeping back into public and even political consciousness. In the U.K., an all-party parliamentary panel issued a report called "Return of the Population Growth Factor" and called for stronger efforts to slow that growth. And the concern in the U.K.

is not just about the people "over there" in developing countries. In early 2009 Jonathon Porritt, chair of the government's Sustainable Development Commission, whacked a hornet's nest by calling parents of more than two children "irresponsible" and blasting mainstream environmental groups for "betraying" their members by fearing to call for small families. "It is the ghost at the table," Porritt said of population in an interview with the *Daily Telegraph,* a London broadsheet. Blog comments on his remarks, most of them supportive, soared into the thousands.

Meanwhile, in Australia, as summer temperatures hovered near 117 degrees Fahrenheit (47 degrees Celsius) and murderous flames converted forests into carbon dioxide, a new book entitled *Overloading Australia: How Governments and Media Dither and Deny on Population* issued an unusual ecological battle cry: ignore all admonitions to conserve the country's increasingly scarce water supplies until the government eliminates "baby bonuses" in the tax code and clamps down on immigration. A former premier of New South Wales spoke at the book's launch.

With comments such as these gaining attention—and in some circles, approval—are environmentalists and eventually policy makers likely to renew the decades-old call for "population control"? Would they be wise to do so?

A Number of Us

Two big questions present themselves as population reemerges from the shadows: Can any feasible downshift in population growth actually put the environment on a more sustainable path? And if so, are there measures that the public and policy makers would support that could actually bring about such a change?

Nature, of course, couldn't care less how many of us there are. What matters to the environment are the sums of human pulls and pushes, the extractions of resources and the injections of wastes. When these exceed key tipping points, nature and its systems can change quickly and dramatically. But the magnitudes of environmental impacts stem not just from our numbers but also from behaviors we learn from our parents and cultures. Broadly speaking, if population is the number of us, then consumption is the way each of us behaves. In this unequal world, the behavior of a dozen people in one place sometimes has more environmental impact than does that of a few hundred somewhere else.

Consider how these principles relate to global warming. The greenhouse gases already released into the atmosphere are likely to bring us quite close to the 3.6 degree F (two degree C) increase from the preindustrial global temperature average that many scientists see as the best-guess threshold of potential climate catastrophe. Already the earth is experiencing harsher droughts, fiercer storms and higher sea levels. If the scientists are right, these impacts will worsen for decades or centuries. Indeed, even if we ended all emissions tomorrow, additional warming is on the way thanks to the momentum built into the earth's intricate climate system. (The oceans, for example, have yet to come into equilibrium with the extra heat-trapping capacity of the atmosphere. As the oceans continue to warm, so will the land around them.)

Our species' demographic growth since its birth in Africa 200,000 years ago clearly contributed to this crisis. If world population had stayed stable at roughly 300 million people—a number that demographers believe characterized humanity from the birth of Christ to A.D. 1000 and that equals the population of just the U.S. today—there would not be enough of us to have the effect of relocating the coastlines even if we all drove Hummers. But instead we kept growing our numbers, which are projected to reach 9.1 billion by midcentury.

Humanity's consumption behaviors consequently did and do matter, and in this arena, all people have not been created equal. Greenhouse gas release has been linked overwhelmingly, at least up until recently, to the high-consumption habits of the industrial nations. As a result, in an ethical outrage as big as all outdoors, the coming shifts in climate and sea level will most harm the world's poor, who are least responsible for the atmosphere's composition, and will least harm the wealthy, who bear the biggest responsibility.

All-Consuming Passions

What part can the size of the human race play in finding a happy ending to this morality play? Population scenarios cannot directly address the inequity in emissions patterns—but they are far from unimportant.

Countries with the highest emissions per capita tend to have smaller families on average, whereas those with low emissions per capita tend to have larger ones. Americans, for example, consumed 8.6 tons of oil or its commercial energy equivalent per capita in 2007, according to data kept by British Petroleum; Indians consumed just 0.4 ton per capita. (These figures somewhat distort the gap because they exclude biomass and other noncommercial forms of energy, for which data are unreliable.)

So while India gained 17 million people in that year and the U.S. gained three million, by this simplified math the U.S. growth in population counted for the equivalent of an additional 25.6 million tons of oil consumed, whereas India's much greater growth counted for only 6.6 million additional tons. With such large disparities, the climate would be better served if the Americans emulated Indian consumption than if India emulated U.S. population.

End of story? For a variety of reasons, not quite. Population is not a contrasting force to consumption but something very close to its parent. Alone, each of us has no significant impact on the planet, even when our collective behavior overwhelms its natural processes. Historically, population has grown fastest when per capita consumption is modest. Later, consumption tends to explode on the base of a population that is large, but it is by then growing more slowly. Throughout the 19th century, the U.S. population grew at rates typical of Africa today. That century of rapid growth helped to make 21st-century America (with 307 million people now) a consumption behemoth.

The same one-two punch of population growth followed by consumption growth is now occurring in China (1.34 billion people) and India (1.2 billion). Per capita commercial energy use has been growing so rapidly in both countries (or at least it

Human Population Growth.

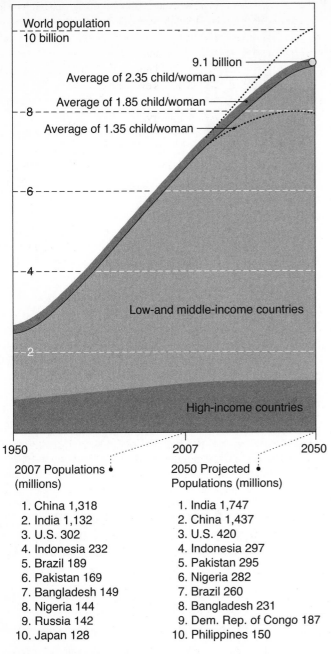

2007 Populations (millions)

1. China 1,318
2. India 1,132
3. U.S. 302
4. Indonesia 232
5. Brazil 189
6. Pakistan 169
7. Bangladesh 149
8. Nigeria 144
9. Russia 142
10. Japan 128

2050 Projected Populations (millions)

1. India 1,747
2. China 1,437
3. U.S. 420
4. Indonesia 297
5. Pakistan 295
6. Nigeria 282
7. Brazil 260
8. Bangladesh 231
9. Dem. Rep. of Congo 187
10. Philippines 150

The challenge to sustainability: For most of its history, the human race has numbered no more than several million and has expanded only slowly. As late as A.D 1000, our species was smaller than the current population of the U.S. Only in the past few centuries have our numbers exploded, especially (during recent decades) in low-and middle-income nations, with increases in consumption habits following suit. Projections suggest that by 2050 or so, the population will probably stabilize around 9.1 billion. But very small changes in fertility could shift that figure up or down by about a billion—with a powerful impact on innumerable sustainability issues.

Americans by 2080. Population and consumption thus feed on each other's growth to expand humans' environmental footprint exponentially over time.

Moreover, because every human being consumes and disposes of multiple natural resources, a birth that does not occur averts consumption impacts in every direction. A person reducing her carbon footprint, conversely, does not automatically use less water. A wind turbine displaces coal-fired electricity but hardly prevents the depletion of forests (now disappearing in the tropics at the rate of one Kentucky-size swath a year) or fisheries (at current depletion rates facing exhaustion by the middle of the century). But unlike wind turbines, humans reproduce themselves. So every smaller generation means that the multipliers of consumption linked to population also shrink on into the future.

Because most environmental challenges emerge on scales of decades and centuries, population growth packs a long-term wallop. With respect to saving the planet, over a few short years it is hard for smaller families to beat sharp reductions in per capita consumption. Since the early 1990s, however, published calculations have demonstrated that slower population growth over decades yields significant reductions of greenhouse gas emissions even in countries where per capita fossil-fuel consumption is modest.

Slower population growth that leads to eight billion people in 2050 rather than to the currently projected 9.1 billion would save one billion to two billion tons of carbon annually by 2050, according to estimates by climate scientist Brian O'Neill of the National Center for Atmospheric Research and his colleagues. The subsequent savings in emissions would grow year by year ever afterward—while the billion-plus fewer people would need less land, forest products, water, fish and other foodstuffs.

Those improvements still would not be enough on their own to avert significant climate change. Other similar billion-ton savings in emissions (what Princeton University professors Stephen Pacala and Robert Socolow have dubbed "stabilization wedges") are desperately needed and can come only from reduction in fossil-fuel consumption through energy efficiency, low-carbon technologies and changes in way of life. If two billion automobiles getting 30 miles per gallon traveled only 5,000 miles a year instead of 10,000, that change would save another billion tons of carbon emissions. So would replacing coal-fired power plants that produce 1.4 trillion watts of electricity with equivalent plants burning natural gas. But without a population that stops growing, comparable technology improvements or lifestyle downshifts will be needed indefinitely to keep greenhouse gas emissions sustainable.

The complications that population growth poses to every environmental problem are not to be dismissed. In fact, they are accepted and understood best by the governments of poorer countries, where the impacts of dense and rapidly growing populations are most obvious. During the past few years, most of the reports that developing countries have filed with the U.N. on how they plan to adapt to climate change mention population growth as a complicating factor.

was through 2007 on the eve of the economic meltdown) that if the trends continue unabated the typical Chinese will outconsume the typical American before 2040, with Indians surpassing

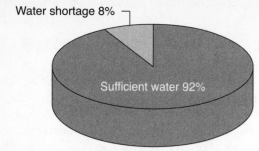

Water shortage 8%

Sufficient water 92%

1995 population: 5.7 billion

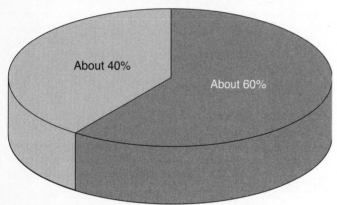

About 40%

About 60%

2050 population: 9.1 billion (projected)
More of the population will suffer water shortages.

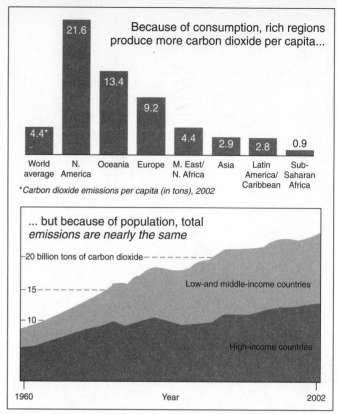

Because of consumption, rich regions produce more carbon dioxide per capita...

21.6 — N. America
13.4 — Oceania
9.2 — Europe
4.4* — World average
4.4 — M. East/N. Africa
2.9 — Asia
2.8 — Latin America/Caribbean
0.9 — Sub-Saharan Africa

Carbon dioxide emissions per capita (in tons), 2002

... but because of population, total *emissions are nearly the same*

20 billion tons of carbon dioxide
15
10

Low-and middle-income countries

High-income countries

1960   Year   2002

Consumption and the greenhouse gap: Citizens of industrial nations produce far more climate-warming carbon dioxide per capita than their peers in poorer countries. Because of population size, however, the developing world now produces slightly more of the gas. Thus, population exerts a powerful multiplier effect on the toll of consumption on the earth.

Instruments of Policy

A commonsense strategy for dealing with rising environmental risk would be to probe every reasonable opportunity for shifting to sustainability as quickly, easily and inexpensively as possible. No single energy strategy—whether nuclear, efficiency, wind, solar or geothermal—shows much promise on its own for eliminating the release of carbon dioxide into the air. Obstacles such as high up-front costs hamper most of those energy strategies even as part of a collective fix for the climate problem. No single change in land use will turn soils and plants into net absorbers of heat-trapping gases. Without technological breakthroughs in energy or land use, only higher prices for fossil fuels show much potential for edging down per capita emissions—a "solution" that policy makers have yet to grapple with effectively.

Given the long-term contribution that a turnaround in population growth could make in easing our most recalcitrant challenges, why doesn't the idea get more respect and attention? Politicians' apathy toward long-term solutions is part of the answer. But the more obvious reason is the discomfort most of us feel in grappling with the topics of sex, contraception, abortion, immigration and family sizes that differ by ethnicity and income. What in the population mix is *not* a hot button? Especially when the word "control" is added, and when the world's biggest religions have fruitful multiplication embedded in their philosophical DNA. And so critics from left, right and the intellectual center gang up on the handful of environmentalists and other activists who try to get population into national and global discussions.

Population and consumption feed on each other's growth to expand humans' environmental footprint exponentially.

Yet newly released population data from the U.N. show that developed countries, from the U.S. to Spain, have been experiencing (at least up through the beginnings of the economic crisis in 2008), if not baby booms, at least reproductive "rat-a-tat-tats." For the first time since the 1970s, the average number of children born to U.S. women has topped 2.1—the number at which parents replace themselves in the populations of developed and many developing countries. Even if net immigration ended tomorrow, continuation of that fertility rate would guarantee further growth in U.S. population for decades to come.

Those who do consider population to be a key to the problem typically say little about which policies would spare the planet many more billions of people. Should we restructure tax rates to favor small families? Propagandize the benefits of small families for the planet? Reward family-planning workers for clients they have sterilized? Each of those steps alone or in combination might help bend birthrates downward for a time, but none has proved to affect demographic trends over the long term or, critically, to gain and keep public support. When the

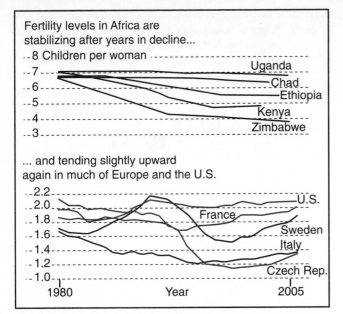

Fertility levels in Africa are
stabilizing after years in decline...

Uganda
Chad
Ethiopia
Kenya
Zimbabwe

... and tending slightly upward
again in much of Europe and the U.S.

U.S.
France
Sweden
Italy
Czech Rep.

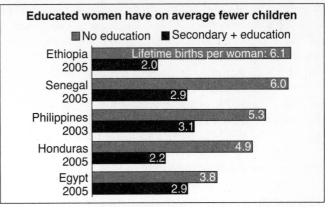

Educated women have on average fewer children

■ No education   ■ Secondary + education

Ethiopia 2005 — Lifetime births per woman: 6.1 / 2.0
Senegal 2005 — 6.0 / 2.9
Philippines 2003 — 5.3 / 3.1
Honduras 2005 — 4.9 / 2.2
Egypt 2005 — 3.8 / 2.9

Education and fertility: Data from around the world testify to a robust trend: birthrates fall where women have more access to education. Improving women's access to schooling (and the opportunities it opens) may be one of the most powerful ways to reduce population growth.

Reason for concern: Declines in fertility rates cannot be taken for granted. In parts of Africa, the rates seem to be flattening out well above the replacement rate. Surprisingly, the U.S. and parts of Europe seem to be experiencing a small but significant increase in fertility, compounding the population increases from immigration.

government of India rewarded health workers for meeting sterilization quotas in 1976, the zeal of some of them for wielding scalpels regardless of their patients' wishes contributed to the downfall of Indira Gandhi's government in 1977.

And how can we reduce consumption? Ideas such as cap-and-trade plans for limiting greenhouse gas emissions and allowing companies to trade emission rights are based on the same principle: raise the price of what harms the environment to reduce consumption of it. Beyond the consumption cuts, however, such schemes don't have much to recommend them. Governments can also eliminate subsidies of polluting behavior, an approach that is more palatable—except to the often powerful interests that benefit from the subsidies. Or governments can subsidize low consumption through tax deductions and credits, but the funds to do so on the needed scale will likely be increasingly scarce.

The Zen of Population

Mostly ignored in the environmental debates about population and consumption is that nearly all the world's nations agreed to an altogether different approach to the problem of growth 15 years ago, one that bases positive demographic outcomes on decisions individuals make in their own self-interest. (If only something comparable could be imagined to shrink consumption.) The strategy that 179 nations signed onto at a U.N. conference in Cairo in 1994 was: forget population control and instead help every woman bear a child in good health when she wants one.

That approach, which powerfully supports reproductive liberty, might sound counterintuitive for shrinking population growth, like handing a teenager the keys to the family car without so much as a lecture. But the evidence suggests that what women want—and have always wanted—is not so much to have *more*

children as to have *more for* a smaller number of children they can reliably raise to healthy adulthood. Women left to their own devices, contraceptive or otherwise, would collectively "control" population while acting on their own intentions.

More than 200 million women in developing countries are sexually active without effective modern contraception even though they do not want to be pregnant anytime soon, according to the Guttmacher Institute, a reproductive health research group. By the best estimates, some 80 million pregnancies around the world are unintended. Although the numbers aren't strictly comparable—many unplanned pregnancies end in abortion—the unintended pregnancies exceed the 78 million by which world population grows every year.

In the U.S., which is well informed and spends nearly 20 cents per dollar of economic activity on health care, nearly one out of every two pregnancies is unintended. That proportion has not changed much for decades. In every nation, rich and poor, in which a choice of contraceptives is available and is backed up by reasonably accessible safe abortion for when contraception fails, women have two or fewer children. Furthermore, educating girls reduces birthrates. Worldwide, according to a calculation provided for this article by demographers at the International Institute for Applied Systems Analysis in Austria, women with no schooling have an average of 4.5 children, whereas those with a few years of primary school have just three. Women who complete one or two years of secondary school have an average of 1.9 children apiece—a figure that over time leads to a decreasing population. With one or two years of college, the average childbearing rate falls even further, to 1.7. And when women enter the workforce, start businesses, inherit assets and otherwise interact with men on an equal footing, their desire for more than a couple of children fades even more dramatically.

Forget population control and instead help every woman bear a child in good health when she wants one.

41

True, old-style population control seems to have helped slow population growth in China. The country's leaders brag that their one-child policy has spared the world's climate 300 million greenhouse gas emitters, the population equivalent of a U.S. that never happened. But most of the drop in Chinese fertility occurred before that coercive policy went into effect in 1979, as the government brought women by the millions into farm and industry collectives and provided them with the family planning they needed to stay on the job. Many developing countries—from Thailand and Colombia to Iran—have experienced comparable declines in family size by getting better family-planning services and educational opportunities to more women and girls in more places.

With President Obama in the White House and Democrats dominant in Congress, the signs are good that the U.S. will support the kind of development abroad and reproductive health at home most likely to encourage slower population growth. Like almost all politicians, however, Obama never mentions population or the way it bridges problems from health and education all the way to food, energy security and climate change.

Bringing population back into the public conversation is risky, but the world has come a long way in understanding that the subject is only one part of most of today's problems and that "population control" can't really control population. Handing control of their lives and their bodies to women—the right thing to do for countless other reasons—can. There is no reason to fear the discussion.

ROBERT ENGELMAN is vice president for programs at the Worldwatch Institute and author of *More: Population, Nature, and What Women Want* (Island Press).

Why Migration Matters

The world total of international migrants has more than doubled in just 25 years; about 25 million were added in just the first 5 years of the twenty-first century.

KHALID KOSER

Migration has always mattered—but today it matters more than ever before. The increasing importance of migration derives from its growing scale and its widening global reach, but also from a number of new dynamics. These include the feminization of migration, the growth of so-called irregular migration, and migration's inextricable linkages with globalization in terms of economic growth, development, and security. Climate change, moreover, is certain to raise migration still higher on nations' and international institutions' policy agendas.

The history of migration begins with humanity's very origins in the Rift Valley of Africa. It was from there that Homo sapiens emerged about 120,000 years ago, subsequently migrating across Africa, through the Middle East to Europe and Central and South Asia, and finally to the New World, reaching the Bering Straits about 20,000 years ago. Then, in the ancient world, Greek colonization and Roman expansion depended on migration; significant movements of people were also associated with the Mesopotamian, Incan, Indus, and Zhou empires. Later we see major migrations such as those involving the Vikings along the shorelines of the Atlantic and North Sea, and the Crusaders to the Holy Land.

In more recent history—in other words, in the past two or three centuries—it is possible to discern, according to migration historian Robin Cohen, a series of major migration periods or events. In the eighteenth and nineteenth centuries, one of the most prominent migration events was the forced transportation of slaves. About 12 million people were taken, mainly from West Africa, to the New World (and also, in lesser numbers, across the Indian Ocean and the Mediterranean Sea). One of the reasons this migration is considered so important, other than its scale, is that it still resonates for descendants of slaves and for African Americans in particular. After slavery's collapse, indentured laborers from China, India, and Japan moved overseas in significant numbers—1.5 million from India alone—to work the plantations of the European powers.

European expansion, especially during the nineteenth century, brought about large-scale voluntary migration away from Europe, particularly to the colonies of settlement, dominions, and the Americas. The great mercantile powers—Britain, the Netherlands, Spain, and France—all promoted settlement of their nationals abroad, not just workers but also peasants, dissident soldiers, convicts, and orphans. Migration associated with expansion largely came to an end with the rise of anticolonial movements toward the end of the nineteenth century, and indeed over the next decades some significant reverse flows back to Europe occurred, for example of the so-called *pieds noirs* to France.

The next period of migration was marked by the rise of the United States as an industrial power. Between the 1850s and the Great Depression of the 1930s, millions of workers fled the stagnant economies and repressive political regimes of northern, southern, and eastern Europe and moved to the United States. (Many fled the Irish famine as well.) Some 12 million of these migrants landed at Ellis Island in New York Harbor. Opportunities for work in the United States also attracted large numbers of Chinese migrants in the first wave of the so-called Chinese diaspora, during the last 50 years of the nineteenth century.

The next major period of migration came after World War II, when the booming postwar economies in Europe, North America, and Australia needed labor. This was the era when, for example, many Turkish migrants arrived to work in Germany and many North Africans went to France and Belgium. It was also the period when, between 1945 and 1972, about 1 million Britons migrated to Australia as so-called "Ten Pound Poms" under an assisted passage scheme. During the same era but in other parts of the world, decolonization continued to have an impact on migration, most significantly in the movement of millions of Hindus and Muslims after the partition of India in 1947 and of Jews and Palestinians after the creation of Israel.

By the late 1970s, and in part as a consequence of the 1973 oil crisis, the international migrant labor boom had ended in Europe, though in the United States it continued into the 1990s. Now, with the global economy's momentum shifting decisively to Asia, labor migration on that continent has grown heavily, and it is still growing. How much longer this will be true, given the current global financial crisis, is a matter open to debate.

More and More

As even this (inevitably selective) overview of international migration's history should make clear, large movements of people have always been associated with significant global events like revolutions, wars, and the rise and fall of empires; with epochal changes like economic expansion, nation building, and political transformations; and with enduring challenges like conflict, persecution, and dispossession.

Nevertheless, one reason to argue that migration matters more today than ever before is sheer numbers. If we define an international migrant as a person who stays outside his usual country of residence for at least one year, there are about 200 million such migrants worldwide. This is roughly equivalent to the population of the fifth-most populous country on earth, Brazil. In fact, 1 in every 35 people in the world today is an international migrant.

Of course, a less dramatic way to express this statistic is to say that only 3 percent of the world's population is composed of international migrants. (In migration, statistics are often used to alarm rather than to inform.) And it is also worth noting that internal migration is a far more significant phenomenon than is international migration (China alone has at least 130 million internal migrants). Still, the world total of international migrants has more than doubled in just 25 years; about 25 million were added in just the first 5 years of the twenty-first century.

And international migration affects many more people than just those who migrate. According to Stephen Castles and Mark Miller, authors of the influential volume *The Age of Migration,* "There can be few people in either industrialized or less developed countries today who do not have personal experience of migration and its effects; this universal experience has become the hallmark of the age of migration." In host countries, migrants' contributions are felt keenly in social, cultural, and economic spheres. Throughout the world, people of different national origins, who speak different languages and practice different customs and religions, are coming into unprecedented contact with each other. For some this is a threat, for others an opportunity.

Migration is also a far more global process than ever before, as migrants today travel both from and to all of the world's regions. In 2005 (the most recent year for which global data are available) there were about 60 million international migrants in Europe, 44 million in Asia, 41 million in North America, 16 million in Africa, and 6 million each in Latin America and Australia. A significant portion of the world's migrants—about 35 million—lived in the United States. The Russian Federation was the second-largest host country for migrants, with about 13 million living there. Following in the rankings were Germany, Ukraine, and India, each with between 6 million and 7 million migrants.

It is much harder to say which countries migrants come from, largely because origin countries tend not to keep count of how many of their nationals are living abroad. It has been estimated that at least 35 million Chinese currently live outside their country, along with 20 million Indians and 8 million Filipinos. But in fact the traditional distinctions among migrants' countries of origin, transit, and destination have become increasingly blurred. Today almost every country in the world fulfills all three roles—migrants leave them, pass through them, and head for them.

A World of Reasons

The reasons for the recent rise in international migration and its widening global reach are complex. The factors include growing global disparities in development, democracy, and demography; in some parts of the world, job shortages that will be exacerbated by the current economic downturn; the segmentation of labor markets in high-income economies, a situation that attracts migrant workers to so-called "3D" jobs (dirty, difficult, or dangerous); revolutions in communications and transportation, which result in more people than ever before knowing about life elsewhere and having the ability to travel there; migration networks that allow existing migrant and ethnic communities to act as magnets for further migration; and a robust migration industry, including migrant smugglers and human traffickers, that profits from international migration.

In addition to being bigger, international migration today is also a more complex phenomenon than it has been in the past, as people of all ages and types move for a wide variety of reasons. For example, child migration appears to be on the increase around the world. Migrants with few skills working "3D" jobs make important contributions to the global economy, but so do highly skilled migrants and students. Some people move away from their home countries permanently, but an increasing proportion moves only temporarily, or circulates between countries. And though an important legal distinction can be made between people who move for work purposes and those who flee conflict and persecution, in reality the two can be difficult to distinguish, as members of the two groups sometimes move together in so-called "mixed flows."

One trend of particular note is that women's representation among migrants has increased rapidly, starting in the 1960s and accelerating in the 1990s. Very nearly half the world's authorized migrants in 2005 were women, and more female than male authorized migrants resided in Europe, North America, Latin America and the Caribbean, the states of the former Soviet Union, and Oceania. What is more, whereas women have traditionally migrated to join their partners, an increasing proportion who migrate today do so independently. Indeed, they are often primary breadwinners for families that they leave behind.

A number of reasons help explain why women comprise an increasing proportion of the world's migrants. One is that global demand for foreign labor, especially in more developed countries, is becoming increasingly gender-selective. That is, more jobs are available in the fields typically staffed by women—services, health care, and entertainment. Second, an increasing number of countries have extended the right of family reunion to migrants, allowing them to be joined by their spouses and children. Third, in some countries of origin, changes in gender relations mean that women enjoy more freedom than previously to migrate independently. Finally, in trends especially evident in Asia, there has been growth in migration of women for domestic work (this is sometimes called the "maid trade"); in organized migration for marriage (with the women sometimes referred to as "mail-order brides"); and in the trafficking of women, above all into the sex industry.

Most Irregular

Another defining characteristic of the new global migration is the growth of irregular migration and the rapid rise of this phenomenon in policy agendas. Indeed, of all the categories of international migrants, none attracts as much attention or divides opinion as consistently as irregular migrants—people often described as "illegal," "undocumented," or "unauthorized."

Almost by definition, irregular migration defies enumeration (although most commentators believe that its scale is increasing).

A commonly cited estimate holds that there are around 40 million irregular migrants worldwide, of whom perhaps one-third are in the United States. There are between 3.5 million and 5 million irregular migrants in the Russian Federation, and perhaps 5 million in Europe. Each year, an estimated 2.5 million to 4 million migrants are thought to cross international borders without authorization.

One reason that it is difficult to count irregular migrants is that even this single category covers people in a range of different situations. It includes migrants who enter or remain in a country without authorization; those who are smuggled or trafficked across an international border; those who seek asylum, are not granted it, and then fail to observe a deportation order; and people who circumvent immigration controls, for example by arranging bogus marriages or fake adoptions.

What is more, an individual migrant's status can change—often rapidly. A migrant can enter a country in an irregular fashion but then regularize her status, for example by applying for asylum or entering a regularization program. Conversely, a migrant can enter regularly then become irregular by working without a permit or overstaying a visa. In Australia, for example, British citizens who have stayed beyond the expiration of their visas account for by far the largest number of irregular migrants.

The Rich Get Richer

International migration matters more today than ever because of its new dimensions and dynamics, but even more because of its increased impact—on the global economy, on international politics, and on society. Three impacts are particularly worth noting: international migration's contribution to the global economy; the significance of migration for development; and the linkages between migration and security.

Kodak, Atlantic Records, RCA, NBC, Google, Intel, Hotmail, Sun, Microsoft, Yahoo, eBay—all these US firms were founded or cofounded by migrants. It has been estimated that international migrants make a net contribution to the US economy of $60 billion, and that half of the scientists, engineers, and holders of PhD degrees in the United States were born overseas. It is often suggested (though this is hard to substantiate) that migrants are worth more to the British economy than is North Sea oil. Worldwide migrant labor is thought to earn at least $20 trillion. In some of the Gulf states, migrants comprise 90 percent of the labor force.

Such a selection of facts and figures can suggest a number of conclusions about international migration's significance for the global economy. First, migrants are often among the most dynamic and entrepreneurial members of society. This has always been the case. In many ways the history of US economic growth is the history of migrants: Andrew Carnegie (steel), Adolphus Busch (beer), Samuel Goldwyn (movies), and Helena Rubenstein (cosmetics) were all migrants. Second, migrants fill labor market gaps both at the top end and the bottom end—a notion commonly captured in the phrase "Mi-grants do the work that natives are either unable or unwilling to do." Third, the significance of migrant labor varies across countries but more importantly across economic sectors. In the majority of advanced economies, migrant workers are over-represented in agriculture, construction, heavy industry, manufacturing, and services—especially food, hospitality, and domestic services. (It is precisely these sectors that the global financial crisis is currently hitting hardest.) Finally, migrant workers contribute

significantly more to national economies than they take away (through, for example, pensions and welfare benefits). That is, migrants tend to be young and they tend to work.

This last conclusion explains why migration is increasingly considered one possible response to the demographic crisis that affects increasing numbers of advanced economies (though it does not affect the United States yet). In a number of wealthy countries, a diminishing workforce supports an expanding retired population, and a mismatch results between taxes that are paid into pension and related programs and the payments that those programs must make. Importing youthful workers in the form of migrants appears at first to be a solution—but for two reasons, it turns out to be only a short-term response. First, migrants themselves age and eventually retire. Second, recent research indicates that, within a generation, migrants adapt their fertility rates to those that prevail in the countries where they settle. In other words, it would not take long for migrants to exacerbate rather then relieve a demographic crisis.

The Poor Get Richer

International migration does not affect only the economies of countries to which migrants travel—it also strongly affects the economies of countries from which migrants depart, especially in the realm of development in poorer countries. The World Bank estimates that each year migrants worldwide send home about $300 billion. This amounts to triple the value of official development assistance, and is the second-largest source of external funding for developing countries after foreign direct investment. The most important recipient countries for remittances are India ($27 billion), China ($26 billion), Mexico ($25 billion), and the Philippines ($17 billion). The top countries from which remittances are dispatched are the United States ($42 billion), Saudi Arabia ($16 billion), Switzerland ($14 billion), and Germany ($12 billion).

The impact of remittances on development is hotly debated, and to an extent the impact depends on who receives the money and how it is spent. It is indisputable that remittances can lift individuals and families out of poverty: Annual household incomes in Somaliland are doubled by remittances. Where remittances are spent on community projects such as wells and schools, as is often the case in Mexico, they also have a wider benefit. And remittances make a significant contribution to gross domestic product (GDP) at the national level, comprising for example 37 percent of GDP in Tonga and 27 percent in both Jordan and Lesotho.

Most experts emphasize that remittances should not be viewed as a substitute for official development assistance. One reason is that remittances are private monies, and thus it is difficult to influence how they are spent or invested. Also, remittances fluctuate over time, as is now becoming apparent in the context of the global economic crisis. Finally, it has been suggested that remittances can generate a "culture of migration," encouraging further migration, and even provide a disincentive to work where families come to expect money from abroad. It has to be said, even so, that the net impact of remittances in developing countries is positive.

International migration, moreover, can contribute to development through other means than remittances. For example, it can relieve pressure on the labor markets in countries from which migrants originate, reducing competition and unemployment. Indonesia and the Philippines are examples of countries that deliberately export labor for this reason (as well as to obtain remittance income). In addition, migrants can contribute to their home countries when they return by using their savings and the new skills they have acquired—although the impact they can have really depends on the extent to which necessary infrastructure is in place for them to realize their potential.

At the same time, however, international migration can undermine development through so-called "brain drain." This term describes a situation in which skills that are already in short supply in a country depart that country through migration. Brain drain is a particular problem in sub-Saharan Africa's health sector, as significant numbers of African doctors and nurses work in the United Kingdom and elsewhere in Europe. Not only does brain drain deprive a country of skills that are in high demand—it undermines that country's investment in the education and training of its own nationals.

Safety First

A third impact of international migration—one that perhaps more than any other explains why it has risen toward the top of policy agendas—is the perception that migration constitutes a heightened security issue in the era after 9/11. Discussions of this issue often revolve around irregular migration—which, in public and policy discourses, is frequently associated with the risk of terrorism, the spread of infectious diseases, and criminality.

Such associations are certainly fair in some cases. A strong link, for example, has been established between irregular migrants from Morocco, Algeria, and Syria and the Madrid bombings of March 2004. For the vast majority of irregular migrants, however, the associations are not fair. Irregular migrants are often assigned bad intentions without any substantiation. Misrepresenting evidence can criminalize and demonize all irregular migrants, encourage them to remain underground—and divert attention from those irregular migrants who actually are criminals and should be prosecuted, as well as those who are suffering from disease and should receive treatment.

Irregular migration is indeed associated with risks, but not with the risks most commonly identified. One legitimate risk is irregular migration's threat to the exercise of sovereignty. States have a sovereign right to control who crosses their borders and remains on their territory, and irregular migration challenges this right. Where irregular migration involves corruption and organized crime, it can also become a threat to public security. This is particularly the case when illegal entry is facilitated by migrant smugglers and human traffickers, or when criminal gangs compete for control of migrants' labor after they have arrived.

Irregular migration is indeed associated with risks, but not with the risks most commonly identified.

When irregular migration results in competition for scarce jobs, this can generate xenophobic sentiments within host populations. Importantly, these sentiments are often directed not only at migrants with irregular status but also at established migrants, refugees, and ethnic minorities. When irregular migration receives a great deal of media attention, it can also undermine public confidence in the integrity and effectiveness of a state's migration and asylum policies.

In addition, irregular migration can undermine the "human security" of migrants themselves. The harm done to migrants by irregular migration is often underestimated—in fact, irregular migration can be very dangerous. A large number of people die each year trying to cross land and sea borders while avoiding detection by the authorities. It has been estimated, for example, that as many as 2,000 migrants die each year trying to cross the Mediterranean from Africa to Europe, and that about 400 Mexicans die annually trying to cross the border into the United States.

People who enter a country or remain in it without authorization are often at risk of exploitation by employers and landlords. Female migrants with irregular status, because they are confronted with gender-based discrimination, are often obliged to accept the most menial jobs in the informal sector, and they may face specific health-related risks, including exposure to HIV/AIDS. Such can be the level of human rights abuses involved in contemporary human trafficking that some commentators have compared it to the slave trade.

Migrants with irregular status are often unwilling to seek redress from authorities because they fear arrest and deportation. For the same reason, they do not always make use of public services to which they are entitled, such as emergency health care. In most countries, they are also barred from using the full range of services available both to citizens and to migrants with regular status. In such situations, already hard-pressed nongovernmental organizations, religious bodies, and other civil society institutions are obliged to provide assistance, at times compromising their own legality.

In Hard Times

What might the future of international migration look like? Tentatively at least, the implications of the current global economic crisis for migration are beginning to emerge. Already a slowdown in the movement of people at a worldwide level has been reported, albeit with significant regional and national variations, and this appears to be largely a result of declining job opportunities in destination countries. The economic sectors in which migrants tend to be over-represented have been hit first; as a consequence migrant workers around the world are being laid off in substantial numbers.

Migrant workers around the world are being laid off in substantial numbers.

Interestingly, it appears that most workers are nevertheless not returning home, choosing instead to stay and look for new jobs. Those entitled to draw on social welfare systems can be expected to do so, thus reducing their net positive impact on national economies. (It remains to be seen whether national economic stimulus packages, such as the one recently enacted in the United States, will help migrant workers get back to work.) Scattered cases of xenophobia have been reported around the world, as anxious natives increasingly fear labor competition from migrant workers.

In the last quarter of 2008 remittances slowed down. Some project that in 2009 remittances, for the first time in decades, may shrink. Moreover, changes in exchange rates mean that even if the volume of remittances remains stable, their net value to recipients may decrease. These looming trends hold worrying implications for households, communities, and even national economies in poor countries.

Our experience of previous economic downturns and financial crises—including the Great Depression, the oil crisis of the early 1970s, and the Asian, Russian, and Latin American financial crises between 1997 and 2000—tells us that such crises' impact on international migration is relatively short-lived and that migration trends soon rebound. Few experts are predicting that the current economic crisis will fundamentally alter overall trends toward increased international migration and its growing global reach.

Hot in Here

In the longer term, what will affect migration patterns and processes far more than any financial crisis is climate change. One commonly cited prediction holds that 200 million people will be forced to move as a result of climate change by 2050, although other projections range from 50 million to a startling 1 billion people moving during this century.

In the longer term, what will affect migration patterns and processes far more than any financial crisis is climate change.

The relationship that will develop between climate change and migration appears complex and unpredictable. One type of variable is in climate change events themselves—a distinction is usually made between slow-onset events like rising sea levels and rapid-onset events like hurricanes and tsunamis. In addition, migration is only one of a number of possible responses to most climate change events. Protective measures such as erecting sea walls may reduce the impact. Societies throughout history have adapted to climate change by altering their agricultural and settlement practices.

Global warming, moreover, will make some places better able to support larger populations, as growing seasons are extended, frost risks reduced, and new crops sustained. Where migration does take place, it is difficult to predict whether the movement will mainly be internal or cross-border, or temporary or permanent. And finally, the relationship between climate change and migration may turn out to be indirect. For example, people may flee conflicts that arise over scarce resources in arid areas, rather than flee desertification itself.

Notwithstanding the considerable uncertainty, a consensus has emerged that, within the next 10 years, climate-related international migration will become observably more frequent, and the scale of overall international migration will increase significantly. Such migration will add still further complexity to the migration situation, as the new migrants will largely defy current classifications.

One immediately contentious issue is whether people who cross borders as a result of the effects of climate change should be defined as "climate refugees" or "climate migrants." The former conveys the fact that at least some people will literally need to seek refuge from the impacts of climate change, will find themselves in situations as desperate as those of other refugees, and will deserve international assistance and protection. But the current definition of a refugee in international law does not extend to people fleeing environmental pressures, and few states are willing to amend the law. Equally, the description "climate migrant" underestimates the involuntariness of the movement, and opens up the possibility for such people to be labeled and dealt with as irregular migrants.

Another legal challenge arises with the prospect of the total submergence by rising sea levels of low-lying island states such as the Maldives—namely, how to categorize people who no longer have a state. Will their national flags be lowered outside UN headquarters in New York, and will they be granted citizenship in another country?

The complexities of responding to climate-related movements of people illustrate a more general point, that new responses are required to international migration as it grows in scale and complexity. Most of the legal frameworks and international institutions established to govern migration were established at the end of World War II, in response to a migration reality very different from that existing today, and as a result new categories of migrants are falling into gaps in protection. New actors have also emerged in international migration, including most importantly the corporate sector, and they have very little representation in migration policy decisions at the moment.

Perhaps most fundamentally, a shift in attitude is required, away from the notion that migration can be controlled, focusing instead on trying to manage migration and maximize its benefits.

KHALID KOSER directs the New Issues in Security program at the Geneva Center for Security Policy. He is also a non-resident fellow at the Brookings Institution and author of *International Migration: A Very Short Introduction* (Oxford University Press, 2007).

Pandemic Pandemonium

Josh N. Ruxin

Pandemic. The word can spread fear to billions overnight. One of the few public-health terms that gives Hollywood nightmare plotlines. Literally meaning "all people," a pandemic is an extraordinary global health event in which an epidemic of infectious disease spreads across regions and, potentially, the entire planet. Ebola, avian flu, SARS—each had the potential to spread rapidly and each received extraordinary attention during the past several years. Though they did not result in mass casualties, all wrought worldwide fear.

Throughout the course of human history, pandemics have wreaked havoc. The 1918 flu pandemic may have killed over 20 million people. Even then, 50 percent of the mortality difference among countries can be attributed to a single factor: per capita income. Thus, the poorest country hit, India, suffered the most, while Denmark suffered the least. That differential, however, has not yet made for compelling public policy. After all, science made landmark breakthroughs in the twentieth century, often applying scientific insights from previous centuries in innovative ways to control and, in the case of smallpox, eradicate disease. But in the days of porous borders and unprecedented global travel, viruses and other pathogens may once again have the upper hand. One key question on the table is: will the next pandemic be worse than the ones we currently face?

Viewed from where I live in Rwanda, it's clear that the sheer neglect of health of poor people has set an ideal foundation for pandemics to spread for years under the radar, evade surveillance and, as has been the case with HIV/AIDS, enter our airspace and bodies at a startling rate. The history of global health demonstrates that wealthy nations respond best to dramatic, fast-moving outbreaks like Ebola or avian flu. Unfortunately, today wealthy and poor nations alike face pandemics that move slowly and don't necessarily show symptoms during the first few years of infection.

Today's pandemics have evolved to prey on our greatest weakness: our inability to wage sustained fights against pressing health issues. This creates a doubly challenging situation in a world where disease is often socioeconomically stratified. Rich people don't generally get sick from malaria or tuberculosis (TB), so those diseases—which kill millions each year—have until very recently received far-less attention than they deserve. But now the line between rich and poor countries, and rich and poor people within countries, is murky. Dangerous infections such as drug-resistant tuberculosis can cross the globe by air in

a matter of hours. These are the new, rapidly moving vectors of disease, and they provide a direct line of transmission between the most-vulnerable and least-healthy people on the planet and the wealthiest and healthiest. It augurs for the worst that health systems for the poor have failed miserably to generate the quality and accountability needed to address even the most-basic health needs.

What happens when a poor country loses 30 percent of its adult population to AIDS or to a flu epidemic? There are plenty of military models that assess decision making when a country is attacked by an enemy, but few models to assess the chaos that cuts across all segments of society when it's a disease that acts as antagonist. Plans have also not fully taken into account the impact of rapidly changing demographics on disease spread. The poorest, precisely those most at risk, are reproducing the fastest, so the chance of pandemic is growing faster than the numbers may superficially reveal. And of course, the prevalence of megacities means more poor people are living in close proximity to each other—and with greater opportunity for disease transmission.

Leaders of poor countries appear to be completely unaware of the global connections between the health of their populations and the security and stability required to ensure that they do not fall prey to unforeseen health catastrophes. The dearth of strong and transparent leadership among the world's poorest nations augurs poorly for the health of those nations, and of the world.

Meanwhile, the rich countries also continue to think about pandemics in a very linear and scientific way, which fails to account for the comprehensive economic and political chaos that would accompany a major pandemic. The World Health Organization (WHO), Centers for Disease Control, and, for that matter, the Gates Foundation and other donors, are concentrating their efforts on vaccines and, in the case of the WHO, antiviral stockpiles for a possible outbreak of avian flu. Plans are also being developed for isolation and quarantine, running through scenarios for stopping air traffic and the like. Unfortunately, it's unlikely that the pathogens will be as responsive to our efforts as we hope they will be, leading to widespread chaos, morbidity and mortality.

At a time when oil shocks have the ability to globally increase food insecurity, it may be worthwhile to consider how a pandemic could push people living on the edge into poverty and starvation. With food production suffering greatly, the urban centers that are dependent on daily imports of food could rapidly fall victim. If this sounds a bit like Jared Diamond's arguments in *Collapse,* it's intentional. The world is interconnected, but poor countries are hanging by a thread, and it's a thread that could quickly break if a pandemic hits hard enough.

Poor countries are hanging by a thread, and it's a thread that could quickly break if a pandemic hits hard enough.

Adding to the threat, it may well be that the worst pandemics on the planet are not emerging, but have simply been with us so long that we've grown accustomed to their presence and therefore have done little to address them. Women across sub-Saharan Africa continue to stand a 1 percent chance of dying in childbirth—is that a pandemic? Five hundred thousand kids die from measles every year. Africans suffer from an astonishing estimated 300 million episodes of malaria annually, with a death toll of one million. And now throughout the developing world silent killers like heart disease and diabetes are taking hold.

In the best of cases, pursuing a business-as-usual approach, the wealthy countries may get lucky: the spread of contagion may be stopped at borders and when it crosses, advanced, expensive treatment may be available. But no matter what, the economic and potential political destabilization that would result would cross these borders and be felt in everyone's bank accounts. The moral implications of continuing to adopt a merely defensive stance will guarantee that developing countries will suffer millions dead and may also cultivate the pathogens for future pandemics that will evade the best weapons the richer countries can throw at them.

Some might see the call for health improvement in poor nations in order to save our own skins as either a Machiavellian ploy to help poor people or a sad and ironic commentary on the state of humankind. Whatever the case, rich nations must begin taking health systems for the poor seriously because: new bugs and the resurgence of old ones are likely to emerge where people are sickest or treatment is inconsistent; when pandemics strike, they'll do the most harm to those without health services; and when sicknesses like a new strain of influenza inevitably come, the health personnel in these settings will be much-better equipped to identify and contain them.

If they don't, Hollywood fantasies may well come true; America and Western Europe will panic as they hear of outbreaks far away (and which may well reach inside their borders); Asia, a likely epicenter of a new flu outbreak or other zoonotically spread disease, will see its services strained and its globalizing economies wrecked; and Africa will see its people die in higher rates than everywhere else while its nascent economic connections to the rest of the world stumble. This scenario is, sadly, hardly far-fetched. The SARS epidemic alone cost Asian countries more than $16 billion and spread panic worldwide while claiming fewer than one thousand lives. That experience suggests that estimating the toll of an actual pandemic is virtually incalculable.

The Threats
AIDS

For the past decade, AIDS has garnered attention not only because of its clinical impact, but also because of its downstream effects. South African businesspeople report that they have to hire one additional worker for every manager hired because they expect so much of their workforce to die of AIDS. Social services and even traditional societal mechanisms for handling orphans are disintegrating in despair as the wave of millions of orphans builds.

More than a decade after numerous news media outlets optimistically queried whether we had reached the end of AIDS, there are troubling signs that this pandemic may yet prove to be the world's top infectious killer. The World Bank has estimated that for every six new infections, only one person is put on life-saving anti-retrovirals (ARVs). This means the disease continues to spread virtually unchecked. With 40 million infected, in all likelihood we'll continue to see 3 to 5 million people dying annually for years to come. Undeniably, AIDS has hit hardest in sub-Saharan Africa, where nearly 23 million are infected. At current rates of drug rollout, all but a couple million of them will die during the next ten years. The ramifications for each of those deaths are hidden by the numbers: for each death, roughly another six people are immediately affected emotionally and economically. Seen through this lens, nearly one-third of sub-Saharan Africa is already likely to be impacted by the current pandemic.

AIDS presents a perfect case for why all health must be global. It is not simply a philanthropic service to ensure that basic health needs are met worldwide: it's a biological necessity. AIDS may well have been around for the better part of the last century, but it went largely undetected because it was prevalent among populations with minimal access to health care. By the time it reached people with health care, it had spread across the planet, causing an estimated 25 million deaths to date.

The numbers will get worse. In the developing world there may be little data on resistance, but with more treated people, coupled with inconsistent treatments and fewer treatment options, it is likely that drug resistance will emerge as a major problem. The solutions do remain well within the grasp of our current abilities. Good surveillance and improved monitoring for patients on ARVs in developing countries will lessen the possibility of treatment failure and corresponding resistance. Expanded treatment programs that include better monitoring and access to more than first-line therapy ensure that when treatment does fail, patients have other options. This will ensure that they do not become vessels for advanced strains of the disease. But without action, strains of HIV which can tolerate even the most-sophisticated and most-expensive drug regimens available may well emerge and move around the world just as the first strains did. Thus, AIDS in the West could prove to be the definitive killer that it once was, yet again.

Malaria

Malaria, though hardly as expensive as AIDS to address, has joined the ranks of diseases being tackled on a grand scale. The Global Fund has committed $3.1 billion to the malaria fight, and the United States has launched a bold new malaria initiative. Through the use of insecticide-treated bed nets and new drug therapy, several countries have realized steep declines in malaria morbidity and mortality, one among them Rwanda. In 2000, Rwanda saw an estimated one million cases of malaria. Today, thanks in large part to bed nets, that figure has fallen by more than 60 percent. In 2000, an astonishing 10 percent of all children under five succumbed to malaria; today, those deaths have virtually disappeared. For the first time in decades, serious debate and action is emerging to eradicate or diminish the disease. Bill and Melinda Gates have set the world's sights on complete malaria eradication, a feat that will require massive breakthroughs in technology.

However, this is one fight that must be taken to the far reaches of the earth and be resolutely committed to a sustained effort. Today it is widely hypothesized that the extraordinary illness seen from malaria resulted from the failure to continue pushing the disease back with DDT in the 1960s. Instead, after some notable successes, efforts evaporated, individuals and populations lost their natural immunity, and the disease came back with a vengeance. Anything less than persistent, wholesale control and elimination efforts risks exacerbation of the disease. In the worst-case scenario, malaria could be eliminated from much of the African continent, be maintained at low levels in a few places, develop resistance to the best drugs available, and then see efforts to contain it wane. What would follow would be devastating for the continent. Malaria would return to populations lacking any natural immunity, drugs could prove ineffective, and millions of lives would potentially be lost—every year—particularly among very young children.

Tuberculosis

Tuberculosis has plagued humankind since the fourth millennia BCE. While the disease only recently ceased to be a significant public-health threat in the developed world, TB still claims five thousand lives globally every day, more than SARS, Marburg and avian flu ever have. Nine million people develop active TB each year. Although curative treatment has been around for the last several decades, it has been unevenly applied: in many cases health facilities have not ensured that patients receive a full course of treatment, and, overall, those most in need of treatment have not received it at all. Poor treatment has resulted in fiercer, more-resistant strains of TB. Three percent of all newly diagnosed patients have multi-drug-resistant TB (MDR-TB), making their treatment complicated, expensive and uncertain. In September 2006, the WHO announced a further worsening of the MDR-TB pandemic with multiple reports in all regions of the world of the emergence of extensively resistant strains of TB (XDR-TB) immune to virtually all drugs.

It should not shock Americans that this disease is making its way across the globe when every location is just a plane ride away. Yet the growth of XDR-TB, considered virtually untreatable, has gone largely unnoticed in the United States, where there have been only seventeen cases since 2000. In sub-Saharan Africa, where roughly 23 million people are HIV positive, nearly half will develop TB. If treatment is not well administered, these cases will lead to new strains of resistant TB. There is a direct connection between the AIDS pandemic, TB, and the failure of health systems to appropriately diagnose and treat these diseases. However, unlike AIDS, whose transmission relies on behavior (unsafe sex, intravenous-drug usage), TB is airborne. While the immuno-compromised and malnourished are at greater risk for developing active TB, the main risk factor for contracting it is shared by all: breathing. Those in the developed world have every reason to fear for their immunity.

Influenza

The flu may be the world's greatest risk. Recent models based on the 1918 Spanish flu have estimated that the next outbreak will cause between 51 and 157 million excess deaths, with 95 percent of those occurring in developing countries. Critics have suggested that it's overly optimistic to conclude the carnage will be so low in developed nations. Other estimates conclude that total excess deaths could exceed 300 million with 27 million occurring in rich nations and the large remainder in poor. Without sufficient health-care facilities in developing countries—in both urban and rural locations—the higher death estimates will undoubtedly be realized, as a virulent flu spreads easily and rapidly through the air. Whatever the case, a particularly vicious strain of the flu would undoubtedly be the greatest public-health catastrophe of our time.

So what precisely is at the root of the massive inequities that provide the petri dish for global pandemics? Is it simply disease burden? Transmission routes? Poverty? Corruption and poor governance? Selfishness on a grand scale? All of the above?

At the turn of the twenty-first century, the blame for the burden was placed squarely on wealthy countries. The failure to roll out simple solutions required exponential increases in funding and new initiatives—ironically fueled by one of the most-complex diseases ever faced, AIDS. Drugs and big pharmaceuticals were the scapegoats of the last several years; today, experts cite the lack of nurses and human resources. There is a predictable oscillation in the blame game, but one fact is clear: health worldwide has deteriorated.

This is perhaps most troubling in the context of pandemics because just as environmental catastrophes can spur epidemics, and potentially pandemics, pandemics can quickly take down economies and, potentially, countries. In the wake of avian flu, Southeast Asian economies experienced an enormous economic downturn; tourists have been writing me and asking whether it's safe to go to Brazil in light of the dengue epidemic; the economic, social and political cost of AIDS in sub-Saharan Africa remains to be calculated. Thus, there is a vicious cycle: pandemics can encourage chaos and breakdowns of basic systems, particularly in the poorest and poorly governed nations, and these breakdowns can in turn create better conditions for more disease to emerge. Case in point: during the chaos in Kenya at the turn of this year, 60 percent of patients on antiretroviral therapy and 35 percent of patients on TB drugs were lost to follow-up. It is likely that all those patients stopped their treatment midcourse and are now potentially cultivating resistant strains of both infections.

Policy makers are looking at the direct health consequences of pandemics (Who is sick? How do we treat them?) rather than the indirect health consequences (What other services will fail? What will happen to the food supply?). Had SARS hit anywhere in sub-Saharan Africa, where ventilators and surgical masks are a rare commodity, death rates would have been higher than in Asia. Today the response systems being put in place are to protect the wealthy with vaccines and antivirals, but do not treat those most likely to suffer. Thus, we are preparing for the next pandemic rather than doing everything in our power to prevent it.

Foundations and governments can't seem to get their heads around the fact that no disease can be treated in a vacuum: all efforts must be part of an integrated response, otherwise dollars are sure to be poorly spent. The worst-hit area on the planet for health-systems failure remains sub-Saharan Africa, where governments spend paltry amounts on health, the poor are frequently required to pay for services and there's an uncanny history of serious illnesses evolving. HIV is widely recognized today as having its roots in central Africa; resistant malaria parasites are commonplace; and bizarre outbreaks such as Ebola appear from time to time. When sexually transmitted infections go untreated and open sores ensue, the possibility for transmission increases exponentially, and that transmission doesn't stop at borders.

While epidemics get the press—the recent dengue outbreak in Brazil for example—pandemics tend to quietly work their way through populations, doing enormous harm never garnering the resources or the media attention. That's not to say that rich nations shouldn't be concerned about these epidemics, but there is an uncomfortably consistent trend in global public health to place attention on those subjects and diseases that may not pose the greatest threat to human welfare.

In the next couple of decades, with expanded funding for public health, it will be possible to radically alter the course of the future of human health, particularly in poor countries. However, sticking to traditional approaches will fail to provide macro results and may exacerbate health challenges. The uneven delivery of AIDS medications, tuberculosis drugs and antimalarials, for example, could give rise to resistant parasites, bacteria and viruses capable of beating current technology. Further, the singular focus on just a few diseases and the subspecialization that accompanies it may rob us of the expert diagnosticians who can quickly spot an unusual illness before it gets out of control.

The solution to the frightening scenario of national breakdowns and despair is to beef up efforts to build capacity in the poorest nations to handle their current problems, with an eye to avoiding such chaos. Health systems require serious strengthening. Farmers need improved agricultural techniques to push them away from the brink and toward something resembling stability. Basic infrastructure must be massively expanded and improved. The list is a long one but most everywhere you look, we have scarcely begun. It's time to shake up the public-health establishment and place investments in basic health services for the neglected and poor worldwide.

We need to step up efforts and get it right. The world's health and stability depend on it.

JOSH N. RUXIN is an assistant clinical professor of public health at Columbia University's Mailman School of Public Health. He resides in Rwanda where he directs the Access Project and the Millennium Villages Project Rwanda, and advises Rwanda Community Works.

The Next Breadbasket?

How Africa Could Save the World—and Itself

Elizabeth Chiles Shelburne

I t's been 41 years since Paul Ehrlich predicted imminent mass starvation, in his 1968 jeremiad, *The Population Bomb*. In the years that followed, a green revolution drove crop production rapidly upward, while population growth slowed dramatically; Ehrlich's bomb, rather conspicuously, failed to go off.

Nonetheless, we're still multiplying—global population is on track to reach 9.1 billion by 2050, up from 6.8 billion today. And the green revolution seems to have run its course: rice yields, for instance, are growing at only 1 percent a year, down from 2.3 percent in the 1960s, 1970s, and 1980s. For the past several years, grain

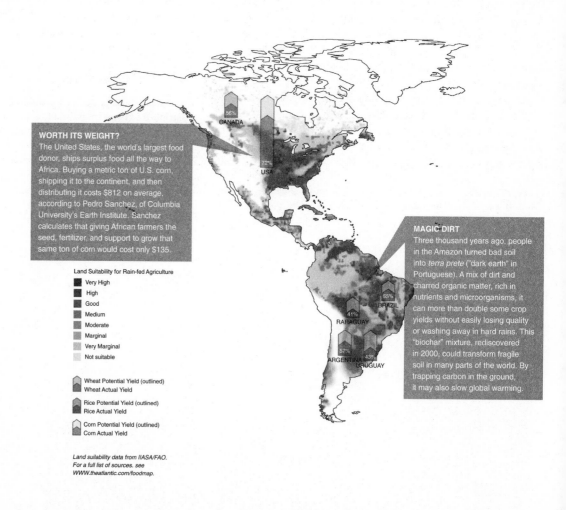

WORTH ITS WEIGHT?
The United States, the world's largest food donor, ships surplus food all the way to Africa. Buying a metric ton of U.S. corn, shipping it to the continent, and then distributing it costs $812 on average, according to Pedro Sanchez, of Columbia University's Earth Institute. Sanchez calculates that giving African farmers the seed, fertilizer, and support to grow that same ton of corn would cost only $135.

MAGIC DIRT
Three thousand years ago, people in the Amazon turned bad soil into *terra preta* ("dark earth" in Portuguese). A mix of dirt and charred organic matter, rich in nutrients and microorganisms, it can more than double some crop yields without easily losing quality or washing away in hard rains. This "biochar" mixture, rediscovered in 2000, could transform fragile soil in many parts of the world. By trapping carbon in the ground, it may also slow global warming.

Land Suitability for Rain-fed Agriculture
- Very High
- High
- Good
- Medium
- Moderate
- Marginal
- Very Marginal
- Not suitable

Wheat Potential Yield (outlined)
Wheat Actual Yield

Rice Potential Yield (outlined)
Rice Actual Yield

Corn Potential Yield (outlined)
Corn Actual Yield

*Land suitability data from IIASA/FAO.
For a full list of sources, see
WWW.theatlantic.com/foodmap.*

production has not kept up with demand; if we are to put enough food on the table in the coming decades, something big will need to change.

Much of the world's arable land is being farmed already, so the lion's share of the increase will need to come through higher yields. In many places, yields *can* increase—if prices rise high enough to make investment in more-intensive agriculture worthwhile. Still, much of the developed world is approaching the ceiling of what is cheaply possible. Sub-Saharan Africa, despite its long history of food insecurity, is one place where yields could increase dramatically; agricultural basics such as good seed and fertilizer would go far in a region that the green revolution bypassed. "We could increase yields in sub-Saharan Africa threefold tomorrow with off-the-shelf technology," says Kenneth Cassman, a well-regarded agronomist who researches potential yields. The problem is the continent's long history of corruption, poor infrastructure, and lack of market access.

Agricultural investment in Africa—and in a few other high-potential places such as Ukraine and Russia—may be the world's best bet for keeping food plentiful and cheap. This investment could bring other benefits too; the World Bank estimates that agricultural development is twice as effective at reducing poverty as other sources of growth. In Asia, as cereal yields rose, poverty rates plummeted. Investment in Africa's agriculture—by donors, farmers, and African governments—may allow the continent to feed the world and save itself.

ELIZABETH CHILES SHELBURNE is a writer based in Boston.

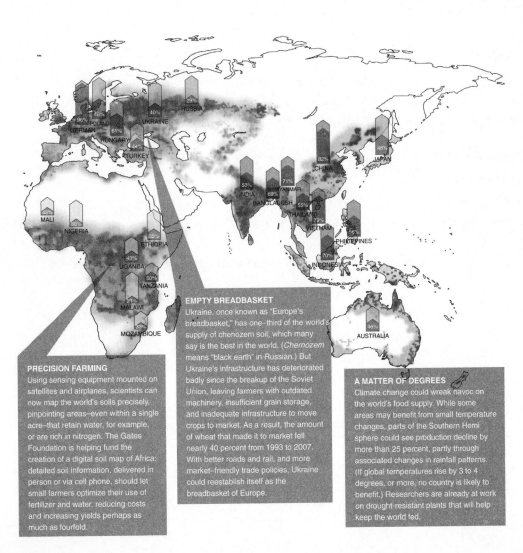

PRECISION FARMING
Using sensing equipment mounted on satellites and airplanes, scientists can now map the world's soils precisely, pinpointing areas–even within a single acre–that retain water, for example, or are rich in nitrogen. The Gates Foundation is helping fund the creation of a digital soil map of Africa: detailed soil information, delivered in person or via cell phone, should let small farmers optimize their use of fertilizer and water, reducing costs and increasing yields perhaps as much as fourfold.

EMPTY BREADBASKET
Ukraine, once known as "Europe's breadbasket," has one–third of the world's supply of chenozem soil, which many say is the best in the world. (*Chernozem* means "black earth" in Russian.) But Ukraine's infrastructure has deteriorated badly since the breakup of the Soviet Union, leaving farmers with outdated machinery, insufficient grain storage, and inadequate infrastructure to move crops to market. As a result, the amount of wheat that made it to market fell nearly 40 percent from 1993 to 2007. With better roads and rail, and more market–friendly trade policies, Ukraine could reestablish itself as the breadbasket of Europe.

A MATTER OF DEGREES
Climate change could wreak havoc on the world's food supply. While some areas may benefit from small temperature changes, parts of the Southern Hemi sphere could see production decline by more than 25 percent, partly through associated changes in rainfall patterns. (If global temperatures rise by 3 to 4 degrees, or more, no country is likely to benefit.) Researchers are already at work on drought-resistant plants that will help keep the world fed.

UNIT 3

The Global Environment and Natural Resources Utilization

Unit Selections

Key Points to Consider

- What are the basic arguments regarding climate change and the ability to mitigate or reverse the impacts of human activities?

- What are the basic environmental challenges that confront both governments and individual consumers?

- Has the international community adequately responded to problems of pollution and threats to our common natural heritage? Why or why not?

- What trends and issues are there in terms of the availability of clean water?

- What is the natural resource picture going to look like 30 years from now?

- How is society, in general, likely to respond to the conflicts between lifestyle and resource conservation?

- The rapid industrialization of China and India has significant impacts beyond their borders. What are some of the environmental impacts?

- Can a sustainable economy be organized and what changes in behavior and values are necessary to accomplish this?

Student Website

www.mhhe.com/cls

Internet References

National Geographic Society
http://www.nationalgeographic.com

National Oceanic and Atmospheric Administration (NOAA)
http://www.noaa.gov

SocioSite: Sociological Subject Areas
http://www.pscw.uva.nl/sociosite/TOPICS

United Nations Environment Programme (UNEP)
http://www.unep.ch

In the eighteenth century, the modern nation-state emerged, and over many generations it evolved to the point where it is now difficult to imagine a world without national governments. These legal entities have been viewed as separate, self-contained units that independently pursue their "national interests." Scholars often described the world as a political community of sovereign units that interact with each other (a concept described as a billiard ball model).

This perspective of the international community as comprised of self-contained and self-directed units has undergone major rethinking in the past 35 years. One of the reasons for this is the international consequences of the growing demands being placed on natural resources. The Middle East, for example, contains a majority of the world's known oil reserves. The United States, Western Europe, China, India, and Japan are dependent on this vital source of energy. The unbalanced oil supply and demand equation has created an unprecedented lack of self-sufficiency for the world's major economic powers.

The increased interdependence of countries is further illustrated by the fact that air and water pollution do not respect political boundaries. One country's smoke is often another country's acid rain. The concept that independent political units control their own destiny makes less sense than it might have 100 years ago. In order to more fully understand why this is so, one must first look at how Earth's natural resources are being utilized and how this may be affecting the climate.

The first two articles examine the debate surrounding global climate change and the challenges facing policymakers. Climate change directly or indirectly impacts everyone, and if these changes are to be successfully addressed, international collaboration will be required. The consequences of basic human activities such as growing and cooking food are profound when multiplied billions of times every day. A single country or even a few countries working together cannot have a significant impact on redressing these problems. Solutions will have to be conceived that are truly global in scope. Just as there are shortages of natural resources, there are also shortages of new ideas for solving many of these problems.

Unit 3 continues by examining specific case studies. Implicit in these discussions is the challenge of moving from the perspective of the environment as primarily an economic resource to be consumed to a perspective that has been defined as "sustainable development." This change is easily called for, but in fact it goes to the core of social values and basic economic activities. Developing sustainable practices, therefore, is a challenge of unprecedented magnitude.

© Getty Images

Nature is not some object "out there" to be visited at a national park. It is the food we eat and the energy we consume. Human beings are joined in the most intimate of relationships with the natural world in order to survive from one day to the next. It is ironic how little time is spent thinking about this relationship. This lack of attention, however, is not likely to continue, for rapidly growing numbers of people and the increased use of energy-consuming technologies are placing unprecedented pressures on Earth's carrying capacity.

Climate Change

BILL MCKIBBEN

"Scientists Are Divided"

No, they're not. In the early years of the global warming debate, there was great controversy over whether the planet was warming, whether humans were the cause, and whether it would be a significant problem. That debate is long since over. Although the details of future forecasts remain unclear, there's no serious question about the general shape of what's to come.

Every national academy of science, long lists of Nobel laureates, and in recent years even the science advisors of President George W. Bush have agreed that we are heating the planet. Indeed, there is a more thorough scientific process here than on almost any other issue: Two decades ago, the United Nations formed the Intergovernmental Panel on Climate Change (IPCC) and charged its scientists with synthesizing the peer-reviewed science and developing broad-based conclusions. The reports have found since 1995 that warming is dangerous and caused by humans. The panel's most recent report, in November 2007, found it is "very likely" (defined as more than 90 percent certain, or about as certain as science gets) that heat-trapping emissions from human activities have caused "most of the observed increase in global average temperatures since the mid-20th century."

If anything, many scientists now think that the IPCC has been too conservative—both because member countries must sign off on the conclusions and because there's a time lag. Its last report synthesized data from the early part of the decade, not the latest scary results, such as what we're now seeing in the Arctic.

In the summer of 2007, ice in the Arctic Ocean melted. It melts a little every summer, of course, but this time was different—by late September, there was 25 percent less ice than ever measured before. And it wasn't a one-time accident. By the end of the summer season in 2008, so much ice had melted that both the Northwest and Northeast passages were open. In other words, you could circumnavigate the Arctic on open water. The computer models, which are just a few years old, said this shouldn't have happened until sometime late in the 21st century. Even skeptics can't dispute such alarming events.

"We Have Time"

Wrong. Time might be the toughest part of the equation. That melting Arctic ice is unsettling not only because it proves the planet is warming rapidly, but also because it will help speed up the warming. That old white ice reflected 80 percent of incoming solar radiation back to space; the new blue water left behind absorbs 80 percent of that sunshine. The process amps up. And there are many other such feedback loops. Another occurs as northern permafrost thaws. Huge amounts of methane long trapped below the ice begin to escape into the atmosphere; methane is an even more potent greenhouse gas than carbon dioxide.

Such examples are the biggest reason why many experts are now fast-forwarding their estimates of how quickly we must shift away from fossil fuel. Indian economist Rajendra Pachauri, who accepted the 2007 Nobel Peace Prize alongside Al Gore on behalf of the IPCC, said recently that we must begin to make fundamental reforms by 2012 or watch the climate system spin out of control; NASA scientist James Hansen, who was the first to blow the whistle on climate change in the late 1980s, has said that we must stop burning coal by 2030. Period.

All of which makes the Copenhagen climate change talks that are set to take place in December 2009 more urgent than they appeared a few years ago. At issue is a seemingly small number: the level of carbon dioxide in the air. Hansen argues that 350 parts per million is the highest level we can maintain "if humanity wishes to preserve a planet similar to that on which civilization developed and to which life on Earth is adapted." But because we're already past that mark—the air outside is currently about 387 parts per million and growing by about 2 parts annually—global warming suddenly feels less like a huge problem, and more like an Oh-My-God Emergency.

"Climate Change Will Help as Many Places as It Hurts"

Wishful thinking. For a long time, the winners-and-losers calculus was pretty standard: Though climate change will cause some parts of the planet to flood or shrivel up, other frigid, rainy regions would at least get some warmer days every year. Or so the thinking went. But more recently, models have begun to show that after a certain point almost everyone on the planet will suffer. Crops might be easier to grow in some places for a few decades as the danger of frost recedes, but over time the threat of heat stress and drought will almost certainly be stronger.

A 2003 report commissioned by the Pentagon forecasts the possibility of violent storms across Europe, megadroughts across the Southwest United States and Mexico, and unpredictable monsoons causing food shortages in China. "Envision Pakistan, India, and China—all armed with nuclear weapons—skirmishing at their borders over refugees, access to shared rivers, and arable land," the report warned. Or Spain and Portugal "fighting over fishing rights—leading to conflicts at sea."

Of course, there are a few places we used to think of as possible winners—mostly the far north, where Canada and Russia could theoretically produce more grain with longer growing seasons, or perhaps explore for oil beneath the newly melted Arctic ice cap. But even those places will have to deal with expensive consequences—a real military race across the high Arctic, for instance.

Want more bad news? Here's how that Pentagon report's scenario played out: As the planet's carrying capacity shrinks, an ancient pattern of desperate, all-out wars over food, water, and energy supplies would reemerge. The report refers to the work of Harvard archaeologist Steven LeBlanc, who notes that wars over resources were the norm until about three centuries ago. When such conflicts broke out, 25 percent of a population's adult males usually died. As abrupt climate change hits home, warfare may again come to define human life. Set against that bleak backdrop, the potential upside of a few longer growing seasons in Vladivostok doesn't seem like an even trade.

"It's China's Fault"

Not so much. China is an easy target to blame for the climate crisis. In the midst of its industrial revolution, China has overtaken the United States as the world's biggest carbon dioxide producer. And everyone has read about the one-a-week pace of power plant construction there. But those numbers are misleading, and not just because a lot of that carbon dioxide was emitted to build products for the West to consume. Rather, it's because China has four times the population of the United States, and per capita is really the only way to think about these emissions. And by that standard, each Chinese person now emits just over a quarter of the carbon dioxide that each American does. Not only that, but carbon dioxide lives in the atmosphere for more than a century. China has been at it in a big way less than 20 years, so it will be many, many years before the Chinese are as responsible for global warming as Americans.

What's more, unlike many of their counterparts in the United States, Chinese officials have begun a concerted effort to reduce emissions in the midst of their country's staggering growth. China now leads the world in the deployment of renewable energy, and there's barely a car made in the United States that can meet China's much tougher fuel-economy standards.

For its part, the United States must develop a plan to cut emissions—something that has eluded Americans for the entire two-decade history of the problem. Although the U.S. Senate voted down the last such attempt, Barack Obama has promised that it will be a priority in his administration. He favors some variation of a "cap and trade" plan that would limit the total amount of carbon dioxide the United States could release, thus putting a price on what has until now been free.

Despite the rapid industrialization of countries such as China and India, and the careless neglect of rich ones such as the United States, climate change is neither any one country's fault, nor any one country's responsibility. It will require sacrifice from everyone. Just as the Chinese might have to use somewhat more expensive power to protect the global environment, Americans will have to pay some of the difference in price, even if just in technology. Call it a Marshall Plan for the environment. Such a plan makes eminent moral and practical sense and could probably be structured so as to bolster emerging green energy industries in the West. But asking Americans to pay to put up windmills in China will be a hard political sell in a country that already thinks China is prospering at its expense. It could be the biggest test of the country's political maturity in many years.

"Climate Change Is an Environmental Problem"

Not really. Environmentalists were the first to sound the alarm. But carbon dioxide is not like traditional pollution. There's no Clean Air Act that can solve it. We must make a fundamental transformation in the most important part of our economies, shifting away from fossil fuels and on to something else. That means, for the United States, it's at least as much a problem for the Commerce and Treasury departments as it is for the Environmental Protection Agency.

And because every country on Earth will have to coordinate, it's far and away the biggest foreign-policy issue we face. (You were thinking terrorism? It's hard to figure out a scenario in which Osama bin Laden destroys Western civilization. It's easy to figure out how it happens with a rising sea level and a wrecked hydrological cycle.)

Expecting the environmental movement to lead this fight is like asking the USDA to wage the war in Iraq. It's not equipped for this kind of battle. It may be ready to save Alaska's Arctic National Wildlife Refuge, which is a noble undertaking but on a far smaller scale. Unless climate change is quickly deghettoized, the chances of making a real difference are small.

"Solving It Will Be Painful"

It depends. What's your definition of painful? On the one hand, you're talking about transforming the backbone of the world's industrial and consumer system. That's certainly expensive. On the other hand, say you manage to convert a lot of it to solar or wind power—think of the money you'd save on fuel.

And then there's the growing realization that we don't have many other possible sources for the economic growth we'll need to pull ourselves out of our current economic crisis. Luckily, green energy should be bigger than IT and biotech combined.

Almost from the moment scientists began studying the problem of climate change, people have been trying to estimate the costs of solving it. The real answer, though, is that it's such a huge transofrmation that no one really knows for sure. The bottom line is, the growth rate in energy use worldwide could be cut in half during the next 15 years and the steps would, net, save more money than they cost. The IPCC included a cost estimate in its latest five-year update on climate change and looked a little further into the future. It found that an attempt to keep carbon levels below about 500 parts per million would shave a little bit off the world's economic growth—but only a little. As in, the world would have to wait until Thanksgiving 2030 to be as rich as it would have been on January 1 of that year. And in return, it would have a much-transformed energy system.

Unfortunately though, those estimates are probably too optimistic. For one thing, in the years since they were published, the science has grown darker. Deeper and quicker cuts now seem mandatory.

But so far we've just been counting the costs of fixing the system. What about the cost of doing nothing? Nicholas Stern, a renowned economist commissioned by the British government to study the question, concluded that the costs of climate change could eventually reach the combined costs of both world wars and the Great Depression. In 2003, Swiss Re, the world's biggest reinsurance company, and Harvard Medical School explained why global warming would be so expensive. It's not just the infrastructure, such as sea walls against rising oceans, for example. It's also that the increased costs of natural disasters begin to compound. The diminishing time between monster storms in places such as the U.S. Gulf Coast could eventually mean that parts of "developed countries would experience developing nation conditions for prolonged periods." Quite simply, we've already done too much damage and waited too long to have any easy options left.

"We Can Reverse Climate Change"

If only. Solving this crisis is no longer an option. Human beings have already raised the temperature of the planet about a degree Fahrenheit. When people first began to focus on global warming (which is, remember, only 20 years ago), the general consensus was that at this point we'd just be standing on the threshold of realizing its consequences—that the big changes would be a degree or two and hence several decades down the road. But scientists seem to have systematically underestimated just how delicate the balance of the planet's physical systems really is.

The warming is happening faster than we expected, and the results are more widespread and more disturbing. Even that rise of 1 degree has seriously perturbed hydrological cycles: Because warm air holds more water vapor than cold air does, both droughts and floods are increasing dramatically. Just look at the record levels of insurance payouts, for instance. Mosquitoes, able to survive in new places, are spreading more malaria and dengue. Coral reefs are dying, and so are vast stretches of forest.

None of that is going to stop, even if we do everything right from here on out. Given the time lag between when we emit carbon and when the air heats up, we're already guaranteed at least another degree of warming.

The only question now is whether we're going to hold off catastrophe. It won't be easy, because the scientific consensus calls for roughly 5 degrees more warming this century unless we do just about everything right. And if our behavior up until now is any indication, we won't.

The Other Climate Changers

Jessica Seddon Wallack and Veerabhadran Ramanathan

Why Black Carbon and Ozone Also Matter

At last, world leaders have recognized that climate change is a threat. And to slow or reverse it, they are launching initiatives to reduce greenhouse gases, especially carbon dioxide, the gas responsible for about half of global warming to date. Significantly reducing emissions of carbon dioxide is essential, as they will likely become an even greater cause of global warming by the end of this century. But it is a daunting task: carbon dioxide remains in the atmosphere for centuries, and it is difficult to get governments to agree on reducing emissions because whereas the benefits of doing so are shared globally, the costs are borne by individual countries. As a result, no government is moving fast enough to offset the impact of past and present emissions. Even if current emissions were cut in half by 2050—one of the targets discussed at the 2008 UN Climate Change Conference—by then, humans' total contribution to the level of carbon dioxide in the atmosphere would still have increased by a third since the beginning of this century.

Meanwhile, little attention has been given to a low-risk, cost-effective, and high-reward option: reducing emissions of light-absorbing carbon particles (known as "black carbon") and of the gases that form ozone. Together, these pollutants' warming effect is around 40-70 percent of that of carbon dioxide. Limiting their presence in the atmosphere is an easier, cheaper, and more politically feasible proposition than the most popular proposals for slowing climate change—and it would have a more immediate effect.

Time is running out. Humans have already warmed the planet by more than 0.5 degrees Celsius since the nineteenth century and produced enough greenhouse gases to make it a total of 2.4 degrees Celsius warmer by the end of this century. If the levels of carbon dioxide and nitrous oxide in the atmosphere continue to increase at current rates and if the climate proves more sensitive to greenhouse gases than predicted, the earth's temperature could rise by as much as five degrees before the century ends.

A temperature change of two to five degrees would have profound environmental and geopolitical effects. It would almost—certainly melt all the Arctic summer sea ice. As a result, the Arctic Ocean would absorb more sunlight, which, in turn, would further amplify the warming. Such a rise could eliminate the Himalayan and Tibetan glaciers, which feed the major

water systems of some of the poorest regions of the world. It would also accelerate the melting of the Greenland and Antarctic ice sheets, raising the sea level worldwide and provoking large-scale emigration from low-lying coastal regions. Cycles of droughts and floods triggered by global warming would spell disaster for agriculture-dependent economies.

Some of global warming's environmental effects would be irreversible; some of its societal impacts, unmanageable. Given these consequences, policymakers worldwide seeking to slow climate change must weigh options beyond just reducing carbon dioxide, especially those that would produce rapid results. Cutting black carbon and ozone is one such strategy.

Powerful Pollutants

The warming effect of carbon dioxide has been known since at least the 1900s, and that of ozone since the 1970s, but the importance of black carbon was discovered only recently. During the past decade, scientists have used sophisticated instruments on drones, aircraft, ships, and satellites to track black carbon and ozone from their sources to remote locations thousands of miles away and measure and model how much atmospheric heating they cause. Black carbon, a widespread form of particulate air pollution, is what makes sooty smoke look blackish or brownish. It is a byproduct of incomplete, inefficient combustion—a sign of energy waste as much as energy use. Vehicles and ships fueled by diesel and cars with poorly maintained engines release it. So do forest fires and households and factories that use wood, dung, crop waste, or coal for cooking, heating, or other energy needs.

Black carbon alters the environment in two ways. In the sky, the suspended particles absorb sunlight, warming up the atmosphere and in turn the earth itself. On the earth's surface, deposits of black carbon on snowpacks and ice absorb sunlight, thereby heating the earth and melting glaciers. The Arctic sea ice and the Himalayan and Tibetan glaciers, for example, are melting as much as a result of black carbon as they are as a result of the global warming caused by carbon dioxide. The warming effect of black carbon is equal to about 20–50 percent of the effect of carbon dioxide, making it the second- or third-largest contributor to global warming. No one knows exactly how much warming it causes, but even the most conservative estimates indicate a nontrivial impact. And its large contribution to the melting of glaciers and sea ice, one of the most alarming near-term manifestations of climate change, is well documented.

The ozone in the lower level of the atmosphere is another major contributor to global warming that deserves attention. (This is different from the ozone in the stratosphere, which shields life on earth from the sun's ultraviolet rays.) A potent greenhouse gas, its warming effect is equal to about 20 percent of that of carbon dioxide. Unlike black carbon, which exists as particles, ozone is a gas. Ozone in the atmosphere is not emitted directly but formed from other gases, "ozone precursors," such as carbon monoxide (from the burning of fossil fuels or biomass), nitrogen oxides (from lightning, soil, and the burning of fossil fuels), methane (from agriculture, cattle, gas leaks, and the burning of wood), and other hydrocarbons (from the burning of organic materials and fossil fuels, among other sources).

Most important, black carbon and ozone stay in the atmosphere for a much shorter time than does carbon dioxide. Carbon dioxide remains in the atmosphere for centuries—maybe even millennia—before it is absorbed by oceans, plants, and algae. Even if all carbon dioxide emissions were miraculously halted today, it would take several centuries for the amount of carbon dioxide in the atmosphere to approach its preindustrial-era level. In contrast, black carbon stays in the atmosphere for only days to weeks before it is washed away by rain, and ozone (as well as some of its precursors) only stays for weeks to months before being broken down. Nonetheless, because both are widespread and continuously emitted, their atmospheric concentrations build up and cause serious damage to the environment.

Although reducing the emissions of other greenhouse gases, such as methane and halocarbons, could also produce immediate results, black carbon and ozone are the shortest-lived climate-altering pollutants, and they are relatively under-recognized in efforts to stem climate change. Reducing the emissions of these pollutants on earth would quickly lower their concentrations in the atmosphere and, in turn, reduce their impact on global warming.

An Easier Extra Step

Another promising feature of black carbon and ozone precursor emissions is that they can be significantly limited at relatively low cost with technologies that already exist. Although the sources of black carbon and ozone precursors vary worldwide, most emissions can be reduced without necessarily limiting the underlying activity that generated them. This is because, unlike carbon dioxide, black carbon and ozone precursors are not essential byproducts of energy use.

The use of fossil fuels, particularly diesel, is responsible for about 35 percent of black carbon emissions worldwide. Technologies that filter out black carbon have already been invented: diesel particulate filters on cars and trucks, for example, can reduce black carbon emissions by 90 percent or more with a negligible reduction in fuel economy. A recent study by the Clean Air Task Force, a U.S. nonprofit environmental research organization, estimated that retrofitting one million semitrailer trucks with these filters would yield the same benefits for the climate over 20 years as permanently removing over 165,000 trucks or 5.7 million cars from the road.

The remaining 65 percent of black carbon emissions are associated with the burning of biomass—through naturally occurring forest fires, man-made fires for clearing cropland, and the use of organic fuels for cooking, heating, and small-scale industry. Cleaner options for the man-made activities exist. The greenest options for households are stoves powered by the sun or by gas from organic waste, but updated designs for biomass-fueled stoves can also substantially cut the amount of black carbon and other pollutants emitted. Crop waste, dung, wood, coal, and charcoal are the cheapest, but also the least efficient and dirtiest, fuels, and so households tend to shift away from them as soon as other options become reliably available. Thus, the challenge in lowering black carbon emissions is not convincing people to sacrifice their lifestyles, as it is with convincing people to reduce their carbon dioxide emissions. The challenge is to make other options available.

Man-made ozone precursors are mostly emitted through industrial processes and fossil-fuel use, particularly in the transportation sector. These emissions can be reduced by making the combustion process more efficient (for example, through the use of fuel additives) or by removing these gases after combustion (for example, through the use of catalytic converters). Technologies that both minimize the formation of ozone precursors and filter or break down emissions are already widely used and are reducing ozone precursors in the developed world. The stricter enforcement of laws that forbid adulterating gasoline and diesel with cheaper, but dirtier, substitutes would also help.

Fully applying existing emissions-control technologies could cut black carbon emissions by about 50 percent. And that would be enough to offset the warming effects of one to two decades' worth of carbon dioxide emissions. Reducing the human-caused ozone in the lower atmosphere by about 50 percent, which could be possible through existing technologies, would offset about another decade's worth. Within weeks, the heating effect of black carbon would lessen; within months, so, too, would the greenhouse effect of ozone. Within ten years, the earth's overall warming trend would slow down, as would the retreat of sea ice and glaciers. The scientific argument for reducing emissions of black carbon and ozone precursors is clear.

A Political Possibility

Reducing emissions of black carbon and ozone precursors is also a politically promising project. It would yield significant benefits apart from slowing climate change, giving governments economic and developmental incentives to reduce them. Reducing ozone precursors, for its part, would have recognizable agricultural benefits. Ozone lowers crop yields by damaging plant cells and interfering with the production of chlorophyll, the pigment that enables plants to derive energy from sunlight. One recent study estimated that the associated economic loss (at 2000 world prices) ranged from $14 billion to $26 billion, three to five times as large as that attributed to global warming. For policymakers concerned about agricultural productivity and food security, these effects should resonate deeply.

In countries where a large portion of the population still depends on biomass fuels, reducing black carbon emissions from households would improve public health and economic productivity. Nearly 50 percent of the world's population, and up to 95 percent of the rural population in poor countries, relies on solid fuels, including biomass fuels and coal. The resulting indoor air pollution is linked to about a third of the fatal acute respiratory infections among children under five, or about seven percent of child deaths worldwide. Respiratory illnesses associated with the emissions from solid fuels are the fourth most important cause of excess mortality in developing countries (after malnutrition, unsafe sex, and waterborne diseases).

These health problems perpetuate poverty. Exposure to pollutants early in life harms children's lung development, and children who suffer from respiratory illnesses are less likely to attend school. Air pollution leaves the poor, who often earn a living from manual labor, especially worse off. Collectively, workers in India lose an estimated 1.6–2.0 billion days of work every year to the effects of indoor air pollution. Reducing black carbon emissions from households would thus promote economic growth and, particularly for rural women and children, improve public health.

Furthermore, both black carbon and ozone precursor emissions tend to have localized consequences, and governments are more likely to agree to emissions-reduction strategies that can deliver local benefits. With carbon dioxide and other long-lasting, far-spreading greenhouse gases, emissions anywhere contribute to global warming everywhere. But the effects of black carbon and ozone are more confined. When it first enters the atmosphere, black carbon spreads locally and then, within a week, dissipates more regionally before disappearing from the atmosphere entirely in the form of precipitation. Ozone precursors, too, are more regionally confined than carbon dioxide, although background levels of ozone are increasing around the globe.

Because the effects of black carbon and ozone are mostly regional, the benefits from reducing them would accrue in large part to the areas where reductions were achieved. The melting of the Himalayan and Tibetan glaciers is almost reason enough for countries in South and East Asia to take rapid action to eliminate black carbon emissions. So is the retreat of the Arctic sea ice for countries bordering the Arctic Ocean. Regional groupings are also more likely than larger collections of countries to have dense networks of the economic, cultural, and diplomatic ties that sustain difficult negotiations. Moreover, both black carbon and ozone can be contained through geographically targeted strategies because many of the sources of black carbon and ozone are largely fixed. And so even if one country in a region seeks to regulate emissions, that country's polluting activities are unlikely to move to another country with less stringent policies—a common concern with agreements to reduce carbon dioxide emissions.

Cleaning Up

So what can be done to curb black carbon and ozone precursor emissions? A logical first step is for governments, international development agencies, and philanthropists to increase financial support for reduction efforts. Although some money for this is currently available, neither pollutant has emerged as a mainstream target for public or private funding. Simply recognizing black carbon and ozone as environmental problems on par with carbon dioxide would make policymakers more inclined to spend development funds and the "green" portions of stimulus packages on initiatives to tackle them. Developed countries could put their contributions toward customizing emissions-reduction technologies for the developing world and promoting their deployment—an important gesture of goodwill that would kick-start change.

Regardless of the source of the funding, aid should support the deployment of clean-energy options for households and small industries in the developing world and of emissions-reduction technologies for transportation around the world. This could mean distributing solar lanterns and stoves that use local fuel sources more efficiently or paying for small enterprises to shift to cleaner technologies. The specific fixes for small-scale industry will vary by economic activity—making brick kilns cleaner is different from making tea and spice driers more efficient—but the number of possible customers for the new technologies offers some economies of scale. When it comes to transportation, policy options include subsidizing engine and filter upgrades, shifting to cleaner fuels, and removing the incentives, created by government subsidies that favor some fuels over others, for adulterating fuel and for using diesel.

Deploying technologies to reduce emissions from so many culturally embedded activities, from cooking to driving, will not be easy. Enforcing emissions controls on many small, mobile polluters is harder than regulating larger sources, such as power plants. And in customizing technologies, close attention will need to be paid to the varied needs of households and industry. But creating and enforcing regulations and subsidizing and disseminating energy-efficient technologies are challenges that have been met before. The "green revolution"—the remarkable growth in agricultural productivity that occurred in the second half of the twentieth century—introduced radical changes to small-scale farming. Other development initiatives have influenced fertility, gender equality, schooling, and other household decisions more sensitive than those about cooking and driving.

Moreover, the infrastructure for international financial and technological transfers already exists in the form of the World Bank, regional development banks, and UN programs that have supported development around the world for decades. The Global Environment Facility, a development and environmental fund that started as a World Bank program and is now the world's largest funder of environmental projects, is well suited to finance cleaner technologies.

Governments and international agencies should also finance technology that tracks air quality, which is generally undermonitored. In the major cities of most developing countries, the number of sensors has not kept up with the growth in population or economic activity. In rural areas, air pollution is not tracked at all. Improving the monitoring of air quality and disseminating the data would inform policymakers and environmental activists. And tracking individuals' emissions—through indoor air-pollution monitors or devices attached to cars' tailpipes—could help motivate people to curb their emissions. Experimental initiatives to measure individuals' carbon footprints and energy use have been shown to change people's behavior in some settings.

Aid alone will not be enough, however. International organizations must also help governments identify and act on opportunities that mitigate climate change and promote development. International development institutions, such as the UN Environment Program and the multilateral and regional development banks, could sponsor research, set up interministerial working groups, and establish standards for monitoring and reporting public expenditures. These initiatives would make it easier to identify possible areas of coordination among public health, agricultural, environmental, and anti-poverty programs. In most countries, domestic institutions are not designed to encourage cooperation among different authorities. Pitching the reduction of black carbon and ozone precursor emissions as public health and agricultural policies could help such efforts compete for scarce funds; enabling the clearer calculation of the environmental benefits of development policies would make policy-making more informed. Much in the same way that international development organizations currently support good governance to improve infrastructure and services, they should also promote better environmental governance.

Responding Regionally

The current piecemeal approach to climate science—in particular, the tendency to treat air pollution and climate change as separate issues—has at times led to bad policy. The decision of many countries to promote diesel as a means to encourage fuel efficiency, for example, may have had the inadvertent effect of increasing black carbon emissions. And air-pollution laws designed to reduce the use of sulfate aerosols, which cause acid rain, have ironically led to more warming because sulfates also have a cooling effect. Had policymakers instead integrated efforts to reduce air pollution with those to slow global warming, they could have ensured that the reduction of sulfates was accompanied by an equivalent reduction in greenhouse gases.

A single global framework would be the ideal way to integrate various strategies for mitigating climate change. Bilateral or multilateral agreements are more feasible for getting started on reducing black carbon and ozone precursor emissions. These can strengthen governments' incentives to act by discouraging free-riding and by motivating governments to take into account the larger-scale impacts of their own emissions. Because the sources of black carbon and ozone vary from region to region, agreements to reduce them need to be tailored to suit regional conditions. In the Northern Hemisphere, for example, ozone precursors mostly come from industrial processes and transportation, whereas in the Southern Hemisphere, especially tropical regions, they mostly come from natural emissions (soils, plants, and forest fires). The sources of black carbon vary by region, too: in Europe and North America, transportation and industrial activity play a larger role than the burning of biomass, whereas the reverse is true in developing regions.

The impact of emissions on the climate is scientifically complex, and it depends on a number of factors that have not yet been adequately taken into account when devising climate models. The challenge, then, is to quickly create agreements that consider the complex links between human activities, emissions, and climate change and that can adjust over time as the scientific understanding of the problem evolves. Regional air-pollution agreements are easier to update than global agreements with many signatories. The UN Convention on Long-Range Transboundary Air Pollution (most of whose signatories are European or Central Asian states) and its subsequent pollutant-specific protocols provide a ready model for regional agreements on short-lived climate-changing pollutants. The specific provisions of these agreements are based on the costs of reductions, scientists' knowledge of the sources and distribution of air pollution, and the ability to measure reductions—considerations that should also inform the regulation of black carbon and ozone precursor emissions. Moreover, these agreements commit countries to particular actions, not just specific outcomes. This is wise, given that emissions are difficult to monitor and quantify precisely.

Black carbon and ozone can also be built into existing bilateral discussions. The High-Level India-EU Dialogue, a working group of scientists and policymakers from Europe and India, is one such existing forum. In February 2009, it was already urging governments from Europe and India to work together to recognize and reduce the threat from black carbon. Participants proposed an interdisciplinary research project that would determine the effects of biomass-based cooking and heating on health and the climate and assess the obstacles to a large-scale deployment of cleaner stoves. Black carbon and ozone are also natural candidates for U.S.-Chinese cooperation on energy and climate change: China would reap public health and agricultural benefits from reducing emissions, and the United States would earn goodwill for helping China do so.

By building on existing air-pollution agreements, the risk of distracting climate-change negotiations from the substantial task of promoting the reduction of carbon dioxide emissions could be avoided. Putting black carbon and ozone on the table in high-level climate talks could backfire if developing nations thought that they would be tacitly admitting responsibility for global warming by committing to reducing emissions of black carbon and ozone precursors or believed that the issue was an effort by developed countries to divert attention from the need for them to reduce their carbon dioxide emissions. Therefore, efforts to reduce emissions of black carbon and ozone precursors should be presented not as substitutes for commitments to reducing carbon dioxide emissions but as ways to quickly achieve local environmental and economic benefits.

The Low-Hanging Fruit

Historically, initiatives to slow global warming have focused on reducing the emissions of carbon dioxide and other greenhouse gases and largely ignored the role played by air pollution. This strategy makes sense for the long run, since carbon dioxide emissions are, and will continue to be, the most important factor in climate change. But in the short run, it alone will not be enough. Some scientists have proposed geoengineering—manipulating the climate through the use of technology—as a potential option of last resort, but the reduction of black carbon and ozone precursor emissions offers a less risky opportunity for achieving the same end.

Such an approach would quickly lower the level of black carbon and ozone in the atmosphere, offsetting the impact of decades of greenhouse gas emissions, decelerating the rush toward a dangerously warm planet, and giving efforts to reduce carbon dioxide emissions time to get off the ground. These pollutants are also tractable policy targets: they can be reduced through the use of existing technologies, institutions, and strategies, and doing so would lead to local improvements in air quality, agricultural output, and public health. In short, reducing black carbon and ozone precursor emissions is a low-risk, high-potential addition to the current arsenal of strategies to mitigate climate change.

At the current rate of global warming, the earth's temperature stands to careen out of control. Now is the time to look carefully at all the possible brakes that can be applied to slow climate change, hedge against near-term climate disasters, and buy time for technological innovations. Of the available strategies, focusing on reducing emissions of black carbon and ozone precursors is the low-hanging fruit: the costs are relatively low, the implementation is feasible, and the benefits would be numerous and immediate.

JESSICA SEDDON WALLACK is Director of the Center for Development Finance at the Institute for Financial Management and Research, in Chennai, India. **VEERABHADRAN RAMANATHAN** is Distinguished Professor of Climate and Atmospheric Sciences at the Scripps Institute of Oceanography at the University of California, San Diego; Distinguished Visiting Fellow at the Energy and Resources Institute, in New Delhi; and a recipient of the 2009 Tyler Prize for Environmental Achievement.

Water of Life in Peril

Sharon Palmer, RD

Water, water, everywhere, nor any drop to drink.
— from *The Rime of the Ancient Mariner*
by Samuel Taylor Coleridge

It's a thirsty planet. For its 6.6 billion inhabitants—a number that continues to swell—the faucet is beginning to run dry. As the world's population tripled in the 20th century, the demand for water resources multiplied sixfold. And as our population continues to grow, becoming more urbanized and industrialized, so does its greed for water.

But the supply is dwindling due to pollution and contamination. Billions of people lack basic water services, and millions die each year from water-related diseases. In 1999, the United Nations Environment Programme (UNEP) reported that 200 scientists in 50 countries had identified water shortage as one of the two most troublesome problems for the new millennium, the other being global warming.

Even though water covers roughly two thirds of the Earth's surface, most of it is not suitable for human use. Only 0.08% of the world's total water supply is available for consumption because a mere 2.5% of it is not salty, and two thirds of that amount is tucked away in icecaps and glaciers. Of the remaining supply, much is in remote areas and comes in monsoons and floods, which is difficult to capture. To make matters worse, pollution is making more of the Earth's available water unfit for use. Just look to Central Asia's Aral Sea environmental crisis as an illustration of how pollution can poison water runoff to rivers and soil.

"Pollution of water due to industrial urbanization performed in an unplanned way, making clean freshwater less accessible, is the most pressing water global issue right now," reported Shaikh Halim, executive director of the Village Education Resource Center in Bangladesh, at this year's World Water Week.

When there's not enough water coming from rainwater and surface water, governments turn to subterranean supplies of groundwater. In turn, rivers, wetlands, and lakes that depend on groundwater can dry out and be replaced with saline seawater. According to the UNEP, water tables are falling by roughly 3 meters per year across much of the developing world. Some of the world's biggest cities, such as Bangkok, Cairo, Kolkata, London, Mexico City, and Jakarta, are dependent on groundwater. While the impact of using up rivers and lakes is obvious, the overuse of groundwater is virtually invisible to the public.

Adding to the problem is the fact that people in some parts of the world literally fight over water. More than 260 river basins are shared by two or more countries, and without strong agreements, transboundary tensions arise over water use. For example, the dispute over water resources has been a feature of the Arab-Israeli conflict since its beginning. Experts call for more international attention to develop groundwater agreements among the nations of such regions.

And lastly, it's not just humans who suffer from a water shortage. The reduction of available water can have repercussions on aquatic ecosystems and countless species that are dependent on them.

Draining the Water Supply

According to the World Water Vision Report published in 2000 by the World Water Council, "There is a water crisis today. But the crisis is not about having too little water to satisfy our needs. It is a crisis of managing water so badly that billions of people—and the environment—suffer badly."

You may think that the sheer volume of humans drinking, cooking, and washing with water is what's putting a drain on the supply, but this utilization of water is just a drop in the bucket compared with how water is used in other endeavors. The biggest abuser of water by far is irrigation, which wastes an enormous amount in inefficiency and evaporation. An estimated 60% of the total water pumped for irrigation is wasted before it even reaches the crop. Water withdrawals for irrigation comprise 66% of the total withdrawals, with up to 90% in arid areas. In Asia, it makes up 86% of total annual water used compared with 49% in North and Central America and 38% in Europe.

Agriculture is a thirsty business. It takes approximately 1,000 liters of water to produce 1 kilogram (kg) of wheat; 1,400 liters to produce 1 kg of rice; and 13,000 liters to produce 1 kg of beef. By 2020, a projected 17% more water will be needed to feed the world than is currently available. Even "eco-friendly" biofuel is a water-gulping industry. Last year in Nebraska, the nation's third-leading ethanol producer, it took 2 billion gallons of water at 15 ethanol plants to create 676 million gallons of the alternative fuel.

"Rivers and lakes are virtually emptied for part of the year as a result of heavy withdrawals for irrigation. Groundwater tables are significantly lowered as a result of this development. While we drink a few liters of water per day, we literally eat one or a few tons of water each day. Water provision to agriculture for food, biofuels, and commercial products are therefore a water problem at another order of magnitude," says Professor Jan Lundqvist, a food and nutrition expert at Stockholm International Water Institute. Domestic households, industry, and evaporation from reservoirs contribute to the water supply drain in a smaller way.

Americans rank highest among the world's water consumers. According to the Pacific Institute for Studies in Development, Environment, and Security in Oakland, Calif., America is sixth in the world behind New Zealand, Armenia, Barbados, Cuba, and the United Arab Emirates for per capita water withdrawals. Europeans use significantly less water per person for domestic purposes than Americans due to more efficient systems like low-flush toilets, as well as abundant rainfall throughout the year, which reduces the need to water gardens in the summer.

The World Water Council reports that part of the problem with valuing water as a resource is that it is underpriced. Subsidies for agricultural use are common in developed and developing countries, but by removing such subsidies and allowing water prices to rise, pushes for conservation and more efficient technology can flourish.

Deep Impact of Climate Change

It is widely accepted that climate change will have a major impact on water resources. At World Water Week, distinguished speakers from around the world discussed the link between water and climate, human societies, and ecosystems, emphasizing an immediate need for adaptation measures. The United Nations Development Programme's Human Development Report 2007 (http://hdr.undp .org) points out that massive human development costs will result from climate change unless we dramatically reduce carbon emissions within the next decade. A shift in attitudes among governments to take climate and water issues more seriously with commitments to decrease carbon emissions is critical.

"Climate risks are wavering heavily on the lives of the poor, and those living in poverty are not able to withstand the shocks," said Claes Johansson, a report coauthor, at World Water Week.

Future predictions for global climate change recently released by the UN Intergovernmental Panel on Climate Change are estimating that between 250 million and 980 million people, mostly in Africa, could find themselves without fresh water by 2050.

Water for the World's Poor

Perhaps it's difficult to grasp the meaning of a water crisis when a simple twist of the faucet handle unleashes an endless gush of clean, safe water. But this isn't the case in many of the poorest countries in the world. Nearly one third of the world's population lives in countries that are stressed for water. In Asia, per capita availability declined by 40% to 60% between 1955 and 1990, with projections that most Asian countries will have severe water problems by the year 2025. Most of Africa has always been short of water.

The daily per capita use of water in residential areas is 350 liters in North America and Japan, 200 liters in Europe, and 10 to 20 liters in sub-Saharan Africa. The UN developed the Millennium Development Goals targeted at reducing poverty and ensuring sustainable development, with goal No. 7, target 10 reading, "Halve, by 2015, the proportion of people without sustainable access to safe water and basic sanitation."

Malawi's story is a vivid example of the chain of water insecurity. Stacia Nordin, RD, and her husband, who is a social worker, began HIV/AIDS prevention work through the U.S. Peace Corps in Malawi, Africa, in 1997. Noticing that food and water security were critical in the region, they began working to promote permaculture, a philosophy that observes how nature replenishes its soil, conserves its water resources, and adapts to an area's specific

Global Water Resources

Tap into these resources to learn more about the global water crisis.

Co-operative Programme on Water and Climate:
www.waterandclimate.org

National Wildlife Federation:
www.nwf.org

Stockholm International Water Institute:
www.siwi.org

The UN Millennium Development Goals:
www.un.org/millenniumgoals

United Nations Environment Programme:
www.unep.org

World Business Council for Sustainable Development:
www.wbcsd.ch

World Water Council:
www.worldwatercouncil.org

World Water Week:
www.worldwaterweek.org

climate. "Water is a more serious problem than food security in some cases. Unclean water is often the root cause of illness for children suffering from malnutrition. For health, sanitation, and agricultural reasons, water is going to be a crisis if not addressed in an integrated manner," says Nordin.

The problems in the Malawi water supply stem from people treating the Earth carelessly by failing to manage the water, the Nordins say. In a healthy system, rainwater should be filtered through the earth's layers, but when people destroy the earth, the rain runs across the surface, collecting manures, bacteria, and harmful chemicals with it, depositing it directly into rivers, wells, and lakes. This causes water to become infected and able to transmit a variety of diseases such as typhoid, cholera, and other diarrheal diseases, as well as causing the water sources to diminish.

In Malawi, rainwater is not captured from rooftops; it is pushed into man-made water drains without being used. Water in rivers and lakes is abused by using synthetic chemicals that cause eutrophication, an explosive growth of plant matter in water that suffocates the animal life; overfishing, which removes the balance in the water source, causing areas of stagnation; and erosion, which deposits top soil and organic and nonorganic materials into water sources. The rivers and lakes must be dredged to remove the materials so the hydroelectric power plant can work properly. Flooding wipes out infrastructure such as homes, roads, and bridges and takes the lives of humans and other animals.

Right to Water, Right to Life

The moral and ethical right to water and sanitation has been planted in cultural and religious traditions around the world. The UN proclaimed that the right to water is "indispensable for leading a life in human dignity" and "a prerequisite for the realization of other human rights."

With access to safe water, child mortality between the ages of 0 to 4 could be reduced, far more children could go to school between the ages of 5 and 14, more productivity could occur among people aged 15 and 59, and people could expect to live longer after the age of 60.

The American Dietetic Association's position on the issue is as follows: "The public has the right to a safe food and water supply. The association supports collaboration among dietetics professionals, academics, representatives of the agricultural and food industries, and appropriate government agencies to ensure the safety of the food and water supply by providing education to the public and industry, promoting technologic innovation and applications and supporting further research."

Safe Water and Sanitation for the Masses

It's not just a matter of sufficient water; it's a matter of safe water for many countries in the world. Safe drinking water and sanitation is critical to preserve human health, especially in children. Water-related diseases are the most common cause of illness and death in developing countries. According to the World Health Organization, 1.6 million children die each year because of unsafe water, poor sanitation, and a lack of hygiene. But the efforts to combat preventable diseases, create better hygiene conditions, and provide more access to safe water continue to face challenges. For instance, the use of fresh water supplies can be extended by reusing water for agriculture, but there are risks that the soil and products from the field may be contaminated.

With the upcoming International Year of Sanitation in 2008, global attention will focus on the need for improved health and hygiene. Helmut Lehn, PhD, of the Institute for Technology Assessment and Systems Analysis in Germany, said at World Water Week that the most pressing water global issue now is "sustainable sanitation for all. We need to ensure better governance and make advanced technology options available to more people."

The UN Millennium Project Task Force on Water and Sanitation identified key recommendations to end the global water and sanitation crisis (http://mirror.undp.org/unmillenniumproject/facts/tf7_e.htm), which emphasize that governments must commit to moving the sanitation crisis to the top of their agendas with an increase in investments for sustainable water and sanitation.

A Watery Solution

How do we tackle the vast problem of preserving our precious water resources? The UN calls for governments to take immediate action to reverse the decline of water resources. Across the globe, more can be done for water conservation through better planning, management, and technology. "We have to be smart. We have to use conservation . . . recycling, reduction of demand, and land management. If we do that, we should be alright for the next 50 years," said Peter Rogers, PhD, of Harvard University at World Water Week.

Some countries are putting these challenges into action. Singapore has been placed on a pedestal for being a model of water efficiency. PUB Singapore, the creator of NEWater, was awarded the 2007 Stockholm Industry Award for transforming the urban nation into a vision of sustainable water management practice by focusing on sound policy, technology investment, close partnerships with business and community, and cost-effective policy implementation. PUB provided 100% of Singapore's water using four national taps: imported, desalinized, rain-captured, and recycled water.

Changes in the public's behavior are also key to preserving water. The World Water Institute encourages people to consider lifestyle choices in water consumption, such as food selections. After all, it takes 130 times more water to produce a kilogram of beef than it does to produce a kilogram of potatoes.

"Given the fact that water for our daily bread is the most significant part of society's water budget, it is important to look at our food habits," says Lundqvist, who notes that a recent study for the Swedish Environmental Advisory Council included information on how much water was used to produce food (www.sou.gov.se/mvb/pdf/WEBB-%20PDF.pdf), illustrating the "water footprint" in the food supply.

Lundqvist also points out that wastage and losses in the food chain are substantial, from the field where food is produced to actual food intake. All the food that is lost and wasted consumed water in connection with its production. "It is very important that individuals acquire a better knowledge of these connections. In urban centers, where people are far away from where food is produced and where the main water challenges are, this is a huge educational issue," says Lundqvist.

In the end, human ingenuity may be our greatest asset when it comes to plugging the leak. Better irrigation systems that drip water directly onto plants, as well as a shift to less water-intensive crops, can make a difference. Improved capture and storage of flood runoff can increase water supply. Though desalination is energy intensive and produces large quantities of waste products, it may pose answers in the future. Uganda's Water Minister Maria Mutagamba emphasizes the benefits of rainwater harvesting through local, low-cost rainwater harvesting tanks. More investments need to occur in water technology projects to stimulate innovative thinking. Getting beyond the basic levels of corporate social responsibility is one of the main goals of the World Council for Sustainable Development. For instance, water supplies destined for mining operations may be tapped along the way to give communities water.

Nordin suggests that food and nutrition professionals educate themselves on solutions to the water challenge, adding, "They should support programs that work toward sustainable water management and implement personal practices that save water."

Björn Guterstam of Global Water Partnership in Sweden said at World Water Week, "Change is necessary for individual survival and global survival. If we do not change our lifestyle, nothing will happen. We have to internalize it, especially in the Western world."

SHARON PALMER, RD, is a contributing editor at *Today's Dietitian* and a freelance food and nutrition writer in southern California.

Troubled Waters

The sea is suffering, mostly at the hand of man, says John Grimond.

All of us have in our veins the exact same percentage of salt in our blood that exists in the ocean . . .
And when we go back to the sea . . . we are going back from whence we came.

THE ECONOMIST

Human beings no longer thrive under the water from which their ancestors emerged, but their relationship with the sea remains close. Over half the world's people live within 100 kilometres (62 miles) of the coast; a tenth are within 10km. On land at least, the sea delights the senses and excites the imagination. The sight and smell of the sea inspire courage and adventure, fear and romance. Though the waves may be rippling or mountainous, the waters angry or calm, the ocean itself is eternal. Its moods pass. Its tides keep to a rhythm. It is unchanging.

Or so it has long seemed. Appearances deceive, though. Large parts of the sea may indeed remain unchanged, but in others, especially in the surface and coastal waters where 90% of marine life is to be found, the impact of man's activities is increasingly plain. This should hardly be a surprise. Man has changed the landscape and the atmosphere. It would be odd if the seas, which he has for centuries used for food, for transport, for dumping rubbish and, more recently, for recreation, had not also been affected.

The evidence abounds. The fish that once seemed an inexhaustible source of food are now almost everywhere in decline: 90% of large predatory fish (the big ones such as tuna, swordfish and sharks) have gone, according to some scientists. In estuaries and coastal waters, 85% of the large whales have disappeared, and nearly 60% of the small ones. Many of the smaller fish are also in decline. Indeed, most familiar sea creatures, from albatrosses to walruses, from seals to oysters, have suffered huge losses.

All this has happened fairly recently. Cod have been caught off Nova Scotia for centuries, but their systematic slaughter began only after 1852; in terms of their biomass (the aggregate mass of the species), they are now 96% depleted. The killing of turtles in the Caribbean (99% down) started in the 1700s. The hunting of sharks in the Gulf of Mexico (45–99%, depending on the variety) got going only in the 1950s.

The habitats of many of these creatures have also been affected by man's activities. Cod live in the bottom layer of the ocean. Trawlermen in pursuit of these and other groundfish like pollock and haddock drag steel weights and rollers as well as nets behind their boats, devastating huge areas of the sea floor as they go. In the Gulf of Mexico, trawlers ply back and forth year in year out, hauling vast nets that scarify the seabed and allow no time for plant and animal life to recover. Off New England, off west Africa, in the Sea of Okhotsk north of Japan, off Sri Lanka, wherever fish can still be found, it is much the same story.

Coral reefs, whose profusion of life and diversity of ecosystems make them the rainforests of the sea, have suffered most of all. Once home to prolific concentrations of big fish, they have attracted human hunters prepared to use any means, even dynamite, to kill their prey. Perhaps only 5% of coral reefs can now be considered pristine, a quarter have been lost and all are vulnerable to global warming.

A hotter atmosphere has several effects on the sea. First, it means higher average temperatures for surface waters. One consequence for coral reefs is that the symbiosis between the corals and algae that constitute a living reef is breaking down. As temperatures rise, the algae leave or are expelled, the corals take on a bleached, white appearance and may then die.

Hotter Water, Slimier Slime

Warming also has consequences for ice: it melts. Melting sea ice affects ecosystems and currents. It does not affect sea levels, because floating ice is already displacing water of a weight equal to its own. But melting glaciers and ice sheets on land are bringing quantities of fresh water into the sea, whose level has been rising at an average of nearly 2 millimetres a year for over 40 years, and the pace is getting faster. Recent studies suggest that the sea level may well rise by a total of 80 centimetres this century, though the figure could plausibly be as much as 2 metres.

The burning over the past 100 years or so of fossil fuels that took half a billion years to form has suddenly, in geological terms, put an enormous amount of carbon dioxide into the atmosphere. About a third of this CO_2 is taken up by the sea, where it forms carbonic acid. The plants and animals that have evolved over time to thrive in slightly alkaline surface waters—their pH is around 8.3—are now having to adapt to a 30% increase in the acidity of their surroundings. Some will no doubt flourish, but if the trend continues, as it will for at least some decades, clams, mussels, conches and all creatures that grow shells made of calcium carbonate will struggle. So will corals, especially those whose skeletons are composed of aragonite, a particularly unstable form of calcium carbonate.

Man's interference does not stop with CO_2. Knowingly and deliberately, he throws plenty of rubbish into the sea, everything from sewage to rubber tyres and from plastic packaging to toxic waste. Inadvertently, he also lets flame retardants, bunker oil, and heavy metals seep into the mighty ocean, and often invasive species too. Much of the harm done by such pollutants is invisible to the eye: it shows up only in the analysis of dead polar bears or in tuna served in New York sushi bars.

Increasingly, though, swimmers, sailors, and even those who monitor the sea with the help of satellites are encountering highly visible algal blooms known as red tides. These have always occurred naturally, but they have increased in frequency, number and size in recent years, notably since man-made nitrogen fertilisers came into widespread use in the 1950s. When rainwater contaminated with these fertilisers and other nutrients reaches the sea, as it does where the Mississippi runs into the Gulf of Mexico, an explosion of toxic algae and bacteria takes place, killing fish, absorbing almost all the oxygen, and leaving a microbially dominated ecosystem, often based on a carpet of slime.

Each of these phenomena would be bad enough on its own, but all appear to be linked, usually synergistically. Slaughter one species in the food web and you set off a chain of alterations above or below. Thus the near extinction of sea otters in the northern Pacific led to a proliferation of sea urchins, which then laid waste an entire kelp forest that had hitherto sustained its own ecosystem. If acidification kills tiny sea snails known as pteropods, as it is likely to, the Pacific salmon that feed upon these planktonic creatures may also die. Then other fish may move in, preventing the salmon from coming back, just as other species did when cod were all but fished out in Georges Bank, off New England.

Whereas misfortunes that came singly might not prove fatal, those that come in combination often prove overwhelming. The few coral reefs that remain pristine seem able to cope with the warming and acidification that none can escape, but most of the reefs that have also suffered overfishing or pollution have succumbed to bleaching or even death. Biodiversity comes with interdependence, and the shocks administered by mankind in recent decades have been so numerous and so severe that the natural balance of marine life is everywhere disturbed.

Are these changes reversible? Most scientists believe that fisheries, for instance, could be restored to health with the right policies, properly enforced. But many of the changes are speeding up, not slowing down. Some, such as the acidification of the seas, will continue for years to come simply because of events already in train or past. And some, such as the melting of the Arctic ice cap, may be close to the point at which an abrupt, and perhaps irreversible, series of happenings is set in motion.

It is clear, in any event, that man must change his ways. Humans could afford to treat the sea as an infinite resource when they were relatively few in number, capable of only rather inefficient exploitation of the vasty deep and without as yet a taste for fossil fuels. A world of 6.7 billion souls, set to become 9 billion by 2050, can no longer do so. The possibility of widespread catastrophe is simply too great.

Acacia Avenue

How to Save Indonesia's Dwindling Rainforests

As a spectacle, the four-hour drive to Teluk Binjai from Pekanbaru, capital of Riau province on the island of Sumatra, tends to the monochrome. Mile after mile of palm-oil plantation alternates with mile after mile of regimented lines of acacia trees, grown for pulpwood. Only an occasional banana grove or superannuated rubber plantation offers a spot of variety. Mountainously laden timber lorries ply the interprovincial highway, their loads of acacia logs almost brushing as they pass. In one direction is the mill of Indah Kiat Pulp and Paper, a subsidiary of APP, part of the Sinar Mas group; in the other that of APRIL, Sumatra's other big pulp-and-paper producer.

Off the main road, small patches of "natural" forest survive alongside the swathe of broad sandy corridor cut by a logging company. Some has been cleared fairly recently. Shrouded in white smoke, the peat soil still smoulders under the blackened tree-stumps. Gaunt and barkless, some trees still stand, like skeletal ghosts stalking a battlefield. Underneath, already oil palms are pushing up, planted by local farmers to feed Indonesia's latest commodity boom.

In Teluk Binjai, a village of 400 families sprawling along the bank of the Kampar river, and its neighbour, Teluk Meranti, farmers feel squeezed. Living inside a logging concession, their access to the forest behind their farms is already curtailed. They want to be granted rights to 5,000 hectares of forest on the other side of the river, in the Kampar peninsula. This area of 700,000 hectares of peat forest, home to tigers, sunbears, hawk-eagles, and other endangered species, is now being fought over by plantation companies, forest residents, and local and international NGOs.

The stretch the villagers have their eye on is also part of a concession. They admit they have no legal right to the land, but they say the concession to convert it to acacia is illegal, since the area is supposedly protected. And the villagers claim customary rights. Their families have used the forest for generations. They still depend on it for rattan, fuel, honeybees, hunting, and wood to build their houses and boats. But they use the resource responsibly, claims Muhammad Yusuf, a local farmers' leader: "We only take the best trees." And no more than they need.

Illegally, some farmers are already staking out claims across the river in the sought-after stretch of forest. One, in his second year there, says the village chief in Meranti granted him a six-hectare claim after his coconut grove in Teluk Binjai was destroyed in a land-clearing fire. He is planting oil palms. Speaking in a tiny hut, against the whine of a chainsaw from the nearby rainforest, he says he is too poor to send his 12- and 14-year-old sons to school. They are working in his fields, helping convert another small patch of peatland, and adding to Indonesia's alarming emissions of carbon dioxide.

Stop It, for Peat's Sake

Indonesia's logging of its rainforests has long been identified as a big contributor to the world's emissions of greenhouse gases (GHGs), and hence to global warming. This is one reason for the shocking statistic that Indonesia trails only China and America as an emitter of carbon. But now attention is also turning to the soil beneath the trees, and especially to peat. Al Gore, a former American vice-president and a vigorous climate-change campaigner, has pointed to evidence that the top two metres of soil contain three times as much carbon as the entire vegetation on the planet, and that soil degradation, such as the burning of peatland, is the main cause of Indonesia's high level of emissions.

According to Greenpeace, an environmental NGO, Riau's peatlands have the highest concentration of carbon stored per hectare anywhere in the world. As elsewhere in Indonesia, peat in Riau is disappearing. The trees growing on it are harvested and the land is either abandoned or converted to a plantation. Every year 1.8 billion tonnes of GHG emissions are released by the degradation and burning of Indonesia's peatlands. By the calculation of WWF, an NGO, between 1990 and 2007 Riau alone produced more CO_2 per year than Germany is saving to meet its commitments under the Kyoto protocol.

Small-scale settlers like those clearing the bit of forest opposite Teluk Binjai are a tiny part of the problem. Far more significant, in Riau ("the deforestation centre of Indonesia," according to Yumiko Uryo of WWF) and across Indonesia, are large-scale commercial operations: illegal logging and the conversion of forest land by big plantation companies. By WWF's estimate, of the forest cover in Riau lost in the past 25 years, 29% was cleared for palm-oil plantations and 24% for pulpwood by the big producers themselves—not counting large areas cleared by their suppliers.

The extent of illegal logging, like every other statistic on Indonesia's forests, is disputed. By one reckoning, 73% of the $1.6 billion-worth of forest products (not including raw logs, whose export is banned) the EU imported from Indonesia last year came from illegally felled timber. But that is a guess, derived by deducting the timber that can be shown to be legal, a process complicated by the often murky ownership of the original forest lands. The Indonesian government reckons that no more than 10% of exports are illegal. It is working with the EU to devise a licensing system for timber exporters which would then be applied globally. Indonesia also faces difficulties in America. Congress, inspired by an unlikely coalition of domestic timber producers and NGOs, last year amended the Lacey act, a law dating from 1900 that bans the illegal commercial transportation of wildlife. It now covers the produce of illegal logging as well.

Protection of the forest against illegal loggers and enforcement of the law are said to have improved since 1997, when forest fires in Sumatra and Kalimantan (Indonesian Borneo) smothered much of South-East Asia in a noxious, choking haze. The fires were spread by a prolonged drought brought by an El Niño weather pattern. Many were lit to clear land illegally logged. And even now the legal arrival of a logging company in an area is often accompanied by criminals chopping away at the edge of the concession. Decentralisation has complicated efforts to enforce the law. Local authorities resent efforts by the central government to assert control.

Hotspots of Bother

Indonesia's government denies it is doing as much to cook the planet as its critics allege. Agus Purnomo, a former director of WWF in Indonesia who now heads the secretariat of the National Council on Climate Change, says that the country's third place in the carbon-emissions tables is a hangover from the disastrous El Niño of the late 1990s. With no serious forest fire for four years, he claims Indonesia has slid down to number 15 or 20. He reckons that the "hotspots" (small-scale forest fires) recorded this year—3,764 in Riau alone by July, according to a count by satellite—are "not a big issue." Hotspots are now designated as crime scenes, he says, so that no one is allowed to plant oil palms there. If caught, those who caused them are prosecuted and sometimes jailed.

He points out that it is in Indonesia's own interests to do its bit to reduce GHG-emissions and hence global warming. A study this year by the Economy and Environment Programme for South-East Asia, based in Singapore, mapped vulnerability to climate change across the region, divided into 530 subnational districts. Of the ten most endangered by climate change, seven were on Indonesia's most populous island, Java, which would become increasingly prone to droughts, floods, landslides and a rise in the sea level.

Even more immediately, Riau, for example, is suffering a localised haze at the moment. It is not quite the eye-stinging, throat-burning, aviation-disrupting peasouper seen in 1997, but still the town of Dumai recorded a surge in acute respiratory illnesses in June and July.

Blucher Doloksaribu, who heads the provincial government's Geophysical, Climatology and Meteorology Board, reckons

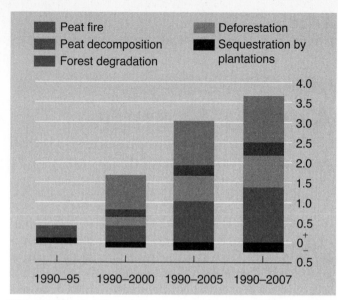

Watch It Grow Cumulative carbon-dioxide emissions in Riau provice; gigatonnes
Source: WWF

Riau is already suffering its own local, accelerated version of global warming. As forest cover has shrunk from 78% in 1982 to 27% today, minimum temperatures in Riau have increased, he estimates, by an average of 2°C.

After a de facto two-year moratorium for an investigation into alleged corruption, logging has resumed in earnest in Riau this year. Green activists link this to the elections and the need for parties to raise funds.

The big pulp-and-paper and palm-oil companies have several lines of defence against attacks from greens. Responding to growing concern about the impact of palm-oil plantations, the big producers and consumers have joined a round-table on sustainable production. The firms insist that they do follow the law, logging only the "production" forests for which they have bought concessions. But their critics allege that they also buy from less scrupulous subcontractors, and that this year the pressure is especially intense since the moratorium had forced pulp companies to eat into their plantation forests earlier than they would normally have done.

The firms also defend their own practices as responsible and sustainable. Sinar Mas, for example, has set aside some 72,000 hectares (an area bigger than Singapore) of "production forest" as a protected "biosphere," where the trees and wildlife will be preserved. Some even argue that palm-oil and acacia plantations can actually help reduce GHG emissions, though scientists scoff at this notion when the plantations are on cleared natural forest and, especially, peatland.

But Gandhi Sulistyanto, Sinar Mas's managing director, also points to the huge economic benefits his business brings Indonesia, directly and indirectly supporting millions of people and producing more than one-tenth of Indonesia's exports. More than half of Sinar Mas's exports go to China and India. So, despite boasting of his firm's green credentials, and his concern for minimising carbon emissions and saving biodiversity, he cannot conceal his impatience with NGOs: "They care about the orangutans [which are indeed threatened by the spread of plantations], not the *orangs* [people]."

The Great Green Hope: REDD

Mr Sulistyanto hopes Sinar Mas's biosphere in Riau may yet bring the firm some income from an initiative known as Reduced Emissions from Deforestation and Degradation (REDD). This is an idea that sounds almost too sensible to have gained currency. Since developed countries have become rich partly by cutting down their trees, and since old forests are better at storing carbon than new ones, it seems fair for the rich world to pay the poor world to stop logging (rather than, as at present, merely to plant new trees, under the so-called Clean Development Mechanism). There is a lot to preserve. More than half of Indonesia is still covered in forest. Sumatra may be a lost cause, like much of Kalimantan. But there is still, for example, Papua.

REDD forms part of the negotiations on a successor to the Kyoto protocol, which will reach a climax at meetings in Copenhagen this December. The idea may be better known in Indonesia than anywhere else. Businesses are already earmarking scraps of their concessions; Merrill Lynch, a big American investment bank, is nurturing a project; less established "carbon traders" are setting up shop in Indonesia; villagers in places like Teluk Binjai have visions of leisurely retirement at the international taxpayer's expense; and the government is creating a complex bureaucratic infrastructure. The forestry ministry has already issued rules on the sort of conservation projects that might be eligible, as well as guidelines on splitting the revenue.

But so far forest carbon credits remain a small, voluntary market. Gordon Brown, Britain's prime minister, has said a deal at Copenhagen should include transfers of $100 billion a year to the developing world, which would include funds for preserving forests. But there are plenty of question-marks still: the price of carbon, for one thing; how the money should best be used; and whether it would really be paid in perpetuity.

Agus Purnomo of Indonesia's climate-change council is a sceptic. He finds it hard to believe that the sort of money needed to compensate for the loss of deforestation revenue would be forthcoming. The range at present under discussion—$3–10 per tonne of carbon emissions saved—would be wholly inadequate. He agrees with many that the main point of Copenhagen must be "deep, deep cuts" in rich-world emissions. "You cannot leave saving the atmosphere to poor people."

So it is not easy to be optimistic about Indonesia's forests. Ahead of big international gatherings the government makes big promises. It has, for example, banned the conversion of land where the peat is more than three metres deep. But green groups say that hardly helps, since peat bogs have varying depths, and draining a shallow part will erode the rest. The commercial pressures are bound to grow. The conversion of acacia and eucalyptus as cellulose for biofuels will add a new market, and the development of palm-oil micro-refineries will make it much easier to get the fruit to a refinery within 24 hours of harvesting. Perhaps most urgently, a renewed El Niño is brewing, threatening drought and devastating forest fires.

For the government, carbon emissions will become an ever more galling issue. Just as the country seems ready to take its place on the international stage, gaining credit for its peacefulness, its stability and its pluralism, it will find itself under attack, however unfairly, as a vandal on a planetary scale.

Cry of the Wild

Last week four gorillas were slaughtered in Congo. With hunting on the rise, our most majestic animals are facing a new extinction crisis.

SHARON BEGLEY

On the lush plains of Congo's Virunga National Park last week, the convoy of porters rounded the final hill and trooped into camp. They gently set down the wooden frame they had carried for miles, and with it the very symbol of the African jungle: a 600-pound silverback mountain gorilla. A leader of a troop often visited by tourists, his arms and legs were lashed to the wood, his head hanging low and spots of blood speckling his fur. The barefoot porters, shirts torn and pants caked with dust from their trek, lay him beside three smaller gorillas, all females, who had also been killed, then silently formed a semicircle around the bodies. As the stench of death wafted across the camp in the waning afternoon light, a park warden stepped forward. "What man would do this?" he thundered. He answered himself: "Not even a beast would do this."

Park rangers don't know who killed the four mountain gorillas found shot to death in Virunga, but it was the seventh killing of the critically endangered primates in two months. Authorities doubt the killers are poachers, since the gorillas' bodies were left behind and an infant—who could bring thousands of dollars from a collector—was found clinging to its dead mother in one of the earlier murders. The brutality and senselessness of the crime had conservation experts concerned that the most dangerous animal in the world had found yet another excuse to slaughter the creatures with whom we share the planet. "This area must be immediately secured," said Deo Kujirakwinja of the Wildlife Conservation Society's Congo Program, "or we stand to lose an entire population of these endangered animals."

Back when the Amazon was aflame and the forests of Southeast Asia were being systematically clear-cut, biologists were clear about what posed the greatest threat to the world's wildlife, and it wasn't men with guns. For decades, the chief threat was habitat destruction. Whether it was from impoverished locals burning a forest to raise cattle or a multinational denuding a tree-covered Malaysian hillside, wildlife was dying because species were being driven from their homes. Yes, poachers killed tigers and other trophy animals—as they had since before Theodore Roosevelt—and subsistence hunters took monkeys for bushmeat to put on their tables, but they were not a primary danger.

That has changed. "Hunting, especially in Central and West Africa, is much more serious than we imagined," says Russell Mittermeier, president of Conservation International. "It's huge," with the result that hunting now constitutes the pre-eminent threat to some species. That threat has been escalating over the past decade largely because the opening of forests to logging and mining means that roads connect once impenetrable places to towns. "It's easier to get to where the wildlife is and then to have access to markets," says conservation biologist Elizabeth Bennett of the Wildlife Conservation Society. Economic forces are also at play. Thanks to globalization, meat, fur, skins and other animal parts "are sold on an increasingly massive scale across the world," she says. Smoked monkey carcasses travel from Ghana to New York and London, while gourmets in Hanoi and Guangzhou feast on turtles and pangolins (scaly anteaters) from Indonesia. There is a thriving market for bushmeat among immigrants in Paris, New York, Montreal, Chicago and other points in the African diaspora, with an estimated 13,000 pounds of bushmeat—much of it primates—arriving every month in seven European and North American cities alone. "Hunting and trade have already resulted in widespread local extinctions in Asia and West Africa," says Bennett. "The world's wild places are falling silent."

When a company wins a logging or mining concession, it immediately builds roads wide enough for massive trucks where the principal access routes had been dirt paths no wider than a jaguar. "Almost no tropical forests remain across Africa and Asia which are not penetrated by logging or other roads," says Bennett. Hunters and weapons follow, she notes, "and wildlife flows cheaply and rapidly down to distant towns where it is either sold directly or links in to global markets." How quickly can opening a forest ravage the resident wildlife? Three weeks after a logging company opened up one Congo forest, the density of animals fell more than 25 percent; a year after a logging road went into forest areas in Sarawak, Malaysia, in 2001, not a single large mammal remained.

A big reason why hunting used to pale next to habitat destruction is that as recently as the 1990s animals were killed mostly for subsistence, with locals taking only what they needed to live. Governments and conservation groups helped reduce even that through innovative programs giving locals an economic stake in the preservation of forests and the survival of wildlife. In the mountains of Rwanda, for instance, tourists pay $500 to spend an hour with the majestic mountain gorillas, bolstering the economy of the surrounding region. But recent years have brought a more dangerous kind of hunter, and not only because they use AK-47s and even land mines to hunt.

The problem now is that hunting, even of supposedly protected animals, is a global, multimillion-dollar business. Eating bushmeat "is now a status symbol," says Thomas Brooks of Conservation International. "It's not a subsistence issue. It's not a poverty issue. It's considered supersexy to eat bushmeat." Exact figures are hard to come by, but what conservation groups know about is sobering. Every year a single province in Laos exports $3.6 million worth of wildlife, including pangolins, cats, bears and primates. In Sumatra, about 51 tigers were killed each year between 1998 and 2002; there are currently an estimated 350 tigers left on the island (down from 1,000 or so in the 1980s) and fewer than 5,000 in the world.

If a wild population is large enough, it can withstand hunting. But for many species that "if" has not existed for decades. As a result, hunting in Kilum-Ijim, Cameroon, has pushed local elephants, buffalo, bushbuck, chimpanzees, leopards and lions to the brink of extinction. The common hippopotamus, which in 1996 was classified as of "least concern" because its numbers seemed to be healthy, is now "vulnerable": over the past 10 years its numbers have fallen as much as 20 percent, largely because the hippos are illegally hunted for meat and ivory. Pygmy hippos, classified as "vulnerable" in 2000, by last year had become endangered, at risk of going extinct. Logging has allowed bushmeat hunters to reach the West African forests where the hippos live; fewer than 3,000 remain.

Setting aside parks and other conservation areas is only as good as local enforcement. "Half of the major protected areas in Southeast Asia have lost at least one species of large mammal due to hunting, and most have lost many more," says Bennett. In Thailand's Doi Inthanon and Doi Suthep National Parks, for instance, elephants, tigers and wild cattle have been hunted into oblivion, as has every primate and hornbill in Sarawak's Kubah National Park. The world-famous Project Tiger site in India's Sariska National Park has no tigers, biologists announced in 2005. Governments cannot afford to pay as many rangers as are needed to patrol huge regions, and corruption is rife. The result is "empty-forest syndrome": majestic landscapes where flora and small fauna thrive, but where larger wildlife has been hunted out.

Which is not to say the situation is hopeless. With governments and conservationists recognizing the extinction threat posed by logging and mining, they are taking steps to ensure that animals do not come out along with the wood and minerals. In one collaboration, the government of Congo and the WCS work with a Swiss company, Congolaise Industrielle des Bois—which has a logging concession near Nouabalé-Ndoki National Park—to ensure that employees and their families hunt only for their own food needs; the company also makes sure that bushmeat does not get stowed away on logging trucks as illegal hunters try to take their haul to market. Despite the logging, gorillas, chimps, forest elephants and bongos are thriving in the park.

Anyone who thrills at the sight of man's distant cousins staring silently through the bush can only hope that the executions of Virunga's gorillas is an aberration. At the end of the week, UNESCO announced that it was sending a team to investigate the slaughter.

UNIT 4
Political Economy

Unit Selections

Key Points to Consider

- Are those who argue that the globalization is inevitable overly optimistic? Why or why not?

- What are some of the impediments to a truly global political economy?

- How has globalization accelerated the growth of criminal behavior?

- What is the nature of the debate surrounding international efforts to overcome extreme poverty?

- What transformations will societies that are heavy users of fossil fuels undergo in order to meet future energy needs?

- How are the political economies of traditional societies different from those of the consumer-oriented societies?

- What are some of the barriers that make it difficult for nonindustrial countries to develop?

- How are China and other emerging countries trying to alter their ways of doing business in order to meet the challenges of globalization? Are they likely to succeed?

- What economic challenges do countries like Japan and the United States face in the years to come?

Student Website
www.mhhe.com/cls

Internet References

Belfer Center for Science and International Affairs (BCSIA)
http://ksgwww.harvard.edu/csia
U.S. Agency for International Development
http://www.usaid.gov
The World Bank Group
http://www.worldbank.org

A defining characteristic of the twentieth century was the intense struggle between proponents of two economic ideologies. At the heart of the conflict was the question of what role government should play in the management of a country's economy. For some, the dominant capitalist economic system appeared to be organized primarily for the benefit of a few wealthy people. From their perspective, the masses were trapped in poverty, supplying cheap labor to further enrich the privileged elite. These critics argued that the capitalist system could be changed only by gaining control of the political system and radically changing the ownership of the means of production. In striking contrast to this perspective, others argued that the best way to create wealth and eliminate poverty was through the profit motive, which encouraged entrepreneurs to create new products and businesses. An open and competitive marketplace, from this point of view, minimized government interference and was the best system for making decisions about production, wages, and the distribution of goods and services.

Violent conflict at times characterized the contest between capitalism and socialism/communism. The Russian and Chinese revolutions overthrew the old social order and created radical changes in the political and economic systems in these two important countries. The political structures that were created to support new systems of agricultural and industrial production (along with the centralized planning of virtually all aspects of economic activity) eliminated most private ownership of property. These two revolutions were, in short, unparalleled experiments in social engineering.

The economic collapse of the Soviet Union and the dramatic market reforms in China have recast the debate about how to best structure contemporary economic systems. Some believe that with the end of communism and the resulting participation of hundreds of millions of new consumers in the global market, an unprecedented new era has been entered. Many have noted that this process of "globalization" is being accelerated by a revolution in communication and computer technologies. Proponents of this view argue that a new global economy is emerging that will ultimately eliminate national economic systems.

Others are less optimistic about the prospects of globalization. They argue that the creation of a single economic system where there are no boundaries to impede the flow of both capital and goods and services does not mean a closing of the gap between the world's rich and poor. Rather, they argue that multinational corporations and global financial institutions will have fewer legal constraints on their behavior, and this will lead to not only increased risks of global financial crises but also greater exploitation of workers and the accelerated destruction of the environment. Further, these critics point out that the unintended globalization of drug trafficking and other criminal behaviors is developing more rapidly than appropriate remedies can be developed.

The use of the term "political economy" for the title of this unit recognizes that economic and political systems are not separate. All economic systems have some type of marketplace

© C. Borland/PhotoLink/Getty Images

where goods and services are bought and sold. Government (either national or international) regulates these transactions to some degree; that is, government sets the rules that regulate the marketplace.

One of the most important concepts in assessing the contemporary political economy is "development." For the purposes of this unit, the term *development* is defined as an improvement in the basic aspects of life: lower infant mortality rates, longer life expectancy, lower disease rates, higher rates of literacy, healthier diets, and improved sanitation. Judged by these standards, some countries are more developed than others. A fundamental question that a thoughtful reader must consider is whether globalization is resulting in increased development not only for a few people but also for all of those participating in the global political economy.

The unit is organized into three sections. The first is a general discussion of the concept of globalization. How is it defined and what are some of the differing perspectives on this process? For example, is the idea of a global economy wishful thinking by those who sit on top of the power hierarchy, self-deluded into believing that globalization is an inexorable force that will evolve in its own way, following its own rules? Or will there continue to be the traditional tensions of nation–state power politics that transcend global economic processes, that is, conflict between the powerful and those who are either ascending or descending in power?

Following the first section are two sets of case studies. The first focuses on specific countries and/or economic sectors. The second set of case studies examines the global energy sector. All of the case studies have been selected to challenge the reader to develop her or his own conclusions about the positive and negative consequences of the globalization process. Does the contemporary global political economy result in increasing the gap between economic winners and losers, or can everyone positively benefit from its system of wealth creation and distribution?

Globalization and Its Contents

Peter Marber

Ask ten different people to define the term "globalization" and you are likely to receive ten different answers. For many, the meaning of globalization has been shaped largely by media coverage of an angry opposition: from right-wing nationalist xenophobes and left-wing labor leaders who fear rampant economic competition from low-wage countries to social activists who see a conspiracy on the part of multinational corporations to seek profits no matter what the cost to local cultures and economic equality to environmentalists who believe the earth is being systematically ravaged by capitalism run amok. "Globalization"—as if it were a machine that could be turned off—has been presented as fundamentally flawed and dangerous. But "globalization" is a term that encompasses all cross-border interactions, whether economic, political, or cultural. And behind the negative headlines lies a story of human progress and promise that should make even the most pessimistic analysts view globalization in an entirely different light.

Two decades ago, globalization was hardly discussed. At the time, less than 15 percent of the world's population participated in true global trade. Pessimism colored discussions of the Third World, of "lesser developed" or "backward" countries. Pawns in the Cold War's global chess game, these countries conjured images of famine, overpopulation, military dictatorship, and general chaos. At the time, the prospect of the Soviet Union or Communist China integrating economically with the West, or of strongman regimes in Latin America or Asia abandoning central planning, seemed farfetched. The possibility of these countries making meaningful socioeconomic progress and attaining Western standards of living appeared utterly unrealistic. Yet the forces of globalization were already at work.

On average, people are living twice as long as they did a century ago. Moreover, the world's aggregate material infrastructure and productive capabilities are hundreds—if not thousands—of times greater than they were a hundred years ago.[1] Much of this acceleration has occurred since 1950, with a powerful upsurge in the last 25 years. No matter how one measures wealth—whether by means of economic, bio-social, or financial indicators—there have been gains in virtually every meaningful aspect of life in the last two generations, and the trend should continue upward at least through the middle of the twenty-first century.

Most people are living longer, healthier, fuller lives. This is most evident in poor parts of the world. For example, since 1950, life expectancy in emerging markets (countries with less than one-third the per capita income of the United States, or nearly 85 percent of the world's population) has increased by more than 50 percent, reaching levels the West enjoyed only two generations ago. These longevity gains are linked to lower infant mortality, better nutrition (including an 85 percent increase in daily caloric intake), improved sanitation, immunizations, and other public health advances.

Literacy rates in developing countries have also risen dramatically in the last 50 years. In 1950, only a third of the people in Eastern Europe and in parts of Latin [America] living in these countries (roughly 800 million) could read or write; today nearly two-thirds—more than 3.2 billion people—are literate. And while it took the United States and Great Britain more than 120 years to increase average formal education from 2 years in the early nineteenth century to 12 years by the mid-twentieth century, some fast-growing developing countries, like South Korea, have accomplished this feat in fewer than 40 years.

The world now has a far more educated population with greater intellectual capacity than at any other time in history. This is particularly clear in much of Asia, where mass public education has allowed billions of people to increase their productivity and integrate in the global economy as workers and consumers. Similar trends can be seen in Eastern Europe and in parts of Latin America. This increase in human capital has led to historic highs in economic output and financial assets per capita.

During the twentieth century, economic output in the United States and other West European countries often doubled in less than 30 years, and Japan's postwar economy doubled in less than 16 years. In recent decades, developing country economies have surged so quickly that some—like South Korea in the 1960s and 1970s, or China in recent years—have often doubled productive output in just 7 to 10 years.

We often forget that poverty was the human living standard for most of recorded history. Until approximately two hundred years ago, virtually everyone lived at a subsistence level. As the economist John Maynard Keynes wrote in 1931 in *Essays in Persuasion*: "From the earliest times of which we have record—back, say, to two thousand years before Christ—down to the beginning of the eighteenth century, there was no very great change in the standard life of the average man living in civilized centers of the earth. Ups and downs certainly. Visitation

	1950	2000	2050
Global Output, Per Capita ($)	586	6,666	15,155
Global Financial Market			
Capitalization, Per Capita ($)	158	13,333	75,000
Percent of Global GDP			
Emerging Markets	5	50	55
Industrial Countries	95	75	45
Life Expectancy (years)			
Emerging Markets	41	64	76
Industrial Countries	65	77	82
Daily Caloric Intake			
Emerging Markets	1200	2600	3000
Industrial Countries	2200	3100	3200
Infant Mortality (per 1000)			
Emerging Markets	140	65	10
Industrial Countries	30	8	4
Literacy Rate (per 100)			
Emerging Markets	33	64	90
Industrial Countries	95	98	99

Sources: Bloomberg, World Bank, United Nations, and author's estimates.
Output and financial market capitalization figures are inflation-adjusted.

Figure 1   Measured Global Progress, 1950–2050E.

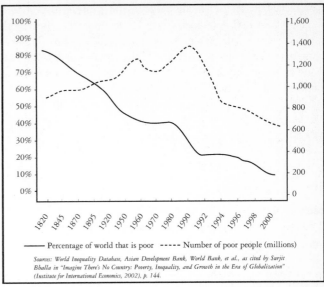

— Percentage of world that is poor - - - - Number of poor people (millions)

Sources: World Inequality Database, Asian Development Bank, World Bank, et al., as cited by Surjit Bhalla in "Imagine There's No Country: Poverty, Inequality, and Growth in the Era of Globalization" (Institute for International Economics, 2002), p. 144.

Figure 2   Historic World Poverty Levels, 1820–2000.

of plague, famine, and war. Golden intervals. But no progressive violent change. This slow rate of progress was due to two reasons—to the remarkable absence of technical improvements and the failure of capital to accumulate." Beginning in the early nineteenth century, this picture began to change. The proportion of the world's population living in poverty declined from over 80 percent in 1820 to under 15 percent in 2000; moreover, the actual number of people living in poverty over that period declined, even as the world's population exploded from something over 1 billion to more than 6 billion.

The application of mass production technology, together with excess capital (or "profit") and a free market technologies—is at the root of our modern prosperity. Upon further examination, one can see the virtuous cycle that connects human progress, technology, and globalization. Let's take two countries, one being richer than the other. The richer country has a more educated workforce, with nearly 99 percent literacy, while the poor one has only 50 percent literacy. Due to its less educated workforce and lack of infrastructure, the poor country might only be able to participate in global trade through exporting commodities—let's say fruits and vegetables. The rich country grows fruits and vegetables as well, but it also produces clothing and light manufactured goods such as radios. In the classic Ricardo/Smith models of comparative advantage and free trade, the wealthy country should utilize its skilled workforce to produce more clothing and radios for domestic consumption and export, and it should import more fruits and vegetables from the poorer country. This would, in turn, provide the poorer country with capital to improve education and infrastructure.

As this trade pattern creates profits for both countries, human capital can be mutually developed. Eventually, the poorer country (by boosting literacy and education) should develop its own ability to produce clothes and radios. Over time, the wealthier country—having reinvested profits in higher education, research and development, etc.—will begin to produce higher-tech goods rather than clothes and radios, perhaps televisions and cars. At this stage, the wealthy country would export its cars and televisions, and import clothes and radios. In turn, the poorer country begins to import agricultural products from an even poorer third country while exporting clothing and radios to both countries. As participating countries make progress through crossborder trade and the continuous upgrading of their workforces, it follows naturally that patterns of labor and employment will evolve over time.

It is sometimes argued that free trade harms economic growth and the poor by causing job losses, particularly in wealthier countries. But trade liberalization works by encouraging a shift of labor and capital from import-competitive sectors to more dynamic export industries where comparative advantages lie. Therefore, the unemployment caused by open trade can be expected to be temporary, being offset by job creation in other export sectors (which often requires some transition time). Output losses due to this transitional unemployment should also be small relative to long-term gains in national income (and lower prices) due to production increases elsewhere. In other words, these short-term labor adjustments should be seen as lesser evils when compared to the costs of continued economic stagnation and isolation that occur without open trade.

The shifting U.S. labor pattern from low-wage agricultural labor to manufacturing to higher-paid office and service employment during the nineteenth and twentieth centuries resulted largely from trade. Similar shifts are now seen all over the globe. In the 1950 and 1960s, the United States imported electronics from Japan, and exported cars and other heavy goods. In the 1970s, we began importing small cars from Japan. In the last 30-odd years, Japan has seen its dominance in electronics and economy cars wither amid competition from China and South

Korea. But Japan has made a successful push upmarket into larger, pricier luxury cars and sport utility vehicles. While these markets were shifting over the last three decades, jobs were lost, gained, and relocated in the United States and abroad. But living standards in America, Japan, South Korea, and China have all improved dramatically over that same time.

Working Less, Producing More

There is a growing consensus that international trade has a positive effect on per capita income. A 1999 World Bank study estimates that increasing the ratio of trade to national output by one percentage point raises per capita income by between 0.5 and 2 percent.[2] But the most dramatic illustration of how greater prosperity is spread through globalization is by our increased purchasing power. Ultimately, what determines wealth is the ability to work less and consume more. The time needed for an average American worker to earn the purchase price of various goods and services decreased dramatically during the twentieth century.

In 1919, it took an American worker 30 minutes of labor to earn enough to buy a pound of ground beef. This number dropped to 23 minutes in 1950, 11 minutes in 1975, and 6 minutes in 1997.[3] But this downward trend is even more impressive with respect to manufactured goods and services. For example, in 1895 the list price for an American-made bicycle in the Montgomery Ward catalog was $65. Today an American can buy a Chinese-manufactured 21-speed bike at any mass retailer for the same amount. But an average American needed to work some 260 hours in 1895 to earn the purchase price of the old bicycle, whereas it would take the average worker less than 5 hours to earn enough to buy today's bicycle.[4] In our own lifetimes, the costs of goods and services, everything from televisions to household appliances to telephone calls, computers, and airplane travel have plummeted relative to income—and not just in the United States.

Around the world, both basic commodities and items once considered luxury items now fill store shelves and pantries as increasing output and income have lifted most people above the subsistence level. The 50 most populous countries average more than 95 televisions per 100 households. In the 25 wealthiest countries, there are approximately 450 automobiles per 1,000 people, and China is now among the fastest-growing markets for cars, clothes, computers, cellular phones, and hundreds of household items.

This deflationary effect has also led to a radically improved quality of life. In 1870, the average American worker labored 3,069 hours per year—or six 10-hour days a week. By 1950, the average hours worked had fallen to 2,075.[5] Today, that number is closer to 1,730.[6] This pattern has been repeated around the world. In 1960, the average Japanese worker toiled 2,432 hours a year over a six-day work week; by 1988, this figure had dropped to 2,111 hours a year, and by 2000 it was down to 1,878 hours. There were even more dramatic reductions in European countries like France, Germany, and Sweden.[7] The Nobel Prize–winning economist Robert William Fogel estimates that the average American's lifetime working hours will have declined from 182,100 in 1880 to a projected 75,900 by 2040, with similar trends in other wealthy industrial countries. Fogel notes that while work took up 60 percent of an American's life in 1870, by 1990 it only took up about 30 percent. Between 1880 and 1990, the average American's cumulative lifetime leisure time swelled from 48,300 hours to a remarkable 246,000 hours, or 22 years.[8] This is a pattern of improvement in the human condition that we first saw in the industrialized West and then in Japan, and which is now spreading to dozens of developing countries that are integrating into the global economy.

A Thriving Middle Class

The recent surge in progress is certainly tied to technological advances, but it is also due to the adoption of free-market practices. Cross-border trade has ballooned by a factor of 20 over the past 50 years and now accounts for more than 20 percent of global output, according to the World Bank. Indeed, trade—which grew twice as fast as global output in the 1990s—will continue to drive economic specialization and growth. The global economy is becoming more sophisticated, segmented, and diversified.

The adoption of free-market practices has gone hand-in-hand with greater political freedoms. At the beginning of the twentieth century, less than 10 percent of the world's population had the right to vote, according to Freedom House. By 1950, approximately 35 percent of the global population in less than a quarter of the world's countries enjoyed this right. By 2000, more than two-thirds of the world's countries had implemented universal suffrage.

These symbiotic developments have helped completely recompose the world's "middle class"—those with a per capita income of roughly $10–40 per day, adjusted for inflation and purchasing power parity (PPP). According to the United Nations, in 1960 two-thirds of the world's middle-class citizens lived in the industrialized world—that is, in the United States, Canada, Western Europe, Japan, and Australia. By 1980, over 60 percent of the global middle class lived in developing countries, and by 2000 this number had reached a remarkable 83 percent. It is anticipated that India and China combined could easily produce middle classes of 400–800 million people over the next two generations—roughly the size of the current middle-class populations of the United States, Western Europe, and Japan combined.

A thriving middle class is an important component of economic, political, and social stability that comes with globalization. According to the World Bank, a higher share of income for the middle class is associated with increased national income and growth, improved health, better infrastructure, sounder economic policies, less instability and civil war, and more social modernization and democracy. There are numerous studies that also suggest that increasing wealth promotes gender equality, greater voter participation, income equality, greater concern for the environment, and more transparency in the business and political arenas, all of the quality-of-life issues that concern globalization skeptics.[9]

Measuring Inequality

Even if they concede that the world is wealthier overall, many critics of globalization cite the dangers of growing income inequality. Although the science of analyzing such long-term trends is far from perfect, there are indicators that point toward measurable progress even on this front.[10] The preoccupation with income or gross national product (GNP) as the sole measure of progress is unfortunate. Income is one measure of wealth, but not the only one. And income comparisons do not always reflect informal or unreported economic activity, which tends to be more prevalent in poor countries.

Many social scientists use Gini coefficients (a measure of income dispersion between and within countries) to bolster their arguments about inequality. The lower the Gini figure (between one and zero), the more equal income distribution tends to be. Unfortunately, the Gini index does not take into consideration purchasing power parity, the age dispersion of a population, and other variables that affect the overall picture. When adjusted for PPP, the Gini index for world income distribution decreased from 0.59 to 0.52 between 1965 and 1997, an improvement of nearly 12 percent.[11] Poverty rate trends are also cited by condemners of globalization, but this approach is problematic as well. The impoverished are often defined as those who earn 50 percent less than the median income in a country. But because 50 percent of median American income is very different than 50 percent of median income in Bangladesh, poverty rates may not tell us as much about human progress as we might think.

We can better gauge human progress by examining broader trends in bio-social development than income-centered analyses. A yardstick like the United Nations Development Program's human development index (HDI), for example, which looks at not only income but also life expectancy and education (including literacy and school enrollment), with the higher numbers denoting greater development, provides a clearer picture of global well-being:

	1960	1993	2002
OECD Countries	.80	.91	.91
Developing Countries	.26	.56	.70
Least Developed Countries	.16	.33	.44

What these numbers show is not only that human development has improved overall but that differentials between rich and poor countries are closing. While the HDI figure for wealthy OECD countries in 1960 was five times greater than that for the least developed countries (and three times higher than that for developing countries), those gaps were nearly halved by 1993. And in the most intense period of recent globalization, from 1993 to 2002, these gaps closed even further.

This by no means negates the reality of poverty in many parts of the world. There are still an estimated 1 billion people living in "abject" poverty today, but the World Bank estimates that this number should decline by 50 percent by 2015, if current growth trends hold.

Potholes on the Road to Globalization

The great gains and momentum of the last 25 years should not be seen as sufficient or irreversible. There are still formidable impediments to continued progress, the four most serious being protectionism, armed conflict, environmental stress, and demographic imbalances.

- *Protectionism.* One of the responses to globalization has been the attempt to pull inward, to save traditional industries and cultures, and to expel foreigners and foreign ideas. In India, consumers have protested against McDonald's restaurants for violating Hindu dietary laws. In France, angry farmers have uprooted genetically engineered crops, saying they threatened domestic control over food production.

  Possibly the most harmful protectionism today relates to global agricultural policy. Farming subsidies in wealthy countries now total approximately $350 billion a year, or seven times the $50 billion that such countries provide annually in foreign aid to the developing world.[12] Global trade policies may exclude developing countries from $700 billion in commerce annually, denying them not only needed foreign currency but also the commercial and social interaction necessary to bio-social progress.[13]

  Protectionism in the form of tariffs, rigid labor and immigration laws, capital controls, and regressive tax structures also should be resisted. Wealthy countries should not cling to old industries like apparel or agriculture; it is far more profitable, economically and socially, to look forward and outward, to focus on growing higher-skill industries—like aviation, pharmaceuticals, and entertainment—and to embrace new markets. In turn, poorer countries have generally grown richer through economic interaction with foreign countries, by refocusing nationalistic energies and policies toward future-oriented, internationally engaged commercial activity. The late-twentieth-century march away from closed economies has improved the lives of billions of people. To bow to nationalistic calls for protectionist policies could slow and even reverse this momentum.

- *Armed Conflict.* Countries cannot compete economically, cultivate human capital, or develop financial markets in the midst of armed conflict. According to the Stockholm International Peace Research Institute, there were 57 major armed conflicts in 45 different locations between 1990 and 2001; all but 3 of these were civil wars, which inflict deep economic damage and stunt development. In addition to ongoing civil wars, there are a number of potential cross-border powder kegs (beyond the recent U.S. invasions of Afghanistan and Iraq): Kashmir, over which nuclearized India and Pakistan have been at odds for decades; Taiwan, over which China claims sovereignty; Israel and its Arab neighbors; and the Korean peninsula. The economic, political, and cultural uncertainty surrounding these areas of potential conflict restricts the flow of capital, and paralyzes businesses, investors, and consumers.

To the extent that defense budgets continue to grow in tandem with global tensions and economic resources are used for military purposes, there will be fewer resources devoted to the development of human capital and economic competitiveness.

- *Environmental Stress.* There is no getting around the fact that the success of globalization is underscored by dramatic increases in consumption. With increased consumption comes environmental degradation. Damage to the environment, current or projected, can impede economic progress in many ways. Climatic changes attributed to greenhouse gas emissions and pressure on natural resources are serious problems. Resource scarcity is only one issue we will have to confront as 2–3 billion more people consume like middle-class Americans over the next 50 years. In the face of these environmental dangers, a host of new regulations may be enacted locally or globally. Increased environmental awareness among wealthier populations may lead to domestic policies that will raise costs to businesses and consumers, which in turn could curb economic expansion.

One step in the right direction would be increased public spending on alternative and renewable energy sources in the wealthier countries. The world is clearly underpowered, and the need for diversified energy grows as we speak. The benefits of a burgeoning alternative energy sector could be multiplicative. First, it might spur new economic growth areas for employment in rich countries, supplying them with potential technologies for export while reducing their reliance on foreign oil. Second, it might encourage developing countries that are over-reliant on oil exports to develop and modernize their economies and societies. Third, it would allow developing countries to build their infrastructures with a more diversified, sustainable energy approach than the first wave of industrializing countries.

- *Demographic Imbalances.* There are sharply contrasting population trends around the globe: developing nations are experiencing a youth bulge while industrialized countries are aging rapidly. This divergence may present a variety of challenges to globalization. In poorer developing countries, the youth bulge equals economic opportunity but is also potentially disruptive. In more than 50 of these countries, 50 percent of the population is under the age of 25. In some cases, half the population is under 20, and in extreme cases, even younger. These developing nations are also among the poorest, the fastest urbanizing, and the least politically or institutionally developed, making them susceptible to violence and instability. The large number of unemployed, disenfranchised young men in these countries may explain the growth of Islamic fundamentalism and the existence of pillaging bands of armed warriors in sub-Saharan Africa. Large young

populations may also lead to unregulated, unlawful migration that can create long-lasting instability.[14]

While the youth bulge can cause problems that derail global progress, the richest countries may fall victim to their past success. Prosperity, while providing more lifestyle choices and wellness, also results in lower birth rates and increasing longevity which could dampen long-term economic demand. The aging of wealthier populations also stresses public pension schemes that were conceived under different demographic circumstances—eras of robust population and consumption growth. In economies where populations are stagnant or shrinking, the specter of lengthy "aging recessions"—characterized by vicious cycles of falling demand for consumer goods (and deflation), collapsing asset values (including real estate), shrinking corporate profits, deteriorating household and financial institution balance sheets, weakening currencies, and soaring budget pressures—looms large.

Preparing for the Best, Not the Worst

Globalization and its major engines—burgeoning human capital, freer markets, increasing cross-border interaction—have created a new world order that has incited passionate debate, pro and con. However, both sides have more in common than one might imagine.

First, if human capital is a key component of improved living standards, it is arguable that increased spending on education should become a priority in rich and poor countries alike. Wealthier nations continually need to boost productivity and comparative advantage, while poorer countries need to develop skills to compete in the global economy. By adding to the numbers of the educated, there will be a wider base of workers and consumers to contribute to the virtuous cycle of prosperity we have witnessed in the last 50 years.

Second, boosting human capital in poor countries through increased financial and technical aid should also help broaden the marketplace in terms of workers and consumers. Appropriating an extra $100 billion in aid each year—a drop in the bucket for the 20 richest countries—could help some 2 billion people overcome their daily struggles with malnutrition, HIV/AIDS, malaria, and dirty drinking water, thereby increasing the number of healthy, productive workers and consumers.

Third, reorienting wealthy country subsidies away from low-tech areas like agriculture and mining toward higher-tech industries (including alternative energy development) would accelerate comparative advantage and stimulate greater trade. With wealthy countries focusing on higher-value-added industries for domestic consumption and export, poorer countries could pick up the slack in lower-skilled sectors where they can begin to engage the global economy. Over time, the poorer countries would become larger markets for goods and services. This, along with the two attitudinal and policy shifts mentioned above, could have a positive effect on the well-being of the world's population.

Even with its positive trends, globalization is not a perfect process. It is not a panacea for every problem for every person at every moment in time. It is a messy, complicated web of inter-dependent relationships, some long-term, some fleeting. But globalization is too often cited as creating a variety of human miseries such as sweatshop labor, civil war, and corruption—as if such ills never existed before 1980. Poverty is more at the root of such miseries. That is why the wholesale rejection of globalization—without acknowledging its tremendously posi-tive record in alleviating poverty—is shortsighted. Indeed, one could see how simply embracing globalization as inevitable—rather than debating its definition and purported shortcom-ings—could potentially foster more cross-border coordination on a variety of issues such as drug trafficking, ethnic cleansing, illegal immigration, famine, epidemic disease, environmental stress, and terrorism.

Emotion and confusion have unfortunately tainted the glo-balization debate both in the United States and abroad, and the focus is often on anecdotal successes or failures. Anxi-eties and economies may ebb and flow in the short run, but the responsibility to manage these progressive evolutions and revolutions—with worldwide human prosperity as the goal—should be our consistent aim in both government and the marketplace.

Notes

Many of the issues and arguments presented here in abbrevi-ated form are examined at greater length in my book, *Money Changes Everything: How Global Prosperity Is Reshaping Our Needs, Values, and Lifestyles* (Upper Saddle River, NJ: FT Pren-tice Hall, 2003).

1. See Angus Maddison, *Monitoring the World Economy: 1820–1992* (Paris: OECD, 1995).

2. Jeffrey A. Frankel and David Romer, "Does Trade Growth Cause Growth?" *American Economic Review,* vol. 89 (June 1999), pp. 379–99.

3. W. Michael Cox and Richard Alm, *Time Well Spent: The Declining Real Cost of Living in America*, annual report (Dallas: Federal Reserve Bank, 1997), p. 4.

4. Based on average U.S. industrial wages of approximately $15 per hour in 2000.

5. W. Michael Cox and Richard Alm, *These Are the Good Old Days: A Report on US Living Standards*, annual report (Dallas: Federal Reserve Bank, 1994), p. 7.

6. Robert William Fogel, *The Fourth Great Awakening and the Future of Egalitarianism* (Chicago: University of Chicago Press, 2000), p. 185.

7. Ibid., p. 186.

8. Ibid., pp. 184–90.

9. See Marber, *Money Changes Everything.* For more on specific shifts in attitudes and values relative to economic development, the University of Michigan's Ron Inglehart's seminal Human Values Surveys are an invaluable resource.

10. For a balanced study of this subject, see Arne Mechoir, Kjetil Telle, and Henrik Wiig, *Globalisation and Inequality: World Income and Living Standards, 1960–1998*, Norwegian Ministry of Foreign Affairs, Report 6B:2000, October 2000, available at http://odin.dep.no/archive/udvedlegg/01/01/rev_016.pdf.

11. Ibid., p. 14.

12. James Wolfensohn, "How Rich Countries Keep the Rest of the World in Poverty," *Irish Independent*, September 30, 2002.

13. Ibid.

14. See Michael Teitelbaum, "Are North/South Population Growth Differentials a Prelude to Conflict?" at http://www.csis.org/gai/Graying/speeches/teitelbaum.html.

PETER MARBER is an author, professional money manager, and faculty member at the School of International and Public Affairs at Columbia University.

From *World Policy Journal,* Winter 2004/2005, pp. 29–30, 33–37. Copyright © 2005 by The World Policy Institute. Reprinted by permission.

Article 19

It's a Flat World, After All

THOMAS L. FRIEDMAN

In 1492 Christopher Columbus set sail for India, going west. He had the Nina, the Pinta and the Santa Maria. He never did find India, but he called the people he met "Indians" and came home and reported to his king and queen: "The world is round." I set off for India 512 years later. I knew just which direction I was going. I went east. I had Lufthansa business class, and I came home and reported only to my wife and only in a whisper: "The world is flat."

And therein lies a tale of technology and geoeconomics that is fundamentally reshaping our lives—much, much more quickly than many people realize. It all happened while we were sleeping, or rather while we were focused on 9/11, the dot-com bust and Enron—which even prompted some to wonder whether globalization was over. Actually, just the opposite was true, which is why it's time to wake up and prepare ourselves for this flat world, because others already are, and there is no time to waste.

I wish I could say I saw it all coming. Alas, I encountered the flattening of the world quite by accident. It was in late February [2004], and I was visiting the Indian high-tech capital, Bangalore, working on a documentary for the Discovery Times channel about outsourcing. In short order, I interviewed Indian entrepreneurs who wanted to prepare my taxes from Bangalore, read my X-rays from Bangalore, trace my lost luggage from Bangalore and write my new software from Bangalore. The longer I was there, the more upset I became—upset at the realization that while I had been off covering the 9/11 wars, globalization had entered a whole new phase, and I had missed it. I guess the eureka moment came on a visit to the campus of Infosys Technologies, one of the crown jewels of the Indian outsourcing and software industry. Nandan Nilekani, the Infosys C.E.O., was showing me his global video-conference room, pointing with pride to a wall-size flat-screen TV, which he said was the biggest in Asia. Infosys, he explained, could hold a virtual meeting of the key players from its entire global supply chain for any project at any time on that supersize screen. So its American designers could be on the screen speaking with their Indian software writers and their Asian manufacturers all at once. That's what globalization is all about today, Nilekani said. Above the screen there were eight clocks that pretty well summed up the Infosys workday: 24/7/365. The clocks were labeled U.S. West, U.S. East, G.M.T., India, Singapore, Hong Kong, Japan, Australia.

"Outsourcing is just one dimension of a much more fundamental thing happening today in the world," Nilekani explained. "What happened over the last years is that there was a massive investment in technology, especially in the bubble era, when hundreds of millions of dollars were invested in putting broadband connectivity around the world, undersea cables, all those things." At the same time, he added, computers became cheaper and dispersed all over the world, and there was an explosion of e-mail software, search engines like Google and proprietary software that can chop up any piece of work and send one part to Boston, one part to Bangalore and one part to Beijing, making it easy for anyone to do remote development. When all of these things suddenly came together around 2000, Nilekani said, they "created a platform where intellectual work, intellectual capital, could be delivered from anywhere. It could be disaggregated, delivered, distributed, produced and put back together again—and this gave a whole new degree of freedom to the way we do work, especially work of an intellectual nature. And what you are seeing in Bangalore today is really the culmination of all these things coming together."

At one point, summing up the implications of all this, Nilekani uttered a phrase that rang in my ear. He said to me, "Tom, the playing field is being leveled." He meant that countries like India were now able to compete equally for global knowledge work as never before—and that America had better get ready for this. As I left the Infosys campus that evening and bounced along the potholed road back to Bangalore, I kept chewing on that phrase: "The playing field is being leveled."

"What Nandan is saying," I thought, "is that the playing field is being flattened. Flattened? Flattened? My God, he's telling me the world is flat!"

Here I was in Bangalore—more than 500 years after Columbus sailed over the horizon, looking for a shorter route to India using the rudimentary navigational technologies of his day, and returned safely to prove definitively that the world was round—and one of India's smartest engineers, trained at his country's top technical institute and backed by the most modern technologies of his day, was telling me that the world was flat, as flat as that screen on which he can host a meeting of his whole global supply chain. Even more interesting, he was citing this development as a new milestone in human progress and a great opportunity for India and the world—the fact that we had made our world flat!

This has been building for a long time. Globalization 1.0 (1492 to 1800) shrank the world from a size large to a size medium, and the dynamic force in that era was countries globalizing for resources and imperial conquest. Globalization 2.0 (1800 to 2000) shrank the world from a size medium to a size small, and it was spearheaded by companies globalizing for markets and labor. Globalization 3.0 (which started around 2000) is shrinking the world from a size small to a size tiny and flattening the playing field at the same time. And while the dynamic force in Globalization 1.0 was countries globalizing and the dynamic force in Globalization 2.0 was companies globalizing, the dynamic force in Globalization 3.0—the thing that gives it its unique character—is individuals and small groups globalizing. Individuals must, and can, now ask: where do I fit into the global competition and opportunities of the day, and how can I, on my own, collaborate with others globally? But Globalization 3.0 not only differs from the previous eras in how it is shrinking and flattening the world and in how it is empowering individuals. It is also different in that Globalization 1.0 and 2.0 were driven primarily by European and American companies and countries. But going forward, this will be less and less true. Globalization 3.0 is not only going to be driven more by individuals but also by a much more diverse—non-Western, nonwhite—group of individuals. In Globalization 3.0, you are going to see every color of the human rainbow take part.

"Today, the most profound thing to me is the fact that a 14-year-old in Romania or Bangalore or the Soviet Union or Vietnam has all the information, all the tools, all the software easily available to apply knowledge however they want," said Marc Andreessen, a co-founder of Netscape and creator of the first commercial Internet browser. "That is why I am sure the next Napster is going to come out of left field. As bioscience becomes more computational and less about wet labs and as all the genomic data becomes easily available on the Internet, at some point you will be able to design vaccines on your laptop."

Andreessen is touching on the most exciting part of Globalization 3.0 and the flattening of the world: the fact that we are now in the process of connecting all the knowledge pools in the world together. We've tasted some of the downsides of that in the way that Osama bin Laden has connected terrorist knowledge pools together through his Qaeda network, not to mention the work of teenage hackers spinning off more and more lethal computer viruses that affect us all. But the upside is that by connecting all these knowledge pools we are on the cusp of an incredible new era of innovation, an era that will be driven from left field and right field, from West and East and from North and South. Only 30 years ago, if you had a choice of being born a B student in Boston or a genius in Bangalore or Beijing, you probably would have chosen Boston, because a genius in Beijing or Bangalore could not really take advantage of his or her talent. They could not plug and play globally. Not anymore. Not when the world is flat, and anyone with smarts, access to Google and a cheap wireless laptop can join the innovation fray.

When the world is flat, you can innovate without having to emigrate. This is going to get interesting. We are about to see creative destruction on steroids.

How did the world get flattened, and how did it happen so fast?

It was a result of 10 events and forces that all came together during the 1990's and converged right around the year 2000. Let me go through them briefly. The first event was 11/9. That's right—not 9/11, but 11/9. Nov. 9, 1989, is the day the Berlin Wall came down, which was critically important because it allowed us to think of the world as a single space. "The Berlin Wall was not only a symbol of keeping people inside Germany; it was a way of preventing a kind of global view of our future," the Nobel Prize-winning economist Amartya Sen said. And the wall went down just as the windows went up—the breakthrough Microsoft Windows 3.0 operating system, which helped to flatten the playing field even more by creating a global computer interface, shipped six months after the wall fell.

The second key date was 8/9. Aug. 9, 1995, is the day Netscape went public, which did two important things. First, it brought the Internet alive by giving us the browser to display images and data stored on Web sites. Second, the Netscape stock offering triggered the dot-com boom, which triggered the dot-com bubble, which triggered the massive overinvestment of billions of dollars in fiber-optic telecommunications cable. That overinvestment, by companies like Global Crossing, resulted in the willy-nilly creation of a global undersea-underground fiber network, which in turn drove down the cost of transmitting voices, data and images to practically zero, which in turn accidentally made Boston, Bangalore and Beijing next-door neighbors overnight. In sum, what the Netscape revolution did was bring people-to-people connectivity to a whole new level. Suddenly more people could connect with more other people from more different places in more different ways than ever before.

No country accidentally benefited more from the Netscape moment than India. "India had no resources and no infrastructure," said Dinakar Singh, one of the most respected hedge-fund managers on Wall Street, whose parents earned doctoral degrees in biochemistry from the University of Delhi before emigrating to America. "It produced people with quality and by quantity. But many of them rotted on the docks of India like vegetables. Only a relative few could get on ships and get out. Not anymore, because we built this ocean crosser, called fiber-optic cable. For decades you had to leave India to be a professional. Now you can plug into the world from India. You don't have to go to Yale and go to work for Goldman Sachs." India could never have afforded to pay for the bandwidth to connect brainy India with high-tech America, so American shareholders paid for it. Yes, crazy overinvestment can be good. The overinvestment in railroads turned out to be a great boon for the American economy. "But the railroad overinvestment was confined to your own country and so, too, were the benefits," Singh said. In the case of the digital railroads, "it was the foreigners who benefited." India got a free ride.

The first time this became apparent was when thousands of Indian engineers were enlisted to fix the Y2K—the year 2000—computer bugs for companies from all over the world. (Y2K should be a national holiday in India. Call it "Indian Interdependence Day," says Michael Mandelbaum, a foreign-policy analyst at Johns Hopkins.) The fact that the Y2K work could be outsourced to Indians was made possible by the first two flat-teners, along with a third, which I call "workflow." Workflow is shorthand for all the software applications, standards and electronic transmission pipes, like middleware, that connected all those computers and fiber-optic cable. To put it another way, if the Netscape moment connected people to people like never before, what the workflow revolution did was connect applications to applications so that people all over the world could work together in manipulating and shaping words, data and images on computers like never before.

Indeed, this breakthrough in people-to-people and application-to-application connectivity produced, in short order, six more flatteners—six new ways in which individuals and companies could collaborate on work and share knowledge. One was "outsourcing." When my software applications could connect seamlessly with all of your applications, it meant that all kinds of work—from accounting to software-writing—could be digitized, disaggregated and shifted to any place in the world where it could be done better and cheaper. The second was "offshoring." I send my whole factory from Canton, Ohio, to Canton, China. The third was "open-sourcing." I write the next operating system, Linux, using engineers collaborating together online and working for free. The fourth was "insourcing." I let a company like UPS come inside my company and take over my whole logistics operation—everything from filling my orders online to delivering my goods to repairing them for customers when they break. (People have no idea what UPS really does today. You'd be amazed!). The fifth was "supply-chaining." This is Wal-Mart's specialty. I create a global supply chain down to the last atom of efficiency so that if I sell an item in Arkansas, another is immediately made in China. (If Wal-Mart were a country, it would be China's eighth-largest trading partner.) The last new form of collaboration I call "informing"—this is Google, Yahoo and MSN Search, which now allow anyone to collaborate with, and mine, unlimited data all by themselves.

So the first three flatteners created the new platform for collaboration, and the next six are the new forms of collaboration that flattened the world even more. The 10th flattener I call "the steroids," and these are wireless access and voice over Internet protocol (VoIP). What the steroids do is turbocharge all these new forms of collaboration, so you can now do any one of them, from anywhere, with any device.

The world got flat when all 10 of these flatteners converged around the year 2000. This created a global, Web-enabled playing field that allows for multiple forms of collaboration on research and work in real time, without regard to geography, distance or, in the near future, even language. "It is the creation of this platform, with these unique attributes, that is the truly important sustainable breakthrough that made what you call the flattening of the world possible," said Craig Mundie, the chief technical officer of Microsoft.

No, not everyone has access yet to this platform, but it is open now to more people in more places on more days in more ways than anything like it in history. Wherever you look today—whether it is the world of journalism, with bloggers bringing down Dan Rather; the world of software, with the Linux code writers working in online forums for free to challenge Microsoft; or the world of business, where Indian and Chinese innovators are competing against and working with some of the most advanced Western multinationals—hierarchies are being flattened and value is being created less and less within vertical silos and more and more through horizontal collaboration within companies, between companies and among individuals.

Do you recall "the IT revolution" that the business press has been pushing for the last 20 years? Sorry to tell you this, but that was just the prologue. The last 20 years were about forging, sharpening and distributing all the new tools to collaborate and connect. Now the real information revolution is about to begin as all the complementarities among these collaborative tools start to converge. One of those who first called this moment by its real name was Carly Fiorina, the former Hewlett-Packard C.E.O., who in 2004 began to declare in her public speeches that the dot-com boom and bust were just "the end of the beginning." The last 25 years in technology, Fiorina said, have just been "the warm-up act." Now we are going into the main event, she said, "and by the main event, I mean an era in which technology will truly transform every aspect of business, of government, of society, of life."

As if this flattening wasn't enough, another convergence coincidentally occurred during the 1990's that was equally important. Some three billion people who were out of the game walked, and often ran, onto the playing field. I am talking about the people of China, India, Russia, Eastern Europe, Latin America and Central Asia. Their economies and political systems all opened up during the course of the 1990s so that their people were increasingly free to join the free market. And when did these three billion people converge with the new playing field and the new business processes? Right when it was being flattened, right when millions of them could compete and collaborate more equally, more horizontally and with cheaper and more readily available tools. Indeed, thanks to the flattening of the world, many of these new entrants didn't even have to leave home to participate. Thanks to the 10 flatteners, the playing field came to them!

It is this convergence—of new players, on a new playing field, developing new processes for horizontal collaboration—that I believe is the most important force shaping global economics and politics in the early 21st century. Sure, not all three billion can collaborate and compete. In fact, for most people the world is not yet flat at all. But even if we're talking about only 10 percent, that's 300 million people—about twice the size of the American work force. And be advised: the Indians and Chinese are not racing us to the bottom. They are racing us to the top. What China's leaders really want is that the next generation of underwear and airplane wings not just be "made in China" but also be "designed in China." And that is where things are heading. So in 30 years we will have gone from "sold in China" to "made in China" to "designed in China" to "dreamed up in China"—or from China as collaborator with the worldwide manufacturers on nothing to China as a low-cost, high-quality, hyperefficient collaborator with worldwide manufacturers on everything. Ditto India. Said

Craig Barrett, the C.E.O. of Intel, "You don't bring three billion people into the world economy overnight without huge consequences, especially from three societies"—like India, China and Russia—"with rich educational heritages."

That is why there is nothing that guarantees that Americans or Western Europeans will continue leading the way. These new players are stepping onto the playing field legacy free, meaning that many of them were so far behind that they can leap right into the new technologies without having to worry about all the sunken costs of old systems. It means that they can move very fast to adopt new, state-of-the-art technologies, which is why there are already more cellphones in use in China today than there are people in America.

If you want to appreciate the sort of challenge we are facing, let me share with you two conversations. One was with some of the Microsoft officials who were involved in setting up Microsoft's research center in Beijing, Microsoft Research Asia, which opened in 1998—after Microsoft sent teams to Chinese universities to administer I.Q. tests in order to recruit the best brains from China's 1.3 billion people. Out of the 2,000 top Chinese engineering and science students tested, Microsoft hired 20. They have a saying at Microsoft about their Asia center, which captures the intensity of competition it takes to win a job there and explains why it is already the most productive research team at Microsoft: "Remember, in China, when you are one in a million, there are 1,300 other people just like you."

The other is a conversation I had with Rajesh Rao, a young Indian entrepreneur who started an electronic-game company from Bangalore, which today owns the rights to Charlie Chaplin's image for mobile computer games. "We can't relax," Rao said. "I think in the case of the United States that is what happened a bit. Please look at me: I am from India. We have been at a very different level before in terms of technology and business. But once we saw we had an infrastructure that made the world a small place, we promptly tried to make the best use of it. We saw there were so many things we could do. We went ahead, and today what we are seeing is a result of that. There is no time to rest. That is gone. There are dozens of people who are doing the same thing you are doing, and they are trying to do it better. It is like water in a tray: you shake it, and it will find the path of least resistance. That is what is going to happen to so many jobs—they will go to that corner of the world where there is the least resistance and the most opportunity. If there is a skilled person in Timbuktu, he will get work if he knows how to access the rest of the world, which is quite easy today. You can make a website and have an e-mail address and you are up and running. And if you are able to demonstrate your work, using the same infrastructure, and if people are comfortable giving work to you and if you are diligent and clean in your transactions, then you are in business."

Instead of complaining about outsourcing, Rao said, Americans and Western Europeans would "be better off thinking about how you can raise your bar and raise yourselves into doing something better. Americans have consistently led in innovation over the last century. Americans whining—we have never seen that before."

Rao is right. And it is time we got focused. As a person who grew up during the cold war, I'll always remember driving down the highway and listening to the radio, when suddenly the music would stop and a grim-voiced announcer would come on the air and say: "This is a test. This station is conducting a test of the Emergency Broadcast System." And then there would be a 20-second high-pitched siren sound. Fortunately, we never had to live through a moment in the cold war when the announcer came on and said, "This is a not a test."

That, however, is exactly what I want to say here: "This is not a test."

The long-term opportunities and challenges that the flattening of the world puts before the United States are profound. Therefore, our ability to get by doing things the way we've been doing them—which is to say not always enriching our secret sauce—will not suffice any more. "For a country as wealthy as we are, it is amazing how little we are doing to enhance our natural competitiveness," says Dinakar Singh, the Indian-American hedge-fund manager. "We are in a world that has a system that now allows convergence among many billions of people, and we had better step back and figure out what it means. It would be a nice coincidence if all the things that were true before were still true now, but there are quite a few things you actually need to do differently. You need to have a much more thoughtful national discussion."

If this moment has any parallel in recent American history, it is the height of the cold war, around 1957, when the Soviet Union leapt ahead of America in the space race by putting up the Sputnik satellite. The main challenge then came from those who wanted to put up walls; the main challenge to America today comes from the fact that all the walls are being taken down and many other people can now compete and collaborate with us much more directly. The main challenge in that world was from those practicing extreme Communism, namely Russia, China and North Korea. The main challenge to America today is from those practicing extreme capitalism, namely China, India and South Korea. The main objective in that era was building a strong state, and the main objective in this era is building strong individuals.

Meeting the challenges of flatism requires as comprehensive, energetic and focused a response as did meeting the challenge of Communism. It requires a president who can summon the nation to work harder, get smarter, attract more young women and men to science and engineering and build the broadband infrastructure, portable pensions and health care that will help every American become more employable in an age in which no one can guarantee you lifetime employment.

We have been slow to rise to the challenge of flatism, in contrast to Communism, maybe because flatism doesn't involve ICBM missiles aimed at our cities. Indeed, the hot line, which used to connect the Kremlin with the White House, has been replaced by the help line, which connects everyone in America to call centers in Bangalore. While the other end of the hot line might have had Leonid Brezhnev threatening nuclear war, the other end of the help line just has a soft voice eager to help you sort out your AOL bill or collaborate with you on a new piece of software. No, that voice has none of the menace of Nikita Khrushchev pounding a shoe on the table at the United Nations, and it has none of the sinister snarl of the bad guys in "From Russia with Love." No, that voice on the help line just has a friendly Indian lilt that masks any sense of threat or challenge. It simply says: "Hello, my name is Rajiv. Can I help you?"

No, Rajiv, actually you can't. When it comes to responding to the challenges of the flat world, there is no help line we can call. We have to dig into ourselves. We in America have all the basic economic and educational tools to do that. But we have not been improving those tools as much as we should. That is why we are in what Shirley Ann Jackson, the 2004 president of the American Association for the Advancement of Science and president of Rensselaer Polytechnic Institute, calls a "quiet crisis"—one that is slowly eating away at America's scientific and engineering base.

"If left unchecked," said Jackson, the first African-American woman to earn a Ph.D. in physics from M.I.T., "this could challenge our pre-eminence and capacity to innovate." And it is our ability to constantly innovate new products, services and companies that has been the source of America's horn of plenty and steadily widening middle class for the last two centuries. This quiet crisis is a product of three gaps now plaguing American society. The first is an "ambition gap." Compared with the young, energetic Indians and Chinese, too many Americans have gotten too lazy. As David Rothkopf, a former official in the Clinton Commerce Department, puts it, "The real entitlement we need to get rid of is our sense of entitlement." Second, we have a serious numbers gap building. We are not producing enough engineers and scientists. We used to make up for that by importing them from India and China, but in a flat world, where people can now stay home and compete with us, and in a post-9/11 world, where we are insanely keeping out many of the first-round intellectual draft choices in the world for exaggerated security reasons, we can no longer cover the gap. That's a key reason companies are looking abroad. The numbers are not here. And finally we are developing an education gap. Here is the dirty little secret that no C.E.O. wants to tell you: they are not just outsourcing to save on salary. They are doing it because they can often get better-skilled and more productive people than their American workers.

These are some of the reasons that Bill Gates, the Microsoft chairman, warned the governors' conference in a Feb. 26 speech that American high-school education is "obsolete." As Gates put it: "When I compare our high schools to what I see when I'm traveling abroad, I am terrified for our work force of tomorrow. In math and science, our fourth graders are among the top students in the world. By eighth grade, they're in the middle of the pack. By 12th grade, U.S. students are scoring near the bottom of all industrialized nations. . . . The percentage of a population with a college degree is important, but so are sheer numbers. In 2001, India graduated almost a million more students from college than the United States did. China graduates twice as many students with bachelor's degrees as the U.S., and they have six times as many graduates majoring in engineering. In the international competition to have the biggest and best supply of knowledge workers, America is falling behind."

We need to get going immediately. It takes 15 years to train a good engineer, because, ladies and gentlemen, this really is rocket science. So parents, throw away the Game Boy, turn off the television and get your kids to work. There is no sugar-coating this: in a flat world, every individual is going to have to run a little faster if he or she wants to advance his or her standard of living. When I was growing up, my parents used to say to me, "Tom, finish your dinner—people in China are starving." But after sailing to the edges of the flat world for a year, I am now telling my own daughters, "Girls, finish your homework—people in China and India are starving for your jobs."

I repeat, this is not a test. This is the beginning of a crisis that won't remain quiet for long. And as the Stanford economist Paul Romer so rightly says, "A crisis is a terrible thing to waste."

THOMAS L. FRIEDMAN is the author of "*The World Is Flat: A Brief History of the Twenty-First Century,*" to be published this week by Farrar, Straus & Giroux and from which this article is adapted. His column appears on the Op-Ed page of *The Times,* and his television documentary "Does Europe Hate Us?" was shown on the Discovery Channel on April 7, 2005.

Why the World Isn't Flat

Globalization has bound people, countries, and markets closer than ever, rendering national borders relics of a bygone era—or so we're told. But a close look at the data reveals a world that's just a fraction as integrated as the one we thought we knew. In fact, more than 90 percent of all phone calls, Web traffic, and investment is local. What's more, even this small level of globalization could still slip away.

PANKAJ GHEMAWAT

Ideas will spread faster, leaping borders. Poor countries will have immediate access to information that was once restricted to the industrial world and traveled only slowly, if at all, beyond it. Entire electorates will learn things that once only a few bureaucrats knew. Small companies will offer services that previously only giants could provide. In all these ways, the communications revolution is profoundly democratic and liberating, leveling the imbalance between large and small, rich and poor. The global vision that Frances Cairncross predicted in her *Death of Distance* appears to be upon us. We seem to live in a world that is no longer a collection of isolated, "local" nations, effectively separated by high tariff walls, poor communications networks, and mutual suspicion. It's a world that, if you believe the most prominent proponents of globalization, is increasingly wired, informed, and, well, "flat."

It's an attractive idea. And if publishing trends are any indication, globalization is more than just a powerful economic and political transformation; it's a booming cottage industry. According to the U.S. Library of Congress's catalog, in the 1990s, about 500 books were published on globalization. Between 2000 and 2004, there were more than 4,000. In fact, between the mid-1990s and 2003, the rate of increase in globalization-related titles more than doubled every 18 months.

Amid all this clutter, several books on the subject have managed to attract significant attention. During a recent TV interview, the first question I was asked—quite earnestly—was why I still thought the world was round. The interviewer was referring of course to the thesis of *New York Times* columnist Thomas L. Friedman's bestselling book *The World Is Flat.* Friedman asserts that 10 forces—most of which enable connectivity and collaboration at a distance—are "flattening" the Earth and leveling a playing field of global competitiveness, the likes of which the world has never before seen.

It sounds compelling enough. But Friedman's assertions are simply the latest in a series of exaggerated visions that also include the "end of history" and the "convergence of tastes." Some writers in this vein view globalization as a good thing—an escape from the ancient tribal rifts that have divided humans, or an opportunity to sell the same thing to everyone on Earth. Others lament its cancerous spread, a process at the end of which everyone will be eating the same fast food. Their arguments are mostly characterized by emotional rather than cerebral appeals, a reliance on prophecy, semiotic arousal (that is, treating everything as a sign), a focus on technology as the driver of change, an emphasis on education that creates "new" people, and perhaps above all, a clamor for attention. But they all have one thing in common: They're wrong.

In truth, the world is not nearly as connected as these writers would have us believe. Despite talk of a new, wired world where information, ideas, money, and people can move around the planet faster than ever before, just a fraction of what we consider globalization actually exists. The portrait that emerges from a hard look at the way companies, people, and states interact is a world that's only beginning to realize the potential of true global integration. And what these trend's backers won't tell you is that globalization's future is more fragile than you know.

The 10 Percent Presumption

The few cities that dominate international financial activity—Frankfurt, Hong Kong, London, New York—are at the height of modern global integration; which is to say, they are all relatively well connected with one another. But when you examine the numbers, the picture is one of extreme connectivity at the local level, not a flat world. What do such statistics reveal? Most types of economic activity that could be conducted either within or across borders turn out to still be quite domestically concentrated.

One favorite mantra from globalization champions is how "investment knows no boundaries." But how much of all the capital being invested around the world is conducted by companies outside of their home countries? The fact is, the total amount of the world's capital formation that is generated from foreign direct investment (FDI) has been less than 10 percent for the last three years for which data are available (2003–05). In other words, more than 90 percent of the fixed investment around the world is still domestic. And though merger waves can push the ratio higher, it has never reached 20 percent. In a thoroughly globalized environment, one would expect this number to be much higher—about 90 percent, by my calculation. And FDI isn't an odd or unrepresentative example.

The levels of internationalization associated with cross-border migration, telephone calls, management research and education, private charitable giving, patenting, stock investment, and trade, as a fraction of gross domestic product (GDP), all stand much closer to 10 percent than 100 percent. The biggest exception in absolute terms—the trade-to-GDP—recedes most of the way back down toward 20 percent if you adjust for certain kinds of double-counting. So if someone asked me to guess the internationalization level of some activity about which I had no particular information, I would guess it to be much closer to 10 percent—than to 100 percent. I call this the "10 Percent Presumption."

More broadly, these and other data on cross-border integration suggest a semiglobalized world, in which neither the bridges nor the barriers between countries can be ignored. From this perspective, the most astonishing aspect of various writings on globalization is the extent of exaggeration involved. In short, the levels of internationalization in the world today are roughly an order of magnitude lower than those implied by globalization proponents.

A Strong National Defense

If you buy into the more extreme views of the globalization triumphalists, you would expect to see a world where national borders are irrelevant, and where citizens increasingly view themselves as members of ever broader political entities. True, communications technologies have improved dramatically during the past 100 years. The cost of a three-minute telephone call from New York to London fell from $350 in 1930 to about 40 cents in 1999, and it is now approaching zero for voice-over-Internet telephony. And the Internet itself is just one of many newer forms of connectivity that have progressed several times faster than plain old telephone service. This pace of improvement has inspired excited proclamations about the pace of global integration. But it's a huge leap to go from predicting such changes to asserting that declining communication costs will obliterate the effects of distance. Although the barriers at borders have declined significantly, they haven't disappeared.

To see why, consider the Indian software industry—a favorite of Friedman and others. Friedman cites Nandan Nilekani, the CEO of the second-largest such firm, Infosys, as his muse for the notion of a flat world. But what Nilekani has pointed out privately is that while Indian software programmers can now serve the United States from India, access is assured, in part, by U.S. capital being invested—quite literally—in that outcome. In other words, the success of the Indian IT industry is not exempt

from political and geographic constraints. The country of origin matters—even for capital, which is often considered stateless.

Or consider the largest Indian software firm, Tata Consultancy Services (TCS). Friedman has written at least two columns in the *New York Times* on TCS's Latin American operations: "[I]n today's world, having an Indian company led by a Hungarian-Uruguayan servicing American banks with Montevidean engineers managed by Indian technologists who have learned to eat Uruguayan veggie is just the new normal," Friedman writes. Perhaps. But the real question is why the company established those operations in the first place. Having worked as a strategy advisor to TCS since 2000, I can testify that reasons related to the tyranny of time zones, languages, and the need for proximity to clients' local operations loomed large in that decision. This is a far cry from globalization proponents' oft-cited world in which geography, language, and distance don't matter.

Trade flows certainly bear that theory out. Consider Canadian-U.S. trade, the largest bilateral relationship of its kind in the world. In 1988, before the North American Free Trade Agreement (NAFTA) took effect, merchandise trade levels between Canadian provinces—that is, within the country—were estimated to be 20 times as large as their trade with similarly sized and similarly distant U.S. states. In other words, there was a built-in "home bias." Although NAFTA helped reduce this ratio of domestic to international trade—the home bias—to 10 to 1 by the mid-1990s, it still exceeds 5 to 1 today. And these ratios are just for merchandise; for services, the ratio is still several times larger. Clearly, the borders in our seemingly "borderless world" still matter to most people.

Geographical boundaries are so pervasive, they even extend to cyberspace. If there were one realm in which borders should be rendered meaningless and the globalization proponents should be correct in their overly optimistic models, it should be the Internet. Yet Web traffic within countries and regions has increased far faster than traffic between them. Just as in the real world, Internet links decay with distance. People across the world may be getting more connected, but they aren't connecting with each other. The average South Korean Web user may be spending several hours a day online—connected to the rest of the world in theory—but he is probably chatting with friends across town and e-mailing family across the country rather than meeting a fellow surfer in Los Angeles. We're more wired, but no more "global."

Just look at Google, which boasts of supporting more than 100 languages and, partly as a result, has recently been rated the most globalized website. But Google's operation in Russia (cofounder Sergey Brin's native country) reaches only 28 percent of the market there, versus 64 percent for the Russian market leader in search services, Yandex, and 53 percent for Rambler.

Indeed, these two local competitors account for 91 percent of the Russian market for online ads linked to Web searches. What has stymied Google's expansion into the Russian market? The biggest reason is the difficulty of designing a search engine to handle the linguistic complexities of the Russian language. In addition, these local competitors are more in tune with the Russian market, for example, developing payment methods through traditional banks to compensate for the dearth of credit cards. And, though Google has doubled its reach since 2003, it's had to set up a Moscow office in Russia and hire Russian software engineers, underlining the continued importance of physical location. Even now, borders between countries define—and constrain—our movements more than globalization breaks them down.

Turning Back the Clock

If globalization is an inadequate term for the current state of integration, there's an obvious rejoinder: Even if the world isn't quite flat today, it will be tomorrow. To respond, we have to look at trends, rather than levels of integration at one point in time. The results are telling. Along a few dimensions, integration reached its all-time high many years ago. For example, rough calculations suggest that the number of long-term international migrants amounted to 3 percent of the world's population in 1900—the high-water mark of an earlier era of migration—versus 2.9 percent in 2005.

Along other dimensions, it's true that new records are being set. But this growth has happened only relatively recently, and only after long periods of stagnation and reversal. For example, FDI stocks divided by GDP peaked before World War I and didn't return to that level until the 1990s. Several economists have argued that the most remarkable development over the long term was the declining level of internationalization between the two World Wars. And despite the records being set, the current level of trade intensity falls far short of completeness, as the Canadian-U.S. trade data suggest. In fact, when trade economists look at these figures, they are amazed not at how much trade there is, but how little.

It's also useful to examine the considerable momentum that globalization proponents attribute to the constellation of policy changes that led many countries—particularly China, India, and the former Soviet Union—to engage more extensively with the international economy. One of the better-researched descriptions of these policy changes and their implications is provided by economists Jeffrey Sachs and Andrew Warner:

"The years between 1970 and 1995, and especially the last decade, have witnessed the most remarkable institutional harmonization and economic integration among nations in world history. While economic integration was increasing throughout the 1970s and 1980s, the extent of integration has come sharply into focus only since the collapse of communism in 1989. In 1995, one dominant global economic system is emerging."

Yes, such policy openings are important. But to paint them as a sea change is inaccurate at best. Remember the 10 Percent Presumption, and that integration is only beginning. The policies that we fickle humans enact are surprisingly reversible. Thus, Francis Fukuyama's *The End of History,* in which liberal democracy and technologically driven capitalism were supposed to have triumphed over other ideologies, seems quite quaint today. In the wake of Sept. 11, 2001, Samuel Huntington's *Clash of Civilizations* looks at least a bit more prescient. But even if you stay on the economic plane, as Sachs and Warner mostly do, you quickly see counterevidence to the supposed decisiveness of policy openings. The so-called Washington Consensus around market-friendly policies ran up against the 1997 Asian currency crisis and has since frayed substantially—for example, in the swing toward neopopulism across much of Latin America. In terms of economic outcomes, the number of countries—in Latin America, coastal Africa, and the former Soviet Union—that have dropped out of the "convergence club" (defined in terms of narrowing productivity and structural gaps vis-à-vis the advanced industrialized countries) is at least as impressive as the number of countries that have joined the club. At a multilateral level, the suspension of the Doha round of trade talks in the summer of 2006—prompting *The Economist* to run a cover titled "The Future of Globalization" and depicting a beached wreck—is no promising omen. In addition, the recent wave of cross-border mergers and acquisitions seems to be encountering more protectionism, in a broader range of countries, than did the previous wave in the late 1990s.

Of course, given that sentiments in these respects have shifted in the past 10 years or so, there is a fair chance that they may shift yet again in the next decade. The point is, it's not only possible to turn back the clock on globalization-friendly policies, it's relatively easy to imagine it happening. Specifically, we have to entertain the possibility that deep international economic integration may be inherently incompatible with national sovereignty—especially given the tendency of voters in many countries, including advanced ones, to support more protectionism, rather than less. As Jeff Immelt, CEO of GE, put it in late 2006, "If you put globalization to a popular vote in the U.S., it would lose." And even if cross-border integration continues on its upward path, the road from here to there is unlikely to be either smooth or straight. There will be shocks and cycles, in all likelihood, and maybe even another period of stagnation or reversal that will endure for decades. It wouldn't be unprecedented.

The champions of globalization are describing a world that doesn't exist. It's a fine strategy to sell books and even describe a potential environment that may someday exist. Because such episodes of mass delusion tend to be relatively short-lived even when they do achieve broad currency, one might simply be tempted to wait this one out as well. But the stakes are far too high for that. Governments that buy into the flat world are likely to pay too much attention to the "golden straitjacket" that Friedman emphasized in his earlier book, *The Lexus and the Olive Tree,* which is supposed to ensure that economics matters more and more and politics less and less. Buying into this version of an integrated world—or worse, using it as a basis for policy-making—is not only unproductive. It is dangerous.

PANKAJ GHEMAWAT is the Anselmo Rubiralta professor of global strategy at IESE Business School and the Jaime and Josefina Chua Tiampo professor of business administration at Harvard Business School. His new book is *Redefining Global Strategy* (Boston: Harvard Business School Press, September 2007).

Can Extreme Poverty Be Eliminated?

**Market economics and globalization are lifting the bulk
of humanity out of extreme poverty, but special measures
are needed to help the poorest of the poor.**

Jeffrey D. Sachs

Almost everyone who ever lived was wretchedly poor. Famine, death from childbirth, infectious disease and countless other hazards were the norm for most of history. Humanity's sad plight started to change with the Industrial Revolution, beginning around 1750. New scientific insights and technological innovations enabled a growing proportion of the global population to break free of extreme poverty.

Two and a half centuries later more than five billion of the world's 6.5 billion people can reliably meet their basic living needs and thus can be said to have escaped from the precarious conditions that once governed everyday life. One out of six inhabitants of this planet, however, still struggles daily to meet some or all of such critical requirements as adequate nutrition, uncontaminated drinking water, safe shelter and sanitation as well as access to basic health care. These people get by on $1 a day or less and are overlooked by public services for health, education and infrastructure. Every day more than 20,000 die of dire poverty, for want of food, safe drinking water, medicine or other essential needs.

For the first time in history, global economic prosperity, brought on by continuing scientific and technological progress and the self-reinforcing accumulation of wealth, has placed the world within reach of eliminating extreme poverty altogether. This prospect will seem fanciful to some, but the dramatic economic progress made by China, India and other low-income parts of Asia over the past 25 years demonstrates that it is realistic. Moreover, the predicted stabilization of the world's population toward the middle of this century will help by easing pressures on Earth's climate, ecosystems and natural resources—pressures that might otherwise undo economic gains.

EXTREME POVERTY could become a thing of the past in a few decades if the affluent countries of the world pony up a small percentage of their wealth to help the planet's 1.1 billion indigent populations out of conditions of dire poverty.

Although economic growth has shown a remarkable capacity to lift vast numbers of people out of extreme poverty, progress is neither automatic nor inevitable. Market forces and free trade are not enough. Many of the poorest regions are ensnared in a poverty trap: they lack the financial means to make the necessary investments in infrastructure, education, health care systems and other vital needs. Yet the end of such poverty is feasible if a concerted global effort is undertaken, as the nations of the world promised when they adopted the Millennium Development Goals at the United Nations Millennium Summit in 2000. A dedicated cadre of development agencies, international financial institutions, nongovernmental organizations and communities throughout the developing world already constitute a global network of expertise and goodwill to help achieve this objective.

This past January my colleagues and I on the U.N. Millennium Project published a plan to halve the rate of extreme poverty by 2015 (compared with 1990) and to achieve other quantitative targets for reducing hunger, disease and environmental degradation. In my recent book, *The End of Poverty,* I argue that a large-scale and targeted public investment effort could in fact eliminate this problem by 2025, much as smallpox was eradicated globally. This hypothesis is controversial, so I am pleased to have the opportunity to clarify its main arguments and to respond to various concerns that have been raised about it.

Beyond Business as Usual

Economists have learned a great deal during the past few years about how countries develop and what roadblocks can stand in their way. A new kind of development economics needs to emerge, one that is better grounded in science—a "clinical economics" akin to modern medicine. Today's medical professionals understand that disease results from a vast array of interacting factors and conditions: pathogens, nutrition, environment, aging, individual and population genetics, and lifestyle. They also know that one key to proper treatment is the

Crossroads for Poverty

The Problem

- Much of humankind has succeeded in dragging itself out of severe poverty since the onset of the Industrial Revolution in the mid-18th century, but about 1.1 billion out of today's 6.5 billion global inhabitants are utterly destitute in a world of plenty.
- These unfortunates, who get by on less than $1 a day, have little access to adequate nutrition, safe drinking water and shelter, as well as basic sanitation and health care services. What can the developed world do to lift this huge segment of the human population out of extreme poverty?

The Plan

- Doubling affluent nations' international poverty assistance to about $160 billion a year would go a long way toward ameliorating the terrible predicament faced by one in six humans. This figure would constitute about 0.5 percent of the gross national product (GNP) of the planet's rich countries. Because these investments do not include other categories of aid, such as spending on major infrastructure projects, climate change mitigation or post conflict reconstruction, donors should commit to reaching the long stand target of 0.7 percent of GNP by 2015.
- These donations, often provided to local groups, would need to be closely monitored and audited to ensure that they are correctly targeted toward those truly in need.

ability to make an individualized diagnosis of the source of illness. Likewise, development economists need better diagnostic skills to recognize that economic pathologies have a wide variety of causes, including many outside the traditional ken of economic practice.

Public opinion in affluent countries often attributes extreme poverty to faults with the poor themselves—or at least with their governments. Race was once thought the deciding factor. Then it was culture: religious divisions and taboos, caste systems, a lack of entrepreneurship, gender inequities. Such theories have waned as societies of an ever widening range of religions and cultures have achieved relative prosperity. Moreover, certain supposedly immutable aspects of culture (such as fertility choices and gender and caste roles) in fact change, often dramatically, as societies become urban and develop economically.

Most recently, commentators have zeroed in on "poor governance," often code words for corruption. They argue that extreme poverty persists because governments fail to open up their markets, provide public services and clamp down on bribe taking. It is said that if these regimes cleaned up their acts, they, too, would flourish. Development assistance efforts have become largely a series of good governance lectures.

The availability of cross-country and time-series data now allows experts to make much more systematic analyses. Although debate continues, the weight of the evidence indicates that governance makes a difference but is not the sole determinant of economic growth. According to surveys conducted by Transparency International, business leaders actually perceive many fast-growing Asian countries to be more corrupt than some slow-growing African ones.

Geography—including natural resources, climate, topography, and proximity to trade routes and major markets—is at least as important as good governance. As early as 1776, Adam Smith argued that high transport costs inhibited development in the inland areas of Africa and Asia. Other geographic features, such as the heavy disease burden of the tropics, also interfere. One recent study by my Columbia University colleague Xavier Sala-i-Martin demonstrated once again that tropical countries saddled with malaria have experienced slower growth than those free from the disease. The good news is that geographic factors shape, but do not decide, a country's economic fate. Technology can offset them: drought can be fought with irrigation systems, isolation with roads and mobile telephones, diseases with preventive and therapeutic measures.

The other major insight is that although the most powerful mechanism for reducing extreme poverty is to encourage overall economic growth, a rising tide does not necessarily lift all boats. Average income can rise, but if the income is distributed unevenly the poor may benefit little, and pockets of extreme poverty may persist (especially in geographically disadvantaged regions). Moreover, growth is not simply a free-market phenomenon. It requires basic government services: infrastructure, health, education, and scientific and technological innovation. Thus, many of the recommendations of the past two decades emanating from Washington—that governments in low-income countries should cut back on their spending to make room for the private sector—miss the point. Government spending, directed at investment in critical areas, is itself a vital spur to growth, especially if its effects are to reach the poorest of the poor.

The Poverty Trap

So what do these insights tell us about the region most afflicted by poverty today, Africa? Fifty years ago tropical Africa was roughly as rich as subtropical and tropical Asia. As Asia boomed, Africa stagnated. Special geographic factors have played a crucial role.

Foremost among these is the existence of the Himalaya Mountains, which produce southern Asia's monsoon climate and vast river systems. Well-watered farmlands served as the starting points for Asia's rapid escape from extreme poverty during the past five decades. The Green Revolution of the 1960s and 1970s introduced high-yield grains, irrigation and fertilizers, which ended the cycle of famine, disease and despair.

It also freed a significant proportion of the labor force to seek manufacturing jobs in the cities. Urbanization, in turn, spurred growth, not only by providing a home for industry and innovation but also by prompting greater investment in a healthy and skilled labor force. Urban residents cut their fertility rates and

Globalization, Poverty and Foreign Aid

Average citizens in affluent nations often have many questions about the effects of economic globalization on rich and poor nations and about how developing countries spend the aid they receive. Here are a few brief answers:

Is Globalization Making the Rich Richer and the Poor Poorer?

Generally, the answer is no. Economic globalization is supporting very rapid advances of many impoverished economies, notably in Asia. International trade and foreign investment inflows have been major factors in China's remarkable economic growth during the past quarter century and in India's fast economic growth since the early 1990s. The poorest of the poor, notably in sub-Saharan Africa, are not held back by globalization; they are largely bypassed by it.

Is Poverty the Result of Exploitation of the Poor by the Rich?

Affluent nations have repeatedly plundered and exploited poor countries through slavery, colonial rule and unfair trade practices. Yet it is perhaps more accurate to say that exploitation is the result of poverty (which leaves impoverished countries vulnerable to abuse) rather than the cause of it. Poverty is generally the result of low productivity per worker, which reflects poor health, lack of job-market skills, patchiness of infrastructure (roads, power plants, utility lines, shipping ports), chronic malnutrition and the like. Exploitation has played a role in producing some of these conditions, but deeper factors [geographic isolation, endemic disease, ecological destruction, challenging conditions for food production] have tended to be more important and difficult to overcome without external help.

Will Higher Incomes in Poor Countries Mean Lower Incomes in Rich Countries?

By and large, economic development is a positive-sum process, meaning that all can partake in it without causing some to suffer. In the past 200 years, the world as a whole has achieved a massive increase in economic output rather than a shift in economic output to one region at the expense of another. To be sure, global environmental constraints are already starting to impose themselves. As today's poor countries develop, the climate, fisheries and forests are coming under increased strain. Overall global economic growth is compatible with sustainable management of the ecosystems on which all humans depend—indeed, wealth can be good for the environment—but only if public policy and technologies encourage sound practices and the necessary investments are made in environmental sustainability.

Do U.S. Private Contributions Make Up for the Low Levels of U.S. Official Aid?

Some have claimed that while the U.S. government budget provides relatively little assistance to the poorest countries, the private sector makes up the gap. In fact, the Organization for Economic Cooperation and Development has estimated that private foundations and nongovernmental organizations give roughly $6 billion a year in international assistance, or 0.05 percent of U.S. gross national product (GNP). In that case, total U.S. international aid is around 0.21 percent of GNP—still among the lowest ratios of all donor nations.

—J.D.S.

thus were able to spend more for the health, nutrition and education of each child. City kids went to school at a higher rate than their rural cousins. And with the emergence of urban infrastructure and public health systems, city populations became less disease-prone than their counterparts in the countryside, where people typically lack safe drinking water, modern sanitation, professional health care and protection from vector-borne ailments such as malaria.

Africa did not experience a green revolution. Tropical Africa lacks the massive floodplains that facilitate the large-scale and low-cost irrigation found in Asia. Also, its rainfall is highly variable, and impoverished farmers have been unable to purchase fertilizer. The initial Green Revolution research featured crops, especially paddy rice and wheat, not widely grown in Africa (high-yield varieties suitable for it have been developed in recent years, but they have not yet been disseminated sufficiently). The continent's food production per person has actually been falling, and Africans' caloric intake is the lowest in the world; food insecurity is rampant. Its labor force has remained tethered to subsistence agriculture.

Compounding its agricultural woes, Africa bears an overwhelming burden of tropical diseases. Because of climate and the endemic mosquito species, malaria is more intensively transmitted in Africa than anywhere else. And high transport costs isolate Africa economically. In East Africa, for example, the rainfall is greatest in the interior of the continent, so most people live there, far from ports and international trade routes.

Much the same situation applies to other impoverished parts of the world, notably the Andean and Central American highlands and the landlocked countries of Central Asia. Being economically isolated, they are unable to attract much foreign investment (other than for the extraction of oil, gas and precious minerals). Investors tend to be dissuaded by the high transport costs associated with the interior regions. Rural areas therefore remain stuck in a vicious cycle of poverty, hunger, illness and illiteracy. Impoverished areas lack adequate internal savings to make the needed investments because most households live hand to mouth. The few high-income families, who do accumulate savings, park them overseas rather than at home. This capital flight includes not only financial capital but also the human variety, in the form of skilled workers—doctors, nurses, scientists and engineers, who frequently leave in search of improved economic opportunities abroad. The poorest countries are often, perversely, net exporters of capital.

Put Money Where Mouths Are

The technology to overcome these handicaps and jump-start economic development exists. Malaria can be controlled using bed nets, indoor pesticide spraying and improved medicines. Drought-prone countries in Africa with nutrient depleted soils can benefit enormously from drip irrigation and greater use of fertilizers. Landlocked countries can be connected by paved highway networks, airports and fiber-optic cables. All these projects cost money, of course.

Many larger countries, such as China, have prosperous regions that can help support their own lagging areas. Coastal eastern China, for instance, is now financing massive public investments in western China. Most of today's successfully developing countries, especially smaller ones, received at least some backing from external donors at crucial times. The critical scientific innovations that formed the underpinnings of the Green Revolution were bankrolled by the Rockefeller Foundation, and the spread of these technologies in India and elsewhere in Asia was funded by the U.S. and other donor governments and international development institutions.

We in the U.N. Millennium Project have listed the investments required to help today's impoverished regions cover basic needs in health, education, water, sanitation, food production, roads and other key areas. We have put an approximate price tag on that assistance and estimated how much could be financed by poor households themselves and by domestic institutions. The remaining cost is the "financing gap" that international donors need to make up.

For tropical Africa, the total investment comes to $110 per person a year. To place this into context, the average income in this part of the world is $350 per annum, most or all of which is required just to stay alive. The full cost of the total investment is clearly beyond the funding reach of these countries. Of the $110, perhaps $40 could be financed domestically, so that $70 per capita would be required in the form of international aid.

Adding it all up, the total requirement for assistance across the globe is around $160 billion a year, double the current rich-country aid budget of $80 billion. This figure amounts to approximately 0.5 percent of the combined gross national product (GNP) of the affluent donor nations. It does not include other humanitarian projects such as postwar Iraqi reconstruction or Indian Ocean tsunami relief. To meet these needs as well, a reasonable figure would be 0.7 percent of GNP, which is what all donor countries have long promised but few have fulfilled. Other organizations, including the International Monetary Fund, the World Bank and the British government, have reached much the same conclusion.

When polled, Americans greatly overestimate how much foreign aid the U.S. gives—by as much as 30 times.

Foreign Aid: How Should the Money Be Spent?

Here is a breakdown of the needed investment for three typical low-income African countries to help them achieve the Millennium Development Goals. For all nations given aid, the average total annual assistance per person would come to around $110 a year. These investments would be financed by both foreign aid and the countries themselves.

Investment Area	Average per Year between 2005–2015 ($ per capita)		
	Ghana	Tanzania	Uganda
Hunger	7	8	6
Education	19	14	5
Gender equality	3	3	3
Health	25	35	34
Water supply and sanitation	8	7	5
Improving slum conditions	2	3	2
Energy	15	16	12
Roads	10	22	20
Other	10	10	10
Total	100	117	106

Calculated from data from Investing in Development [U.N. Millennium Project, Earth Scan Publications, 2005]. Numbers do not sum to totals because of rounding.

We believe these investments would enable the poorest countries to cut poverty by half by 2015 and, if continued, to eliminate it altogether by 2025. They would not be "welfare payments" from rich to poor but instead something far more important and durable. People living above mere subsistence levels would be able to save for their futures; they could join the virtuous cycle of rising incomes, savings and technological inflows. We would be giving a billion people a hand up instead of a handout.

If rich nations fail to make these investments, they will be called on to provide emergency assistance more or less indefinitely. They will face famine, epidemics, regional conflicts and the spread of terrorist havens. And they will condemn not only the impoverished countries but themselves as well to chronic political instability, humanitarian emergencies and security risks.

The debate is now shifting from the basic diagnosis of extreme poverty and the calculations of financing needs to the practical matter of how assistance can best be delivered. Many people believe that aid efforts failed in the past and that care is needed to avoid the repetition of failure. Some of these concerns are well grounded, but others are fueled by misunderstandings.

When pollsters ask Americans how much foreign aid they think the U.S. gives, they greatly overestimate the amount by as much as 30 times. Believing that so much money has been donated and so little has been done with it, the public concludes that these programs have "failed." The reality is rather different.

U.S. official assistance to sub-Saharan Africa has been running at $2 billion to $4 billion a year, or roughly $3 to $6 for every African. Most of this aid has come in the form of "technical cooperation" (which goes into the pockets of consultants), food contributions for famine victims and the cancellation of unpaid debts. Little of this support has come in a form that can be invested in systems that improve health, nutrition, food production and transport. We should give foreign aid a fair chance before deciding whether it works or not.

A second common misunderstanding concerns the extent to which corruption is likely to eat up the donated money. Some foreign aid in the past has indeed ended up in the equivalent of Swiss bank accounts. That happened when the funds were provided for geopolitical reasons rather than development; a good example was U.S. support for the corrupt regime of Mobutu Sese Seko of Zaire (now the Democratic Republic of the Congo) during part of the cold war. When assistance has been targeted at development rather than political goals, the outcomes have been favorable, ranging from the Green Revolution to the eradication of smallpox and the recent near-eradication of polio.

The aid package we advocate would be directed toward those countries with a reasonable degree of good governance and operational transparency. In Africa, these countries include Ethiopia, Ghana, Mali, Mozambique, Senegal and Tanzania. The money would not be merely thrown at them. It would be provided according to a detailed and monitored plan, and new rounds of financing would be delivered only as the work actually got done. Much of the funds would be given directly to villages and towns to minimize the chances of their getting diverted by central governments. All these programs should be closely audited.

Western society tends to think of foreign aid as money lost. But if supplied properly, it is an investment that will one day yield huge returns, much as U.S. assistance to Western Europe and East Asia after World War II did. By prospering, today's impoverished countries will wean themselves from endless charity. They will contribute to the international advance of science, technology and trade. They will escape political instability, which leaves many of them vulnerable to violence, narcotics trafficking, civil war and even terrorist takeover. Our own security will be bolstered as well. As U.N. Secretary-General Kofi Annan wrote earlier this year: "There will be no development without security, and no security without development."

The author, **JEFFREY D. SACHS,** directs the Earth Institute at Columbia University and the United Nations Millennium Project. An economist, Sachs is well known for advising governments in Latin America, Eastern Europe, the former Soviet Union, Asia and Africa on economic reforms and for his work with international agencies to promote poverty reduction, disease control and debt reduction in poor countries. A native of Detroit, he received his BA, MA and PhD degrees from Harvard University.

The Ideology of Development

WILLIAM EASTERLY

A dark ideological specter is haunting the world. It is almost as deadly as the tired ideologies of the last century—communism, fascism, and socialism—that failed so miserably. It feeds some of the most dangerous trends of our time, including religious fundamentalism. It is the half-century-old ideology of Developmentalism. And it is thriving.

Like all ideologies, Development promises a comprehensive final answer to all of society's problems, from poverty and illiteracy to violence and despotic rulers. It shares the common ideological characteristic of suggesting there is only one correct answer, and it tolerates little dissent. It deduces this unique answer for everyone from a general theory that purports to apply to everyone, everywhere. There's no need to involve local actors who reap its costs and benefits. Development even has its own intelligentsia, made up of experts at the International Monetary Fund (IMF), World Bank, and United Nations.

The power of Developmentalism is disheartening, because the failure of all the previous ideologies might have laid the groundwork for the opposite of ideology—the freedom of individuals and societies to choose their destinies. Yet, since the fall of communism, the West has managed to snatch defeat from the jaws of victory, and with disastrous results. Development ideology is sparking a dangerous counterreaction. The "one correct answer" came to mean "free markets," and, for the poor world, it was defined as doing whatever the IMF and the World Bank tell you to do. But the reaction in Africa, Central Asia, Latin America, the Middle East, and Russia has been to fight against free markets. So, one of the best economic ideas of our time, the genius of free markets, was presented in one of the worst possible ways, with unelected outsiders imposing rigid doctrines on the xenophobic unwilling.

The backlash has been so severe that other failed ideologies are gaining new adherents throughout these regions. In Nicaragua, for instance, IMF and World Bank structural adjustments failed so conspicuously that the pitiful Sandinista regime of the 1980s now looks good by comparison. Its leader, Daniel Ortega, is back in power. The IMF's actions during the Argentine financial crisis of 2001 now reverberate a half decade later with Hugo Chavez, Venezuela's illiberal leader, being welcomed with open arms in Buenos Aires. The heavy-handed directives of the World Bank and IMF in Bolivia provided the soil from which that country's neosocialist president, Evo Morales, sprung. The disappointing payoff following eight structural adjustment loans to Zimbabwe and $8 billion in foreign aid during the 1980s and 1990s helped Robert Mugabe launch a vicious counterattack on democracy. The IMF-World Bank—Jeffrey Sachs application of "shock therapy" to the former Soviet Union has created a lasting nostalgia for communism. In the Middle East, $154 billion in foreign aid between 1980 and 2001, 45 structural adjustment loans, and "expert" advice produced zero per capita GDP growth that helped create a breeding ground for Islamic fundamentalism.

This blowback against "globalization from above" has spread to every corner of the Earth. It now threatens to kill sensible, moderate steps toward the freer movement of goods, ideas, capital, and people.

Development's Politburo

The ideology of Development is not only about having experts design your free market for you; it is about having the experts design a comprehensive, technical plan to solve all the problems of the poor. These experts see poverty as a purely technological problem, to be solved by engineering and the natural sciences, ignoring messy social sciences such as economics, politics, and sociology.

Sachs, Columbia University's celebrity economist, is one of its main proprietors. He is now recycling his theories of overnight shock therapy, which failed so miserably in Russia, into promises of overnight global poverty reduction. "Africa's problems," he has said, "are . . . solvable with practical and proven technologies." His own plan features hundreds of expert interventions to solve every last problem of the poor—from green manure, breast-feeding education, and bicycles to solar-energy systems, school uniforms for AIDS orphans, and windmills. Not to mention such critical interventions as "counseling and information services for men to address their reproductive health needs." All this will be done, Sachs says, by "a united and effective United Nations country team, which coordinates in one place the work of the U.N. specialized agencies, the IMF, and the World Bank."

So the admirable concern of rich countries for the tragedies of world poverty is thus channeled into fattening the international aid bureaucracy, the self-appointed priesthood of Development. Like other ideologies, this thinking favors collective goals such as national poverty reduction, national economic growth, and the global Millennium Development Goals, over the aspirations of individuals. Bureaucrats who write poverty-reduction frameworks outrank individuals who actually reduce poverty by, say, starting a business. Just as Marxists favored world revolution and socialist internationalism, Development stresses world goals over the autonomy of societies to choose their own path. It favors doctrinaire abstractions such as "market-friendly policies," "good investment climate," and "pro-poor globalization" over the freedom of individuals.

Development also shares another Marxist trait: It aspires to be scientific. Finding the one correct solution to poverty is seen as a scientific problem to be solved by the experts. They are always sure they know the answer, vehemently reject disagreement, and then later change their answers. In psychiatry, this is known as Borderline Personality Disorder. For the Development Experts, it's a way of life. The answer at first was aid-financed investment and industrialization in poor countries, then it was market-oriented government policy reform, then it was fixing institutional problems such as corruption, then it was globalization, then it was the Poverty Reduction Strategy to achieve the Millennium Development Goals.

One reason the answers keep changing is because, in reality, high-growth countries follow a bewildering variety of paths to development, and the countries with high growth rates are constantly changing from decade to decade. Who could be more different than successful developers such as China and Chile, Botswana and Singapore, Taiwan and Turkey, or Hong Kong and Vietnam? What about the many countries who tried to emulate these rising stars and failed? What about the former stars who have fallen on hard times, like the Ivory Coast, which was one of the fastest developers of the 1960s and 1970s, only to become mired in a civil war? What about Mexico, which saw rapid growth until 1980 and has had slow growth ever since, despite embracing the experts' reforms?

The experts in Developmentalism's Politburo don't bother themselves with such questions. All the previous answers were right; they were just missing one more "necessary condition" that the experts have only just now added to the list. Like all ideologies, Development is at the same time too rigid to predict what will work in the messy real world and yet flexible enough to forever escape falsification by real-world events. The high church of Development, the World Bank, has guaranteed it can never be wrong by making statements such as, "different policies can yield the same result, and the same policy can yield different results, depending on country institutional contexts and underlying growth strategies." Of course, you still need experts to figure out the contexts and strategies.

Resistance is Futile

Perhaps more hypocritical yet is Development's simple theory of historical inevitability. Poor societies are not just poor, the experts tell us, they are "developing" until they reach the final stage of history, or "development," in which poverty will soon end. Under this historiography, an end to starvation, tyranny, and war are thrown in like a free toaster on an infomercial. The experts judge all societies on a straight line, per capita income,

with the superior countries showing the inferior countries the image of their own future. And the experts heap scorn on those who resist the inevitabilities on the path to development.

One of today's leading Developmentalists, *New York Times* columnist Thomas Friedman, can hardly conceal his mockery of those who resist the march of history, or "the flattening of the world." "When you are Mexico," Friedman has written, "and your claim to fame is that you are a low-wage manufacturing country, and some of your people are importing statuettes of your own patron saint from China, because China can make them and ship them all the way across the Pacific more cheaply than you can produce them . . . you have got a problem. [T]he only way for Mexico to thrive is with a strategy of reform . . . the more Mexico just sits there, the more it is going to get run over." Friedman seems blissfully unaware that poor Mexico, so far from God yet so close to American pundits, has already tried much harder than China to implement the experts' "strategy of reform."

The self-confidence of Developmentalists like Friedman is so strong that they impose themselves even on those who accept their strategies. This year, for instance, Ghana celebrated its 50th anniversary as the first black African nation to gain independence. Official international aid donors to Ghana told its allegedly independent government, in the words of the World Bank: "We Partners are here giving you our pledge to give our best to make lives easier for you in running your country." Among the things they will do to make your life easier is to run your country for you.

Unfortunately, Development ideology has a dismal record of helping any country actually develop. The regions where the ideology has been most influential, Latin America and Africa, have done the worst. Luckless Latins and Africans are left chasing yesterday's formulas for success while those who ignored the Developmentalists found homegrown paths to success. The nations that have been the most successful in the past 40 years did so in such a variety of different ways that it would be hard to argue that they discovered the "correct answer" from development ideology. In fact, they often conspicuously violated whatever it was the experts said at the time. The East Asian tigers, for instance, chose outward orientation on their own in the 1960s, when the experts' conventional wisdom was industrialization for the home market. The rapid growth of China over the past quarter century came when it was hardly a poster child for either the 1980s Washington Consensus or the 1990s institutionalism of democracy and cracking down on corruption.

What explains the appeal of development ideology despite its dismal track record? Ideologies usually arise in response to tragic situations in which people are hungry for clear and comprehensive solutions. The inequality of the Industrial Revolution bred Marxism, and the backwardness of Russia its Leninist offshoot. Germany's defeat and demoralization in World War I birthed Nazism. Economic hardship accompanied by threats to identity led to both Christian and Islamic fundamentalism. Similarly, development ideology appeals to those who want a definitive, complete answer to the tragedy of world poverty and inequality. It answers the question, "What is to be done?" to borrow the title of Lenin's 1902 tract. It stresses collective social outcomes that must be remedied by collective, top-down action by the intelligentsia, the revolutionary vanguard, the development expert. As Sachs explains, "I have . . . gradually come to understand through my scientific research and on the ground advisory work the awesome power in our generation's hands to end the massive suffering of the extreme poor . . . although introductory economics textbooks preach individualism and decentralized markets, our safety and prosperity depend at least as much on collective decisions."

Freeing the Poor

Few realize that Americans in 1776 had the same income level as the average African today. Yet, like all the present-day developed nations, the United States was lucky enough to escape poverty before there were Developmentalists. In the words of former IMF First Deputy Managing Director Anne Krueger, development in the rich nations "just happened." George Washington did not have to deal with aid partners, getting structurally adjusted by them, or preparing poverty-reduction strategy papers for them. Abraham Lincoln did not celebrate a government of the donors, by the donors, and for the donors. Today's developed nations were free to experiment with their own pragmatic paths toward more government accountability and freer markets. Individualism and decentralized markets were good enough to give rise to penicillin, air conditioning, high-yield corn, and the automobile—not to mention better living standards, lower mortality, and the iPod.

The opposite of ideology is freedom, the ability of societies to be unchained from foreign control. The only "answer" to poverty reduction is freedom from being told the answer. Free societies and individuals are not guaranteed to succeed. They will make bad choices. But at least they bear the cost of those mistakes, and learn from them. That stands in stark contrast to accountability-free Developmentalism. This process of learning from mistakes is what produced the repositories of common sense that make up mainstream economics. The opposite of Development ideology is not anything goes, but the pragmatic use of time-tested economic ideas—the benefits of specialization, comparative advantage, gains from trade, market-clearing prices, trade-offs, budget constraints—by individuals, firms, governments, and societies as they find their own success.

History proves just how much good can come from individuals who both bear the costs and reap the benefits of their own choices when they are free to make them. That includes local politicians, activists, and businesspeople who are groping their way toward greater freedom, contrary to the Developmentalists who oxymoronically impose freedom of choice on other people. Those who best understood the lessons of the 20th century were not the ideologues asking, "What is to be done?" They were those asking, "How can people be more free to find their own solutions?"

The ideology of Development should be packed up in crates and sent off to the Museum of Dead Ideologies, just down the hall from Communism, Socialism, and Fascism. It's time to recognize that the attempt to impose a rigid development ideology on the world's poor has failed miserably. Fortunately, many poor societies are forging their own path toward greater freedom and prosperity anyway. That is how true revolutions happen.

WILLIAM EASTERLY is professor of economics at New York University.

Reprinted in entirety by McGraw-Hill with permission from *FOREIGN POLICY,* July/August 2007. www.foreignpolicy.com. © 2007 Washingtonpost.Newsweek Interactive, LLC.

Article 23

The Quiet Coup

The crash has laid bare many unpleasant truths about the United States. One of the most alarming; says a former chief economist of the International Monetary Fund, is that the finance industry has effectively captured our government—a state of affairs that more typically describes emerging markets, and is at the center of many emerging-market crises. If the IMF's staff could speak freely about the U.S., it would tell us what it tells all countries in this situation: Recovery will fail unless we break the financial oligarchy that is blocking essential reform. And if we are to prevent a true depression, we're running out of time.

SIMON JOHNSON

One thing you learn rather quickly when working at the International Monetary Fund is that no one is ever very happy to see you. Typically, your "clients" come in only after private capital has abandoned them, after regional trading-bloc partners have been unable to throw a strong enough lifeline, after last-ditch attempts to borrow from powerful friends like China or the European Union have fallen through. You're never at the top of anyone's dance card.

The reason, of course, is that the IMF specializes in telling its clients what they don't want to hear. I should know; I pressed painful changes on many foreign officials during my time there as chief economist in 2007 and 2008. And I felt the effects of IMF pressure, at least indirectly, when I worked with governments in Eastern Europe as they struggled after 1989, and with the private sector in Asia and Latin America during the crises of the late 1990s and early 2000s. Over that time, from every vantage point, I saw firsthand the steady flow of officials—from Ukraine, Russia, Thailand, Indonesia, South Korea, and elsewhere—trudging to the fund when circumstances were dire and all else had failed.

Every crisis is different, of course. Ukraine faced hyperinflation in 1994; Russia desperately needed help when its short-term-debt rollover scheme exploded in the summer of 1998; the Indonesian rupiah plunged in 1997, nearly leveling the corporate economy; that same year, South Korea's 30-year economic miracle ground to a halt when foreign banks suddenly refused to extend new credit.

But I must tell you, to IMF officials, all of these crises looked depressingly similar. Each country, of course, needed a loan, but more than that, each needed to make big changes so that the loan could really work. Almost always, countries in crisis need to learn to live within their means after a period of excess—exports must be increased, and imports cut—and

the goal is to do this without the most horrible of recessions. Naturally, the fund's economists spend time figuring out the policies—budget, money supply, and the like—that make sense in this context. Yet the economic solution is seldom very hard to work out.

No, the real concern of the fund's senior staff, and the biggest obstacle to recovery, is almost invariably the politics of countries in crisis.

Typically, these countries are in a desperate economic situation for one simple reason—the powerful elites within them overreached in good times and took too many risks. Emerging-market governments and their private-sector allies commonly form a tight-knit—and, most of the time, genteel—oligarchy, running the country rather like a profit-seeking company in which they are the controlling shareholders. When a country like Indonesia or South Korea or Russia grows, so do the ambitions of its captains of industry. As masters of their mini-universe, these people make some investments that clearly benefit the broader economy, but they also start making bigger and riskier bets. They reckon—correctly, in most cases—that their political connections will allow them to push onto the government any substantial problems that arise.

In Russia, for instance, the private sector is now in serious trouble because, over the past five years or so, it borrowed at least $490 billion from global banks and investors on the assumption that the country's energy sector could support a permanent increase in consumption throughout the economy. As Russia's oligarchs spent this capital, acquiring other companies and embarking on ambitious investment plans that generated jobs, their importance to the political elite increased. Growing political support meant better access to lucrative contracts, tax breaks, and subsidies. And foreign investors could not have been more pleased; all other things

98

being equal, they prefer to lend money to people who have the implicit backing of their national governments, even if that backing gives off the faint whiff of corruption.

But inevitably, emerging-market oligarchs get carried away; they waste money and build massive business empires on a mountain of debt. Local banks, sometimes pressured by the government, become too willing to extend credit to the elite and to those who depend on them. Overborrowing always ends badly, whether for an individual, a company, or a country. Sooner or later, credit conditions become tighter and no one will lend you money on anything close to affordable terms.

The downward spiral that follows is remarkably steep. Enormous companies teeter on the brink of default, and the local banks that have lent to them collapse. Yesterday's "public-private partnerships" are relabeled "crony capitalism." With credit unavailable, economic paralysis ensues, and conditions just get worse and worse. The government is forced to draw down its foreign-currency reserves to pay for imports, service debt, and cover private losses. But these reserves will eventually run out. If the country cannot right itself before that happens, it will default on its sovereign debt and become an economic pariah. The government, in its race to stop the bleeding, will typically need to wipe out some of the national champions—now hemorrhaging cash—and usually restructure a banking system that's gone badly out of balance. It will, in other words, need to squeeze at least some of its oligarchs.

Squeezing the oligarchs, though, is seldom the strategy of choice among emerging-market governments. Quite the contrary: at the outset of the crisis, the oligarchs are usually among the first to get extra help from the government, such as preferential access to foreign currency, or maybe a nice tax break, or—here's a classic Kremlin bailout technique—the assumption of private debt obligations by the government. Under duress, generosity toward old friends takes many innovative forms. Meanwhile, needing to squeeze *someone,* most emerging-market governments look first to ordinary working folk—at least until the riots grow too large.

Treasury and the Fed just worked out a transaction and claimed it was the best that could be done. This was late-night, backroom dealing, pure and simple.

Eventually, as the oligarchs in Putin's Russia now realize, some within the elite have to lose out before recovery can begin. It's a game of musical chairs: there just aren't enough currency reserves to take care of everyone, and the government cannot afford to take over private-sector debt completely.

So the IMF staff looks into the eyes of the minister of finance and decides whether the government is serious yet. The fund will give even a country like Russia a loan eventually, but first it wants to make sure Prime Minister Putin is ready, willing, and able to be tough on some of his friends. If he is not ready to throw former pals to the wolves, the fund can wait. And when he is ready, the fund is happy to make helpful suggestions—particularly with regard to wresting control of the banking system from the hands of the most incompetent and avaricious "entrepreneurs."

Of course, Putin's ex-friends will fight back. They'll mobilize allies, work the system, and put pressure on other parts of the government to get additional subsidies. In extreme cases, they'll even try subversion—including calling up their contacts in the American foreign-policy establishment, as the Ukrainians did with some success in the late 1990s.

Many IMF programs "go off track" (a euphemism) precisely because the government can't stay tough on erstwhile cronies, and the consequences are massive inflation or other disasters. A program "goes back on track" once the government prevails or powerful oligarchs sort out among themselves who will govern—and thus win or lose—under the IMF-supported plan. The real fight in Thailand and Indonesia in 1997 was about which powerful families would lose their banks. In Thailand, it was handled relatively smoothly. In Indonesia, it led to the fall of President Suharto and economic chaos.

From long years of experience, the IMF staff knows its program will succeed—stabilizing the economy and enabling growth—only if at least some of the powerful oligarchs who did so much to create the underlying problems take a hit. This is the problem of all emerging markets.

Becoming a Banana Republic

In its depth and suddenness, the U.S. economic and financial crisis is shockingly reminiscent of moments we have recently seen in emerging markets (and only in emerging markets): South Korea (1997), Malaysia (1998), Russia and Argentina (time and again). In each of those cases, global investors, afraid that the country or its financial sector wouldn't be able to pay off mountainous debt, suddenly stopped lending. And in each case, that fear became self-fulfilling, as banks that couldn't roll over their debt did, in fact, become unable to pay. This is precisely what drove Lehman Brothers into bankruptcy on September 15, causing all sources of funding to the U.S. financial sector to dry up overnight. Just as in emerging-market crises, the weakness in the banking system has quickly rippled out into the rest of the economy, causing a severe economic contraction and hardship for millions of people.

But there's a deeper and more disturbing similarity: elite business interests—financiers, in the case of the U.S.—played a central role in creating the crisis, making ever-larger gambles, with the implicit backing of the government, until the inevitable collapse. More alarming, they are now using their influence to prevent precisely the sorts of reforms that are needed, and fast, to pull the economy out of its nosedive. The government seems helpless, or unwilling, to act against them.

Top investment bankers and government officials like to lay the blame for the current crisis on the lowering of U.S. interest rates after the dotcom bust or, even better—in a "buck stops somewhere else" sort of way—on the flow of savings out of China. Some on the right like to complain about Fannie Mae or Freddie Mac, or even about longer-standing efforts to promote broader homeownership. And, of course, it is axiomatic to everyone that the regulators responsible for "safety and soundness" were fast asleep at the wheel.

But these various policies—lightweight regulation, cheap money, the unwritten Chinese-American economic alliance, the promotion of homeownership—had something in common. Even though some are traditionally associated with Democrats and some with Republicans, they *all* benefited the financial sector. Policy changes that might have forestalled the crisis but would have limited the financial sector's profits— such as Brooksley Born's now-famous attempts to regulate credit-default swaps at the Commodity Futures Trading Commission, in 1998—were ignored or swept aside.

The financial industry has not always enjoyed such favored treatment. But for the past 25 years or so, finance has boomed, becoming ever more powerful. The boom began with the Reagan years, and it only gained strength with the deregulatory policies of the Clinton and George W. Bush administrations. Several other factors helped fuel the financial industry's ascent. Paul Volcker's monetary policy in the 1980s, and the increased volatility in interest rates that accompanied it, made bond trading much more lucrative. The invention of securitization, interest-rate swaps, and credit-default swaps greatly increased the volume of transactions that bankers could make money on. And an aging and increasingly wealthy population invested more and more money in securities, helped by the invention of the IRA and the 401(k) plan. Together, these developments vastly increased the profit opportunities in financial services.

Not surprisingly, Wall Street ran with these opportunities. From 1973 to 1985, the financial sector never earned more than 16 percent of domestic corporate profits. In 1986, that figure reached 19 percent. In the 1990s, it oscillated between 21 percent and 30 percent, higher than it had ever been in the postwar period. This decade, it reached 41 percent. Pay rose just as dramatically. From 1948 to 1982, average compensation in the financial sector ranged between 99 percent and 108 percent of the average for all domestic private industries. From 1983, it shot upward, reaching 181 percent in 2007.

The great wealth that the financial sector created and concentrated gave bankers enormous political weight—a weight not seen in the U.S. since the era of J.P. Morgan (the man). In that period, the banking panic of 1907 could be stopped only by coordination among private-sector bankers: no government entity was able to offer an effective

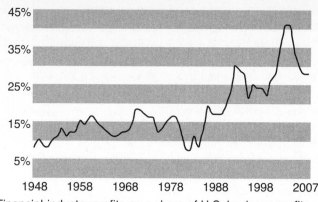

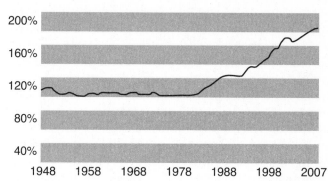
Financial-industry profits as a share of U.S. business profits.

Pay per worker in the financial sector as a percentage of average U.S. compensation.

response. But that first age of banking oligarchs came to an end with the passage of significant banking regulation in response to the Great Depression; the reemergence of an American financial oligarchy is quite recent.

The Wall Street—Washington Corridor

Of course, the U.S. is unique. And just as we have the world's most advanced economy, military, and technology, we also have its most advanced oligarchy.

In a primitive political system, power is transmitted through violence, or the threat of violence: military coups, private militias, and so on. In a less primitive system more typical of emerging markets, power is transmitted via money: bribes, kickbacks, and offshore bank accounts. Although lobbying and campaign contributions certainly play major roles in the American political system, old-fashioned corruption— envelopes stuffed with $100 bills—is probably a sideshow today, Jack Abramoff notwithstanding.

Instead, the American financial industry gained political power by amassing a kind of cultural capital—a belief system. Once, perhaps, what was good for General Motors was good for the country. Over the past decade, the attitude took hold that what was good for Wall Street was good for the country. The banking-and-securities industry has become one of the top contributors to political campaigns, but at the peak of its influence, it did not have to buy favors the way, for example, the tobacco companies or military contractors might have to. Instead, it benefited from the fact that Washington insiders already believed that large financial institutions and free-flowing capital markets were crucial to America's position in the world.

One channel of influence was, of course, the flow of individuals between Wall Street and Washington. Robert Rubin, once the co-chairman of Goldman Sachs, served in Washington as Treasury secretary under Clinton, and later became chairman of Citigroup's executive committee. Henry Paulson, CEO of Goldman Sachs during the long boom, became Treasury secretary under George W. Bush. John Snow, Paulson's predecessor, left to become chairman of Cerberus Capital Management, a large private-equity firm that also counts Dan Quayle among its executives. Alan Greenspan, after leaving the Federal Reserve, became a consultant to Pimco, perhaps the biggest player in international bond markets.

These personal connections were multiplied many times over at the lower levels of the past three presidential administrations, strengthening the ties between Washington and Wall Street. It has become something of a tradition for Goldman Sachs employees to go into public service after they leave the firm. The flow of Goldman alumni—including Jon Corzine, now the governor of New Jersey, along with Rubin and Paulson—not only placed people with Wall Street's worldview in the halls of power; it also helped create an image of Goldman (inside the Beltway, at least) as an institution that was itself almost a form of public service.

Wall Street is a very seductive place, imbued with an air of power. Its executives truly believe that they control the levers that make the world go round. A civil servant from Washington invited into their conference rooms, even if just for a meeting, could be forgiven for falling under their sway. Throughout my time at the IMF, I was struck by the easy access of leading financiers to the highest U.S. government officials, and the interweaving of the two career tracks. I vividly remember a meeting in early 2008—attended by top policy makers from a handful of rich countries—at which the chair casually proclaimed, to the room's general approval, that the best preparation for becoming a central-bank governor was to work first as an investment banker.

A whole generation of policy makers has been mesmerized by Wall Street, always and utterly convinced that whatever the banks said was true. Alan Greenspan's pronouncements in favor of unregulated financial markets are well known. Yet Greenspan was hardly alone. This is what Ben Bernanke, the man who succeeded him, said in 2006: "The management of market risk and credit risk has become increasingly sophisticated . . . Banking organizations of all sizes have made substantial strides over the past two decades in their ability to measure and manage risks."

Of course, this was mostly an illusion. Regulators, legislators, and academics almost all assumed that the managers of these banks knew what they were doing. In retrospect, they didn't. AIG's Financial Products division, for instance, made $2.5 billion in pretax profits in 2005, largely by selling underpriced insurance on complex, poorly understood securities. Often described as "picking up nickels in front of a steamroller," this strategy is profitable in ordinary years, and catastrophic in bad ones. As of last fall, AIG had outstanding insurance on more than $400 billion in securities. To date, the U.S. government, in an effort to rescue the company, has committed about $180 billion in investments and loans to cover losses that AIG's sophisticated risk modeling had said were virtually impossible.

Wall Street's seductive power extended even (or especially) to finance and economics professors, historically confined to the cramped offices of universities and the pursuit of Nobel Prizes. As mathematical finance became more and more essential to practical finance, professors increasingly took positions as consultants or partners at financial institutions. Myron Scholes and Robert Merton, Nobel laureates both, were perhaps the most famous; they took board seats at the hedge fund Long-Term Capital Management in 1994, before the fund famously flamed out at the end of the decade. But many others beat similar paths. This migration gave the stamp of academic legitimacy (and the intimidating aura of intellectual rigor) to the burgeoning world of high finance.

As more and more of the rich made their money in finance, the cult of finance seeped into the culture at large. Works like *Barbarians at the Gate, Wall Street,* and *Bonfire of the Vanities*—all intended as cautionary tales—served only to increase Wall Street's mystique. Michael Lewis noted in *Portfolio* last year that when he wrote *Liar's Poker,* an insider's account of the financial industry, in 1989, he had hoped the book might provoke outrage at Wall Street's hubris and excess. Instead, he found himself "knee-deep in letters from students at Ohio State who wanted to know if I had any other secrets to share . . . They'd read my book as a how-to manual." Even Wall Street's criminals, like Michael Milken and Ivan Boesky, became larger than life. In a society that celebrates the idea of making money, it was easy to infer that the interests of the financial sector were the same as the interests of the country—and that the winners in the financial sector knew better what was good for America than did the career civil servants in Washington. Faith in free financial markets grew into conventional wisdom—trumpeted on the editorial pages of *The Wall Street Journal* and on the floor of Congress.

From this confluence of campaign finance, personal connections, and ideology there flowed, in just the past decade, a river of deregulatory policies that is, in hindsight, astonishing:

- insistence on free movement of capital across borders;
- the repeal of Depression-era regulations separating commercial and investment banking;

- a congressional ban on the regulation of credit-default swaps;
- major increases in the amount of leverage allowed to investment banks;
- a light (dare I say *invisible?*) hand at the Securities and Exchange Commission in its regulatory enforcement;
- an international agreement to allow banks to measure their own riskiness;
- and an intentional failure to update regulations so as to keep up with the tremendous pace of financial innovation.

The mood that accompanied these measures in Washington seemed to swing between nonchalance and outright celebration: finance unleashed, it was thought, would continue to propel the economy to greater heights.

America's Oligarchs and the Financial Crisis

The oligarchy and the government policies that aided it did not alone cause the financial crisis that exploded last year. Many other factors contributed, including excessive borrowing by households and lax lending standards out on the fringes of the financial world. But major commercial and investment banks—and the hedge funds that ran alongside them—were the big beneficiaries of the twin housing and equity-market bubbles of this decade, their profits fed by an ever-increasing volume of transactions founded on a relatively small base of actual physical assets. Each time a loan was sold, packaged, securitized, and resold, banks took their transaction fees, and the hedge funds buying those securities reaped ever-larger fees as their holdings grew.

Because everyone was getting richer, and the health of the national economy depended so heavily on growth in real estate and finance, no one in Washington had any incentive to question what was going on. Instead, Fed Chairman Greenspan and President Bush insisted metronomically that the economy was fundamentally sound and that the tremendous growth in complex securities and credit-default swaps was evidence of a healthy economy where risk was distributed safely.

In the summer of 2007, signs of strain started appearing. The boom had produced so much debt that even a small economic stumble could cause major problems, and rising delinquencies in subprime mortgages proved the stumbling block. Ever since, the financial sector and the federal government have been behaving exactly the way one would expect them to, in light of past emerging-market crises.

By now, the princes of the financial world have of course been stripped naked as leaders and strategists—at least in the eyes of most Americans. But as the months have rolled by, financial elites have continued to assume that their position as the economy's favored children is safe, despite the wreckage they have caused.

Stanley O'Neal, the CEO of Merrill Lynch, pushed his firm heavily into the mortgage-backed-securities market at its peak in 2005 and 2006; in October 2007, he acknowledged, "The bottom line is, we—I—got it wrong by being overexposed to subprime, and we suffered as a result of impaired liquidity in that market. No one is more disappointed than I am in that result." O'Neal took home a $14 million bonus in 2006; in 2007, he walked away from Merrill with a severance package worth $162 million, although it is presumably worth much less today.

In October, John Thain, Merrill Lynch's final CEO, reportedly lobbied his board of directors for a bonus of $30 million or more, eventually reducing his demand to $10 million in December; he withdrew the request, under a firestorm of protest, only after it was leaked to *The Wall Street Journal.* Merrill Lynch as a whole was no better: it moved its bonus payments, $4 billion in total, forward to December, presumably to avoid the possibility that they would be reduced by Bank of America, which would own Merrill beginning on January 1. Wall Street paid out $18 billion in year-end bonuses last year to its New York City employees, after the government disbursed $243 billion in emergency assistance to the financial sector.

In a financial panic, the government must respond with both speed and overwhelming force. The root problem is uncertainty—in our case, uncertainty about whether the major banks have sufficient assets to cover their liabilities. Half measures combined with wishful thinking and a wait-and-see attitude cannot overcome this uncertainty. And the longer the response takes, the longer the uncertainty will stymie the flow of credit, sap consumer confidence, and cripple the economy—ultimately making the problem much harder to solve. Yet the principal characteristics of the government's response to the financial crisis have been delay, lack of transparency, and an unwillingness to upset the financial sector.

The response so far is perhaps best described as "policy by deal": when a major financial institution gets into trouble, the Treasury Department and the Federal Reserve engineer a bailout over the weekend and announce on Monday that everything is fine. In March 2008, Bear Stearns was sold to JPMorgan Chase in what looked to many like a gift to JPMorgan. (Jamie Dimon, JPMorgan's CEO, sits on the board of directors of the Federal Reserve Bank of New York, which, along with the Treasury Department, brokered the deal.) In September, we saw the sale of Merrill Lynch to Bank of America, the first bailout of AIG, and the takeover and immediate sale of Washington Mutual to JPMorgan— all of which were brokered by the government. In October, nine large banks were recapitalized on the same day behind closed doors in Washington. This, in turn, was followed by additional bailouts for Citigroup, AIG, Bank of America, Citigroup (again), and AIG (again).

Some of these deals may have been reasonable responses to the immediate situation. But it was never clear (and still isn't) what combination of interests was being served, and how. Treasury and the Fed did not act according to any publicly articulated principles, but just worked out a transaction and claimed it was the best that could be done under the circumstances. This was late-night, backroom dealing, pure and simple.

Throughout the crisis, the government has taken extreme care not to upset the interests of the financial institutions, or to question the basic outlines of the system that got us here. In September 2008, Henry Paulson asked Congress for $700 billion to buy toxic assets from banks, with no strings attached and no judicial review of his purchase decisions. Many observers suspected that the purpose was to overpay for those assets and thereby take the problem off the banks' hands—indeed, that is the only way that buying toxic assets would have helped anything. Perhaps because there was no way to make such a blatant subsidy politically acceptable, that plan was shelved.

Instead, the money was used to recapitalize banks, buying shares in them on terms that were grossly favorable to the banks themselves. As the crisis has deepened and financial institutions have needed more help, the government has gotten more and more creative in figuring out ways to provide banks with subsidies that are too complex for the general public to understand. The first AIG bailout, which was on relatively good terms for the taxpayer, was supplemented by three further bailouts whose terms were more AIG-friendly. The second Citigroup bailout and the Bank of America bailout included complex asset guarantees that provided the banks with insurance at below-market rates. The third Citigroup bailout, in late February, converted government-owned preferred stock to common stock at a price significantly higher than the market price—a subsidy that probably even most *Wall Street Journal* readers would miss on first reading. And the convertible preferred shares that the Treasury will buy under the new Financial Stability Plan give the conversion option (and thus the upside) to the banks, not the government.

This latest plan—which is likely to provide cheap loans to hedge funds and others so that they can buy distressed bank assets at relatively high prices—has been heavily influenced by the financial sector, and Treasury has made no secret of that. As Neel Kashkari, a senior Treasury official under both Henry Paulson and Tim Geithner (and a Goldman alum) told Congress in March, "We had received inbound unsolicited proposals from people in the private sector saying, 'We have capital on the sidelines; we want to go after [distressed bank] assets.'" And the plan lets them do just that: "By marrying government capital—taxpayer capital—with private-sector capital and providing financing, you can enable those investors to then go after those assets at a price that makes sense for the investors and at a price that makes sense for the banks." Kashkari didn't mention anything about what makes sense for the third group involved: the taxpayers.

Even leaving aside fairness to taxpayers, the government's velvet-glove approach with the banks is deeply troubling, for

one simple reason: it is inadequate to change the behavior of a financial sector accustomed to doing business on its own terms, at a time when that behavior *must* change. As an unnamed senior bank official said to *The New York Times* last fall, "It doesn't matter how much Hank Paulson gives us, no one is going to lend a nickel until the economy turns." But there's the rub: the economy can't recover until the banks are healthy and willing to lend.

The Way Out

Looking just at the financial crisis (and leaving aside some problems of the larger economy), we face at least two major, interrelated problems. The first is a desperately ill banking sector that threatens to choke off any incipient recovery that the fiscal stimulus might generate. The second is a political balance of power that gives the financial sector a veto over public policy, even as that sector loses popular support.

Big banks, it seems, have only gained political strength since the crisis began. And this is not surprising. With the financial system so fragile, the damage that a major bank failure could cause—Lehman was small relative to Citigroup or Bank of America—is much greater than it would be during ordinary times. The banks have been exploiting this fear as they wring favorable deals out of Washington. Bank of America obtained its second bailout package (in January) after warning the government that it might not be able to go through with the acquisition of Merrill Lynch, a prospect that Treasury did not want to consider.

The challenges the United States faces are familiar territory to the people at the IMF. If you hid the name of the country and just showed them the numbers, there is no doubt what old IMF hands would say: nationalize troubled banks and break them up as necessary.

> If you hid the name of the country and just showed them the numbers, there is no doubt what old IMF hands would say: nationalize troubled banks and break them up.

In some ways, of course, the government has already taken control of the banking system. It has essentially guaranteed the liabilities of the biggest banks, and it is their only plausible source of capital today. Meanwhile, the Federal Reserve has taken on a major role in providing credit to the economy—the function that the private banking sector is supposed to be performing, but isn't. Yet there are limits to what the Fed can do on its own; consumers and businesses are still dependent on banks that lack the balance sheets and the incentives to make the loans the economy needs, and the government has no real control over who runs the banks, or over what they do.

At the root of the banks' problems are the large losses they have undoubtedly taken on their securities and loan portfolios. But they don't want to recognize the full extent of their losses, because that would likely expose them as insolvent. So they talk down the problem, and ask for handouts that aren't enough to make them healthy (again, they can't reveal the size of the handouts that would be necessary for that), but are enough to keep them upright a little longer. This behavior is corrosive: unhealthy banks either don't lend (hoarding money to shore up reserves) or they make desperate gambles on high-risk loans and investments that could pay off big, but probably won't pay off at all. In either case, the economy suffers further, and as it does, bank assets themselves continue to deteriorate—creating a highly destructive vicious cycle.

To break this cycle, the government must force the banks to acknowledge the scale of their problems. As the IMF understands (and as the U.S. government itself has insisted to multiple emerging-market countries in the past), the most direct way to do this is nationalization. Instead, Treasury is trying to negotiate bailouts bank by bank, and behaving as if the banks hold all the cards—contorting the terms of each deal to minimize government ownership while forswearing government influence over bank strategy or operations. Under these conditions, cleaning up bank balance sheets is impossible.

Nationalization would not imply permanent state ownership. The IMF's advice would be, essentially: scale up the standard Federal Deposit Insurance Corporation process. An FDIC "intervention" is basically a government-managed bankruptcy procedure for banks. It would allow the government to wipe out bank shareholders, replace failed management, clean up the balance sheets, and then sell the banks back to the private sector. The main advantage is immediate recognition of the problem so that it can be solved before it grows worse.

The government needs to inspect the balance sheets and identify the banks that cannot survive a severe recession. These banks should face a choice: write down your assets to their true value and raise private capital within 30 days, or be taken over by the government. The government would write down the toxic assets of banks taken into receivership—recognizing reality—and transfer those assets to a separate government entity, which would attempt to salvage whatever value is possible for the taxpayer (as the Resolution Trust Corporation did after the savings-and-loan debacle of the 1980s). The rump banks—cleansed and able to lend safely, and hence trusted again by other lenders and investors—could then be sold off.

Cleaning up the megabanks will be complex. And it will be expensive for the taxpayer; according to the latest IMF numbers, the cleanup of the banking system would probably cost close to $1.5 trillion (or 10 percent of our GDP) in the long term. But only decisive government action—exposing the full extent of the financial rot and restoring some set of banks to publicly verifiable health—can cure the financial sector as a whole.

This may seem like strong medicine. But in fact, while necessary, it is insufficient. The second problem the U.S. faces—the power of the oligarchy—is just as important as the immediate crisis of lending. And the advice from the IMF on this front would again be simple: break the oligarchy.

Oversize institutions disproportionately influence public policy; the major banks we have today draw much of their power from being too big to fail. Nationalization and re-privatization would not change that; while the replacement of the bank executives who got us into this crisis would be just and sensible, ultimately, the swapping-out of one set of powerful managers for another would change only the names of the oligarchs.

Ideally, big banks should be sold in medium-size pieces, divided regionally or by type of business. Where this proves impractical—since we'll want to sell the banks quickly—they could be sold whole, but with the requirement of being broken up within a short time. Banks that remain in private hands should also be subject to size limitations.

This may seem like a crude and arbitrary step, but it is the best way to limit the power of individual institutions in a sector that is essential to the economy as a whole. Of course, some people will complain about the "efficiency costs" of a more fragmented banking system, and these costs are real. But so are the costs when a bank that is too big to fail—a financial weapon of mass self-destruction—explodes. Anything that is too big to fail is too big to exist.

To ensure systematic bank breakup, and to prevent the eventual reemergence of dangerous behemoths, we also need to overhaul our antitrust legislation. Laws put in place more than 100 years ago to combat industrial monopolies were not designed to address the problem we now face. The problem in the financial sector today is not that a given firm might have enough market share to influence prices; it is that one firm or a small set of interconnected firms, by failing, can bring down the economy. The Obama administration's fiscal stimulus evokes FDR, but what we need to imitate here is Teddy Roosevelt's trust-busting.

Caps on executive compensation, while redolent of populism, might help restore the political balance of power and deter the emergence of a new oligarchy. Wall Street's main attraction—to the people who work there and to the government officials who were only too happy to bask in its reflected glory—has been the astounding amount of money that could be made. Limiting that money would reduce the allure of the financial sector and make it more like any other industry.

Still, outright pay caps are clumsy, especially in the long run. And most money is now made in largely unregulated private hedge funds and private-equity firms, so lowering pay would be complicated. Regulation and taxation should be part of the solution. Over time, though, the largest part may involve more transparency and competition, which would bring financial-industry fees down. To those who say this would drive financial activities to other countries, we can now safely say: fine.

Two Paths

To paraphrase Joseph Schumpeter, the early-20th-century economist, everyone has elites; the important thing is to change them from time to time. If the U.S. were just another country, coming to the IMF with hat in hand, I might be fairly optimistic about its future. Most of the emerging-market crises that I've mentioned ended relatively quickly, and gave way, for the most part, to relatively strong recoveries. But this, alas, brings us to the limit of the analogy between the U.S. and emerging markets.

Emerging-market countries have only a precarious hold on wealth, and are weaklings globally. When they get into trouble, they quite literally run out of money—or at least out of foreign currency, without which they cannot survive. They must make difficult decisions; ultimately, aggressive action is baked into the cake. But the U.S., of course, is the world's most powerful nation, rich beyond measure, and blessed with the exorbitant privilege of paying its foreign debts in its own currency, which it can print. As a result, it could very well stumble along for years—as Japan did during its lost decade—never summoning the courage to do what it needs to do, and never really recovering. A clean break with the past—involving the takeover and cleanup of major banks—hardly looks like a sure thing right now. Certainly no one at the IMF can force it.

In my view, the U.S. faces two plausible scenarios. The first involves complicated bank-by-bank deals and a continual drumbeat of (repeated) bailouts, like the ones we saw in February with Citigroup and AIG. The administration will try to muddle through, and confusion will reign.

Boris Fyodorov, the late finance minister of Russia, struggled for much of the past 20 years against oligarchs, corruption, and abuse of authority in all its forms. He liked to say that confusion and chaos were very much in the interests of the powerful—letting them take things, legally and illegally, with impunity. When inflation is high, who can say what a piece of property is really worth? When the credit system is supported by byzantine government arrangements and backroom deals, how do you know that you aren't being fleeced?

Our future could be one in which continued tumult feeds the looting of the financial system, and we talk more and more about exactly how our oligarchs became bandits and how the economy just can't seem to get into gear.

The second scenario begins more bleakly, and might end that way too. But it does provide at least some hope that we'll be shaken out of our torpor. It goes like this: the global economy continues to deteriorate, the banking system in east-central Europe collapses, and—because eastern Europe's banks are mostly owned by western European banks—justifiable fears of government insolvency spread throughout the Continent. Creditors take further hits and confidence falls further. The Asian economies that export manufactured goods are devastated, and the commodity producers in Latin America and Africa are not much better off. A dramatic worsening of the global environment forces the U.S. economy, already staggering, down onto both knees. The baseline growth rates used in the administration's current budget are increasingly seen as unrealistic, and the rosy "stress scenario" that the U.S. Treasury is currently using to evaluate banks' balance sheets becomes a source of great embarrassment.

Under this kind of pressure, and faced with the prospect of a national and global collapse, minds may become more concentrated.

The conventional wisdom among the elite is still that the current slump "cannot be as bad as the Great Depression." This view is wrong.

The conventional wisdom among the elite is still that the current slump "cannot be as bad as the Great Depression." This view is wrong. What we face now could, in fact, be worse than the Great Depression—because the world is now so much more interconnected and because the banking sector is now so big. We face a synchronized downturn in almost all countries, a weakening of confidence among individuals and firms, and major problems for government finances. If our leadership wakes up to the potential consequences, we may yet see dramatic action on the banking system and a breaking of the old elite. Let us hope it is not then too late.

SIMON JOHNSON, a professor at MIT's Sloan School of Management, was the chief economist at the International Monetary Fund during 2007 and 2008. He blogs about the financial crisis at baselinescenario.com, along with James Kwak, who also contributed to this essay.

The Case against the West

America and Europe in the Asian Century

KISHORE MAHBUBANI

There is a fundamental flaw in the West's strategic thinking. In all its analyses of global challenges, the West assumes that it is the source of the solutions to the world's key problems. In fact, however, the West is also a major source of these problems. Unless key Western policymakers learn to understand and deal with this reality, the world is headed for an even more troubled phase.

The West is understandably reluctant to accept that the era of its domination is ending and that the Asian century has come. No civilization cedes power easily, and the West's resistance to giving up control of key global institutions and processes is natural. Yet the West is engaging in an extraordinary act of self-deception by believing that it is open to change. In fact, the West has become the most powerful force preventing the emergence of a new wave of history, clinging to its privileged position in key global forums, such as the UN Security Council, the International Monetary Fund, the World Bank, and the G-8 (the group of highly industrialized states), and refusing to contemplate how the West will have to adjust to the Asian century.

Partly as a result of its growing insecurity, the West has also become increasingly incompetent in its handling of key global problems. Many Western commentators can readily identify specific failures, such as the Bush administration's botched invasion and occupation of Iraq. But few can see that this reflects a deeper structural problem: the West's inability to see that the world has entered a new era.

Apart from representing a specific failure of policy execution, the war in Iraq has also highlighted the gap between the reality and what the West had expected would happen after the invasion. Arguably, the United States and the United Kingdom intended only to free the Iraqi people from a despotic ruler and to rid the world of a dangerous man, Saddam Hussein. Even if George W. Bush and Tony Blair had no malevolent intentions, however, their approaches were trapped in the Western mindset of believing that their interventions could lead only to good, not harm or disaster. This led them to believe that the invading U.S. troops would be welcomed with roses thrown at their feet by happy Iraqis. But the twentieth century showed that no country welcomes foreign invaders. The notion that any Islamic nation would approve of Western military boots on its soil was ridiculous. Even in the early twentieth century, the British

invasion and occupation of Iraq was met with armed resistance. In 1920, Winston Churchill, then British secretary for war and air, quelled the rebellion of Kurds and Arabs in British-occupied Iraq by authorizing his troops to use chemical weapons. "I am strongly in favor of using poisoned gas against uncivilized tribes," Churchill said. The world has moved on from this era, but many Western officials have not abandoned the old assumption that an army of Christian soldiers can successfully invade, occupy, and transform an Islamic society.

Many Western leaders often begin their speeches by remarking on how perilous the world is becoming. Speaking after the August 2006 discovery of a plot to blow up transatlantic flights originating from London, President Bush said, "The American people need to know we live in a dangerous world." But even as Western leaders speak of such threats, they seem incapable of conceding that the West itself could be the fundamental source of these dangers. After all, the West includes the best-managed states in the world, the most economically developed, those with the strongest democratic institutions. But one cannot assume that a government that rules competently at home will be equally good at addressing challenges abroad. In fact, the converse is more likely to be true. Although the Western mind is obsessed with the Islamist terrorist threat, the West is mishandling the two immediate and pressing challenges of Afghanistan and Iraq. And despite the grave threat of nuclear terrorism, the Western custodians of the nonproliferation regime have allowed that regime to weaken significantly. The challenge posed by Iran's efforts to enrich uranium has been aggravated by the incompetence of the United States and the European Union. On the economic front, for the first time since World War II, the demise of a round of global trade negotiations, the Doha Round, seems imminent. Finally, the danger of global warming, too, is being mismanaged.

Yet Westerners seldom look inward to understand the deeper reasons these global problems are being mismanaged. Are there domestic structural reasons that explain this? Have Western democracies been hijacked by competitive populism and structural short-termism, preventing them from addressing long-term challenges from a broader global perspective?

Fortunately, some Asian states may now be capable of taking on more responsibilities, as they have been strengthened by implementing Western principles. In September 2005, Robert

Zoellick, then U.S. deputy secretary of state, called on China to become a "responsible stakeholder" in the international system. China has responded positively, as have other Asian states. In recent decades, Asians have been among the greatest beneficiaries of the open multilateral order created by the United States and the other victors of World War II, and few today want to destabilize it. The number of Asians seeking a comfortable middle-class existence has never been higher. For centuries, the Chinese and the Indians could only dream of such an accomplishment; now it is within the reach of around half a billion people in China and India. Their ideal is to achieve what the United States and Europe did. They want to replicate, not dominate, the West. The universalization of the Western dream represents a moment of triumph for the West. And so the West should welcome the fact that the Asian states are becoming competent at handling regional and global challenges.

The Middle East Mess

Western Policies have been most harmful in the Middle East. The Middle East is also the most dangerous region in the world. Trouble there affects not just seven million Israelis, around four million Palestinians, and 200 million Arabs; it also affects more than a billion Muslims worldwide. Every time there is a major flare-up in the Middle East, such as the U.S. invasion of Iraq or the Israeli bombing of Lebanon, Islamic communities around the world become concerned, distressed, and angered. And few of them doubt the problems origin: the West.

The invasion and occupation of Iraq, for example, was a multidimensional error. The theory and practice of international law legitimizes the use of force only when it is an act of self-defense or is authorized by the UN Security Council. The U.S.-led invasion of Iraq could not be justified on either count. The United States and the United Kingdom sought the Security Council's authorization to invade Iraq, but the council denied it. It was therefore clear to the international community that the subsequent war was illegal and that it would do huge damage to international law.

This has created an enormous problem, partly because until this point both the United States and the United Kingdom had been among the primary custodians of international law. American and British minds, such as James Brierly, Philip Jessup, Hersch Lauterpacht, and Hans Morgenthau, developed the conceptual infrastructure underlying international law, and American and British leaders provided the political will to have it accepted in practice. But neither the United States nor the United Kingdom will admit that the invasion and the occupation of Iraq were illegal or give up their historical roles as the chief caretakers of international law. Since 2003, both nations have frequently called for Iran and North Korea to implement UN Security Council resolutions. But how can the violators of UN principles also be their enforcers?

One rare benefit of the Iraq war may be that it has awakened a new fear of Iran among the Sunni Arab states. Egypt, Jordan, and Saudi Arabia, among others, do not want to deal with two adversaries and so are inclined to make peace with Israel. Saudi Arabia's King Abdullah used the opportunity of the special Arab League summit meeting in March 2007 to relaunch his long-standing proposal for a two-state solution to the Israeli-Palestinian conflict. Unfortunately, the Bush administration did not seize the opportunity—or revive the Taba accords that President Bill Clinton had worked out in January 2001, even though they could provide a basis for a lasting settlement and the Saudis were prepared to back them. In its early days, the Bush administration appeared ready to support a two-state solution. It was the first U.S. administration to vote in favor of a UN Security Council resolution calling for the creation of a Palestinian state, and it announced in March 2002 that it would try to achieve such a result by 2005. But here it is 2008, and little progress has been made.

The United States has made the already complicated Israeli-Palestinian conflict even more of a mess. Many extremist voices in Tel Aviv and Washington believe that time will always be on Israel's side. The pro-Israel lobby's stranglehold on the U.S. Congress, the political cowardice of U.S. politicians when it comes to creating a Palestinian state, and the sustained track record of U.S. aid to Israel support this view. But no great power forever sacrifices its larger national interests in favor of the interests of a small state. If Israel fails to accept the Taba accords, it will inevitably come to grief. If and when it does, Western incompetence will be seen as a major cause.

Never Say Never

Nuclear nonproliferation is another area in which the West, especially the United States, has made matters worse. The West has long been obsessed with the danger of the proliferation of weapons of mass destruction, particularly nuclear weapons. It pushed successfully for the near-universal ratification of the Biological and Toxin Weapons Convention, the Chemical Weapons Convention, and the Nuclear Nonproliferation Treaty (NPT).

But the West has squandered many of those gains. Today, the NPT is legally alive but spiritually dead. The NPT was inherently problematic since it divided the world into nuclear haves (the states that had tested a nuclear device by 1967) and nuclear have-nots (those that had not). But for two decades it was reasonably effective in preventing horizontal proliferation (the spread of nuclear weapons to other states). Unfortunately, the NPT has done nothing to prevent vertical proliferation, namely, the increase in the numbers and sophistication of nuclear weapons among the existing nuclear weapons states. During the Cold War, the United States and the Soviet Union agreed to work together to limit proliferation. The governments of several countries that could have developed nuclear weapons, such as Argentina, Brazil, Germany, Japan, and South Korea, restrained themselves because they believed the NPT reflected a fair bargain between China, France, the Soviet Union, the United Kingdom, and the United States (the five official nuclear weapons states and five permanent members of the UN Security Council) and the rest of the world. Both sides agreed that the world would be safer if the five nuclear states took steps to reduce their arsenals and worked toward the eventual goal of universal disarmament and the other states refrained from acquiring nuclear weapons at all.

So what went wrong? The first problem was that the NPT's principal progenitor, the United States, decided to walk away from the postwar rule-based order it had created, thus eroding the infrastructure on which the NPT's enforcement depends. During the time I was Singapore's ambassador to the UN, between 1984 and 1989, Jeane Kirkpatrick, the U.S. ambassador to the UN, treated the organization with contempt. She infamously said, "What takes place in the Security Council more closely resembles a mugging than either a political debate or an effort at problem-solving." She saw the postwar order as a set of constraints, not as a set of rules that the world should follow and the United States should help preserve. This undermined the NPT, because with no teeth of its own, no self-regulating or sanctioning mechanisms, and a clause allowing signatories to ignore obligations in the name of "supreme national interest," the treaty could only really be enforced by the UN Security Council. And once the United States began tearing holes in the fabric of the overall system, it created openings for violations of the NPT and its principles. Finally, by going to war with Iraq without UN authorization, the United States lost its moral authority to ask, for example, Iran to abide by Security Council resolutions.

Another problem has been the United States'—and other nuclear weapons states'—direct assault on the treaty. The NPT is fundamentally a social contract between the five nuclear weapons states and the rest of the world, based partly on the understanding that the nuclear powers will eventually give up their weapons. Instead, during the Cold War, the United States and the Soviet Union increased both the quantity and the sophistication of their nuclear weapons: the United States' nuclear stockpile peaked in 1966 at 31,700 warheads, and the Soviet Union's peaked in 1986 at 40,723. In fact, the United States and the Soviet Union developed their nuclear stockpiles so much that they actually ran out of militarily or economically significant targets. The numbers have declined dramatically since then, but even the current number of nuclear weapons held by the United States and Russia can wreak enormous damage on human civilization.

The nuclear states' decision to ignore Israel's nuclear weapons program was especially damaging to their authority. No nuclear weapons state has ever publicly acknowledged Israel's possession of nuclear weapons. Their silence has created a loophole in the NPT and delegitimized it in the eyes of Muslim nations. The consequences have been profound. When the West sermonizes that the world will become a more dangerous place when Iran acquires nuclear weapons, the Muslim world now shrugs.

India and Pakistan were already shrugging by 1998, when they tested their first nuclear weapons. When the international community responded by condemning the tests and applying sanctions on India, virtually all Indians saw through the hypocrisy and double standards of their critics. By not respecting their own obligations under the NPT, the five nuclear states had robbed their condemnations of any moral legitimacy; criticisms from Australia and Canada, which have also remained silent about Israel's bomb, similarly had no moral authority. The near-unanimous rejection of the NPT by the Indian establishment, which is otherwise very conscious of international opinion, showed how dead the treaty already was.

The world has lost its trust in the five nuclear weapons states and now sees them as the NPT's primary violators.

From time to time, common sense has entered discussions on nuclear weapons. President Ronald Reagan said more categorically than any U.S. president that the world would be better off without nuclear weapons. Last year, with the NPT in its death throes and the growing threat of loose nuclear weapons falling into the hands of terrorists forefront in everyone's mind, former Secretary of State George Shultz, former Defense Secretary William Perry, former Secretary of State Henry Kissinger, and former Senator Sam Nunn warned in *The Wall Street Journal* that the world was "now on the precipice of a new and dangerous nuclear era." They argued, "Unless urgent new actions are taken, the U.S. soon will be compelled to enter a new nuclear era that will be more precarious, psychologically disorienting, and economically even more costly than was Cold War deterrence." But these calls may have come too late. The world has lost its trust in the five nuclear weapons states and now sees them as the NPT's primary violators rather than its custodians. Those states' private cynicism about their obligations to the NPT has become public knowledge.

Contrary to what the West wants the rest of the world to believe, the nuclear weapons states, especially the United States and Russia, which continue to maintain thousands of nuclear weapons, are the biggest source of nuclear proliferation. Mohamed ElBaradei, the director general of the International Atomic Energy Agency, warned in *The Economist* in 2003, "The very existence of nuclear weapons gives rise to the pursuit of them. They are seen as a source of global influence, and are valued for their perceived deterrent effect. And as long as some countries possess them (or are protected by them in alliances) and others do not, this asymmetry breeds chronic global insecurity." Despite the Cold War, the second half of the twentieth century seemed to be moving the world toward a more civilized order. As the twenty-first century unfurls, the world seems to be sliding backward.

Irresponsible Stakeholders

After leading the world toward a period of spectacular economic growth in the second half of the twentieth century by promoting global free trade, the West has recently been faltering in its global economic leadership. Believing that low trade barriers and increasing trade interdependence would result in higher standards of living for all, European and U.S. economists and policymakers pushed for global economic liberalization. As a result, global trade grew from seven percent of the world's GDP in 1940 to 30 percent in 2005.

But a seismic shift has taken place in Western attitudes since the end of the Cold War. Suddenly, the United States and Europe no longer have a vested interest in the success of the East Asian economies, which they see less as allies and more as competitors. That change in Western interests was reflected in the fact that the West provided little real help to East Asia during the Asian financial crisis of 1997–98. The entry of China into the global marketplace, especially after its admission to the World Trade Organization, has made a huge difference in both economic and psychological terms. Many Europeans have lost confidence in their ability to compete with the Asians. And many Americans have lost confidence in the virtues of competition.

There are some knotty issues that need to be resolved in the current global trade talks, but fundamentally the negotiations are stalled because the conviction of the Western "champions" of free trade that free trade is good has begun to waver. When Americans and Europeans start to perceive themselves as losers in international trade, they also lose their drive to push for further trade liberalization. Unfortunately, on this front at least, neither China nor India (nor Brazil nor South Africa nor any other major developing country) is ready to take over the West's mantle. China, for example, is afraid that any effort to seek leadership in this area will stoke U.S. fears that it is striving for global hegemony. Hence, China is lying low. So, too, are the United States and Europe. Hence, the trade talks are stalled. The end of the West's promotion of global trade liberalization could well mean the end of the most spectacular economic growth the world has ever seen. Few in the West seem to be reflecting on the consequences of walking away from one of the West's most successful policies, which is what it will be doing if it allows the Doha Round to fail.

At the same time that the Western governments are relinquishing their stewardship of the global economy, they are also failing to take the lead on battling global warming. The awarding of the Nobel Peace Prize to former U.S. Vice President Al Gore, a longtime environmentalist, and the UN's Intergovernmental Panel on Climate Change confirms there is international consensus that global warning is a real threat. The most assertive advocates for tackling this problem come from the U.S. and European scientific communities, but the greatest resistance to any effective action is coming from the U.S. government. This has left the rest of the world confused and puzzled. Most people believe that the greenhouse effect is caused mostly by the flow of current emissions. Current emissions do aggravate the problem, but the fundamental cause is the stock of emissions that has accumulated since the Industrial Revolution. Finding a just and equitable solution to the problem of greenhouse gas emissions must begin with assigning responsibility both for the current flow and for the stock of greenhouse gases already accumulated. And on both counts the Western nations should bear a greater burden.

The West has to learn to share power and responsibility for the management of global issues with the rest of the world.

When it comes to addressing any problem pertaining to the global commons, such as the environment, it seems only fair that the wealthier members of the international community should shoulder more responsibility. This is a natural principle of justice. It is also fair in this particular case given the developed countries' primary role in releasing harmful gases into the atmosphere. R. K. Pachauri, chair of the Intergovernmental Panel on Climate Change, argued last year, "China and India are certainly increasing their share, but they are not increasing their

per capita emissions anywhere close to the levels that you have in the developed world." Since 1850, China has contributed less than 8 percent of the world's total emissions of carbon dioxide, whereas the United States is responsible for 29 percent and western Europe is responsible for 27 percent. Today, India's per capita greenhouse gas emissions are equivalent to only 4 percent of those of the United States and 12 percent of those of the European Union. Still, the Western governments are not clearly acknowledging their responsibilities and are allowing many of their citizens to believe that China and India are the fundamental obstacles to any solution to global warming.

Washington might become more responsible on this front if a Democratic president replaces Bush in 2009. But people in the West will have to make some real concessions if they are to reduce significantly their per capita share of global emissions. A cap-and-trade program may do the trick. Western countries will probably have to make economic sacrifices. One option might be, as the journalist Thomas Friedman has suggested, to impose a dollar-per-gallon tax on Americans' gasoline consumption. Gore has proposed a carbon tax. So far, however, few U.S. politicians have dared to make such suggestions publicly.

Temptations of the East

The Middle East, nuclear proliferation, stalled trade liberalization, and global warming are all challenges that the West is essentially failing to address. And this failure suggests that a systemic problem is emerging in the West's stewardship of the international order—one that Western minds are reluctant to analyze or confront openly. After having enjoyed centuries of global domination, the West has to learn to share power and responsibility for the management of global issues with the rest of the world. It has to forgo outdated organizations, such as the Organization for Economic Cooperation and Development, and outdated processes, such as the G-8, and deal with organizations and processes with a broader scope and broader representation. It was always unnatural for the 12 percent of the world population that lived in the West to enjoy so much global power. Understandably, the other 88 percent of the world population increasingly wants also to drive the bus of world history.

First and foremost, the West needs to acknowledge that sharing the power it has accumulated in global forums would serve its interests. Restructuring international institutions to reflect the current world order will be complicated by the absence of natural leaders to do the job. The West has become part of the problem, and the Asian countries are not yet ready to step in. On the other hand, the world does not need to invent any new principles to improve global governance; the concepts of domestic good governance can and should be applied to the international community. The Western principles of democracy, the rule of law, and social justice are among the world's best bets. The ancient virtues of partnership and pragmatism can complement them.

Democracy, the foundation of government in the West, is based on the premise that each human being in a society is an equal stakeholder in the domestic order. Thus, governments are selected on the basis of "one person, one vote." This has produced long-term stability and order in Western societies. In order to produce long-term stability and order worldwide, democracy should be the cornerstone of global society, and the planet's 6.6 billion inhabitants should become equal stakeholders. To inject the spirit of democracy into global governance and global decision-making, one must turn to institutions with universal representation, especially the UN. UN institutions such as the World Health Organization and the World Meteorological Organization enjoy widespread legitimacy because of their universal membership, which means their decisions are generally accepted by all the countries of the world.

The problem today is that although many Western actors are willing to work with specialized UN agencies, they are reluctant to strengthen the UN's core institution, the UN General Assembly, from which all these specialized agencies come. The UN General Assembly is the most representative body on the planet, and yet many Western countries are deeply skeptical of it. They are right to point out its imperfections. But they overlook the fact that this imperfect assembly enjoys legitimacy in the eyes of the people of this imperfect world. Moreover, the General Assembly has at times shown more common sense and prudence than some of the most sophisticated Western democracies. Of course, it takes time to persuade all of the UN's members to march in the same direction, but consensus building is precisely what gives legitimacy to the result. Most countries in the world respect and abide by most UN decisions because they believe in the authority of the UN. Used well, the body can be a powerful vehicle for making critical decisions on global governance.

The world today is run not through the General Assembly but through the Security Council, which is effectively run by the five permanent member states. If this model were adopted in the United States, the U.S. Congress would be replaced by a selective council comprised of only the representatives from the country's five most powerful states. Would the populations of the other 45 states not deem any such proposal absurd? The West must cease its efforts to prolong its undemocratic management of the global order and find ways to effectively engage the majority of the world's population in global decision-making.

Another fundamental principle that should underpin the global order is the rule of law. This hallowed Western principle insists that no person, regardless of his or her status, is above the law. Ironically, while being exemplary in implementing the rule of law at home, the United States is a leading international outlaw in its refusal to recognize the constraints of international law. Many Americans live comfortably with this contradiction while expecting other countries to abide by widely accepted treaties. Americans react with horror when Iran tries to walk away from the NPT. Yet they are surprised that the world is equally shocked when Washington abandons a universally accepted treaty such as the Comprehensive Test Ban Treaty.

The Bush administration's decision to exempt the United States from the provisions of international law on human rights is even more damaging. For over half a century, since Eleanor Roosevelt led the fight for the adoption of the Universal Declaration of Human Rights, the United States was the global champion of human rights. This was the result of a strong ideological conviction that it was the United States' God-given duty to create a more civilized world. It also made for a good ideological weapon during the Cold War: the free United States was fighting the unfree Soviet Union. But the Bush administration has stunned the world by walking away from universally accepted human rights conventions, especially those on torture. And much as the U.S. electorate could not be expected to tolerate an attorney general who broke his own laws from time to time, how can the global body politic be expected to respect a custodian of international law that violates these very rules?

Finally, on social justice, Westerns nations have slackened. Social justice is the cornerstone of order and stability in modern Western societies and the rest of the world. People accept inequality as long as some kind of social safety net exists to help the dispossessed. Most western European governments took this principle to heart after World War II and introduced welfare provisions as a way to ward off Marxist revolutions seeking to create socialist societies. Today, many Westerners believe that they are spreading social justice globally with their massive foreign aid to the developing world. Indeed, each year, the members of the Organization for Economic Cooperation and Development, according to the organization's own estimates, give approximately $104 billion to the developing world. But the story of Western aid to the developing world is essentially a myth. Western countries have put significant amounts of money into their overseas development assistance budgets, but these funds' primary purpose is to serve the immediate and short-term security and national interests of the donors rather than the long-term interests of the recipients.

Some Asian countries are now ready to join the West in becoming responsible custodians of the global order.

The experience of Asia shows that where Western aid has failed to do the job, domestic good governance can succeed. This is likely to be Asia's greatest contribution to world history. The success of Asia will inspire other societies on different continents to emulate it. In addition, Asia's march to modernity can help produce a more stable world order. Some Asian countries are now ready to join the West in becoming responsible custodians of the global order; as the biggest beneficiaries of the current system, they have powerful incentives to do so. The West is not welcoming Asia's progress, and its short-term interests in preserving its privileged position in various global institutions are trumping its long-term interests in creating a more just and stable world order. Unfortunately, the West has gone from being the world's primary problem solver to being its single biggest liability.

KISHORE MAHBUBANI is Dean of the Lee Kuan Yew School of Public Policy at the National University of Singapore. This essay is adapted from his latest book, *The New Asian Hemisphere: The Irresistible Shift of Global Power to the East* (Public Affairs, 2008).

"Chimerica" Is Headed for Divorce

Niall Ferguson

When does a rising power become a threat? There is seldom a single moment. A century ago, Anglo-German antagonism was still a relatively new phenomenon; an alliance between the two empires seemed plausible as late as 1899. Likewise, the United States took time to identify Japan as a serious rival in the Pacific region; it was not until the 1930s that relations really soured. In both cases, the perception of a strategic threat was slow to grow. But grow it did—and ultimately it led to war. Could the same be happening to the United States and China today? Are we imperceptibly but inexorably slipping from cooperation to competition?

Back in early 2007, it seemed as if China and America were so intertwined they'd become one economy: I called it "Chimerica." *The Chinese did the* saving, the Americans the spending. The Chinese did the exporting, the Americans the importing. The Chinese did the lending, the Americans the borrowing.

As the Chinese strategy was based on export-led growth, they had no desire to see their currency appreciate against the dollar. So they intervened consistently in currency markets, and as a result, they now have international reserves totaling $2.1 trillion. About 70 percent of these are in dollar-denominated securities, and a large proportion of these are in U.S. government bonds. The unintended effect of this was to help finance the U.S. current-account deficit at very low interest rates. Without those low long-term rates, it's hard to believe that the U.S. real-estate market would have bubbled the way it did between 2002 and 2007.

For a time Chimerica seemed like a marriage made in heaven: both economies grew so fast that they accounted for about 40 percent of global growth between 1998 and 2007. The big question now is whether or not this marriage is on the rocks. America's highly indebted consumers just can't borrow anymore. The U.S. savings rate is soaring upward, and U.S. imports from China have slumped, down 18 percent between May 2008 and May 2009. Of course, that doesn't mean the Chinese are going to stop buying dollars. They dare not allow their currency to appreciate when so many jobs in the export sector are under threat. But it does mean that they are questioning the Chimerica strategy.

It's a bit like one of those marriages between a compulsive saver and a chronic spender. Such partnerships can work for a certain period of time, but eventually the penny-pincher gets disillusioned with the spendthrift. Every time Chinese officials express concern about U.S. fiscal or monetary policy, it reminds me of one of those domestic tiffs in which the saver says to the spender: "You maxed out on the credit cards once too often, honey."

Let's look at the numbers. China's holdings of U.S. Treasuries rose to $801.5 billion in May, an increase of 5 percent from $763.5 billion in April. Call it $40 billion a month. And let's imagine the Chinese do that every month through this fiscal year. That would be a credit line to the U.S. government of $480 billion. Given that the total deficit is forecast to be about $2 trillion, that means the Chinese may finance less than a quarter of total federal-government borrowing—whereas a few years ago they were financing virtually the whole deficit.

The trouble is that the Chinese clearly feel they have enough U.S. government bonds. Their great anxiety is that the Obama administration's very lax fiscal policy, plus the Federal Reserve's policy of quantitative easing (in layman's terms, printing money), are going to cause one or both of two things to happen: the price of U.S. bonds could fall and/or the purchasing power of the dollar could fall. Either way the Chinese lose. Their current strategy is to shift their purchases to the short end of the yield curve, buying Treasury bills instead of 10-year bonds. But that doesn't address the currency risk. In a best-selling book titled *Currency Wars,* Chinese economist Song Hongbing warned that the United States has a bad habit of stiffing its creditors by letting the dollar slide. This, he points out, is what happened to the Japanese in the 1980s. First their currency strengthened against the dollar. Then their economy tanked.

What is China's alternative if it seeks a divorce from America? Call it the empire option. Instead of continuing in this unhappy marriage, the Chinese can go it alone, counting on their growing economic might (according to Goldman Sachs, China's gross domestic product could equal that of the United States by 2027) to buy them global power in their own right. In some ways they've already begun doing this. Their naval strategy clearly implies a challenge to U.S. hegemony in the Asia-Pacific region. Their investments in African minerals and infrastructure look distinctly imperial too. And now the official line from Prime Minister Wen Jiabao is to "hasten the implementation of our 'going out' strategy and combine the utilization of foreign exchange reserves with the 'going out' of our enterprises." That sounds like a Chinese campaign to buy up foreign assets—exchanging dodgy dollars for copper mines.

At the same time, crucially, the Chinese need to have their own domestic consumers step up to take the place of over leveraged Americans. China's economy is, above all, a manufacturing concern; if no one is going to the shopping malls, China's companies are just building their inventories. So a post-Chimerican China needs to be not only an empire, but also a consumer society. This will boost China's internal market as well as trade with its Asian neighbors, and will spur the development of an Asian economic bloc.

The global implications of this divorce are huge. Imagine a new Cold War, but one in which the two superpowers are economically the same size. Or, if you prefer an older analogy, imagine a rerun of the Anglo-German antagonism of the early 1900s, with America in the role of Britain, and China in the role of imperial Germany. This is a better analogy because it captures the fact that a high level of economic integration does not necessarily prevent the growth of strategic rivalry and, ultimately, conflict.

We are a very long way from outright warfare, of course. The tectonic plates of geopolitics don't move that fast. But the danger signs are there. In a succession of official and semi-official statements, Chinese spokesmen have signaled their interest in a substitute for the dollar in the form of International Monetary Fund Special Drawing Rights, or even gold. At the very least, a gradual increase in the share of euros and yen in Chinese reserves must surely be in the cards. But they could go further than that. It's not impossible that, at some point within the next five to 10 years, the Chinese will feel ready to remove their capital controls and allow their own currency, the renminbi, to develop as a freely convertible international currency. At that point, the Chimerican marriage will be over. Not too surprising, really. As the name implied, such an unbalanced relationship was always something of chimera.

FERGUSON, a *Newsweek* contributor, is author of *The Ascent of Money: A Financial History of the World.*

Promises and Poverty

**Starbucks calls its coffee worker-friendly—
but in Ethiopia, a day's pay is a dollar.**

TOM KNUDSON

Gemadro, Ethiopia—Tucked inside a fancy black box, the $26-a-pound Starbucks Black Apron Exclusives coffee promised to be more than just another bag of beans.

Not only was the premium coffee from a remote plantation in Ethiopia "rare, exotic, cherished," according to Starbucks advertising, it was grown in ways that were good for the environment—and for local people, too.

Companies routinely boast about what they're doing for the planet, in part because guilt-ridden consumers expect as much—and are willing to pay extra for it. But, in this case, Starbucks' eco-friendly sales pitch does not begin to reflect the complex story of coffee in East Africa.

Inside the front flap of Starbucks' box are African arabica beans grown on a plantation in a threatened mountain rain forest. Behind the lofty phrases on the back label are coffee workers who make less than a dollar a day and a dispute between plantation officials and neighboring tribal people, who accuse the plantation of using their ancestral land and jeopardizing their way of life.

"We used to hunt and fish in there, and also we used to have honeybee hives in trees," one tribal member, Mikael Yatola, said through a translator. "But now we can't do that. . . . When we were told to remove our beehives from there, we felt deep sorrow, deep sadness."

25 New U.S. Stores per Week

Few companies have so dramatically conquered the American retail landscape as Starbucks. Last year, the $7.8 billion company opened an average of 25 new stores a week in the United States alone. Nowhere is Starbucks a more common sight than in environmentally conscious California, which has 2,350 outlets, more than New York, Massachusetts, Florida, Oregon and Washington—Starbucks' home state—combined.

No coffee company claims to do more for the environment and Third World farmers than Starbucks either. In full-page ads in *The New York Times,* in brochures and on its Web page, Starbucks says that it pays premium prices for premium beans, protects tropical forests and enhances the lives of farmers by building schools, clinics and other projects.

In places, Starbucks delivers on those promises, certainly more so than other multinational coffee companies. In parts of Latin America, for instance, its work has helped improve water quality, educate children and protect biodiversity.

Inside many Starbucks outlets across America, the African décor is hard to miss. There are photographs and watercolors of quaint coffee-growing scenes from Ethiopia to Tanzania to Zimbabwe. Yet such images clash with the reality of African life.

They don't show the industrial arm of coffee—the large farms and estates that encroach on wild forest regions. They don't reveal that even in the best of times in Ethiopia, the birthplace of wild coffee and the source of some of Starbucks' priciest offerings, there is barely enough for the peasant coffee farmers who still grow most of the nation's beans.

Even where Starbucks has built its bricks-and-mortar projects in Ethiopia, poverty remains a cornerstone of life, visible in the soot-stained cooking pots, spindly legs and ragged T-shirts, in the mad scramble of children for a visitor's cookie or empty water bottle.

"We plant coffee, harvest coffee but we never get anything out of it," said Muel Alema, a rail-thin coffee farmer who lives near a Starbucks-funded footbridge spanning

113

a narrow chasm in Ethiopia's famous Sidamo coffee-growing region.

Alema's tattered shirt looked years old. So did his mud-splattered thongs. The red coffee berries he sold to a local buyer last fall were mixed with mountains of others, stripped of their pulp and sold as beans to distant companies—like other farmers, he did not know which ones—that made millions selling Sidamo coffee. Only $220 dribbled back to him.

This February, after Alema paid workers to pick the beans and bought grain for his family, just $110 remained—not enough, he said, to feed his wife and three children, to buy them clothes until the crop ripens again.

'A Marketing Genius'

Starbucks conveys a different image on the white foil bags of Ethiopia Sidamo whole bean coffee it sells for $10.45 a pound. "Good coffee, doing good," says lettering on the side.

"We believe there's a connection between the farmers who grow our coffees, us and you. That's why we work together with coffee-growing communities—paying prices that help farmers support their families . . . and funding projects like building a bridge in Ethiopia's Sidamo region to help farmers get to market safely. . . . By drinking this coffee, you're helping to make a difference."

And while the Sidamo footbridge does make travel safer, it is but a simple yellow-brown concrete slab, 10 paces long.

Dean Cycon, founder of Dean's Beans, an organic coffee company in Massachusetts, calls Starbucks "a marketing genius."

"They put out cleverly crafted material that makes the consumer feel they are doing everything possible," Cycon said. "But there is no institutional commitment. They do it to capture a market and shut up the activists."

Starbucks officials insist such critics have it wrong. As proof, they point to Latin America, the source of the bulk of the company's beans.

"You go to Nariño, Colombia. We built 1,800 (coffee) washing stations and sanitation facilities and homes," said Dub Hay, Starbucks senior vice president for global coffee procurement. "It's literally changed the face of that whole area."

"The same is true throughout Latin America," Hay added. "They call it the Starbucks effect."

Starbucks' dealings in Latin America have drawn some fire. Near the El Triunfo Biosphere Reserve in Chiapas, Mexico, for instance, farmers cut off relations about three years ago over a dispute about selling to an exporter instead of directly to Starbucks. The new arrangement, farmers said, would drain profits from peasant growers.

Starbucks, the farmers charged in a memo to coffee buyers, was supporting "a pseudo-fair trade system, adapted to their own neo-liberal interests, to dismantle structures and advances that we have made."

In an e-mailed response to The Bee, Starbucks vice president for global communications, Frank Kern, wrote that the Chiapas farmers were ultimately "given the opportunity to ship directly to us as they requested, but they were unable to manage it."

Sharper Focus on Africa

In Ethiopia, Starbucks says, it spent $25,000 on three footbridges in 2004. The company estimates the structures are used by 70,000 farmers and family members—about 1 percent of those who depend upon coffee for income. Some Ethiopian coffee leaders say there is a better way to help.

"If we are paid a (coffee) price which is decent, the people can make the bridge on their own," said Tadesse Meskela, general manager of the Oromia Coffee Farmers' Cooperative Union of 100,000 farmers, which has sold to Starbucks. "We don't have to be always beggars."

Starbucks won't disclose what it pays for Ethiopian coffee. Instead, it lumps its purchases together into a global average, which last year was $1.42 a pound, 16 cents more than the Fair Trade minimum. Much of that money, though, never makes it into the pockets of farmers but instead is siphoned off by buyers, processors and other middlemen.

Starbucks executives say they want to shrink that supply chain. "You end up at least five levels removed from the farmer and that's where the money goes," said Hay. "And that's a shame." Hay said that as the company buys more coffee from Africa—it plans to double its purchases there to 36 million pounds by 2009—the commerce will spur more progress.

"That's our goal," Hay said. "Africa is 6 percent of our purchases. . . . Seventy percent is from Latin America. So that's where our money has gone."

Making an impact in Ethiopia is undeniably a challenge. Good roads, electricity, potable water don't exist in many places. The climate is often hostile. There are ethnic conflicts, border disputes and rebel movements, and a sea of young faces that gather every time a car stops.

Since 1990, Ethiopia's population has jumped from 52 million to about 80 million: two new Los Angeleses. The more people, the less there is to go around. Ethiopia's

114

per capita annual income is only $180, one of the lowest on Earth.

The environment is hurting, too, as coffee and tea plantations—as well as peasant farmers—spread into once wild areas, raising concern about the demise of one of the country's natural treasures: its biologically rich southwestern rain forest.

However, Samuel Assefa, the Ethiopian ambassador to the United States, said human suffering must be taken into consideration, too.

"We have a population of more than 80 million people, many of them living in rural and impoverished circumstances," he wrote in an e-mail. "Returning all cleared land to rain forest might be a victory for some extreme environmentalists, but it would condemn millions of my fellow citizens to starvation."

Atonement in a Cup

Starbucks has bought coffee from Africa for years. But now it is expanding rapidly there because it wants more of the continent's high-quality arabica beans. In Ethiopia alone, Starbucks purchases jumped 400 percent between 2002 and 2006.

While Starbucks is rapidly cloning retail outlets globally, 79 percent of its revenue last year was made in one caffeine-crazed country: the United States. With just 5 percent of the world's people, the United States drinks one-fifth of its coffee, more than any other nation.

Thanks largely to Starbucks, coffee is no longer just coffee. Now it is a vanilla soy latte, a java chip Frappuccino, a grande zebra mocha or—if you're feeling guilty—a Fair Trade-certified, bird-friendly, shade-grown caramel macchiato.

Starbucks did not pioneer the push for more equitable, conservation-based coffee. But it has woven the theme into everything from the earthy feel of its stores to its own certification program—called Coffee and Farmer Equity practices, or C.A.F.E.—that rewards farmers for meeting social and environmental goals.

"Social justice is becoming increasingly important to consumers," said industry analyst Judith Ganes-Chase as she flashed slides across a screen at a Long Beach coffee conference. One slide read: "Fair Trade is absolution in a cup."

Atonement, though, is not as simple as it may seem.

"It's very comfortable to believe Starbucks is doing the right thing—and to some degree, they are," said Eric Perkunder, a Seattle resident who worked as a Starbucks environmental manager in the 1980s and '90s. "They lull us into complacency. The stores are comfortable. You see pictures of people from origin countries. You believe

certain things they are telling you. But there's more to the story."

Dirt Road, Stick Huts

Part of that story lies in the southwestern corner of Ethiopia, in a swath of mountains not far from the Sudan border. There, a dirt road snakes through one of the country's largest coffee plantations—the Ethiopia Gemadro Estate—and comes to a halt in a dense mat of reeds and grasses.

A narrow path winds through the thicket and spills out into a clearing of stick huts. This is the home of an African Sheka tribe that for generations has lived off the land—catching fish, gathering wild honey and trapping animals in the forest. They call themselves the Shabuyye.

"The land over there used to belong to our forefathers," said Yatola, the tribal member in his 20s, as he nodded toward the plantation.

Conflict with local people and tribes is growing across southwest Ethiopia as coffee and tea plantations spread into the region under the government's effort to sow more development. At Gemadro, 2,496 acres of coffee were planted from 1998 to 2001 on land the company obtained from the government in a countylike jurisdiction called the Sheka Zone.

"One of Ethiopia's last remaining forests, Sheka Forest, is under huge pressure. . . . The rate of deforestation is now increasing and threatens the forest biodiversity . . . and the very livelihood" of forest-dwelling tribes, says the 2006 annual report of Melca Mahiber, an environmental group in the nation's capital, Addis Ababa.

However, Haile Michael Shiferaw, the plantation's manager—who attended the Long Beach coffee conference—said the Gemadro Estate had not displaced any tribe members.

"Before our farm was started," he said, "very few people were living in Gemadro."

Last year, Starbucks bought about 75,000 pounds of coffee from the Gemadro plantation and sold it as one of its "Black Apron Exclusives." At the time, the purchase was the 12th in the series of vintage offerings, six of which originated in Africa.

Starbucks packaged the beans in the fancy black box and inserted a flier touting the plantation's environmental and social track record. It also donated $15,000 to the Gemadro Estate for a school and health clinic.

"With its pure water supply, near pristine growing environment and dedication to conservation-based farming methods, this 2,300-hectare (5,700-acre) farm . . . is setting new standards for progressive, sustainable coffee farming," the flier said. "Gemadro workers and their families enjoy access to clean water, health care, housing and schools, all in keeping with the estate's commitment to maintain the highest standards of social and environmental stewardship."

Family's Income: 66 Cents a Day

Hailu is one of those workers. He stood outside his one-room, dirt-floor home, folded his arms across his chest and said that while he was happy to have a job, he was struggling to support his wife and family on just 6 Ethiopian birr per day—66 cents.

"Life is expensive," he said. "We have to go all the way to the town of Tepi (about 35 miles) for supplies." The round-trip bus ticket costs him four days' pay.

Plantation manager Shiferaw said Gemadro Estate wages are higher than the 55 cents a day workers earn at a government plantation near Tepi. Gemadro workers—most of whom are classified as temporary—also subsequently received a raise to between 77 cents and $1.10 a day, he said, adding, "We pay more than the minimum wage of the country."

That's still not a livable wage, according to the U.S. State Department. In a 2006 report on human rights in Ethiopia, the agency said that "there is no national minimum wage" and that public employees earn about $23 a month; private workers, $27. Those wages, it said, do "not provide a decent standard of living."

The Gemadro Estate is owned by Ethiopian-born Saudi Sheik Mohammed Al Amoudi, ranked by Forbes magazine as one of the world's 100 wealthiest individuals, with a net worth of $8 billion.

Al Amoudi owns many businesses in Ethiopia, from the posh Sheraton Hotel in Addis Ababa where rooms start at $270 a night—about a year's wages on the coffee plantation—to Ethio Agri-CEFT Plc, the farm management company that oversees the plantation.

Asked about the contrast between the sheik's wealth and the plantation wages, Assefa Tekle, Ethio Agri-CEFT's commercial manager, said, "There is no additional income that has been given from Sheik Al Amoudi. So what can you do? You have to be profitable to exist."

Ethiopian Ecology Suffers

Plantation wages are only one issue for workers and neighbors, however. The health care partially supported by Starbucks is another.

"When the estate came, they said they were going to give us adequate health service," said Geremew Gelito, an elder in the tiny village of Gemadro, where many estate workers live. He called the clinic bureaucratic and ineffective.

"As far as the promise of adequate health service, we have not received it," Gelito said. Shiferaw—the farm manager—said there are plans to improve the care. "It is not a very big clinic," he said, "but now we are increasing."

In his office above a furniture store in Addis Ababa, 2½ days' drive to the northeast, the agricultural manager for Ethio Agri-CEFT, Biru Abebe, said he was unaware of any complaints.

"Everybody goes and gets treatment," he said.

That even includes the native tribe, said Tekle, the commercial manager, a claim that exceeds that of Starbucks. "They are people of the environment so the farm has to give assistance."

But tribal member Yatola said the Shabuyye who live just downstream cannot get health care. "The company just gives medical attention to people who work for the company," he charged. Sitting in a stick hut, Yatola looked pensive. "We were isolated before. We didn't interact with anyone," he said as women outside pounded grain into mash with heavy wooden sticks. "But since the company has come, the road has acquainted us with the outside world."

Outsiders show up along the river, catching fish that feed the tribe, Yatola said. "There are less fish—and more people fishing," he said. "When we hear that the company, the way they have operated, they have created a nice relationship with the community, we know it's not true."

What's unfolding in the Gemadro region is not unique. An article in the April 2007 Journal of Agrarian Change points out that as coffee growing expands in southwest Ethiopia, the ecology can suffer.

"Environmental degradation is a serious concern with rates of deforestation estimated at 10,000 hectares per year (25,000 acres) in the coffee growing areas," the article said. "High levels of river pollution are also a major problem near coffee pulping and washing stations."

During the fall harvest, Yatola said, coffee processing pulp appears in the river from somewhere upstream. "The river becomes black, almost like oil," he said. "It smells like a dead horse."

Abebe, Ethio Agri-CEFT's agricultural manager, said the plantation has a lagoon to control pollution, that no waste flows from the Gemadro Estate. "The river is clean throughout the year. There is no pollution from our farm," he said. "Zero."

However, plantation manager Shiferaw said that not long ago valuable coffee beans did show up in the estate's wastewater lagoon, where a handful of workers and area farmers had dumped them in a failed theft attempt. "They are in prison now," he said.

In late February, four months after the bustling coffee harvest season, the Gemadro River looked clean. But in one of the ankle-deep side streams flowing into it, a white truck used to haul coffee was parked in the silvery water, being scrubbed of dirt and grease—a different but obvious pollution source.

"Sometimes it happens," acknowledged Tekle, the commercial manager.

"We don't have any control over that," Abebe said. "That road, though we made it, is a public road, so any truck can go and come."

Deforestation Takes a Toll

Although public, the road into the Gemadro Estate felt private. Armed guards checked vehicles entering or leaving to prevent coffee smuggling.

A row of rusty metal shacks looked like tool sheds, but were in fact worker housing. Even Shiferaw, the plantation manager, acknowledged they were not adequate.

"Yes, some is not. OK?" he said. "But we have a program to improve. When you see the standards of the country, it is better than most."

Along the bumpy dirt road, waxy green rows of coffee trees sprouted in rows, shaded by clumps of taller trees that not long ago were part of a denser, more diverse forest.

To Tadesse Gole—an ecologist in Addis Ababa and a native Ethiopian whose doctoral thesis at the University of Bonn, Germany, focused on preservation of wild arabica coffee—that manicured landscape is a biological calamity.

"This is an Afromontane rain forest—an area of high plant diversity, of unique epiphytic plants that grow on the branches of trees," Gole said. "We lose those plant species. And we lose many of the animals, birds and insects dependent on them."

Gole is the author of a recent study about the environmental and cultural impacts of coffee and tea plantations in Ethiopia, including the Gemadro Estate. The estate has spawned a wave of imitators, Gole said: smaller coffee and tea farms that are toppling more trees.

The estate itself is growing, too.

Last year, the Ethiopian Herald cited the plantation's project manager, Asenake Nigatu, telling the Ethiopian News Agency that Gemadro had "developed coffee on 1,000 hectares (about 2,470 acres) of land" it had obtained from the state investment bureau and had begun "activities to develop additional coffee on 1,500 hectares (about 3,700 acres) of land."

Gole tapped the touchpad on his laptop. An image based on satellite photography popped up showing land use changes in the Gemadro region from 1973 to 1987. A small puddle of red blotches appeared, indicating deforested areas. Gole tapped again, bringing up an image through 2001—three years after the plantation started. The red blotches had spread across the map, like measles. His eyes widened.

"This is quite big," he said.

In his study, prepared for a future book, Gole analyzed coffee planting and forest change across two woredas—local districts—in the Sheka Zone. "The area under forest cover has dropped significantly in all parts," he wrote in the study. One area in particular stood out.

"The highest deforestation rate was observed in Gemadro, with (an) annual deforestation rate of 12.2 percent," he wrote.

But Abebe, the Ethio-Agri CEFT agricultural manager, said Gole's statements are misleading because the region was partially settled and cleared before the plantation came.

Ambassador Assefa agreed. "As I understand it, the land was largely cleared before Gemadro acquired the property," he said.

In addition, Abebe said, Gemadro is helping the land recover by incorporating conservation principles into its practices. To bolster his point, he pointed to an award the estate recently received from the Southern Nations, Nationalities and Peoples' Regional State for, he said, "being a model coffee farm."

Those model practices include planting grasses and reeds to slow erosion, planting shade trees for coffee and leaving 3,200 acres untouched for wildlife, Abebe said, adding that they "have even planted indigenous trees in the appropriate areas."

Gole, however, said such practices come up short. Many trees are non-native, he said, changing the composition of the forests. The plantation's Web site says cover crops planted there include some from South America, Mexico and India.

Struggle over Trademarks

The Ethiopian government's advocacy for its coffee industry—as well as for tea and other rural developments—has drawn international concern about the fate of its highland rain forests. A 2007 article by two German scientists blamed a lack of consistent forest policies.

"Ethiopia's montane rain forests are declining at an alarming rate," scientists Carmen Richerzhagen and Detlef Virchow wrote in the *International Journal of Biotechnology.* "The absence of a land use policy in Ethiopia creates spontaneous decisions on land allocations in a disorganized manner—therefore the forest is always the one to suffer."

But Ethiopia's push to grow more coffee drew plenty of encouragement at a conference in Addis Ababa in

February attended by representatives of the world's leading coffee companies, including Starbucks.

At the time, Starbucks and Ethiopia were locked in a struggle over the government's effort to trademark its famous coffee names—including Muel Alema's Sidamo—to create a distinctive brand that could funnel more profits back to the countryside.

Starbucks fought the effort, saying geographical certification programs, such as those in place for Colombian coffees, keep prices higher by guaranteeing that coffee from Colombia really is from Colombia.

"A trademark does not do that," said Hay, the Starbucks vice president, in a February interview in Addis Ababa. "It could be Sidamo and toilet paper. It doesn't mean anything about the region or the quality."

At times, the dispute turned bitter.

"What I don't understand is why Starbucks is resisting this," said Getachew Mengistie, director general of Ethiopia's Intellectual Property Office. "They are for improving the lives of the farmers. We are for improving the lives of the farmers. Where is the problem?"

In May, the issue was resolved in the government's favor, a positive step, said the ambassador.

"Starbucks is an important supporter of Ethiopia's efforts to control our specialty coffee brands, and it is critical that our relationship isn't about charity but about sound business," Ambassador Assefa said. "While the company only buys a small fraction of Ethiopia's coffee, our agreement will encourage market forces to allow Ethiopian farmers to capture a greater share of retail prices. This broad effort already has benefited thousands of poor farmers and could potentially benefit millions more."

Who Checked the Plantation?

Improving the lives of farmers and the environment is the goal of many coffee certification systems, such as Fair Trade, Rain Forest Alliance and Smithsonian Bird-Friendly. The Gemadro Estate has been approved by the European-based Utz Certified, an organization started by a Dutch coffee roaster and Guatemalan growers.

"It's good," said Yehasab Aschale, Utz's field representative in Ethiopia who said he toured the Gemadro plantation last year. "They are environmentally friendly. They are planting shade trees of the indigenous types. And they are improving the working conditions of the workers."

Starbucks also gave the estate's beans its own C.A.F.E. practices approval last year, signifying that the plantation protected the environment, paid workers fairly and provided them with decent housing.

Yet no one from Starbucks ever inspected the Gemadro plantation for C.A.F.E. certification. Dub Hay—the Starbucks global purchasing executive—said he knew little about the plantation because he hadn't been there. Starbucks bought the coffee after tasting it in Europe, Hay said, adding that a coffee buyer from Switzerland visited at some point.

No one from the company Starbucks pays to oversee C.A.F.E. verification, Scientific Certification Systems of Emeryville, inspected Gemadro either. Instead, the plantation hired and paid an Africa-based company to do the job—a common industry practice.

Then, something out of the ordinary happened: The African company's inspector was fired for doing a poor job, a fact that emerged only after The Bee asked about the verification process.

"Clearly, the inspector didn't do as good, or as thorough, a job as is to be expected in C.A.F.E. practices," said Ted Howes, vice president of corporate social responsibility for Scientific Certification Systems.

Howes declined to release a copy of the inspection report, but he said his company would visit the plantation this year. "There are issues we want to look at more closely," he said.

Dennis Macray, Starbucks' director of corporate responsibility, added that such problems "can happen in any kind of a system. . . . You can have something go wrong."

If the C.A.F.E. certification process was flawed, why did Starbucks certify the beans?

"I can't tell you," Macray said at the Long Beach conference. With that, the trail went cold. Macray did not return follow-up calls. Starbucks spokeswoman Stacey Krum said details are confidential.

Krum, however, defended C.A.F.E. practices in general.

"There isn't a standard code for the coffee industry; this is something we are learning as we go along," she said. "And we are proud of it and confident it is achieving results."

Bee reporter TOM KNUDSON spent three weeks in Ethiopia during his four months of reporting this story, including journeys to the Gemadro Estate, the Sidamo and Yirgacheffe regions, and an international coffee conference in Addis Ababa. He interviewed coffee farmers, plantation workers, tribal people, scientists and coffee industry leaders in Africa and the United States. And he reviewed dozens of studies, reports, books and scientific journal articles about coffee growing and marketing. Travel and research were underwritten by a grant from the Alicia Patterson Foundation in Washington, D.C.

Not Your Father's Latin America

Its troubles continue, but the region has made real progress.

DUNCAN CURRIE

Hugo Chávez likes to boast that history is on his side. During a recent broadcast of his talk show, *Aló Presidente,* the Venezuelan leader informed Barack Obama that "the process of change in Latin America is not going to stop," even if the U.S. deploys naval fleets and fighter planes. It's easy to dismiss such rhetoric as typical Chávez bluster. But is there a nugget of truth in it? Is Venezuela's illiberal "Bolivarian revolution" really sweeping Latin America?

The short answer is no. The longer answer is that, while various small countries have embraced Chávez-style populism, most of the region's large economic powers have not. In general, Latin American officials have greatly improved their fiscal and monetary policies, making their economies less sensitive to external shocks. Though Latin America has not escaped the global recession and is still plagued by many of its perennial troubles—such as widespread corruption, high levels of violent crime, ethnic fissures, and yawning inequality—its recent progress offers grounds for optimism.

We must appreciate just how far Latin America has come. From the late 1970s through the early 2000s, the region went through a seemingly endless series of economic and financial implosions. Meanwhile, frequent military coups and prolonged civil wars stifled its movement toward liberal democracy.

Even after free elections and constitutional government became the norm, inflation remained a scourge, and currency meltdowns continued to wreak havoc. The 2001–02 Argentine financial crisis sparked a full-blown economic collapse and a massive debt default, which fueled severe turmoil in neighboring countries. In mid-2002, the Bush administration endorsed a $30 billion International Monetary Fund bailout for Brazil (which was suffering from its own domestic woes) and dispatched a $1.5 billion Treasury loan to Uruguay. The U.S. took a stemer line on Argentina but eventually supported a new IMF loan package after Argentine economy minister Roberto Lavagna implemented some prudent reforms that mitigated the crisis.

As the global economy recovered, so did Latin America's. Between 2002 and 2008, the region enjoyed its most robust expansion in decades. Unlike the growth spurt during the 1990s, this one led to substantial poverty reduction. According to World Bank estimates, the poverty rate in Latin America and the Caribbean—that is, the share of the population living on less than $4 a day (in purchasing-power-parity terms)—fell from 45.4 percent in 2002 to 32.5 percent in 2008. Over that same period, the rate of extreme poverty (the portion living on less than $2 a day) dropped from 21.5 percent to 13.1 percent.

Had Latin America just gotten lucky? After all, its anti-poverty gains occurred during an era of abundant liquidity, high commodity prices, and booming global trade. But that wasn't the whole story: Latin America also strengthened its fundamentals, taming inflation and accumulating foreign-exchange reserves while slashing its external debt. An April 2008 Inter-American Development Bank study pointed to lingering vulnerabilities but affirmed that economic management in the region had "noticeably improved." More recently, a May 2009 IMF survey said that many Latin American countries "have made strides in strengthening fiscal positions and public debt structures, solidifying financial systems and their regulation, anchoring inflation expectations, and building more credible policy frameworks."

Latin America's experience during the current global slump has underscored these achievements. The downturn has been painful (in some countries, deeply painful) but not cataclysmic. Previous recessions in Latin America triggered banking and currency disasters. Not this one. The region has demonstrated that it is much more resilient now than it was in the past. Alberto Ramos, senior Latin America economist at Goldman Sachs, says the difference is "night and day."

Perhaps the most pleasant surprise of recent Latin American history has been the performance of Brazilian president Luiz. Inácio Lula da Silva, a former union boss whose 2002 election spooked the investment community. Lula's predecessor, Fernando Henrique Cardoso, was a more conservative social democrat who had helped devise and manage the anti-inflationary "Plano Real" during his tenures as Brazilian finance minister (1993–94) and president (1995–2003). As former Federal Reserve chairman Alan Greenspan writes in *The Age of Turbulence,* the Plano Real "successfully brought the nation's roaring inflation to a halt after it had surged more than 5,000 percent during the twelve months between mid-1993 and mid-1994."

Lula, a member of the left-wing Workers' Party and a long-time friend of Cuban dictator Fidel Castro, had fiercely opposed the Plano Real. He had also spent years attacking free-market economics and calling for major social changes. How would he govern as president? "To the surprise of most, myself included," writes Greenspan, "he has largely followed the sensible policies embodied in the Plano Real." Indeed, there has been a great deal of continuity between the Cardoso and Lula administrations. Despite being dogged by assorted scandals, Lula has acquired enormous popularity and international stature.

He is part of a bigger trend: Throughout Latin America, there is a growing center-left political class that broadly agrees with conservatives about the basic tenets of good economic stewardship. "This is a very positive development for the region," says economist Luis Oganes, head of Latin America research at J. P. Morgan. In a 2007 *New Republic* article, foreign-affairs scholar Walter Russell Mcad wrote that "Latin America is now beginning to acquire something it has sorely lacked: a left-of-center political leadership able to combine its mission of serving the poor with a firm commitment to currency stability, the rule of law, and the development of a favorable business climate."

This can be seen in countries such as Chile, Uruguay, and Peru. The Chilean economy remains the most dynamic in Latin America. Since 1990, it has been piloted by the center-left Concertación coalition, which inherited a slew of free-market reforms from the Pinochet dictatorship. Successive Concentación governments "kept the broad thrust of the dictatorship's economic policies, deepened some of them and reformed others," writes journalist Michael Reid in *Forgotten Continent*. "That bestowed democratic legitimacy on the 'Chilean model.'" During the recent commodity boom, Chile saved a hefty chunk of its copper windfall. As the *Wall Street Journal* reports, this enabled it to craft "one of the largest stimulus packages in the world relative to the size of its economy."

In Uruguay, the center-left administration of Pres. Tabaré Vázquez has promoted a solid economic agenda and completed a "trade and investment framework agreement" with the United States. In Peru, Pres. Alan García has effectively repudiated his earlier stint as chief executive in the late 1980s, when he espoused economic populism and unleashed hyper-inflation. Since returning to the presidency in 2006, Garcia has governed as a born-again neoliberal.

His 2006 election campaign reflected a larger ideological struggle. García defeated Ollanta Humala, a radical populist favored by Chávez, after telling voters to choose "between Hugo Chávez and Peru." That same year, conservative Felipe Calderón won a razor-thin victory over leftist Andrés Manuel López Obrador to capture the Mexican presidency. Just as García did in Peru, Calderòn linked his opponent to Chávez. It proved a smart strategy, as Calderón came from behind to triumph.

All of these countries—Brazil, Chile, Uruguay, Peru, and Mexico—have rejected *Chavismo*. All five have inflation-targeting central banks. So does Colombia, which has made greater progress over the past half-decade than any other country in the hemisphere. Pres. Álvaro Uribe took office in 2002 amid a horrendous guerrilla war that threatened to turn Colombia into a failed state. Since then, the government has reclaimed Bogotá, Medellín, and other cities from left-wing rebels; demobilized

thousands of right-wing paramilitaries; dramatically reduced violence; and fostered a more attractive business environment. Prior to the recession, Colombia's GDP was growing at its fastest rate since the 1970s. National police data show that in 2008, the country had 44 percent fewer homicides and 75 percent fewer massacres than it did in 2002.

Yet the number of massacres increased slightly from 2007 to 2008, and new scandals have emerged concerning extrajudicial killings by the army. Uribe helped expose paramilitary infiltration of the political system, but the subsequent discoveries have implicated many of his supporters. As for the drug war, an October 2008 Government Accountability Office report said that Plan Colombia, the vast U.S. aid package begun under President Clinton, had "not fully achieved" its drug-reduction goals but had nonetheless contributed to "major security advances." Uribe is still immensely popular, though he has raised eyebrows by musing about a third term in office. (His current term expires in 2010.) Colombian lawmakers already amended their constitution to let him run for a second term in 2006.

It would be the height of moral confusion to associate Uribe, a staunch democrat, with Latin America's populist rabble. But revising constitutions to extend or abolish term limits is the preferred strategy of Chávez and his ilk. That's what ousted Honduran president Manuel Zelaya was trying to do, via an illegal "referendum," before the supreme court and the military intervened.

His removal trimmed the ranks of Chávez allies. In 2008, Honduras had joined the "Bolivarian Alternative for the Americas," a Chávez-led trade group whose members now include Venezuela, Cuba, Bolivia, Nicaragua, Ecuador, and a few tiny Caribbean nations. Heavily dependent on tourism, the impoverished Caribbean islands are especially susceptible to Chávez's petro-diplomacy. The governments of Bolivia, Nicaragua, and Ecuador feel an ideological attachment to Venezuela. All of them have, to varying degrees, embraced illiberal populism. So has Argentina, where Pres. Cristina Kirchner nationalized the private-pension system late last year.

Though Venezuela, Argentina, and Ecuador posted impressive growth rates when commodity prices were booming, they are now dealing with the consequences of reckless policy decisions. The Kirchner government suffered a crushing setback in Argentina's June 28 congressional elections. "There was definitely a shift to the right in Argentina," says Oganes. In Venezuela, unfortunately, Chávez won a referendum on scrapping term limits this past February, and he has intensified his attacks on independent media outlets and opposition politicians. Chávez is also lending full-throated support to Zelaya as the deposed Honduran leader seeks to reclaim his former office.

Beyond the unrest in Honduras, Central America faces a raft of economic and security challenges. Costa Rica and Panama remain its most stable and prosperous countries. The latter is now led by a conservative supermarket baron named Ricardo Martinelli. El Salvador also has a new president, Mauricio Funes, who represents the FMLN, a former leftist guerrilla outfit turned political party. Funes cites Lula as his model and "has filled the cabinet mostly with moderates," says Michael Shifter, a vice president at the Inter-American Dialogue. But it is unclear whether Funes can genuinely transform the FMLN and curb soaring crime. In neighboring Guatemala, Pres. Álvaro Colom has been hobbled by a sensational murder scandal at a time when his country is being over-whelmed by drug violence.

Meanwhile, such violence continues to generate grisly headlines in Mexico. It has exacerbated a nasty recession (the worst in Latin America), as has the swine-flu panic. President Calderón deserves credit for tackling the narco-gangs with military force. Though his anti-crime campaign is still widely popular, his party got thrashed in Mexico's July 5 congressional elections. That makes it even less likely that Calderón will be able to undertake the tax, energy, and labor-market reforms necessary to boost his country's long-term economic performance.

"To change Mexico, you really need an extraordinary leader," says economist Rafael Amiel, regional managing director for Latin America at IHS Global Insight. "I'm more hopeful about Brazil than Mexico." Like other Latin American countries, both Brazil and Mexico require deep structural changes in order to realize their full growth potential. "The Latin American experience has laid bare the fact that private ownership and fiscal prudence yield only limited benefits in a regime of overbearing taxation and regulation," writes Harvard economist Andrei Shleifer.

While the ongoing recession has aggravated social tensions and reversed some of the region's anti-poverty gains, Latin America's recent record is one of significant progress. "Many countries are on the right track," says Amiel. But a smaller cluster—the Chávez bloc—is clearly on the wrong track. As Shifter puts it, "We have different Latin Americas, and they're moving in very different directions."

It's Still the One

Oil's very future is now being seriously questioned, debated, and challenged. The author of an acclaimed history explains why, just as we need more oil than ever, it is changing faster than we can keep up with.

DANIEL YERGIN

On a still afternoon under a hot Oklahoma sun, neither a cloud nor an ounce of "volatility" was in sight. Anything but. All one saw were the somnolent tanks filled with oil, hundreds of them, spread over the rolling hills, some brand-new, some more than 70 years old, and some holding, inside their silver or rust-orange skins, more than half a million barrels of oil each.

This is Cushing, Oklahoma, the gathering point for the light, sweet crude oil known as West Texas Intermediate—or just WTI. It is the oil whose price you hear announced every day, as in "WTI closed today at. . . ." Cushing proclaims itself, as the sign says when you ride into town, the "pipeline crossroads of the world." Through it passes the network of pipes that carry oil from Texas and Oklahoma and New Mexico, from Louisiana and the Gulf Coast, and from Canada too, into Cushing's tanks, where buyers take title before moving the oil onward to refineries where it is turned into gasoline, jet fuel, diesel, home heating oil, and all the other products that people actually use.

But that is not what makes Cushing so significant. After all, there are other places in the world through which much more oil flows. Cushing plays a unique role in the new global oil industry because WTI is the preeminent benchmark against which other oils are priced. Every day, billions of "paper barrels" of light, sweet crude are traded on the floor of the New York Mercantile Exchange in lower Manhattan and, in ever increasing volumes, at electron speed around the world, an astonishing virtual commerce that no matter how massive in scale, still connects back somehow to a barrel of oil in Cushing changing owners.

That frenetic daily trading has helped turn oil into something new—not only a physical commodity critical to the security and economic viability of nations but also a financial asset, part of that great instantaneous exchange of stocks, bonds, currencies, and everything else that makes up the world's financial portfolio. Today, the daily trade in those "paper barrels"—crude oil futures—is more than 10 times the world's daily consumption of physical barrels of oil. Add in the trades that take place on other exchanges or outside them entirely, and the ratio may be as much as 30 times greater. And though the oil may flow steadily in and out of Cushing at a stately 4 miles per hour, the global oil market is anything but stable.

That's why, as I sat down to work on a new edition of *The Prize* and considered what had changed since the early 1990s, when I wrote this history of the world's most valuable, and misunderstood, commodity, the word "volatility" kept springing to mind. How could it not? Indeed, when people are talking about volatility, they are often thinking oil. On July 11, 2008, WTI hit $147.27. Exactly a year later, it was $59.87. In between, in December, it fell as low as $32.40. (And don't forget a little more than a decade ago, when it was as low as $10 a barrel and consumers were supposedly going to swim forever in a sea of cheap oil.)

These wild swings don't just affect the "hedgers" (oil producers, airlines, heating oil dealers, etc.) and the "speculators," the financial players. They show up in the changing prices at the gasoline station. They stir political passions and feed consumers' suspicions. Volatility also makes it more difficult to plan future energy investments, whether in oil and gas or in renewable and alternative fuels. And it can have a cataclysmic impact on the world economy. After all, Detroit was knocked flat on its back by what happened at the gasoline pump in 2007 and 2008 even before the credit crisis. The enormous impact of these swings is why British Prime Minister Gordon Brown and French President Nicolas Sarkozy were recently moved to call for a global solution to "destructive volatility." But, they were forced to add, "There are no easy solutions."

This volatility is part of the new age of oil. For though Cushing looks pretty much the same as it did when *The Prize* came out, the world of oil looks very different. Some talk today about "the end of oil." If so, others reply, we are entering its very long goodbye. One characteristic of this new age is that oil has developed a split personality—as a physical commodity but also now as a financial asset. Three other defining characteristics of this new age are the globalization of the demand for oil, a vast shift from even a decade ago; the rise of climate change as a political factor shaping decisions on how we will use oil, and how much of it, in the future; and the drive for new technologies that could dramatically affect oil along with the rest of the energy portfolio.

The cast of characters in the oil business has also grown and changed. Some oil companies have become "supermajors," such as ExxonMobil and Chevron, while others, such as Amoco and ARCO, have just disappeared. "Big oil" no longer means the traditional international oil companies, their logos instantly recognizable from corner gas stations, but rather much larger state-owned companies, which, along with governments, today control more than 80 percent of the world's oil reserves. Fifteen of the world's 20 largest oil companies are now state-owned.

The cast of oil traders has also much expanded. Today's global oil game now includes pension funds, institutional money managers, endowments, and hedge funds, as well as individual investors and day traders. The managers at the pension funds and the university endowments see themselves as engaged in "asset allocation," hedging risks and diversifying to protect retirees' incomes and faculty salaries. But, technically, they too are part of the massive growth in the ranks of the new oil speculators.

With all these changes, the very future of this most vital commodity is now being seriously questioned, debated, and challenged, even as the world will need more of it than ever before. Both the U.S. Department of Energy and the International Energy Agency project that, even accounting for gains in efficiency, global energy use will increase almost 50 percent from 2006 to 2030—and that oil will continue to provide 30 percent or more of the world's energy in 2030.

But will it?

$147.27-Closing price per barrel of oil on July 11, 2008. Exactly one year later, it had fallen to $59.87.

From the beginning, oil has been a global industry, going back to 1861 when the first cargo of kerosene was sent from Pennsylvania—the Saudi Arabia of 19th-century oil—to Britain. (The potential crew was so fearful that the kerosene would catch fire that they had to be gotten drunk to shanghai them on board.) But that is globalization of supply, a familiar story. What is decisively new is the globalization of demand.

For decades, most of the market—and the markets that mattered the most—were in North America, Western Europe, and Japan. That's also where the growth was. At the time of the first Gulf War in 1991, China was still an oil exporter.

But now, the growth is in China, India, other emerging markets, and the Middle East. Between 2000 and 2007, the world's daily oil demand increased by 9.4 million barrels. Almost 85 percent of that growth was in emerging markets. There were many reasons that prices soared all the way to $147.27 last year, ranging from geopolitics to a weak dollar to the impact of financial markets and speculation (in all its manifold meanings). But the starting point was the fundamentals—the surge in oil demand driven by powerful economic growth in emerging markets. This shift may be even more powerful than people recognize: So far this year, more new cars have been sold in China than in the United States. When economic recovery

The Capital of Oil

Within three years of its discovery in 1912, the Cushing field in Oklahoma was producing almost 20 percent of U.S. oil. Two years later, it was supplying a substantial part of the fuel used by the U.S. Army in Europe during World War I. The Cushing area was so prolific that it became known as "the Queen of the Oil Fields," and Cushing became one of those classic wild oil boomtowns of the early 20th century. "Any man with red blood gets oil fever" was the diagnosis of one reporter who visited the area during those days. Production grew so fast around Cushing that pipelines had to be hurriedly built and storage tanks quickly thrown up to hold surplus supplies. By the time production began to decline, a great deal of infrastructure was in place, and Cushing turned into a key oil hub, its network of pipelines used to bring in supplies from elsewhere in Oklahoma and West Texas. Those supplies were stored in the tanks at Cushing before being put into other pipelines and shipped to refineries. When the New York Mercantile Exchange—the NYMEX—started to trade oil futures in 1983, it needed a physical delivery point. Cushing, its boom days long gone, but with its network of pipelines and tank farms and its central location, was the obvious answer. As much as 1.1 million barrels per day pass in and out of Cushing—equivalent to about 6 percent of U.S. oil consumption. But prices for much of the world's crude oil are set against the benchmark of the West Texas Intermediate crude oil—also known as "domestic sweet"—sitting in those 300 or so tanks in Cushing, making this sedate Oklahoma town not only an oil hub but one of the hubs of the world economy.

—Daniel Yergin

takes hold again, what happens to oil demand in such emerging countries will be crucial.

The math is clear: More consumers mean more demand, which means more supplies are needed. But what about the politics? There the forecasts are murkier, feeding a new scenario for international tension—a competition, even a clash, between China and the United States over "scarce" oil resources. This scenario even comes with a well-known historical model—the rivalry between Britain and "rising" Germany that ended in the disaster of World War I.

This scenario, though compelling reading, does not really accord with the way that the world oil market works. The Chinese are definitely new players, willing and able to pay top dollar to gain access to existing and new oil sources and, lately, also making loans to oil-producing countries to ensure future supplies. With more than $2 trillion in foreign reserves, China certainly has the wherewithal to be in the lending business.

But the global petroleum industry is not a go-it-alone business. Because of the risk and costs of large-scale development, companies tend to work in consortia with other companies.

Oil-exporting countries seek to diversify the countries and companies they work with. Inevitably, any country in China's position—whose demand had grown from 2.5 million barrels per day to 8 million in a decade and a half—would be worrying about supplies. Such an increase, however, is not a forecast of inevitable strife; it is a message about economic growth and rising standards of living. It would be much more worrying if, in the face of rising demand, Chinese companies were not investing in production both inside China (the source of half of its supply) and outside its borders.

There are potential flash points in this new world of oil. But they will not come from standard commercial competition. Rather, they arise when oil (along with natural gas) gets caught up in larger foreign-policy issues—most notably today, the potentially explosive crisis over the nuclear ambitions of oil- and gas-rich Iran.

Yet, despite all the talk of an "oil clash" scenario, there seems to be less overall concern than a few years ago and much more discussion about "energy dialogue." The Chinese themselves appear more confident about their increasingly important place in this globalized oil market. Although the risks are still there, the Chinese—and the Indians right alongside them—have the same stake as other consumers in an adequately supplied world market that is part of the larger global economy. Disruption of that economy, as the last year has so vividly demonstrated, does not serve their purposes. Why would the Chinese want to get into a confrontation over oil with the United States when the U.S. export market is so central to their economic growth and when the two countries are so financially interdependent?

Oil is not even the most important energy issue between China and the United States. It is coal. The two countries have the world's largest coal resources, and they are the world's biggest consumers of it. In a carbon-constrained world, they share a strong common interest in finding technological solutions for the emissions released when coal is burned.

And that leads directly to the second defining feature of the new age of oil: climate change. Global warming was already on the agenda when *The Prize* came out. It was back in 1992 that 154 countries signed the Rio Convention, pledging to dramatically reduce CO_2 concentrations in the atmosphere. But only in recent years has climate change really gained traction as a political issue—in Europe early in this decade, in the United States around 2005. Whatever the outcome of December's U.N. climate change conference in Copenhagen, carbon regulation is now part of the future of oil. And that means a continuing drive to reduce oil demand.

How does that get done? How does the world at once meet both the challenge of climate change and the challenge of economic growth—steady expansion in the industrial countries and more dramatic growth in China, India, and other emerging markets as tens of millions of their citizens rise from poverty and buy appliances and cars?

The answer has to be in another defining change—an emphasis on technology to a degree never before seen. The energy business has always been a technology business. After all, the men who figured out in 1859, exactly 150 years ago, how to drill that first oil well—Colonel Drake and his New Haven, Conn., investors—would, in today's lingo, be described as a group of disruptive technology entrepreneurs and venture capitalists. Again and again, in researching oil's history, I was struck by how seemingly insurmountable barriers and obstacles were overcome by technological progress, often unanticipated.

9.4 million-Number of barrels by which the world's daily oil demand rose from 2000 to 2007, with 85 percent coming from the developing world.

But the focus today on technology—all across the energy spectrum—is of unprecedented intensity. In the mid-1990s, I chaired a task force for the U.S. Department of Energy on "strategic energy R&D." Our panel worked very hard for a year and a half and produced what many considered a very worthy report. But there was not all that much follow-through. The Gulf War was over, and the energy problem looked like it had been "solved."

Today, by contrast, the interest in energy technology is enormous. And it will only be further stoked by the substantial increases that are ahead in government support for energy R&D. Much of that spending and effort is aimed at finding alternatives to oil. Yet the challenge is not merely to find alternatives; it is to find alternatives that can be competitive at the massive scale required.

What will those alternatives be? The electric car, which is the hottest energy topic today? Advanced biofuels? Solar systems? New building designs? Massive investment in wind? The evolving smart grid, which can integrate electric cars with the electricity industry? Something else that is hardly on the radar screen yet? Or perhaps a revolution in the internal combustion engine, making it two to three times as efficient as the ones in cars today?

We can make educated guesses. But, in truth, we don't know, and we won't know until we do know. For now, it is clear that the much higher levels of support for innovation—along with considerable government incentives and subsidies—will inevitably drive technological change and thus redraw the curve in the future demand for oil.

Indeed, the biggest surprises might come on the demand side, through conservation and improved energy efficiency. The United States is twice as energy efficient as it was in the 1970s. Perhaps we will see a doubling once again. Certainly, energy efficiency has never before received the intense focus and support that it does today.

Just because we have entered this new age of high-velocity change does not mean this story is about the imminent end of oil. Consider the "peak oil" thesis—shorthand for the presumption that the world has reached the high point of production and is headed for a downward slope. Historically, peak-oil thinking gains attention during times when markets are tight and prices are rising, stoking fears of a permanent shortage. In 2007 and 2008, the belief system built around peak oil helped drive prices to $147.27. (It was actually the fifth time that the world had supposedly "run out" of oil. The first such episode was in the 1880s; the last instance before this most recent time was in the 1970s.)

However, careful examination of the world's resource base—including my own firm's analysis of more than 800 of the largest oil fields—indicates that the resource endowment of the planet is sufficient to keep up with demand for decades to come. That, of course, does not mean that the oil will actually make it to consumers. Any number of "aboveground" risks and obstacles can stand in the way, from government policies that restrict access to tax systems to civil conflict to geopolitics to rising costs of exploration and production to uncertainties about demand. As has been the case for decades and decades, the shifting relations between producing and consuming countries, between traditional oil companies and state-owned oil companies, will do much to determine what resources are developed, and when, and thus to define the future of the industry.

There are two further caveats. Many of the new projects will be bigger, more complex, and more expensive. In the 1990s, a "megaproject" might have cost $500 million to $1 billion. Today, the price tag is more like $5 billion to $10 billion. And an increasing part of the new petroleum will come in the form of so-called "unconventional oil"—from ultradeep waters, Canadian oil sands, and the liquids that are produced with natural gas.

But through all these changes, one constant of the oil market is that it is not constant. The changing balance of supply and demand—shaped by economics, politics, technologies, consumer tastes, and accidents of all sorts—will continue to move

prices. Economic recovery, expectations thereof, the pent-up demand for "demand," a shift into oil as a "financial asset"—some combination of these could certainly send oil prices up again, even with the current surplus in the market. Yet, the quest for stability is also a constant for oil, whether in reaction to the boom-and-bust world of northwest Pennsylvania in the late 19th century, the 10-cents-a-barrel world of Texas oil in the 1930s, or the $147.27 barrel of West Texas Intermediate in July 2008.

Certainly, the roller-coaster ride of oil prices over the last couple of years, as oil markets and financial markets have become more integrated, has made volatility a central pre-occupation for policymakers who do not want to see their economies whipsawed by huge price swings. Yet without the flexibility and liquidity of markets, there is no effective way to balance supply and demand, no way for consumers and producers to hedge their risks. Nor is there a way to send signals to these consumers and producers about how much oil to use and how much money to invest—or signals to would-be innovators about tomorrow's opportunities.

One part of the solution is not only enhancement of the already considerable regulation of the financial markets where oil is traded, but also greater transparency and better understanding of who the players are in the rapidly expanding financial oil markets. But regulatory changes cannot eliminate market cycles or repeal the laws of supply and demand in the world's largest organized commodity market. Those cycles may not be much in evidence amid the quiet tanks and rolling hills at Cushing. But they are inescapably part of the global landscape of the new world of oil.

Daniel Yergin received a Pulitzer Prize for *The Prize: The Epic Quest for Oil, Money and Power,* published in an updated edition this year. He is chairman of IHS Cambridge Energy Research Associates.

Reprinted in entirety by McGraw-Hill with permission from *FOREIGN POLICY*, September/October 2009, pp. 90, 92–95. www.foreignpolicy.com. © 2009 Washingtonpost. Newsweek Interactive, LLC.

Seven Myths about Alternative Energy

As the world looks around anxiously for an alternative to oil, energy sources such as biofuels, solar, and nuclear seem like they could be the magic ticket. They're not."

MICHAEL GRUNWALD

What Comes Next?
Imagining the Post-Oil World

Nothing is as fraught with myths, misperceptions, and outright flights of fancy as the conversation about oil's successors. We asked two authors—award-winning environmental journalist Michael Grunwald and energy consultant David J. Rothkopf—to take aim at some of these myths, and look over the horizon to see which technologies might win the day and which ones could cause unexpected new problems. If fossil fuels are indeed saying their very long goodbye, then their would-be replacements still have a lot to prove.

1. "We Need to Do Everything Possible to Promote Alternative Energy"

Not exactly. It's certainly clear that fossil fuels are mangling the climate and that the status quo is unsustainable. There is now a broad scientific consensus that the world needs to reduce greenhouse gas emissions more than 25 percent by 2020—and more than 80 percent by 2050. Even if the planet didn't depend on it, breaking our addictions to oil and coal would also reduce global reliance on petrothugs and vulnerability to energy-price spikes.

But though the world should do everything sensible to promote alternative energy, there's no point trying to do everything possible. There are financial, political, and technical pressures as well as time constraints that will force tough choices; solutions will need to achieve the biggest emissions reductions for the least money in the shortest time. Hydrogen cars, cold fusion, and other speculative technologies might sound cool, but they could divert valuable resources from ideas that are already achievable and cost-effective. It's nice that someone managed to run his car on liposuction leftovers, but that doesn't mean he needs to be subsidized.

Reasonable people can disagree whether governments should try to pick energy winners and losers. But why not at least agree that governments shouldn't pick losers to be winners? Unfortunately,

that's exactly what is happening. The world is rushing to promote alternative fuel sources that will actually accelerate global warming, not to mention an alternative power source that could cripple efforts to stop global warming.

We can still choose a truly alternative path. But we'd better hurry.

2. "Renewable Fuels Are the Cure for Our Addiction to Oil"

Unfortunately not. "Renewable fuels" sound great in theory, and agricultural lobbyists have persuaded European countries and the United States to enact remarkably ambitious biofuels mandates to promote farm-grown alternatives to gasoline. But so far in the real world, the cures—mostly ethanol derived from corn in the United States or biodiesel derived from palm oil, soybeans, and rapeseed in Europe—have been significantly worse than the disease.

Researchers used to agree that farm-grown fuels would cut emissions because they all made a shockingly basic error. They gave fuel crops credit for soaking up carbon while growing, but it never occurred to them that fuel crops might displace vegetation that soaked up even more carbon. It was as if they assumed that biofuels would only be grown in parking lots. Needless to say, that hasn't been the case; Indonesia, for example, destroyed so many of its lush forests and peat lands to grow palm oil for the European biodiesel market that it ranks third rather than 21st among the world's top carbon emitters.

In 2007, researchers finally began accounting for deforestation and other land-use changes created by biofuels. One study found that it would take more than 400 years of biodiesel use to "pay back" the carbon emitted by directly clearing peat for palm oil. Indirect damage can be equally devastating because on a hungry planet, food crops that get diverted to fuel usually end up getting replaced somewhere. For example, ethanol profits are prompting U.S. soybean farmers to switch to corn, so Brazilian soybean farmers are expanding into cattle pastures to pick up the slack and Brazilian ranchers are invading the Amazon rain forest, which is why another study pegged corn ethanol's payback period at 167 years. It's simple economics: The mandates increase demand for grain, which boosts prices, which makes it lucrative to ravage the wilderness.

Deforestation accounts for 20 percent of global emissions, so unless the world can eliminate emissions from all other sources—cars, coal, factories, cows—it needs to back off forests. That means limiting agriculture's footprint, a daunting task as the world's population grows—and an impossible task if vast expanses of cropland are converted to grow middling amounts of fuel. Even if the United States switched its entire grain crop to ethanol, it would only replace one fifth of U.S. gasoline consumption.

This is not just a climate disaster. The grain it takes to fill an SUV tank with ethanol could feed a hungry person for a year; biofuel mandates are exerting constant upward pressure on global food prices and have contributed to food riots in dozens of poorer countries. Still, the United States has quintupled its ethanol production in a decade and plans to quintuple its biofuel production again in the next decade. This will mean more money for well-subsidized grain farmers, but also more malnutrition, more deforestation, and more emissions. European leaders have paid a bit more attention to the alarming critiques of biofuels—including one by a British agency that was originally established to promote biofuels—but they have shown no more inclination to throw cold water on this $100 billion global industry.

3. "If Today's Biofuels Aren't the Answer, Tomorrow's Biofuels Will Be"

Doubtful. The latest U.S. rules, while continuing lavish support for corn ethanol, include enormous new mandates to jump-start "second-generation" biofuels such as cellulosic ethanol derived from switchgrass. In theory, they would be less destructive than corn ethanol, which relies on tractors, petroleum-based fertilizers, and distilleries that emit way too much carbon. Even first-generation ethanol derived from sugar cane—which already provides half of Brazil's transportation fuel—is considerably greener than corn ethanol. But recent studies suggest that any biofuels requiring good agricultural land would still be worse than gasoline for global warming. Less of a disaster than corn ethanol is still a disaster.

Back in the theoretical world, biofuels derived from algae, trash, agricultural waste, or other sources could help because they require no land or at least unspecific "degraded lands," but they always seem to be "several" years away from large-scale commercial development. And some scientists remain hopeful that fast-growing perennial grasses such as miscanthus can convert sunlight into energy efficiently enough to overcome the land-use dilemmas—someday. But for today, farmland happens to be very good at producing the food we need to feed us and storing the carbon we need to save us, and not so good at generating fuel. In fact, new studies suggest that if we really want to convert biomass into energy, we're better off turning it into electricity.

Then what should we use in our cars and trucks? In the short term . . . gasoline. We just need to use less of it.

Instead of counterproductive biofuel mandates and ethanol subsidies, governments need fuel-efficiency mandates to help the world's 1 billion drivers guzzle less gas, plus subsidies for mass transit, bike paths, rail lines, telecommuting, carpooling, and other activities to get those drivers out of their cars. Policymakers also need to eliminate subsidies for roads to nowhere, mandates that require excess parking and limit dense development in urban areas, and other sprawl-inducing policies. None of this is as enticing as inventing a magical new fuel, but it's doable, and it would cut emissions.

In the medium term, the world needs plug-in electric cars, the only plausible answer to humanity's oil addiction that isn't decades away. But electricity is already the source of even more emissions than oil. So we'll need an answer to humanity's coal addiction, too.

4. "Nuclear Power Is the Cure for Our Addiction to Coal"

Nope. Atomic energy is emissions free, so a slew of politicians and even some environmentalists have embraced it as a clean alternative to coal and natural gas that can generate power when there's no sun or wind. In the United States, which already gets nearly 20 percent of its electricity from nuclear plants, utilities are thinking about new reactors for the first time since the Three Mile Island meltdown three decades ago—despite global concerns about nuclear proliferation, local concerns about accidents or terrorist attacks, and the lack of a disposal site for the radioactive waste. France gets nearly 80 percent of its electricity from nukes, and Russia, China, and India are now gearing up for nuclear renaissances of their own.

But nuclear power cannot fix the climate crisis. The first reason is timing: The West needs major cuts in emissions within a decade, and the first new U.S. reactor is only scheduled for 2017—unless it gets delayed, like every U.S. reactor before it. Elsewhere in the developed world, most of the talk about a nuclear revival has remained just talk; there is no Western country with more than one nuclear plant under construction, and scores of existing plants will be scheduled for decommissioning in the coming decades, so there's no way nuclear could make even a tiny dent in electricity emissions before 2020.

The bigger problem is cost. Nuke plants are supposed to be expensive to build but cheap to operate. Unfortunately, they're turning out to be really, really expensive to build; their cost estimates have quadrupled in less than a decade. Energy guru Amory Lovins has calculated that new nukes will cost nearly three times as much as wind—and that was before their construction costs exploded for a variety of reasons, including the global credit crunch, the atrophying of the nuclear labor force, and a supplier squeeze symbolized by a Japanese company's worldwide monopoly on steel-forging for reactors. A new reactor in Finland that was supposed to showcase the global renaissance is already way behind schedule and way, way over budget. This is why plans for new plants were recently shelved in Canada and several U.S. states, why Moody's just warned utilities they'll risk ratings downgrades if they seek new reactors, and why

127

renewables attracted $71 billion in worldwide private capital in 2007—while nukes attracted zero.

It's also why U.S. nuclear utilities are turning to politicians to supplement their existing loan guarantees, tax breaks, direct subsidies, and other cradle-to-grave government goodies with new public largesse. Reactors don't make much sense to build unless someone else is paying; that's why the strongest push for nukes is coming from countries where power is publicly funded. For all the talk of sanctions, if the world really wants to cripple the Iranian economy, maybe the mullahs should just be allowed to pursue nuclear energy.

Unlike biofuels, nukes don't worsen warming. But a nuclear expansion—like the recent plan by U.S. Republicans who want 100 new plants by 2030—would cost trillions of dollars for relatively modest gains in the relatively distant future.

Nuclear lobbyists do have one powerful argument: If coal is too dirty and nukes are too costly, how are we going to produce our juice? Wind is terrific, and it's on the rise, adding nearly half of new U.S. power last year and expanding its global capacity by a third in 2007. But after increasing its worldwide wattage tenfold in a decade—China is now the leading producer, and Europe is embracing wind as well—it still produces less than 2 percent of the world's electricity. Solar and geothermal are similarly wonderful and inexhaustible technologies, but they're still global rounding errors. The average U.S. household now has 26 plug-in devices, and the rest of the world is racing to catch up; the U.S. Department of Energy expects global electricity consumption to rise 77 percent by 2030. How can we meet that demand without a massive nuclear revival?

Wind is terrific, but it produces less than 2 percent of the world's electricity.

We can't. So we're going to have to prove the Department of Energy wrong.

5. "There Is No Silver Bullet to the Energy Crisis"

Probably not. But some bullets are a lot better than others; we ought to give them our best shot before we commit to evidently inferior bullets. And one renewable energy resource is the cleanest, cheapest, and most abundant of them all. It doesn't induce deforestation or require elaborate security. It doesn't depend on the weather. And it won't take years to build or bring to market; it's already universally available.

It's called "efficiency". It means wasting less energy—or more precisely, using less energy to get your beer just as cold, your shower just as hot, and your factory just as productive. It's not about some austerity scold harassing you to take cooler showers, turn off lights, turn down thermostats, drive less, fly less, buy less stuff, eat less meat, ditch your McMansion, and otherwise change your behavior to save energy. Doing less with less is called conservation. Efficiency is about doing more or

the same with less; it doesn't require much effort or sacrifice. Yet more efficient appliances, lighting, factories, and buildings, as well as vehicles, could wipe out one fifth to one third of the world's energy consumption without any real deprivation.

Efficiency isn't sexy, and the idea that we could use less energy without much trouble hangs uneasily with today's more-is-better culture. But the best way to ensure new power plants don't bankrupt us, empower petrodictators, or imperil the planet is not to build them in the first place. "Negawatts" saved by efficiency initiatives generally cost 1 to 5 cents per kilowatt-hour versus projections ranging from 12 to 30 cents per kilowatt-hour from new nukes. That's because Americans in particular and human beings in general waste amazing amounts of energy. U.S. electricity plants fritter away enough to power Japan, and American water heaters, industrial motors, and buildings are as ridiculously inefficient as American cars. Only 4 percent of the energy used to power a typical incandescent bulb produces light; the rest is wasted. China is expected to build more square feet of real estate in the next 15 years than the United States has built in its entire history, and it has no green building codes or green building experience.

But we already know that efficiency mandates can work wonders because they've already reduced U.S. energy consumption levels from astronomical to merely high. For example, thanks to federal rules, modern American refrigerators use three times less energy than 1970s models, even though they're larger and more high-tech.

The biggest obstacles to efficiency are the perverse incentives that face most utilities; they make more money when they sell more power and have to build new generating plants. But in California and the Pacific Northwest, utility profits have been decoupled from electricity sales, so utilities can help customers save energy without harming shareholders. As a result, in that part of the country, per capita power use has been flat for three decades—while skyrocketing 50 percent in the rest of the United States. If utilities around the world could make money by helping their customers use less power, the U.S. Department of Energy wouldn't be releasing such scary numbers.

6. "We Need a Technological Revolution to Save the World"

Maybe. In the long term, it's hard to imagine how (without major advances) we can reduce emissions 80 percent by 2050 while the global population increases and the developing world develops. So a clean-tech Apollo program modeled oil the Manhattan Project makes sense. And we do need carbon pricing to send a message to market makers and innovators to promote low-carbon activities; Europe's cap-and-trade scheme seems to be working well after a rocky start. The private capital already pouring into renewables might someday produce a cheap solar panel or a synthetic fuel or a superpowerful battery or a truly clean coal plant. At some point, after we've milked efficiency for all the negawatts and negabarrels we can, we might need something new.

But we already have all the technology we need to start reducing emissions by reducing consumption. Even if we only hold electricity demand flat, we can subtract a coal-fired megawatt every time we add a wind-powered megawatt. And with a smarter grid, green building codes, and strict efficiency standards for everything from light bulbs to plasma TVs to server farms, we can do better than flat. Al Gore has a reasonably plausible plan for zero-emissions power by 2020; he envisions an ambitious 28 percent decrease in demand through efficiency, plus some ambitious increases in supply from wind, solar, and geothermal energy. But we don't even have to reduce our fossil fuel use to zero to reach our 2020 targets. We just have to use less.

If somebody comes up with a better idea by 2020, great! For now, we should focus on the solutions that get the best emissions bang for the buck.

7. "Ultimately, We'll Need to Change Our Behaviors to Save the World"

Probably. These days, it's politically incorrect to suggest that going green will require even the slightest adjustment to our way of life, but let's face it: Jimmy Carter was right. It wouldn't kill you to turn down the heat and put on a sweater. Efficiency is a miracle drug, but conservation is even better; a Prius saves gas, but a Prius sitting in the driveway while you ride your bike uses no gas. Even energy-efficient dryers use more power than clotheslines.

More with less will be a great start, but to get to 80 percent less emissions, the developed world might occasionally have to do less with less. We might have to unplug a few digital picture frames, substitute teleconferencing for some business travel, and take it easy on the air conditioner. If that's an inconvenient truth, well, it's less inconvenient than trillions of dollars' worth of new reactors, perpetual dependence on hostile petrostates, or a fricasseed planet.

After all, the developing world is entitled to develop. Its people are understandably eager to eat more meat, drive more cars, and live in nicer houses. It doesn't seem fair for the developed world to say: Do as we say, not as we did. But if the developing world follows the developed world's wasteful path to prosperity, the Earth we all share won't be able to accommodate us. So we're going to have to change our ways. Then we can at least say: Do as we're going, not as we did.

Michael Grunwald, a senior correspondent at *Time* magazine, is an award-winning environmental journalist and author of *The Swamp: The Everglades, Florida, and the Politics of Paradise*.

Reprinted in entirety by McGraw-Hill with permission from *FOREIGN POLICY*, September/October 2009, pp. 130–133. www.foreignpolicy.com. © 2009 Washingtonpost. Newsweek Interactive, LLC.

UNIT 5
Conflict

Unit Selections

Key Points to Consider

- Are violent conflicts and warfare increasing or decreasing?

- Where are the major hotspots in the world where conflict is taking place?

- What changes have taken place in recent years in the types of conflicts and who participates?

- How is military doctrine changing to reflect new political realities?

- How is the nature of terrorism different than conventional warfare? What new threats do terrorists pose?

- What are the motivations and attitudes of those who use terror as a political tool?

- What challenges does nuclear proliferation pose to the United States?

- How is the national security policy of the United States likely to change? What about Russia, Iran, and China?

Student Website
www.mhhe.com/cls

Internet References

DefenseLINK
http://www.defenselink.mil
Federation of American Scientists (FAS)
http://www.fas.org
ISN International Relations and Security Network
http://www.isn.ethz.ch
The NATO Integrated Data Service (NIDS)
http://www.nato.int/structur/nids/nids.htm

Do you lock your doors at night? Do you secure your personal property to avoid theft? These are basic questions that have to do with your sense of personal security. Most individuals take steps to protect what they have, including their lives. The same is true for groups of people, including countries.

In the international arena, governments frequently pursue their national interest by entering into mutually agreeable "deals" with other governments. Social scientists call these types of arrangements "exchanges" (i.e., each side gives up something it values in order to gain something in return that it values even more). On an economic level, it functions like this: "I have the oil that you need and am willing to sell it. In return I want to buy from you the agricultural products that I lack." Whether on the governmental level or the personal level ("If you help me with my homework, then I will drive you home this weekend"), exchanges are the process used by most individuals and groups to obtain and protect what is of value. The exchange process, however, can break down. When threats and punishments replace mutual exchanges, conflict ensues. Neither side benefits, and there are costs to both. Further, each may use threats with the expectation that the other will capitulate. But if efforts at intimidation and coercion fail, the conflict may escalate into violent confrontation.

With the end of the cold war, issues of national security and the nature of international conflict have changed. In the late 1980s agreements between the former Soviet Union and the United States led to the elimination of superpower support for participants in low-intensity conflicts in Central America, Africa, and Southeast Asia. Fighting the cold war by proxy is now a thing of the past. In addition, cold war military alliances have either collapsed or have been significantly redefined. Despite these historic changes, there is no shortage of conflicts in the world today.

Many experts initially predicted that the collapse of the Soviet Union would decrease the arms race and diminish the threat of nuclear war. However, some analysts now believe that the threat of nuclear war has in fact increased as control of nuclear weapons has become less centralized and the command structure less reliable. In addition, the proliferation of nuclear weapons into North Korea and South Asia (India and Pakistan) is a growing security issue. Further, there are concerns about both dictatorial governments and terrorist organizations obtaining weapons of mass destruction. What these changing circumstances mean for U.S. policy is a topic of considerable debate.

The unit begins with a unique perspective into the sources of international conflict. It is followed by a series of case studies

© U.S. Air Force

that provide insights into the roots of the drug war in Mexico, terrorism and conflict in the Middle East, and the foreign policy objectives of emerging regional and global powers. The unit concludes with an article on the increasingly complex problem of nuclear weapons proliferation.

As in the case of the other global issues described in this anthology, international conflict is a dynamic problem. It is important to understand that conflicts are not random events, but follow patterns and trends. Forty-five years of cold war established discernable patterns of international conflict as the superpowers deterred each other with vast expenditures of money and technological know-how. The consequence of this stalemate was often a shift to the developing world for conflict by superpower proxy.

The changing circumstances of the post-cold war era generate a series of important new policy questions: Will there be more nuclear proliferation? Is there an increased danger of so-called "rogue" states destabilizing the international arena? Is the threat of terror a temporary or permanent feature of world affairs? Will there be a growing emphasis on low-intensity conflicts related to the interdiction of drugs, or will some other unforeseen issue determine the world's hot spots? Will the United States and its European allies lose interest in security issues that do not directly involve their economic interests and simply look the other way, for example, as age-old ethnic conflicts become brutally violent? Can the international community develop viable institutions to mediate and resolve disputes before they become violent? The answers to these and related questions will determine the patterns of conflict in the twenty-first century.

The Revenge of Geography

People and ideas influence events, but geography largely determines them, now more than ever. To understand the coming struggles, it's time to dust off the Victorian thinkers who knew the physical world best. A journalist who has covered the ends of the Earth offers a guide to the relief map—and a primer on the next phase of conflict.

ROBERT D. KAPLAN

When rapturous Germans tore down the Berlin Wall 20 years ago it symbolized far more than the overcoming of an arbitrary boundary. It began an intellectual cycle that saw all divisions, geographic and otherwise, as surmountable; that referred to "realism" and "pragmatism" only as pejoratives; and that invoked the humanism of Isaiah Berlin or the appeasement of Hitler at Munich to launch one international intervention after the next. In this way, the armed liberalism and the democracy-promoting neoconservatism of the 1990s shared the same universalist aspirations. But alas, when a fear of Munich leads to overreach the result is Vietnam—or in the current case, Iraq.

And thus began the rehabilitation of realism, and with it another intellectual cycle. "Realist" is now a mark of respect, "neocon" a term of derision. The Vietnam analogy has vanquished that of Munich. Thomas Hobbes, who extolled the moral benefits of fear and saw anarchy as the chief threat to society, has elbowed out Isaiah Berlin as the philosopher of the present cycle. The focus now is less on universal ideals than particular distinctions, from ethnicity to culture to religion. Those who pointed this out a decade ago were sneered at for being "fatalists" or "determinists." Now they are applauded as "pragmatists." And this is the key insight of the past two decades—that there are worse things in the world than extreme tyranny, and in Iraq we brought them about ourselves. I say this having supported the war.

So now, chastened, we have all become realists. Or so we believe. But realism is about more than merely opposing a war in Iraq that we know from hindsight turned out badly. Realism means recognizing that international relations are ruled by a sadder, more limited reality than the one governing domestic affairs. It means valuing order above freedom, for the latter becomes important only after the former has been established. It means focusing on what divides humanity rather than on what unites it, as the high priests of globalization would have it. In short, realism is about recognizing and embracing those forces beyond our control that constrain human action—culture, tradition, history, the bleaker tides of passion that lie just beneath the veneer of civilization. This poses what, for realists, is the central question in foreign affairs: Who can do what to whom? And of all the unsavory truths in which realism is rooted, the bluntest, most uncomfortable, and most deterministic of all is geography.

Indeed, what is at work in the recent return of realism is the revenge of geography in the most old-fashioned sense. In the 18th and 19th centuries, before the arrival of political science as an academic specialty, geography was an honored, if not always formalized, discipline in which politics, culture, and economics were often conceived of in reference to the relief map. Thus, in the Victorian and Edwardian eras, mountains and the men who grow out of them were the first order of reality; ideas, however uplifting, were only the second.

And yet, to embrace geography is not to accept it as an implacable force against which humankind is powerless. Rather, it serves to qualify human freedom and choice with a modest acceptance of fate. This is all the more important today, because rather than eliminating the relevance of geography, globalization is reinforcing it. Mass communications and economic integration are weakening many states, exposing a Hobbesian world of small, fractious regions. Within them, local, ethnic, and religious sources of identity are reasserting themselves, and because they are anchored to specific terrains, they are best explained by reference to geography. Like the faults that determine earthquakes, the political future will be defined by conflict and instability with a similar geographic logic. The upheaval spawned by the ongoing economic crisis is increasing the relevance of geography even further, by weakening social orders and other creations of humankind, leaving the natural frontiers of the globe as the only restraint.

So we, too, need to return to the map, and particularly to what I call the "shatter zones" of Eurasia. We need to reclaim those thinkers who knew the landscape best. And we need to update their theories for the revenge of geography in our time.

If you want to understand the insights of geography, you need to seek out those thinkers who make liberal humanists profoundly uneasy—those authors who thought the map determined nearly everything, leaving little room for human agency.

One such person is the French historian Fernand Braudel, who in 1949 published *The Mediterranean and the Mediterranean World in the Age of Philip II*. By bringing demography and nature itself into history, Braudel helped restore geography to its proper place. In his narrative, permanent environmental forces lead to enduring historical trends that preordain political events and regional wars. To Braudel, for example, the poor, precarious soils along the Mediterranean, combined with an uncertain, drought-afflicted climate, spurred ancient Greek and Roman conquest. In other words, we delude ourselves by thinking that we control our own destinies. To understand the present challenges of climate change, warming Arctic seas, and the scarcity of resources such as oil and water, we must reclaim Braudel's environmental interpretation of events.

So, too, must we reexamine the blue-water strategizing of Alfred Thayer Mahan, a U.S. naval captain and author of *The Influence of Sea Power Upon History, 1660–1783*. Viewing the sea as the great "commons" of civilization, Mahan thought that naval power had always been the decisive factor in global political struggles. It was Mahan who, in 1902, coined the term "Middle East" to denote the area between Arabia and India that held particular importance for naval strategy. Indeed, Mahan saw the Indian and Pacific oceans as the hinges of geopolitical destiny, for they would allow a maritime nation to project power all around the Eurasian rim and thereby affect political developments deep into Central Asia. Mahan's thinking helps to explain why the Indian Ocean will be the heart of geopolitical competition in the 21st century—and why his books are now all the rage among Chinese and Indian strategists.

Similarly, the Dutch-American strategist Nicholas Spykman saw the seaboards of the Indian and Pacific oceans as the keys to dominance in Eurasia and the natural means to check the land power of Russia. Before he died in 1943, while the United States was fighting Japan, Spykman predicted the rise of China and the consequent need for the United States to defend Japan. And even as the United States was fighting to liberate Europe, Spykman warned that the postwar emergence of an integrated European power would eventually become inconvenient for the United States. Such is the foresight of geographical determinism.

But perhaps the most significant guide to the revenge of geography is the father of modern geopolitics himself—Sir Halford J. Mackinder—who is famous not for a book but a single article, "The Geographical Pivot of History," which began as a 1904 lecture to the Royal Geographical Society in London. Mackinder's work is the archetype of the geographical discipline, and he summarizes its theme nicely: "Man and not nature initiates, but nature in large measure controls."

His thesis is that Russia, Eastern Europe, and Central Asia are the "pivot" around which the fate of world empire revolves. He would refer to this area of Eurasia as the "heartland" in a later book. Surrounding it are four "marginal" regions of the Eurasian landmass that correspond, not coincidentally, to the four great religions, because faith, too, is merely a function of geography for Mackinder. There are two "monsoon lands": one in the east generally facing the Pacific Ocean, the home of Buddhism; the other in the south facing the Indian Ocean, the home of Hinduism. The third marginal region is Europe, watered by the Atlantic to the west and the home of Christianity. But the most fragile of the four marginal regions is the Middle East, home of Islam, "deprived of moisture by the proximity of Africa" and for the most part "thinly peopled" (in 1904, that is).

Realism is about recognizing and embracing those forces beyond our control that constrain human action. And of all the unsavory truths in which realism is rooted, the bluntest, most uncomfortable, and most deterministic of all is geography.

This Eurasian relief map, and the events playing out on it at the dawn of the 20th century, are Mackinder's subject, and the opening sentence presages its grand sweep:

> When historians in the remote future come to look back on the group of centuries through which we are now passing, and see them fore-shortened, as we to-day see the Egyptian dynasties, it may well be that they will describe the last 400 years as the Columbian epoch, and will say that it ended soon after the year 1900.

Mackinder explains that, while medieval Christendom was "pent into a narrow region and threatened by external barbarism," the Columbian age—the Age of Discovery—saw Europe expand across the oceans to new lands. Thus at the turn of the 20th century, "we shall again have to deal with a closed political system," and this time one of "world-wide scope."

> Every explosion of social forces, instead of being dissipated in a surrounding circuit of unknown space and barbaric chaos, will [henceforth] be sharply re-echoed from the far side of the globe, and weak elements in the political and economic organism of the world will be shattered in consequence.

By perceiving that European empires had no more room to expand, thereby making their conflicts global, Mackinder foresaw, however vaguely, the scope of both world wars.

Mackinder looked at European history as "subordinate" to that of Asia, for he saw European civilization as merely the outcome of the struggle against Asiatic invasion. Europe, he writes, became the cultural phenomenon it is only because of its geography: an intricate array of mountains, valleys, and peninsulas; bounded by northern ice and a western ocean; blocked by seas and the Sahara to the south; and set against the immense, threatening flatland of Russia to the east. Into this confined landscape poured a succession of nomadic, Asian invaders from the naked steppe. The union of Franks, Goths, and Roman provincials against these invaders produced the basis for modern France. Likewise, other European powers originated, or at least matured, through their encounters with Asian nomads. Indeed, it was the Seljuk Turks' supposed ill treatment of Christian pilgrims in Jerusalem that ostensibly led to the Crusades, which Mackinder considers the beginning of Europe's collective modern history.

Russia, meanwhile, though protected by forest glades against many a rampaging host, nevertheless fell prey in the 13th century to the Golden Horde of the Mongols. These invaders decimated and subsequently changed Russia. But because most of Europe knew no such level of destruction, it was able to emerge as the world's political cockpit, while Russia was largely denied access to the European Renaissance. The ultimate land-based empire, with few natural barriers against invasion, Russia would know forevermore what it was like to be brutally conquered. As a result, it would become perennially obsessed with expanding and holding territory.

Key discoveries of the Columbian epoch, Mackinder writes, only reinforced the cruel facts of geography. In the Middle Ages, the peoples of Europe were largely confined to the land. But when the sea route to India was found around the Cape of Good Hope, Europeans suddenly had access to the entire rimland of southern Asia, to say nothing of strategic discoveries in the New World. While Western Europeans "covered the ocean with their fleets," Mackinder tells us, Russia was expanding equally impressively on land, "emerging from her northern forests" to police the steppe with her Cossacks, sweeping into Siberia, and sending peasants to sow the southwestern steppe with wheat. It was an old story: Europe versus Russia, a liberal sea power (like Athens and Venice) against a reactionary land power (like Sparta and Prussia). For the sea, beyond the cosmopolitan influences it bestows by virtue of access to distant harbors, provides the inviolate border security that democracy needs to take root.

In the 19th century, Mackinder notes, the advent of steam engines and the creation of the Suez Canal increased the mobility of European sea power around the southern rim of Eurasia, just as railways were beginning to do the same for land power in the Eurasian heartland. So the struggle was set for the mastery of Eurasia, bringing Mackinder to his thesis:

> As we consider this rapid review of the broader currents of history, does not a certain persistence of geographical relationship become evident? Is not the pivot region of the world's politics that vast area of Euro-Asia which is inaccessible to ships, but in antiquity lay open to the horse-riding nomads, and is today about to be covered with a network of railways?

Just as the Mongols banged at, and often broke down, the gates to the marginal regions surrounding Eurasia, Russia would now play the same conquering role, for as Mackinder writes, "the geographical quantities in the calculation are more measurable and more nearly constant than the human." Forget the czars and the commissars-yet-to-be in 1904; they are but trivia compared with the deeper tectonic forces of geography.

Mackinder's determinism prepared us for the rise of the Soviet Union and its vast zone of influence in the second half of the 20th century, as well as for the two world wars preceding it. After all, as historian Paul Kennedy notes, these conflicts were struggles over Mackinder's "marginal" regions, running from Eastern Europe to the Himalayas and beyond. Cold War containment strategy, moreover, depended heavily on rimland bases across the greater Middle East and the Indian Ocean. Indeed, the U.S. projection of power into Afghanistan and Iraq, and today's tensions with Russia over the political fate of Central Asia and the Caucasus have only bolstered Mackinder's thesis. In his article's last paragraph, Mackinder even raises the specter of Chinese conquests of the "pivot" area, which would make China the dominant geopolitical power. Look at how Chinese migrants are now demographically claiming parts of Siberia as Russia's political control of its eastern reaches is being strained. One can envision Mackinder's being right yet again.

The wisdom of geographical determinism endures across the chasm of a century because it recognizes that the most profound struggles of humanity are not about ideas but about control over territory, specifically the heartland and rimlands of Eurasia. Of course, ideas matter, and they span geography. And yet there is a certain geographic logic to where certain ideas take hold. Communist Eastern Europe, Mongolia, China, and North Korea were all contiguous to the great land power of the Soviet Union. Classic fascism was a predominantly European affair. And liberalism nurtured its deepest roots in the United States and Great Britain, essentially island nations and sea powers both. Such determinism is easy to hate but hard to dismiss.

To discern where the battle of ideas will lead, we must revise Mackinder for our time. After all, Mackinder could not foresee how a century's worth of change would redefine—and enhance—the importance of geography in today's world. One author who did is Yale University professor Paul Bracken, who in 1999 published *Fire in the East*. Bracken draws a conceptual map of Eurasia defined by the collapse of time and distance and the filling of empty spaces. This idea leads him to declare a "crisis of room." In the past, sparsely populated geography acted as a safety mechanism. Yet this is no longer the case, Bracken argues, for as empty space increasingly disappears, the very "finite size of the earth" becomes a force for instability. And as I learned at the U.S. Army's Command and General Staff College, "attrition of the same adds up to big change."

One force that is shrinking the map of Eurasia is technology, particularly the military applications of it and the rising power it confers on states. In the early Cold War, Asian militaries were mostly lumbering, heavy forces whose primary purpose was national consolidation. They focused inward. But as national wealth accumulated and the computer revolution took hold, Asian militaries from the oil-rich Middle East to the tiger economies of the Pacific developed full-fledged, military-civilian postindustrial complexes, with missiles and fiber optics and satellite phones. These states also became bureaucratically more cohesive, allowing their militaries to focus outward, toward other states. Geography in Eurasia, rather than a cushion, was becoming a prison from which there was no escape.

Now there is an "unbroken belt of countries," in Bracken's words, from Israel to North Korea, which are developing ballistic missiles and destructive arsenals. A map of these countries' missile ranges shows a series of overlapping circles: Not only is no one safe, but a 1914-style chain reaction leading to wider war is easily conceivable. "The spread of missiles and weapons of mass destruction in Asia is like the spread of the six-shooter in the American Old West," Bracken writes—a cheap, deadly equalizer of states.

The other force driving the revenge of geography is population growth, which makes the map of Eurasia more claustrophobic still. In the 1990s, many intellectuals viewed the 18th-century English philosopher Thomas Malthus as an overly deterministic thinker because he treated humankind as a species reacting to its physical environment, not a body of autonomous individuals. But as the years pass, and world food and energy prices fluctuate, Malthus is getting more respect. If you wander through the slums of Karachi or Gaza, which wall off multitudes of angry lumpen faithful—young men mostly—one can easily see the conflicts over scarce resources that Malthus predicted coming to pass. In three decades covering the Middle East, I have watched it evolve from a largely rural society to a realm of teeming megacities. In the next 20 years, the Arab world's population will nearly double while supplies of groundwater will diminish.

A Eurasia of vast urban areas, overlapping missile ranges, and sensational media will be one of constantly enraged crowds, fed by rumors transported at the speed of light from one Third World megalopolis to another. So in addition to Malthus, we will also hear much about Elias Canetti, the 20th-century philosopher of crowd psychology: the phenomenon of a mass of people abandoning their individuality for an intoxicating collective symbol. It is in the cities of Eurasia principally where crowd psychology will have its greatest geopolitical impact. Alas, ideas do matter. And it is the very compression of geography that will provide optimum breeding grounds for dangerous ideologies and channels for them to spread.

All of this requires major revisions to Mackinder's theories of geopolitics. For as the map of Eurasia shrinks and fills up with people, it not only obliterates the artificial regions of area studies; it also erases Mackinder's division of Eurasia into a specific "pivot" and adjacent "marginal" zones. Military assistance from China and North Korea to Iran can cause Israel to take military actions. The U.S. Air Force can attack landlocked Afghanistan from Diego Garcia, an island in the middle of the Indian Ocean. The Chinese and Indian navies can project power from the Gulf of Aden to the South China Sea—out of their own regions and along the whole rimland. In short, contra Mackinder, Eurasia has been reconfigured into an organic whole.

The map's new seamlessness can be seen in the Pakistani outpost of Gwadar. There, on the Indian Ocean, near the Iranian border, the Chinese have constructed a spanking new deep-water port. Land prices are booming, and people talk of this still sleepy fishing village as the next Dubai, which may one day link towns in Central Asia to the burgeoning middle-class fleshpots of India and China through pipelines, supertankers, and the Strait of Malacca. The Chinese also have plans for developing other

Indian Ocean ports in order to transport oil by pipelines directly into western and central China, even as a canal and land bridge are possibly built across Thailand's Isthmus of Kra. Afraid of being outflanked by the Chinese, the Indians are expanding their own naval ports and strengthening ties with both Iran and Burma, where the Indian-Chinese rivalry will be fiercest.

Much of Eurasia will eventually be as claustrophobic as the Levant, with geography controlling everything and no room to maneuver. The battle over land between Israelis and Palestinians is a case of utter geographical determinism. This is Eurasia's future as well.

These deepening connections are transforming the Middle East, Central Asia, and the Indian and Pacific oceans into a vast continuum, in which the narrow and vulnerable Strait of Malacca will be the Fulda Gap of the 21st century. The fates of the Islamic Middle East and Islamic Indonesia are therefore becoming inextricable. But it is the geographic connections, not religious ones, that matter most.

This new map of Eurasia—tighter, more integrated, and more crowded—will be even less stable than Mackinder thought. Rather than heartlands and marginal zones that imply separateness, we will have a series of inner and outer cores that are fused together through mass politics and shared paranoia. In fact, much of Eurasia will eventually be as claustrophobic as Israel and the Palestinian territories, with geography controlling everything and no room to maneuver. Although Zionism shows the power of ideas, the battle over land between Israelis and Palestinians is a case of utter geographical determinism. This is Eurasia's future as well.

The ability of states to control events will be diluted, in some cases destroyed. Artificial borders will crumble and become more fissiparous, leaving only rivers, deserts, mountains, and other enduring facts of geography. Indeed, the physical features of the landscape may be the only reliable guides left to understanding the shape of future conflict. Like rifts in the Earth's crust that produce physical instability, there are areas in Eurasia that are more prone to conflict than others. These "shatter zones" threaten to implode, explode, or maintain a fragile equilibrium. And not surprisingly, they fall within that unstable inner core of Eurasia: the greater Middle East, the vast way station between the Mediterranean world and the Indian subcontinent that registers all the primary shifts in global power politics.

This inner core, for Mackinder, was the ultimate unstable region. And yet, writing in an age before oil pipelines and ballistic missiles, he saw this region as inherently volatile, geographically speaking, but also somewhat of a secondary concern. A century's worth of technological advancement and population explosion has rendered the greater Middle East no less volatile but dramatically more relevant, and where Eurasia is most prone to fall apart now is in the greater Middle East's several shatter zones.

I'll never forget what a U.S. military expert told me in Sanaa: "Terrorism is an entrepreneurial activity, and in Yemen you've got over 20 million aggressive, commercial-minded, and well-armed people, all extremely hard-working compared with the Saudis next door. It's the future, and it terrifies the hell out of the government in Riyadh."

The Indian subcontinent is one such shatter zone. It is defined on its landward sides by the hard geographic borders of the Himalayas to the north, the Burmese jungle to the east, and the somewhat softer border of the Indus River to the west. Indeed, the border going westward comes in three stages: the Indus; the unruly crags and canyons that push upward to the shaved wastes of Central Asia, home to the Pashtun tribes; and, finally, the granite, snow-mantled massifs of the Hindu Kush, transecting Afghanistan itself. Because these geographic impediments are not contiguous with legal borders, and because barely any of India's neighbors are functional states, the current political organization of the subcontinent should not be taken for granted. You see this acutely as you walk up to and around any of these land borders, the weakest of which, in my experience, are the official ones—a mere collection of tables where cranky bureaucrats inspect your luggage. Especially in the west, the only border that lives up to the name is the Hindu Kush, making me think that in our own lifetimes the whole semblance of order in Pakistan and southeastern Afghanistan could unravel, and return, in effect, to vague elements of greater India.

In Nepal, the government barely controls the countryside where 85 percent of its people live. Despite the aura bequeathed by the Himalayas, nearly half of Nepal's population lives in the dank and humid lowlands along the barely policed border with India. Driving throughout this region, it appears in many ways indistinguishable from the Ganges plain. If the Maoists now ruling Nepal cannot increase state capacity, the state itself could dissolve.

The same holds true for Bangladesh. Even more so than Nepal, it has no geographic defense to marshal as a state. The view from my window during a recent bus journey was of the same ruler-flat, aquatic landscape of paddy fields and scrub on both sides of the line with India. The border posts are disorganized, ramshackle affairs. This artificial blotch of territory on the Indian subcontinent could metamorphose yet again, amid the gale forces of regional politics, Muslim extremism, and nature itself.

Like Pakistan, no Bangladeshi government, military or civilian, has ever functioned even remotely well. Millions of Bangladeshi refugees have already crossed the border into India illegally. With 150 million people—a population larger than Russia—crammed together at sea level, Bangladesh is vulnerable to the slightest climatic variation, never mind the changes caused by global warming. Simply because of its geography, tens of millions of people in Bangladesh could be inundated with salt water, necessitating the mother of all humanitarian relief efforts. In the process, the state itself could collapse.

Of course, the worst nightmare on the subcontinent is Pakistan, whose dysfunction is directly the result of its utter lack of geographic logic. The Indus should be a border of sorts, but Pakistan sits astride both its banks, just as the fertile and teeming Punjab plain is bisected by the India-Pakistan border. Only the Thar Desert and the swamps to its south act as natural frontiers between Pakistan and India. And though these are formidable barriers, they are insufficient to frame a state composed of disparate, geographically based, ethnic groups—Punjabis, Sindhis, Baluchis, and Pashtuns—for whom Islam has provided insufficient glue to hold them together. All the other groups in Pakistan hate the Punjabis and the army they control, just as the groups in the former Yugoslavia hated the Serbs and the army they controlled. Pakistan's raison d'être is that it supposedly provides a homeland for subcontinental Muslims, but 154 million of them, almost the same number as the entire population of Pakistan, live over the border in India.

To the west, the crags and canyons of Pakistan's North-West Frontier Province, bordering Afghanistan, are utterly porous. Of all the times I crossed the Pakistan-Afghanistan border, I never did so legally. In reality, the two countries are inseparable. On both sides live the Pashtuns. The wide belt of territory between the Hindu Kush mountains and the Indus River is really Pashtunistan, an entity that threatens to emerge were Pakistan to fall apart. That would, in turn, lead to the dissolution of Afghanistan.

The Taliban constitute merely the latest incarnation of Pashtun nationalism. Indeed, much of the fighting in Afghanistan today occurs in Pashtunistan: southern and eastern Afghanistan and the tribal areas of Pakistan. The north of Afghanistan, beyond the Hindu Kush, has seen less fighting and is in the midst of reconstruction and the forging of closer links to the former Soviet republics in Central Asia, inhabited by the same ethnic groups that populate northern Afghanistan. Here is the ultimate world of Mackinder, of mountains and men, where the facts of geography are asserted daily, to the chagrin of U.S.-led forces—and of India, whose own destiny and borders are hostage to what plays out in the vicinity of the 20,000-foot wall of the Hindu Kush.

Another shatter zone is the Arabian Peninsula. The vast tract of land controlled by the Saudi royal family is synonymous with Arabia in the way that India is synonymous with the subcontinent. But while India is heavily populated throughout, Saudi Arabia constitutes a geographically nebulous network of oases separated by massive waterless tracts. Highways and domestic air links are crucial to Saudi Arabia's cohesion. Though India is built on an idea of democracy and religious pluralism, Saudi Arabia is built on loyalty to an extended family. But while India is virtually surrounded by troubling geography and dysfunctional states, Saudi Arabia's borders disappear into harmless desert to the north and are shielded by sturdy, well-governed, self-contained sheikhdoms to the east and southeast.

Where Saudi Arabia is truly vulnerable, and where the shatter zone of Arabia is most acute, is in highly populous Yemen to the south. Although it has only a quarter of Saudi Arabia's land area, Yemen's population is almost as large, so the all-important demographic core of the Arabian Peninsula is crammed into its mountainous southwest corner, where sweeping basalt plateaus, rearing up into sandcastle formations and volcanic plugs, embrace a network of oases densely inhabited since antiquity. Because the Turks and the British never really controlled Yemen, they did not leave behind the strong bureaucratic institutions that other former colonies inherited.

When I traveled the Saudi-Yemen border some years back, it was crowded with pickup trucks filled with armed young men, loyal to this sheikh or that, while the presence of the Yemeni government was negligible. Mudbrick battlements hid the encampments of these rebellious sheikhs, some with their own artillery. Estimates of the number of firearms in Yemen vary, but any Yemeni who wants a weapon can get one easily. Meanwhile, groundwater supplies will last no more than a generation or two.

I'll never forget what a U.S. military expert told me in the capital, Sanaa: "Terrorism is an entrepreneurial activity, and in Yemen you've got over 20 million aggressive, commercial-minded, and well-armed people, all extremely hard-working compared with the Saudis next door. It's the future, and it terrifies the hell out of the government in Riyadh." The future of teeming, tribal Yemen will go a long way to determining the future of Saudi Arabia. And geography, not ideas, has everything to do with it.

The Fertile Crescent, wedged between the Mediterranean Sea and the Iranian plateau, constitutes another shatter zone. The countries of this region—Jordan, Lebanon, Syria, and Iraq—are vague geographic expressions that had little meaning before the 20th century. When the official lines on the map are removed, we find a crude finger-painting of Sunni and Shiite clusters that contradict national borders. Inside these borders, the governing authorities of Lebanon and Iraq barely exist. The one in Syria is tyrannical and fundamentally unstable; the one in Jordan is rational but under quiet siege. (Jordan's main reason for being at all is to act as a buffer for other Arab regimes that fear having a land border with Israel.) Indeed, the Levant is characterized by tired authoritarian regimes and ineffective democracies.

Of all the geographically illogical states in the Fertile Crescent, none is more so than Iraq. Saddam Hussein's tyranny, by far the worst in the Arab world, was itself geographically determined: Every Iraqi dictator going back to the first military coup in 1958 had to be more repressive than the previous one just to hold together a country with no natural borders that seethes with ethnic and sectarian consciousness. The mountains that separate Kurdistan from the rest of Iraq, and the division of the Mesopotamian plain between Sunnis in the center and Shiites in the south, may prove more pivotal to Iraq's stability than the yearning after the ideal of democracy. If democracy doesn't in fairly short order establish sturdy institutional roots, Iraq's geography will likely lead it back to tyranny or anarchy again.

But for all the recent focus on Iraq, geography and history tell us that Syria might be at the real heart of future turbulence in the Arab world. Aleppo in northern Syria is a bazaar city with greater historical links to Mosul, Baghdad, and Anatolia than to Damascus. Whenever Damascus's fortunes declined with the rise of Baghdad to the east, Aleppo recovered its greatness. Wandering through the souks of Aleppo, it is striking how distant and irrelevant Damascus seems: The bazzars are dominated by Kurds, Turks, Circassians, Arab Christians, Armenians, and others, unlike the Damascus souk, which is more a world of Sunni Arabs. As in Pakistan and the former Yugoslavia, each sect and religion in Syria has a specific location. Between Aleppo and Damascus in the increasingly Islamist Sunni heartland. Between Damascus and the Jordanian border are the Druse, and in the mountain stronghold contiguous with Lebanon are the Alawites—both remnants of a wave of Shiism from Persia and Mesopotamia that swept over Syria a thousand years ago.

Elections in Syria in 1947, 1949, and 1954 exacerbated these divisions by polarizing the vote along sectarian lines. The late Hafez al-assad came to power in 1970 after 21 changes of government in 24 years. For three decades, he was the Leonid Brezhnev of the Arab world, staving off the future by failing to build a civil society at home. His sone Bashar will have to open the political system eventually, if only to keep pace with a dynamically changing society armed with satellite dishes and the Internet. But no one knows how stable a post-authoritarian Syria would be. Policymakers must fear the worst. Yet a post-Assad Syria may well do better than post-Saddam Iraq, precisely because its tyranny has been much less severe. Indeed, traveling from Saddam's Iraq to Assad's Syria was like coming up for air.

In addition to its inability to solve the problem of political legitimacy, the Arab world is unable to secure its own environment. The plateau peoples of Turkey will dominate the Arabs in the 21st century because the Turks have water and the Arabs don't. Indeed, to develop its own desperately poor southeast and thereby suppress Kurdish separatism, Turkey will need to divert increasingly large amounts of the Euphrates River from Syria and Iraq. As the Middle East becomes a realm of parched urban areas, water will grow in value relative to oil. The countries with it will retain the ability—and thus the power—to blackmail those without it. Water will be like nuclear energy, thereby making desalinization and dual-use power facilities primary targets of missile strikes in future wars. Not just in the West Bank, but everywhere there is less room to maneuver.

A final shatter zone is the Persian core, stretching from the Caspian Sea to Iran's north to the Persian Gulf to its south. Virtually all of the greater Middle East's oil and natural gas lies in this region. Just as shipping lanes radiate from the Persian Gulf, pipelines are increasingly radiating from the Caspian region to the Mediterranean, the Black Sea, China, and the Indian Ocean. The only country that straddles both energy-producing areas is Iran, as Geoffrey Kemp and

Robert E. Harkavy note in *Strategic Geography and the Changing Middle East.* The Persian Gulf possesses 55 percent of the world's crude-oil reserves, and Iran dominates the whole gulf, from the Shatt al-Arab on the Iraqi border to the Strait of Hormuz in the southeast—a coastline of 1,317 nautical miles, thanks to its many bays, inlets, coves, and islands that offer plenty of excellent places for hiding tanker-ramming speedboats.

It is not an accident that Iran was the ancient world's first superpower. There was a certain geographic logic to it. Iran is the greater Middle East's universal joint, tightly fused to all of the outer cores. Its border roughly traces and conforms to the natural contours of the landscape—plateaus to the west, mountains and seas to the north and south, and desert expanse in the east toward Afghanistan. For this reason, Iran has a far more venerable record as a nation-state and urbane civilization than most places in the Arab world and all the places in the Fertile Crescent. Unlike the geographically illogical countries of that adjacent region, there is nothing artificial about Iran. Not surprisingly, Iran is now being wooed by both India and China, whose navies will come to dominate the Eurasian sea lanes in the 21st century.

Of all the shatter zones in the greater Middle East, the Iranian core is unique: The instability Iran will cause will not come from its implosion, but from a strong, internally coherent Iranian nation that explodes outward from a natural geographic platform to shatter the region around it. The security provided to Iran by its own natural boundaries has historically been a potent force for power projection. The present is no different. Through its uncompromising ideology and nimble intelligence services, Iran runs an unconventional, postmodern empire of substate entities in the greater Middle East: Hamas in Palestine, Hezbollah in Lebanon, and the Sadrist movement in southern Iraq. If the geographic logic of Iranian expansion sounds eerily similar to that of Russian expansion in Mackinder's original telling, it is.

The geography of Iran today, like that of Russia before, determines the most realistic strategy to securing this shatter zone: containment. As with Russia, the goal of containing Iran must be to impose pressure on the contradictions of the unpopular, theocratic regime in Tehran, such that it eventually changes from within. The battle for Eurasia has many, increasingly interlocking fronts. But the primary one is for Iranian hearts and minds, just as it was for those of Eastern Europeans during the Cold War. Iran is home to one of the Muslim world's most sophisticated populations, and traveling there, one encounters less anti-Americanism and anti-Semitism than in Egypt. This is where the battle of ideas meets the dictates of geography.

In this century's fight for Eurasia, like that of the last century, Mackinder's axiom holds true: Man will initiate, but nature will control. Liberal universalism and the individualism of Isaiah Berlin aren't going away, but it is becoming clear that the success of these ideas is in large measure bound and determined by geography. This was always the case, and it is harder to deny now, as the ongoing recession will likely cause the global economy to contract for the first time in six decades. Not only wealth, but political and social order, will erode in many places, leaving only nature's frontiers and men's passions as the main arbiters of that age-old question: Who can coerce whom? We thought globalization had gotten rid of this antiquarian world of musty maps, but now it is returning with a vengeance.

We all must learn to think like Victorians. That is what must guide and inform our newly rediscovered realism. Geographical determinists must be seated at the same honored table as liberal humanists, thereby merging the analogies of Vietnam and Munich. Embracing the dictates and limitations of geography will be especially hard for Americans, who like to think that no constraint, natural or otherwise, applies to them. But denying the facts of geography only invites disasters that, in turn, make us victims of geography.

Better, instead, to look hard at the map for ingenious ways to stretch the limits it imposes, which will make any support for liberal principles in the world far more effective. Amid the revenge of geography, that is the essence of realism and the crux of wise policymaking—working near the edge of what is possible, without slipping into the precipice.

ROBERT D. KAPLAN is national correspondent for *The Atlantic* and senior fellow at the Center for a New American Security.

The Real War in Mexico

How Democracy Can Defeat the Drug Cartels

Shannon O'Neil

Brazen assassinations, kidnappings, and intimidation by drug lords conjure up images of Colombia in the early 1990s. Yet today it is Mexico that is engulfed by escalating violence. Over 10,000 drug-related killings have occurred since President Felipe Calderón took office in December 2006; in 2008 alone, there were over 6,000. Drug cartels have begun using guerrilla-style tactics: sending heavily armed battalions to attack police stations and assassinating police officers, government officials, and journalists. And they have also adopted innovative public relations strategies to recruit supporters and intimidate their enemies: displaying *narcomantas*—banners hung by drug traffickers—in public places and uploading videos of gruesome beheadings to You Tube.

Washington is just waking up to the violence next door. Last December, the U.S. Joint Forces Command's *Joint Operating Environment, 2008* paired Mexico with Pakistan in its discussion of "worstcase scenarios"—states susceptible to "a rapid and sudden collapse." In January, Michael Hayden, the departing CIA chief, claimed that Mexico could become "more problematic than Iraq," and Michael Chertoff, the departing secretary of homeland security, announced that the Department of Homeland Security has a "contingency plan for border violence, so if we did get a significant spillover, we have a surge—if I may use that word—capability." The U.S. media breathlessly proclaims that Mexico is "on the brink."

This rising hysteria clouds the real issues for Mexico and for the United States. The question is not whether the Mexican state will fail. It will not. The Mexican state does, and will continue to, collect taxes, run schools, repair roads, pay salaries, and manage large social programs throughout the country. The civilian-controlled military has already extinguished any real guerrilla threats. The government regularly holds free and fair elections, and its legitimacy, in the eyes of its citizens and of the world, is not questioned.

The actual risk of the violence today is that it will undermine democracy tomorrow. What has changed in Mexico in recent years is not the drug trade but that a fledgling market-based democracy has arisen. Although an authoritarian legacy persists, power now comes from the ballot box. This transformation has coincided with the rise of Mexico's middle class, which, now nearly 30 million strong, has supported more open politics and markets.

But Mexico's democratic system is still fragile. And by disrupting established payoff systems between drug traffickers and government officials, democratization unwittingly exacerbated drug-related violence. The first two freely elected governments have struggled to respond, hampered by electoral competition and the decentralization of political power. Yet in the long run, only through true democratic governance will Mexico successfully conquer, rather than just paper over, its security challenges. For the safety and prosperity of Mexico and the United States, Washington must go beyond its current focus on border control to a more ambitious goal: supporting Mexico's democracy.

Drug Parties

Mexico's escalating violence is in part an unintended side effect of democratization and economic globalization. The chaos, anarchy, and violence of the Mexican Revolution—which began nearly a hundred years ago—scarred the country and enabled the rise of a strong state dominated by a single political party. Created in 1929, the National Revolutionary Party, later renamed the Institutional Revolutionary Party (PRI), systematically extended its control over Mexico's territory and people. It quelled political opposition by incorporating important social groups—including workers, peasants, businesspeople, intellectuals, and the military—into its party structure.

The PRI's reach went beyond politics; it created Mexico's ruling economic and social classes. Through an inwardly focused development model (and later by giving away oil money), the government granted monopolies to private-sector supporters, paid off labor leaders, and doled out thousands of public-sector jobs. It provided plum positions and national recognition for loyal intellectuals, artists, and journalists. Famously called "the perfect dictatorship," the PRI used its great patronage machine (backed, of course, by a strong repressive capacity) to subdue dissident voices—and control Mexico for decades.

Ties between the PRI and illegal traders began in the first half of the twentieth century, during Prohibition. By the end of World War II, the relationship between drug traffickers and the ruling party had solidified. Through the Mexican Ministry of the Interior and the federal police, as well as governorships and other political offices, the government established patron-client relationships with drug traffickers (just as it did with other sectors of the economy and society). This arrangement limited violence against public officials, top traffickers, and civilians; made sure that court investigations never reached the upper ranks of cartels; and defined the rules of the game for traffickers. This compact held even as drug production and transit accelerated in the 1970s and 1980s.

Mexico's political opening in the late 1980s and 1990s disrupted these long-standing dynamics. As the PRI's political monopoly ended, so, too, did its control over the drug trade. Electoral competition nullified the unwritten understandings, requiring drug lords to negotiate with the new political establishment and encouraging rival traffickers to bid for new market opportunities. Accordingly, Mexico's drug-related violence rose first in opposition-led states. After the PRI lost its first governorship, in Baja California in 1989, for example, drug-related violence there surged. In Chihuahua, violence followed an opposition takeover in 1992. When the PRI won back the Chihuahua governorship in 1998, the violence moved to Ciudad Juárez—a city governed by the National Action Party (PAN).

With the election of Vicente Fox, the PAN candidate, as president in 2000, the old model—dependent on PRI dominance—was truly broken. Drug-trafficking organizations took advantage of the political opening to gain autonomy, ending their subordination to the government. They focused instead on buying off or intimidating local authorities in order to ensure the safe transit of their goods.

Democratic competition also hampered the state's capacity to react forcefully. Mexico's powerful presidency—the result of party cohesion rather than institutional design—ended. As Congress' influence grew, legislative gridlock weakened President Fox's hand, delaying judicial and police reforms. Conflicts also emerged between the different levels of government. Federal, state, and local officials—who frequently belonged to different parties—often refused to coordinate policies or even share information. At the extreme, this led to armed standoffs—not with drug dealers but between federal, state, and local police forces, such as the one that occurred in Tijuana in 2005.

The High Tide

As democratization tilted the balance of power from politicians to criminals, the economics of Mexico's drug business also changed. Mexico has a long history of supplying coveted but illegal substances to U.S. consumers, beginning at the turn of the twentieth century with heroin and marijuana. It continued through Prohibition, as drinkers moved south and Mexican rumrunners sent alcohol north. The marijuana trade picked up in the 1960s and 1970s with rising demand from the U.S. counterculture. In the late 1970s and 1980s, U.S. cocaine consumption boomed, and Mexican traffickers teamed up with Colombian drug lords to meet the growing U.S. demand.

In the 1980s and 1990s, the United States cracked down on drug transit through the Caribbean and Miami. As a result, more products started going through Mexico and over the U.S.-Mexican border. In 1991, 50 percent of U.S.-bound cocaine came through Mexico; by 2004, 90 percent of U.S.-bound cocaine

(and large percentages of other drugs) did. Like other Mexican industries, the drug cartels learned to maximize the comparative advantage of sharing a border with the world's largest consumer. As the transit of drugs to the United States grew, Mexican traffickers gained more power vis-à-vis the Colombian cartels.

These changes in business and enforcement accelerated the consolidation and professionalization of Mexico's drug-trafficking organizations. Rising profitability meant larger operations and more money, and as political and market uncertainty grew, the cartels developed increasingly militarized enforcement arms. The most famous of these branches is the Zetas, who were recruited from an elite Mexican army unit in the 1990s by the Gulf cartel. This group now acts independently, supplying hired guns and functioning as a trafficking organization itself. For many Mexicans, its name has come to signify terror and bloodshed.

From this increasingly sophisticated operational structure, Mexico's drug-trafficking organizations aggressively moved into the markets for heroin and methamphetamine in the United States, as well as the expanding European cocaine market. They extended their influence down the production chain into source countries such as Bolivia, Colombia, and Peru. They established beachheads in Central American and Caribbean nations—which in many cases have much weaker institutions and democracies than Mexico—where they worked their way into the countries' economic, social, and political fabric, to devastating effect. They widened and deepened their U.S. distribution route. In the words of a recent Justice Department report, Mexican drug cartels now represent the "biggest organized crime threat to the United States," with operations in some 230 U.S. cities. They also diversified their domestic operations, with participants expanding into kidnapping, extortion, contraband, and human smuggling.

A History of Violence

The current surge in violence is largely a result of these long-term political and economic processes, but President Calderóne self-proclaimed war on drug trafficking has also contributed. Soon after coming into office in December 2006, Calderón sent the army to Nuevo León, Guerrero, Michoacán, and Tijuana, beginning a new phase of government action that now involves some 45,000 troops. Record numbers of interdictions, arrests, and extraditions to the United States have interrupted business as usual. With the older kingpins gone, the second and often third generations of criminal leaders are now vying for territory, control, and power. Many of these aspiring leaders come from the enforcement arms of the cartels—and are accordingly inclined to use even more violence as they try to gain control of fragmented markets. Both the rewriting and the enforcement of illicit contracts mean blood in the streets.

The number of drug-related deaths in 2008 far surpassed those for any other year in Mexican history. Disputes between rival criminal organizations have led to open gun battles on major city streets, often in broad daylight. Death threats have forced dozens of law enforcement and government officials to resign. Extortion rings in many cities prey on businesses, forcing owners to pay to protect their operations and employees. The fear of kidnapping plagues the upper, middle, and working classes alike.

But as concern mounts on both sides of the border, the current situation should be put into perspective. Although unparalleled in scale, today's bloodshed is not unprecedented in type. In the early 1990s, conflict between the Tijuana and Sinaloa cartels engulfed not only the city of Tijuana but also the entire country in violence—including the assassinations of Cardinal Juan Jesus Posadas Ocampo, a Catholic archbishop, and Luis Donaldo Colosio, the PRI's presidential candidate These events stirred up fear in both Washington and Mexico City, spurring the United States to strengthen border controls and revive security collaboration with Mexican counterparts (which had all but disappeared in the wake of the murder of the U.S. Drug Enforcement Administration agent Enrique "Kiki" Camarena in 1985). The violence did not decline until 1997, when the Tijuana cartel successfully solidified its hold over the border crossing to San Diego.

As the carnage subsided in Tijuana, it skyrocketed in Ciudad Juárez, which borders El Paso, Texas. There, the violence initially reflected intracartel fighting following the demise of the Juárez cartel leader Amado Carrillo Fuentes, who died while undergoing plastic surgery to change his appearance. It escalated as both the Tijuana and the Sinaloa organizations attempted to take over the territory of the shaken cartel. This wave of bloodshed did not end until 1999, when Vicente Carrillo Fuentes, Amado's brother, gained clear control of the Juárez cartel.

Simmering narco-conflicts again exploded in 2005, this time in the border town of Nuevo Laredo, when the Sinaloa cartel tried to take over the U.S.-Mexican crossing there (the busiest land border between the two countries), which the Gulf cartel had controlled for years. Shootouts in broad daylight with automatic rifles and rocket-propelled grenades prompted the temporary closing of the U.S. consulate in Nuevo Laredo, and the body count quickly rose to over 180. Among the dead were the editor of the largest daily newspaper in the city and the new police chief—who was killed just six hours after his swearing in. President Fox sent in the army, and Secretary Chertoff revived Operation Stonegarden, an initiative to provide up to $400 million in funding to local law enforcement agencies on the U.S. side of the border. Stability returned when the cartels reached a truce in 2007, with the Sinaloa cartel paying the Gulf cartel for access to the Laredo border crossing.

The Last War

This history does not diminish the current danger. It does, however, highlight the inefficacy of rehashing past policy approaches. This is not the first time Mexico has brought out the military to quell drug related violence. President Miguel de la Madrid mobilized troops in the mid-1980s to fight drug gangs, and every subsequent Mexican president has followed suit (although Calderóne current effort far surpasses former shows of force). The United States, too, provided equipment, training, and capacity building at various points throughout the 1980s and 1990s. If history is any lesson, these approaches will neither stem the violence nor provide real border security.

Instead, the United States needs to develop a comprehensive policy to bolster North American security—one that treats Mexico as an equal and permanent partner. Mexico must continue to challenge the drug cartels, and the United States, in turn, must address its own role in perpetuating the drug trade and drug-related violence. But more important, Mexico and the United States need to work together to broaden their focus beyond immediate security measures—fostering Mexico's democracy and growing middle class. Only then can they overcome the security challenges facing both nations.

The United States needs to take a hard look at its own role in the rising violence in Mexico.

To start, the United States needs to take a hard look at its own role in the escalating violence and instability in Mexico. This means enforcing its own laws—and rethinking its own priorities. When it comes to the gun trade, U.S. law prohibits the sale of weapons to foreign nationals or "straw buyers," who use their clean criminal records to buys arms for others. It also forbids the unlicensed export of guns to Mexico. Nevertheless, over 90 percent of the guns seized in Mexico and traced are found to have come from the United States. These include not just pistols but also cartel favorites such as AR-15s and AK-47-style semiautomatic rifles. To stop this "iron river" of guns, Washington must inspect traffic on the border going south—not just north—and increase the resources for the Bureau of Alcohol, Tobacco, Firearms and Explosives. (Even with recent additional deployments, a mere 250 ATF officers and inspectors cover the 2,000-mile border.) This effort should also include a broader program of outreach and education, encouraging responsible sales at gun shops and shows and deterring potential straw buyers with more explicit warnings of the punishment they would face if caught. Reducing the tools of violence in Mexico is a first step in addressing U.S. responsibility.

Even more important than guns, although less discussed, is money. Estimates of illicit profits range widely, but most believe some $15 billion to $25 billion heads across the U.S. border into the hands of Mexico's drug cartels each year. This money buys guns, people, and power. Compiled from thousands of retail drug sales in hundreds of U.S. cities, much of this money is wired, carried, or transported to the U.S.-Mexican border and then simply driven south in bulk. Mexican criminal organizations then launder the funds by using seemingly legal business fronts, such as used-car lots, import-export businesses, or foreign exchange houses. Laundered money not used to fund criminal operations or pay off officials in Mexico is often sent back to the United States and saved in U.S. bank accounts.

Targeting illicit funds is one of the most effective ways of dealing with drug trafficking. (Incarcerating individuals only briefly disrupts criminal operations, since people are swiftly replaced.) Washington has begun working with Mexican authorities to stop the flow of illicit funds. There have been some successes, such as the passage of an asset forfeiture law in Mexico, the addition of Mexican cartels to the U.S. drug kingpin list, and the strengthening of Mexico's financial intelligence unit. The United States should continue and deepen this bilateral cooperation, further developing financial tools and infrastructure to increase the information and intelligence sharing needed to dismantle money-laundering schemes. At home, the United States should work to replicate the successes of the interagency Foreign Terrorist Asset Tracking Center, which was ramped up after 9/11 to thwart terrorist financing, by creating a similar structure to go after drug-related money.

Law enforcement, however, is not enough. The supply of drugs follows demand. The United States needs to shift the emphasis of its drug policy toward demand reduction. Studies show that a dollar spent on reducing demand in the United States is vastly more effective than a dollar spent on eradication and interdiction abroad and that money designated for the treatment of addicts is five times as effective as that spent on conventional law enforcement. The United States needs to expand its drug-treatment and drug-education programs and other measures to rehabilitate addicts and lessen drugs' allure for those not yet hooked. Reduced demand would lower the drug profits that corrupt officials, buy guns, and threaten Mexico's democracy.

The Other Side

As the United States deals with the problems in its own backyard, it should also be helping Mexico address its challenges. Until just last year, the United States provided less than $40 million a year in security funding to its southern neighbour—in stark contrast to the $600 million designated for Colombia. This changed last June with Congress' passage of the Merida Initiative, which called for supplying $1.4 billion worth of equipment, software, and technical assistance to Mexico's military, police, and judicial forces over three years.

Despite its many laudable elements, the Merida Initiative does not go far enough fast enough. For one thing, it is just too small. The current budget for Plan Colombia is twice as large as Mexico's 2009 allotment—and that is for a country that does not share a border with the United States. And even the support for Plan Colombia pales next to the billions of dollars U.S. drug consumers supply to Mexico's enemies in this confrontation. Compared to other U.S. national security threats, Mexico remains an afterthought.

The spending has also been far too slow. Although $700 million had been released by Congress as of April 2009, only $7 million had been spent. Despite the touted urgency, a cumbersome consultation process between the two countries, combined with a complicated dispersement process (since all of the assistance is in kind, not cash), has meant little headway even as the deaths mount. Most important, the focus of this aid is too narrow, reflecting a misunderstanding of Mexico's fundamental challenge. Unlike Colombia, which had to retake vast swaths of territory from guerrilla groups, paramilitary organizations, and drug cartels, the Mexican state has been able to quell the rising violence when it has deployed large and well-armed military units. So far, the cartels have put up limited resistance in the face of true shows of force by the state—for instance, when the government sent in 7,000 troops to Ciudad Juárez in March 2009. Firepower is not the main issue; sustainability is.

Mexico's Achilles' heel is corruption—which in an electoral democracy cannot be stabilizing the way it was in the days of Mexico's autocracy. Under the PRI, the purpose of government policy was to assert power rather than govern by law. The opacity of court proceedings, the notorious graft of the police forces, and the menacing presence of special law enforcement agencies were essential elements of an overall system of political, economic, and social control. Rather than acting as a check or balance on executive power, the judiciary was often just another arm of the party, used to reward supporters and intimidate opponents. Law enforcement, too, was used to control, rather than protect, the population.

The decline of the PRI and the onset of electoral competition transformed the workings of the executive and legislative branches quite quickly, but the changes have had much less influence over the judicial branch or over law enforcement more generally. Instead, even after the transition to democracy, accountability mechanisms remain either nonexistent or defunct. Most of Mexico's various police forces continue to be largely incapable of objective and thorough investigations, having never received adequate resources or training. Impunity reigns: the chance of being prosecuted, much less convicted, of a crime is extremely low. As a result, Mexicans place little faith in their law enforcement and judicial systems. And as today's democratic government struggles to overcome this history through legislative reform, funding new programs for vetting and training and creating more avenues for citizen involvement, it faces a new threat: increasingly sophisticated, well-funded, and autonomous criminal organizations intent on manipulating the rule of law for their own benefit.

The Merida Initiative provides some funding for institution building, but that is dwarfed by the amount spent on hardware. Furthermore, although Mexico's lawlessness is most intractable at the state and local levels, the Merida funding focuses almost solely on the federal level. This neglects some 325,000 officers—90 percent of the nation's police. It leaves out those on the frontlines who are most likely to face the ultimate Faustian bargain—money or death—from organized crime. The United States should expand Merida's focus to incorporate local and state-level initiatives and training, including vetting mechanisms similar to those envisioned for federal agents, training for local crime labs, training for judges and lawyers, and support for community policing programs. In the end, all lasting security is local.

Disorder on the Border

Improving security will depend above all, however, on other dimensions of the complex U.S.-Mexican relationship—including trade, economic development, and immigration. To really overcome Mexico's security challenges, the United States must move beyond a short-term threat-based mentality to one that considers all these elements in the strategic relationship with its southern neighbor.

The foremost challenge in Mexico today, at least according to most Mexicans, is in fact the growing economic crisis. Even during Mexico's protectionist days, its fortunes rose and fell along with those of its northern neighbor. Today, the economies and general well-being of Mexico and the United States are even more linked. Some 80 percent of Mexico's exports—well over $200 billion worth—go to the United States. Mexico's tourism industry—which brings in $11 billion annually—depends on 15 million American vacationers each year. The large Mexican and Mexican American populations living in the United States—estimated at 12 million and 28 million, respectively—transfer nearly $25 billion a year to family and friends in Mexico.

This relationship runs the other way as well. After Canada, Mexico is the second most important destination for U.S. exports, receiving one-ninth of U.S. goods sent abroad. It is either the primary or the secondary destination for exports from 22 of the 50 U.S. states. Hundreds of thousands—if not millions—of American jobs depend on consumers and industries in Mexico. And increasingly, U.S. citizens depend on Mexico for even more, as over one million individual Americans—from young professionals to adventurous snowbirds—now live there.

The U.S. recession is hitting Mexico's economy exceptionally hard. In January, Mexico's GDP shrank by nearly ten percent year on year as manufacturing tumbled. In March, the Peso sodded to a 16-year low against the dollar. The government now predicts a three-and-a-half percent decline in GDP for 2009, and many private economists are bracing for an even greater fall. Policymakers are beginning to worry about rising unemployment, poverty, and even social unrest. Some ten million Mexicans still live on just $2 a day, and economists predict that the downturn will push more Mexicans into poverty.

Nowhere else are the asymmetries between two such interlinked neighbors so severe. In its own self-interest, the United States should work with Mexico on a new economic development strategy. The United States can start by lessening the barriers to trade with Mexico. This will require resolving the current trucking dispute (fulfilling U.S. obligations under the North American Free Trade Agreement [NAFTA] by allowing Mexican trucks to operate on both sides of the border) and avoiding protectionist measures, such as the recent "Buy American" provision in the stimulus package. It will also require investing in the border itself. Nearly one million people and $1 billion in trade cross the border every day, overwhelming the existing infrastructure and border personnel and leading to long and unpredictable border delays, which limit Mexico's competitiveness. The U.S. Department of Transportation currently estimates that $11 billion more will need to be spent on the U.S. side of the border to catch up with the growing traffic.

The United States should also help create opportunities within Mexico. This means expanding development assistance, rather than just security assistance. At less than $5 million for 2009, current U.S. development aid to Mexico is paltry. Increased assistance should focus on supporting Mexico's efforts to expand its education and infrastructure programs and encourage local entrepreneurship and job creation.

Intertwined with both the economy and security is immigration. Economic opportunities in the United States, and their absence at home, draw millions of Mexicans north. Subsequent remittances provide a lifeline for millions of Mexican households and have brought many families out of poverty and into the bottom rungs of Mexico's middle class. At the same time, immigration to the United States pulls away many of Mexico's best and brightest, limiting the spillover benefits of their work on the larger economy and society.

Most studies show that immigration provides net benefits to the United States, including providing flexible workers to labor-scarce economic sectors, lowering the prices of domestically produced labor-intensive goods and services, and contributing to entitlement programs such as Social Security. The illegality of these human flows, however, has its costs. It depresses local wages and puts pressure on local health and education services, and it can undermine labor rights. In terms of security, the presence of millions of unauthorized workers in the United States gives unsavory elements a place to hide among a larger population forced to live underground. Illicit profits can be hidden in the flow of honestly earned money going back to Mexico, complicating efforts against money laundering.

The United States views immigration as a domestic concern, but when it comes to Mexico, this perspective is both inaccurate and counterproductive. During her April 2009 visit to Mexico, Janet Napolitano, the U.S. secretary of homeland security, announced, with Patricia Espinosa, the Mexican foreign secretary, a new high-level joint working group to make immigration safer and more orderly. This is a step toward greater consultation and cooperation. Still, fundamental and comprehensive immigration reform in the United States is necessary to address the economic and security concerns on both sides of the border. New policies should be designed not only to improve border security and management. They should also regularize the status of the unauthorized work force already in the United States, ensure employer verification and responsibility, and create an expanded flexible worker program to meet changing U.S. economic demands.

Finally, U.S. policy toward Mexico must become more coherent. The U.S. diplomatic presence in Mexico—which includes an embassy, nine consulates, and 14 consular agencies—is one of the largest diplomatic missions in the world. It houses representatives from not only enforcement and investigative agencies, such as the ATF, the Drug Enforcement Administration, and the Department of Homeland Security, but also 37 additional agencies and departments, ranging from the Department of Agriculture to the U.S. Agency for International Development. Disorganization has led to a lack of policy coherence, as no organization is able or willing to take the lead in guiding the overall bilateral relationship. Washington needs to strengthen coordination among the agencies, bringing together the multiple interests and agendas they represent into a more coherent strategy.

Mending Fences

U.S. leaders and the press commonly tout President Calderóne's commitment to fighting the Mexican cartels as something exceptional. Congressman Connie Mack (R-Fla.) has said, for example, "This is a president who has taken the drug cartels head-on, and has not flinched in the fight to rid Mexico of these cowards." Although true, this image misses the real political dynamic behind Calderóne fight. Rather than a quixotic lone crusader, he is a shrewd politician responding to voter demands.

Rather than a lone crusader, Calderón is a shrewd politician responding to voters' demands.

Like his predecessor, Calderón was elected by Mexico's burgeoning middle class—now nearly one-third of the population. Long noted for the disparities between the extremely wealthy and the desperately poor, Mexico now has an economic center that is rapidly expanding. The middle class has grown thanks to NAFTA and Mexico's broader economic opening, a boom in immigration to the United States that has sent billions of dollars back to families at home, and a decade of economic stability and growth that has enabled average citizens to work, save, and plan for the future. Mexico's middle-class families work in small businesses, own their cars and homes, and strive to send their children to college. And as voters, they threw out the PRI in 2000, bringing an end to its 70-year rule. Since then, they have been behind halting steps to create new civil-society organizations and to demand public transparency, judicial reform, and safety. It is these voters who tilted the election in Calderón's favor in 2006—and it is to them he is responding.

Security ranks second only to the economy in terms of voter priorities. Polls show that the middle class (as well as other segments of society) wants the government to take on the narcotraffickers, even if it creates more violence in the short run—and even though many think the government cannot win. Calderón's ratings have risen as he has confronted organized crime, with fully two-thirds of the public supporting his actions.

Mexican middle-class preferences for law and order, fairness, transparency, and democracy benefit Mexico, but they also benefit the United States. Although hardly an antidote for all challenges, a secure and growing middle class would help move Mexico further down the road toward achieving democratic prosperity and toward an increasingly able partnership with the United States. But if this center is diminished or decimated by economic crisis, insecurity, or closing opportunities, Mexico could truly descend into crime-ridden political and economic turmoil.

The best the United States and Mexico can hope for in terms of security is for organized crime in Mexico to become a persistent but manageable law enforcement problem, similar to illegal businesses in the United States. But both the United States and Mexico should hope for more in terms of Mexico's future, and for the future of U.S.-Mexican relations. U.S. policies that help increase accountability, expand economic and social opportunity, and strengthen the rule of law in Mexico will all encourage a more inclusive and more stable democracy there. This will require a difficult conceptual shift in Washington—recognizing Mexico as a permanent strategic partner rather than an often-forgotten neighbor.

SHANNON O'NEIL is Douglas Dillon Fellow for Latin America Studies at the Council on Foreign Relations and Director of the CFR task force on U.S.—Latin American relations.

The Long March to Be a Superpower

The People's Liberation Army is investing heavily to give China the military muscle to match its economic power. But can it begin to rival America?

THE ECONOMIST

The sight is as odd as its surroundings are bleak. Where a flat expanse of mud flats, salt pans and fish farms reaches the Bohai Gulf, a vast ship looms through the polluted haze. It is an aircraft-carrier, the *Kiev,* once the proud possession of the Soviet Union. Now it is a tourist attraction. Chinese visitors sit on the flight deck under Pepsi umbrellas, reflecting perhaps on a great power that was and another, theirs, that is fast in the making.

Inside the *Kiev,* the hangar bay is divided into two. On one side, bored-looking visitors watch an assortment of dance routines featuring performers in ethnic-minority costumes. On the other side is a full-size model of China's new J-10, a plane unveiled with great fanfare in January as the most advanced fighter built by the Chinese themselves (except for the Ukrainian or Russian turbofan engines—but officials prefer not to advertise this). A version of this, some military analysts believe, could one day be deployed on a Chinese ship.

The Pentagon is watching China's aircraft-carrier ambitions with bemused interest. Since the 1980s, China has bought four of them (three from the former Soviet Union and an Australian one whose construction began in Britain during the second world war). Like the *Kiev,* the *Minsk* (berthed near Hong Kong) has been turned into a tourist attraction having first been studied closely by Chinese naval engineers. Australia's carrier, the *Melbourne,* has been scrapped. The biggest and most modern one, the *Varyag,* is in the northern port city of Dalian, where it is being refurbished. Its destiny is uncertain. The Pentagon says it might be put into service, used for training carrier crews, or become yet another floating theme-park.

American global supremacy is not about to be challenged by China's tinkering with aircraft-carriers. Even if China were to commission one—which analysts think unlikely before at least 2015—it would be useless in the most probable area of potential conflict between China and America, the Taiwan Strait. China could far more easily launch its jets from shore. But it would be widely seen as a potent symbol of China's rise as a military power. Some Chinese officers want to fly the flag ever farther afield as a demonstration of China's rise. As China emerges as a trading giant (one increasingly dependent on imported oil), a few of its military analysts talk about the need to protect distant sea lanes in the Malacca Strait and beyond.

This week China's People's Liberation Army (PLA), as the armed forces are known, is celebrating the 80th year since it was born as a group of ragtag rebels against China's then rulers. Today it is vying to become one of the world's most capable forces: one that could, if necessary, keep even the Americans at bay. The PLA has little urge to confront America head-on, but plenty to deter it from protecting Taiwan.

The pace of China's military upgrading is causing concern in the Pentagon. Eric McVadon, a retired rear admiral, told a congressional commission in 2005 that China had achieved a "remarkable leap" in the modernisation of forces needed to overwhelm Taiwan and deter or confront any American intervention. And the pace of this, he said, was "urgently continuing". By Pentagon standards, Admiral McVadon is doveish.

In its annual report to Congress on China's military strength, published in May, the Pentagon said China's "expanding military capabilities" were a "major factor" in altering military balances in East Asia. It said China's ability to project power over long distances remained limited. But it repeated its observation, made in 2006, that among "major and emerging powers" China had the "greatest potential to compete militarily" with America.

Since the mid-1990s China has become increasingly worried that Taiwan might cut its national ties with the mainland. To instil fear into any Taiwanese leader so inclined, it has been deploying short-range ballistic missiles (SRBMs) on the coast facing the island as fast as it can produce them—about 100 a year. The Pentagon says there are now about 900 of these DF-11s (CSS-7) and DF-15s (CSS-6). They are getting more accurate. Salvoes of them might devastate Taiwan's military infrastructure so quickly that any war would be over before America could respond.

Much has changed since 1995 and 1996, when China's weakness in the face of American power was put on stunning display. In a fit of anger over America's decision in 1995 to allow Lee Teng-hui, then Taiwan's president, to make a high-profile trip to his alma mater, Cornell University, China fired ten unarmed

DF-15s into waters off Taiwan. The Americans, confident that China would quickly back off, sent two aircraft-carrier battle groups to the region as a warning. The tactic worked. Today America would have to think twice. Douglas Paal, America's unofficial ambassador to Taiwan from 2002 to 2006, says the "cost of conflict has certainly gone up."

The Chinese are now trying to make sure that American aircraft-carriers cannot get anywhere near. Admiral McVadon worries about their development of DF-21 (CSS-5) medium-range ballistic missiles. With their far higher re-entry velocities than the SRBMs, they would be much harder for Taiwan's missile defences to cope with. They could even be launched far beyond Taiwan into the Pacific to hit aircraft-carriers. This would be a big technical challenge. But Admiral McVadon says America "might have to worry" about such a possibility within a couple of years.

Once the missiles have done their job, China's armed forces could (so they hope) follow up with a panoply of advanced Russian weaponry—mostly amassed in the past decade. Last year the Pentagon said China had imported around $11 billion of weapons between 2000 and 2005, mainly from Russia.

China knows it has a lot of catching up to do. Many Americans may be unenthusiastic about America's military excursions in recent years, particularly about the war in Iraq. But Chinese military authors, in numerous books and articles, see much to be inspired by.

On paper at least, China's gains have been impressive. Even into the 1990s China had little more than a conscript army of ill-educated peasants using equipment based largely on obsolete Soviet designs of the 1950s and outdated cold-war (or even guerrilla-war) doctrine. Now the emphasis has shifted from ground troops to the navy and air force, which would spearhead any attack on Taiwan. China has bought 12 Russian Kilo-class diesel attack submarines. The newest of these are equipped with supersonic Sizzler cruise missiles that America's carriers, many analysts believe, would find hard to stop.

There are supersonic cruise missiles too aboard China's four new Sovremenny-class destroyers, made to order by the Russians and designed to attack aircraft-carriers and their escorts. And China's own shipbuilders have not been idle. In an exhibition marking the 80th anniversary, Beijing's Military Museum displays what Chinese official websites say is a model of a new nuclear-powered attack submarine, the *Shang*. These submarines would allow the navy to push deep into the Pacific, well beyond Taiwan, and, China hopes, help defeat American carriers long before they get close. Last year, much to America's embarrassment, a newly developed Chinese diesel submarine for shorter-range missions surfaced close to the American carrier *Kitty Hawk* near Okinawa without being detected beforehand.

American air superiority in the region is now challenged by more than 200 advanced Russian Su-27 and Su-30 fighters China has acquired since the 1990s. Some of these have been made under licence in China itself. The Pentagon thinks China is also interested in buying Su-33s, which would be useful for deployment on an aircraft-carrier, if China decides to build one.

During the Taiwan Strait crisis of 1995–96, America could be reasonably sure that, even if war did break out (few seriously thought it would), it could cope with any threat from China's nuclear arsenal. China's handful of strategic missiles capable of hitting mainland America were based in silos, whose positions the Americans most probably knew. Launch preparations would take so long that the Americans would have plenty of time to knock them out. China has been working hard to remedy this. It is deploying six road-mobile, solid-fuelled (which means quick to launch) intercontinental DF-31s and is believed to be developing DF-31As with a longer range that could hit anywhere in America, as well as submarine-launched (so more concealable) JL-2s that could threaten much of America too.

All Dressed up and Ready to Fight?

But how much use is all this hardware? Not a great deal is known about the PLA's fighting capability. It is by far the most secretive of the world's big armies. One of the few titbits it has been truly open about in the build-up to the celebrations is the introduction of new uniforms to mark the occasion: more body-hugging and, to howls of criticism from some users of popular Chinese internet sites, more American-looking.

As Chinese military analysts are well aware, America's military strength is not just about technology. It also involves training, co-ordination between different branches of the military ("jointness", in the jargon), gathering and processing intelligence, experience and morale. China is struggling to catch up in these areas too. But it has had next to no combat experience since a brief and undistinguished foray into Vietnam in 1979 and a huge deployment to crush pro-democracy unrest ten years later.

China is even coyer about its war-fighting capabilities than it is about its weaponry. It has not rehearsed deep-sea drills against aircraft-carriers. It does not want to create alarm in the region, nor to rile America. There is also a problem of making all this Russian equipment work. Some analysts say the Chinese have not been entirely pleased with their Su-27 and Su-30 fighters. Keeping them maintained and supplied with spare parts (from Russia) has not been easy. A Western diplomat says China is also struggling to keep its Russian destroyers and submarines in good working order. "We have to be cautious about saying 'wow'," he suggests of the new equipment.

China is making some progress in its efforts to wean itself off dependence on the Russians. After decades of effort, some analysts believe, China is finally beginning to use its own turbofan engines, an essential technology for advanced fighters. But self-sufficiency is still a long way off. The Russians are sometimes still reluctant to hand over their most sophisticated technologies. "The only trustworthy thing [the Chinese] have is missiles," says Andrew Yang of the Chinese Council of Advanced Policy Studies in Taiwan.

The Pentagon, for all its fretting, is trying to keep channels open to the Chinese. Military exchanges have been slowly reviving since their nadir of April 2001, when a Chinese fighter jet hit an American spy plane close to China. Last year, for the first time, the two sides conducted joint exercises—search-and-rescue missions off the coasts of America and China. But these were simple manoeuvres and the Americans learned little from them. The Chinese remain reluctant to engage in anything more complex, perhaps for fear of revealing their weaknesses.

The Russians have gained deeper insights. Two years ago the PLA staged large-scale exercises with them, the first with a foreign army. Although not advertised as such, these were partly aimed at scaring the Taiwanese. The two countries practised blockades, capturing airfields and amphibious landings. The Russians showed off some of the weaponry they hope to sell to the big-spending Chinese.

Another large joint exercise is due to be held on August 9th–17th in the Urals (a few troops from other members of the Shanghai Co-operation Organisation, a six-nation group including Central Asian states, will also take part). But David Shambaugh of George Washington University says the Russians have not been very impressed by China's skills. After the joint exercise of 2005, Russians muttered about the PLA's lack of "jointness", its poor communications and the slowness of its tanks.

China has won much praise in the West for its increasing involvement in United Nations peacekeeping operations. But this engagement has revealed little of China's combat capability. Almost all of the 1,600 Chinese peacekeepers deployed (including in Lebanon, Congo and Liberia) are engineers, transport troops or medical staff.

A series of "white papers" published by the Chinese government since 1998 on its military developments have shed little light either, particularly on how much the PLA is spending and on what. By China's opaque calculations, the PLA enjoyed an average annual budget increase of more than 15% between 1990 and 2005 (nearly 10% in real terms). This year the budget was increased by nearly 18%. But this appears not to include arms imports, spending on strategic missile forces and research and development. The International Institute for Strategic Studies in London says the real level of spending in 2004 could have been about 1.7 times higher than the officially declared budget of 220 billion yuan ($26.5 billion at then exchange rates).

This estimate would make China's spending roughly the same as that of France in 2004. But the different purchasing power of the dollar in the two countries—as well as China's double-digit spending increases since then—push the Chinese total far higher. China is struggling hard to make its army more professional—keeping servicemen for longer and attracting better-educated recruits. This is tough at a time when the civilian economy is booming and wages are climbing. The PLA is having to spend much more on pay and conditions for its 2.3m people.

Keeping the army happy is a preoccupation of China's leaders, mindful of how the PLA saved the party from probable destruction during the unrest of 1989. In the 1990s they encouraged military units to run businesses to make more money for themselves. At the end of the decade, seeing that this was fuelling corruption, they ordered the PLA to hand over its business

to civilian control. Bigger budgets are now helping the PLA to make up for some of those lost earnings.

The party still sees the army as a bulwark against the kind of upheaval that has toppled communist regimes elsewhere. Chinese leaders lash out at suggestions (believed to be supported by some officers) that the PLA should be put under the state's control instead of the party's. The PLA is riddled with party spies who monitor officers' loyalty. But the party also gives the army considerable leeway to manage its own affairs. It worries about military corruption but seldom moves against it, at least openly (in a rare exception to this, a deputy chief of the navy was dismissed last year for taking bribes and "loose morals"). The PLA's culture of secrecy allowed the unmonitored spread of SARS, an often fatal respiratory ailment, in the army's medical system in 2003.

Carrier Trade

The PLA knows its weaknesses. It has few illusions that China can compete head-on with the Americans militarily. The Soviet Union's determination to do so is widely seen in China as the cause of its collapse. Instead China emphasises weaponry and doctrine that could be used to defeat a far more powerful enemy using "asymmetric capabilities".

The idea is to exploit America's perceived weak points such as its dependence on satellites and information networks. China's successful (if messy and diplomatically damaging) destruction in January of one of its own ageing satellites with a rocket was clearly intended as a demonstration of such power. Some analysts believe Chinese people with state backing have been trying to hack into Pentagon computers. Richard Lawless, a Pentagon official, recently said China had developed a "very sophisticated" ability to attack American computer and internet systems.

The Pentagon's fear is that military leaders enamoured of new technology may underestimate the diplomatic consequences of trying it out. Some Chinese see a problem here too. The anti-satellite test has revived academic discussion in China of the need for setting up an American-style national security council that would help military planners co-ordinate more effectively with foreign-policy makers.

But the Americans find it difficult to tell China bluntly to stop doing what others are doing too (including India, which has aircraft-carriers and Russian fighter planes). In May Admiral Timothy Keating, the chief of America's Pacific Command, said China's interest in aircraft-carriers was "understandable". He even said that if China chose to develop them, America would "help them to the degree that they seek and the degree that we're capable." But, he noted, "it ain't as easy as it looks."

A senior Pentagon official later suggested Admiral Keating had been misunderstood. Building a carrier for the Chinese armed forces would be going a bit far. But the two sides are now talking about setting up a military hotline. The Americans want to stay cautiously friendly as the dragon grows stronger.

What Russia Wants

From Gorbachev to Yeltsin to Putin, every new Russian president has drastically altered his country's relationship with the world. How will President Dmitry Medvedev change it again? Here are the clues that reveal what the Kremlin is thinking, and, more importantly, what it really wants.

IVAN KRASTEV

This much we know: In the two decades since the collapse of the Soviet Union, Russia has transformed itself from a one-party state into a one-pipeline state—a semiauthoritarian regime in democratic clothing. At the same time, Russia has grown increasingly independent and unpredictable on the international political scene. And now that Vladimir Putin has successfully installed his handpicked successor, Dmitry Medvedev, he is nowhere near relinquishing his grip on power. Putin's foreign policy is here to stay.

But there's so much we can't know about the direction Russia is heading. It is, at once, a regime that offers its citizens consumer rights but not political freedoms, state sovereignty but not individual autonomy, a market economy but not genuine democracy. It is both a rising global power and a weak state with corrupt and inefficient institutions. The Kremlin's regime seems both rock solid and extremely vulnerable, simultaneously authoritarian and wildly popular. Although Russia's economy has performed well in the past 10 years, it is more dependent on the production and export of natural resources today than it was during Soviet times. Its foreign policy is no less puzzling. Russia may be more democratic today, but it is less predictable and reliable as a world player than was the Soviet Union. The more capitalist and Westernized Russia becomes, the more anti-Western its policies seem. The more successful Russia's foreign policy looks, the more unclear its goals appear.

Russia's contradictory development has succeeded once again in capturing the world's political imagination. Putin's tenure has left most people confused about what role Russia now wants to play in the world. In recent years, for example, Moscow has orchestrated a noisy and confrontational return to the international scene. It decided not to cooperate with the West in taming Iran's nuclear ambitions or in settling the final status of Kosovo. Last year, the Kremlin unilaterally suspended the Treaty on Conventional Armed Forces in Europe. It blocked the work of the Organization for security and Cooperation in Europe. Gazprom, Russia's gas monopoly, aggressively tries to control the energy supply throughout the region. The country's military budget has increased sixfold since 2000. Russian planes are patrolling the Atlantic. Moscow's intelligence network is creeping into all corners of Europe. Not since the hottest days of the Cold War have so many wondered just what was going on behind the Kremlin's closed doors.

Once a Superpower . . .

Some look at Russia and see a wounded enemy readying itself for another round. They interpret Moscow's new assertiveness as a simple overreaction to the humiliation of the 1990s. These realists are quick to blame NATO expansion and Western triumphalism after the Soviet collapse for the direction of Russia's current foreign policy. What Moscow learned in its "decade of humiliation" is that the West respects strength, not shared values. On the other hand, the liberals who shaped the West's policies toward Russia in the 1990s are not in a selfcritical mood. They tend to believe that Putin's foreign policy is simply a new incarnation of Moscow's traditional imperial policies. Plus, though they may concede that the West has lost some of its ability to shape Russian politics, they insist that the West can still focus on the rule of law—if not full democracy. In their view,

Russia's gains in the international arena are temporary and the Putin miracle is a mirage. In short, even the experts are far from unanimous in divining the motives of Russia's recent turn.

It would be easy to assume Russia is simply grasping power for power's sake, or to conclude that just as "there are no ex-KGB officers," there are also no ex-imperial powers. But to understand why the Kremlin acts the way it does, one must first recognize how haunted it is by uncertainty and paranoia. How Russia thinks is closely linked to how Russia's political elites feel. Moscow's current strategy is not merely a reflection of its new economic power or a geopolitical change. It is the expression of the traumatic experience of the collapse of the Soviet Union and the omnipresent political vulnerability of the current regime.

In effect, Russian foreign policy is held hostage by the sense of fragility that marked the Russian experience of the 1990s. It explains Moscow's preference for the pre-World War II international order based on unrestricted sovereignty and sphere-of-influence politics. It explains Russia's open resistance to American hegemony and its opposition to the postmodern European order promoted by the European Union (EU). The EU, with its emphasis on human rights and openness, threatens the Kremlin's monopoly on power. The West's policy of democracy promotion awakens in Moscow the nightmare of ethnic and religious politics and the threat of the territorial disintegration of the Russian Federation. Russia feels threatened by the invasion of Western funded nongovernmental organizations, and the Kremlin is tempted to recreate the police state to prevent foreign interference in its domestic politics. The recent "color" revolutions that shook the post-Soviet space embodied the ultimate threat for Russia: popular revolt orchestrated by remote control. Moscow is in an elusive quest for absolute stability.

Putin's foreign policy—and, by extension, Medvedev's—rests on two key assumptions and one strategic calculation. It assumes the United States is facing a collapse that is not much different from the collapse of Soviet power. It also assumes that the EU—despite being, in Russia's view, a temporary phenomenon—is a threat to the Russian regime by its very existence as a postmodern empire. The calculation is that the next decade presents a strategic window of opportunity for Russia to position itself as a great power in the emerging multipolar world while also securing the legitimacy of the regime, even if that means following a more assertive and confrontational foreign policy.

Unlike China, where the consensus these days is that world order does not collapse over a weekend and that

betting on America's decline is a risky gamble, Russia demonstrates complete confidence in the end of American hegemony. Russian elites are tempted to view the crisis of America's global power as a replay of the crisis of Soviet power in the 1980s. Moscow looks at the United States' debacle in Iraq and sees its own failure in Afghanistan. It views the United States' conflicts with the EU as proof of the dismantling of the informal American empire. In this sense, when Jacques Chirac openly questioned the wisdom of American leadership in the lead-up to the war in Iraq, Russians saw echoes of Lech Walesa's defiance of the Soviet Union at Gdansk. Moscow's policies, in other words, are informed by the assumption that great powers are less stable than they look and their positions are more vulnerable than classical balance-of-power analysis suggests.

Why Russia Fights

Of course, none of these calculations is necessarily comforting to a United States that views itself as the world's preeminent political, economic, and military power, or an EU that sees strength in unity and integration. Russia's resurgence comes at a time when the global hegemony of the United States is in decline and the EU is suffering a profound crisis of self-confidence. Russia's revisionism threatens the very nature of this existing international order. The paradox is that, faced with new Russian revisionism, the West is becoming nostalgic for the old Soviet Union. Even as a longing for a familiar foe has dramatically declined among the Russian public, it is on the rise in Western capitals. In the words of one senior French diplomat, "The Soviet Union was easier to deal with than Russia is today. Sometimes the Soviets were difficult, but you knew they were being obstructive in order to achieve an objective. Now, Russia seeks to block the West systematically on every subject, apparently without purpose." In other words, Russia is not simply a revisionist power—it is something potentially more dangerous: a spoiler at large. The Kremlin's recent actions easily fit this threatening image. In reality, though, Russia is not a spoiler so much as it likes to be viewed as one. Where the West seeks to find aggressiveness and imperial tendencies, it will find uncertainty and vulnerability. Demonizing Russia won't help—pitying it won't help either.

In 10 years' time, Russia will not be a failed state. But neither will it be a mature democracy.

In 10 years' time, Russia will not be a failed state. But neither will it be a mature democracy. Russian foreign policy will remain independent—one that promotes Russia's great-power status in a multipolar world. It will be selectively confrontational. Russia will remain more integrated in the world than it has ever been in its history, and it will remain as suspicious as ever. At base, the Kremlin's strategic dilemma is how to remain integrated in the world while also making the country impervious to political influence from abroad. Russia is a rising global power but also a declining state. The key to understanding the Kremlin's foreign-policy thinking is that simple—and that complicated.

IVAN KRASTEV is editor of *Foreign Policy*'s Bulgarian edition.

Lifting the Veil

Understanding the Roots of Islamic Militancy

HENRY MUNSON

I n the wake of the attacks of September 11, 2001, many intellectuals have argued that Muslim extremists like Osama bin Laden despise the United States primarily because of its foreign policy. Conversely, US President George Bush's administration and its supporters have insisted that extremists loathe the United States simply because they are religious fanatics who "hate our freedoms." These conflicting views of the roots of militant Islamic hostility toward the United States lead to very different policy prescriptions. If US policies have caused much of this hostility, it would make sense to change those policies, if possible, to dilute the rage that fuels Islamic militancy. If, on the other hand, the hostility is the result of religious fanaticism, then the use of brute force to suppress fanaticism would appear to be a sensible course of action.

Groundings for Animosity

Public opinion polls taken in the Islamic world in recent years provide considerable insight into the roots of Muslim hostility toward the United States, indicating that for the most part, this hostility has less to do with cultural or religious differences than with US policies in the Arab world. In February and March 2003, Zogby International conducted a survey on behalf of Professor Shibley Telhami of the University of Maryland involving 2,620 men and women in Egypt, Jordan, Lebanon, Morocco, and Saudi Arabia. Most of those surveyed had "unfavorable attitudes" toward the United States and said that their hostility to the United States was based primarily on US policy rather than on their values. This was true of 67 percent of the Saudis surveyed. In Egypt, however, only 46 percent said their hostility resulted from US policy, while 43 percent attributed their attitudes to their values as Arabs. This is surprising given that the prevailing religious values in Saudi Arabia are more conservative than in Egypt. Be that as it may, a plurality of people in all the countries surveyed said that their hostility toward the United States was primarily based on their opposition to US policy.

The issue that arouses the most hostility in the Middle East toward the United States is the Israeli-Palestinian conflict and what Muslims perceive as US responsibility for the suffering of the Palestinians. A similar Zogby International survey from the summer of 2001 found that more than 80 percent of

the respondents in Egypt, Kuwait, Lebanon, and Saudi Arabia ranked the Palestinian issue as one of the three issues of greatest importance to them. A survey of Muslim "opinion leaders" released by the Pew Research Center for the People and the Press in December 2001 also found that the US position on the Israeli-Palestinian conflict was the main source of hostility toward the United States.

It is true that Muslim hostility toward Israel is often expressed in terms of anti-Semitic stereotypes and conspiracy theories—think, for example, of the belief widely-held in the Islamic world that Jews were responsible for the terrorists attacks of September 11, 2001. Muslim governments and educators need to further eliminate anti-Semitic bias in the Islamic world. However, it would be a serious mistake to dismiss Muslim and Arab hostility toward Israel as simply a matter of anti-Semitism. In the context of Jewish history, Israel represents liberation. In the context of Palestinian history, it represents subjugation. There will always be a gap between how the West and how the Muslim societies perceive Israel. There will also always be some Muslims (like Osama bin Laden) who will refuse to accept any solution to the Israeli-Palestinian conflict other than the destruction of the state of Israel. That said, if the United States is serious about winning the so-called "war on terror," then resolution of the Israeli-Palestinian conflict should be among its top priorities in the Middle East.

Eradicating, or at least curbing, Palestinian terrorism entails reducing the humiliation, despair, and rage that drive many Palestinians to support militant Islamic groups like Hamas and Islamic Jihad. When soldiers at an Israeli checkpoint prevented Ahmad Qurei (Abu al Ala), one of the principal negotiators of the Oslo accords and president of the Palestinian Authority's parliament, from traveling from Gaza to his home on the West Bank, he declared, "Soon, I too will join Hamas." Qurei's words reflected his outrage at the subjugation of his people and the humiliation that Palestinians experience every day at the checkpoints that surround their homes. Defeating groups like Hamas requires diluting the rage that fuels them. Relying on force alone tends to increase rather than weaken their appeal. This is demonstrated by some of the unintended consequences of the US-led invasion and occupation of Iraq in the spring of 2003.

On June 3, 2003, the Pew Research Center for the People and the Press released a report entitled *Views of a Changing World*

June 2003. This study was primarily based on a survey of nearly 16,000 people in 21 countries (including the Palestinian Authority) from April 28 to May 15, 2003, shortly after the fall of Saddam Hussein's regime. The survey results were supplemented by data from earlier polls, especially a survey of 38,000 people in 44 countries in 2002. The study found a marked increase in Muslim hostility toward the United States from 2002 to 2003. In the summer of 2002, 61 percent of Indonesians held a favorable view of the United States. By May of 2003, only 15 percent did. During the same period of time, the decline in Turkey was from 30 percent to 15 percent, and in Jordan it was from 25 percent to one percent.

Indeed, the Bush administration's war on terror has been a major reason for the increased hostility toward the United States. The Pew Center's 2003 survey found that few Muslims support this war. Only 23 percent of Indonesians did so in May of 2003, down from 31 percent in the summer of 2002. In Turkey, support dropped from 30 percent to 22 percent. In Pakistan, support dropped from 30 percent to 16 percent, and in Jordan from 13 percent to two percent. These decreases reflect overwhelming Muslim opposition to the war in Iraq, which most Muslims saw as yet another act of imperial subjugation of Muslims by the West.

The 2003 Zogby International poll found that most Arabs believe that the United States attacked Iraq to gain control of Iraqi oil and to help Israel. Over three-fourths of all those surveyed felt that oil was a major reason for the war. More than three-fourths of the Saudis and Jordanians said that helping Israel was a major reason, as did 72 percent of the Moroccans and over 50 percent of the Egyptians and Lebanese. Most Arabs clearly do not believe that the United States overthrew Saddam Hussein out of humanitarian motives. Even in Iraq itself, where there was considerable support for the war, most people attribute the war to the US desire to gain control of Iraqi oil and help Israel.

Not only has the Bush administration failed to win much Muslim support for its war on terrorism, its conduct of the war has generated a dangerous backlash. Most Muslims see the US fight against terror as a war against the Islamic world. The 2003 Pew survey found that over 70 percent of Indonesians, Pakistanis, and Turks were either somewhat or very worried about a potential US threat to their countries, as were over half of Jordanians and Kuwaitis.

This sense of a US threat is linked to the 2003 Pew report's finding of widespread support for Osama bin Laden. The survey of April and May 2003 found that over half those surveyed in Indonesia, Jordan, and the Palestinian Authority, and almost half those surveyed in Morocco and Pakistan, listed bin Laden as one of the three world figures in whom they had the most confidence "to do the right thing." For most US citizens, this admiration for the man responsible for the attacks of September 11, 2001, is incomprehensible. But no matter how outrageous this widespread belief may be, it is vitally important to understand its origins. If one does not understand why people think the way they do, one cannot induce them to think differently. Similarly, if one does not understand why people act as they do, one cannot hope to induce them to act differently.

The Appeal of Osama bin Laden

Osama bin Laden first engaged in violence because of the occupation of a Muslim country by an "infidel" superpower. He did not fight the Russians in Afghanistan because he hated their values or their freedoms, but because they had occupied a Muslim land. He participated in and supported the Afghan resistance to the Soviet occupation from 1979 to 1989, which ended with the withdrawal of the Russians. Bin Laden saw this war as legitimate resistance to foreign occupation. At the same time, he saw it as a *jihad*, or holy war, on behalf of Muslims oppressed by infidels.

When Saddam Hussein invaded Kuwait in August 1990, bin Laden offered to lead an army to defend Saudi Arabia. The Saudis rejected this offer and instead allowed the United States to establish bases in their kingdom, leading to bin Laden's active opposition to the United States. One can only speculate what bin Laden would have done for the rest of his life if the United States had not stationed hundreds of thousands of US troops in Saudi Arabia in 1990. Conceivably, bin Laden's hostility toward the United States might have remained passive and verbal instead of active and violent. All we can say with certainty is that the presence of US troops in Saudi Arabia did trigger bin Laden's holy war against the United States. It was no accident that the bombing of two US embassies in Africa on August 7, 1998, marked the eighth anniversary of the introduction of US forces into Saudi Arabia as part of Operation Desert Storm.

Part of bin Laden's opposition to the presence of US military presence in Saudi Arabia resulted from the fact that US troops were infidels on or near holy Islamic ground. Non-Muslims are not allowed to enter Mecca and Medina, the two holiest places in Islam, and they are allowed to live in Saudi Arabia only as temporary residents. Bin Laden is a reactionary Wahhabi Muslim who undoubtedly does hate all non-Muslims. But that hatred was not in itself enough to trigger his *jihad* against the United States.

Indeed, bin Laden's opposition to the presence of US troops in Saudi Arabia had a nationalistic and anti-imperialist tone. In 1996, he declared that Saudi Arabia had become an American colony. There is nothing specifically religious or fundamentalist about this assertion. In his book *Chronique d'une Guerre d'Orient*, Gilles Kepel describes a wealthy whiskey-drinking Saudi who left part of his fortune to bin Laden because he alone "was defending the honor of the country, reduced in his eyes to a simple American protectorate."

In 1996, bin Laden issued his first major manifesto, entitled a "Declaration of Jihad against the Americans Occupying the Land of the Two Holy Places." The very title focuses on the presence of US troops in Saudi Arabia, which bin Laden calls an "occupation." But this manifesto also refers to other examples of what bin Laden sees as the oppression of Muslims by infidels. "It is no secret that the people of Islam have suffered from the oppression, injustice, and aggression of the alliance of Jews and Christians and their collaborators to the point that the blood of the Muslims became the cheapest and their wealth was loot in the hands of the enemies," he writes. "Their blood was spilled in Palestine and Iraq."

Bin Laden has referred to the suffering of the Palestinians and the Iraqis (especially with respect to the deaths caused by sanctions) in all of his public statements since at least the mid-1990s. His 1996 "Declaration of Jihad" is no exception. Nonetheless, it primarily focuses on the idea that the Saudi regime has "lost all legitimacy" because it "has permitted the enemies of the Islamic community, the Crusader American forces, to occupy our land for many years." In this 1996 text, bin Laden even contends that the members of the Saudi royal family are apostates because they helped infidels fight the Muslim Iraqis in the Persian Gulf War of 1991.

A number of neo-conservatives have advocated the overthrow of the Saudi regime because of its support for terrorism. It is true that the Saudis have funded militant Islamic movements. It is also true that Saudi textbooks and teachers often encourage hatred of infidels and allow the extremist views of bin Laden to thrive. It is also probably true that members of the Saudi royal family have financially supported terrorist groups. The fact remains, however, that bin Laden and his followers in Al Qaeda have themselves repeatedly called for the overthrow of the Saudi regime, saying that it has turned Saudi Arabia into "an American colony."

If the United States were to send troops to Saudi Arabia once again, this time to overthrow the Saudi regime itself, the main beneficiaries would be bin Laden and those who think like him. On January 27, 2002, a *New York Times* article referenced a Saudi intelligence survey conducted in October 2001 that showed that 95 percent of educated Saudis between the ages of 25 and 41 supported bin Laden. If the United States were to overthrow the Saudi regime, such people would lead a guerrilla war that US forces would inevitably find themselves fighting. This war would attract recruits from all over the Islamic world outraged by the desecration of "the land of the two holy places." Given that US forces are already fighting protracted guerrilla wars in Iraq and Afghanistan, starting a third one in Saudi Arabia would not be the most effective way of eradicating terror in the Middle East.

Those who would advocate the overthrow of the Saudi regime by US troops seem to forget why bin Laden began his holy war against the United States in the first place. They also seem to forget that no one is more committed to the overthrow of the Saudi regime than bin Laden himself. Saudi Arabia is in dire need of reform, but yet another US occupation of a Muslim country is not the way to make it happen.

In December 1998, Palestinian journalist Jamal Abd al Latif Isma'il asked bin Laden, "Who is Osama bin Laden, and what does he want?" After providing a brief history of his life, bin Laden responded to the second part of the question, "We demand that our land be liberated from the enemies, that our land be liberated from the Americans. God almighty, may He be praised, gave all living beings a natural desire to reject external intruders. Take chickens, for example. If an armed soldier enters a chicken's home wanting to attack it, it fights him even though it is just a chicken." For bin Laden and millions of other Muslims, the Afghans, the Chechens, the Iraqis, the Kashmiris, and the Palestinians are all just "chickens" defending their homes against the attacks of foreign soldiers.

In his videotaped message of October 7, 2001, after the attacks of September 11, 2001, bin Laden declared, "What America is tasting now is nothing compared to what we have been tasting for decades. For over 80 years our *umma* has been tasting this humiliation and this degradation. Its sons are killed, its blood is shed, its holy places are violated, and it is ruled by other than that which God has revealed. Yet no one hears. No one responds."

Bin Laden's defiance of the United States and his criticism of Muslim governments who ignore what most Muslims see as the oppression of the Palestinians, Iraqis, Chechens, and others, have made him a hero of Muslims who do not agree with his goal of a strictly Islamic state and society. Even young Arab girls in tight jeans praise bin Laden as an anti-imperialist hero. A young Iraqi woman and her Palestinian friends told Gilles Kepel in the fall of 2001, "He stood up to defend us. He is the only one."

Looking Ahead

Feelings of impotence, humiliation, and rage currently pervade the Islamic world, especially the Muslim Middle East. The invasion and occupation of Iraq has exacerbated Muslim concerns about the United States. In this context, bin Laden is seen as a heroic Osama Maccabeus descending from his mountain cave to fight the infidel oppressors to whom the worldly rulers of the Islamic world bow and scrape.

The violent actions of Osama bin Laden and those who share his views are not simply caused by "hatred of Western freedoms." They result, in part at least, from US policies that have enraged the Muslim world. Certainly, Islamic zealots like bin Laden do despise many aspects of Western culture. They do hate "infidels" in general, and Jews in particular. Muslims do need to seriously examine the existence and perpetuation of such hatred in their societies and cultures. But invading and occupying their countries simply exacerbates the sense of impotence, humiliation, and rage that induce them to support people like bin Laden. Defeating terror entails diluting the rage that fuels it.

Henry Munson is Chair of the Department of Anthropology at the University of Maine.

Tehran's Take
Understanding Iran's U.S. Policy

MOHSEN M. MILANI

Although a great deal has been written about the United States' policy toward Iran, hardly anything comprehensive has been produced about Iran's policy toward the United States. Given Washington's concerns that the United States faces "no greater challenge from a single country than from Iran," as the 2006 National Security Strategy put it, this lack of serious attention is astonishing. What does exist is sensationalistic coverage about Iran's nuclear ambitions and about mad mullahs driven by apocalyptic delusions and a martyr complex. That picture suggests that Iran's policy consists of a series of random hit-and-run assaults on U.S. interests and that its leaders, being irrational and undeterrable, must be eliminated by force.

In fact, Tehran's foreign policy has its own strategic logic. Formulated not by mad mullahs but by calculating ayatollahs, it is based on Iran's ambitions and Tehran's perception of what threatens them. Tehran's top priority is the survival of the Islamic Republic as it exists now. Tehran views the United States as an existential threat and to counter it has devised a strategy that rests on both deterrence and competition in the Middle East.

To deter any possible military actions by the United States and its allies, Iran is improving its retaliatory capabilities by developing the means to pursue asymmetric, low-intensity warfare, both inside and outside the country; modernizing its weapons; building indigenous missile and antimissile systems; and developing a nuclear program while cultivating doubts about its exact capability. And to neutralize the United States' attempts to contain it, the Iranian government is both undermining U.S. interests and increasing its own power in the vast region that stretches from the Levant and the Persian Gulf to the Caucasus and Central Asia. Although it is being careful to avoid a military confrontation with the United States, Tehran is maneuvering to prevent Washington from leading a united front against it and strategically using Iran's oil and gas resources to reward its friends.

Iranian foreign policy today is as U.S.-centric as it was before the 1979 revolution. Mohammad Reza Shah Pahlavi relied on Washington to secure and expand his power; today, the Islamic Republic exploits anti-Americanism to do the same. Policy has been consistent over the years partly because it is determined by the supreme leader, who is also the commander of the security and armed forces and serves for life. Iran's defiance has in some ways undermined the country's national interests, but it has paid huge dividends to the ruling ayatollahs and helped them survive three tumultuous decades in power.

Today, Ayatollah Sayyid Ali Khamenei is the supreme leader, and he makes all the key policy decisions, usually after Iran's major centers of power, including the presidency, have reached a consensus. This means that the outcome of the presidential election in June will have some, although probably limited, ramifications for Iran's foreign policy. President Mahmoud Ahmadinejad and his two major reformist rivals, Mir Hossein Mousavi and Mehdi Karroubi, have all supported engaging in negotiations with Washington—a political taboo just a few years ago. Ahmadinejad would be less likely to compromise than his more moderate competitors, but, thanks to the support he has among major anti-American constituencies inside and outside the Iranian government, he would be in a better position to institutionalize any shift in policy. Although Iran's president can change tactical aspects of the country's foreign policy, he cannot single-handedly alter its essence. Only Khamenei, the ultimate decider, can do that. And he will do that only if a fundamental change in policy would not undermine his own authority and if it enjoys broad support from among the major centers of power.

The Hungry Wolf and the Fat Sheep

The roots of anti-Americanism in Iran—really, an opposition to U.S. policies—can be traced to the 1953 coup against Mohammad Mosaddeq, which was backed by the CIA and MI6. Anti-American sentiment was strengthened when in 1964 Ayatollah Ruhollah Khomeini, who would become Iran's first supreme leader after the revolution, opposed a treaty granting legal immunity to U.S. military advisers in Iran and declared that Iran had become a "U.S. colony." By 1979, the revolutionaries were portraying the Iranian monarch as "America's shah" and had made "independence" a defining slogan of their movement. After the taking of hostages at the U.S. embassy in Tehran that year, anti-Americanism became an enduring feature of the state's Islamic ideology. Since then, Iran's leaders have deftly linked the survival of the Islamic Revolution to Iran's independence, depicting the United States as antithetical to both. No one has drawn this link more vividly than Khomeini: he called the United States "the great Satan" and compared U.S. relations with Iran to those between a hungry wolf and a fat sheep. As hostility between the two states intensified, a Manichaean security paradigm developed in both of them. Each one came to perceive the other as a mortal enemy in a zero-sum game. Anti-Americanism and anti-Iranian feelings became two sides of the same coin.

For decades, the Iranian regime has used anti-Americanism to crush its opponents at home and expand its power abroad. After 1979, documents selectively released by the radical students who occupied the U.S. embassy were invoked to establish links between opponents of the Islamic Republic and the U.S. government. Hundreds of people were consequently defamed, jailed, or exiled. In the 1980s, when the young regime was simultaneously struggling to consolidate its rule and fighting a war with Iraq, allegations that the U.S. government was attempting to stage coups in Tehran and prevent Iran from winning the war strengthened the sentiment.

Over time, anti-American constituencies in Iran have proliferated and gained ground in various institutions. Some of them oppose the United States for purely ideological reasons. Others have substantial economic interests in preventing the normalization of relations between Tehran and Washington: they profit from domestic black markets and international trade routes established to bypass U.S. sanctions. Moreover, the foreign organizations that Iran supports throughout the Middle East, and that Washington considers to be terrorist groups, have created effective lobbies in Iran that thrive on this animosity.

Yet now, as under Khomeini, the intensity of the anti-Americanism prevailing in Iran is ultimately determined by the supreme leader. As president, Khamenei declared in 1981, "We are not like [Salvador] Allende [a Chilean president ousted by a coup allegedly backed by Washington], liberals willing to be snuffed out by the CIA." Today, Khamenei still considers the United States to be an existential threat. Washington surrounds Iran with bases in Bahrain, Kuwait, and Qatar and massive troop buildups in Afghanistan and Iraq. It makes friends with the leaders of Iran's neighbors. And its nuclear-equipped naval carriers patrol the Persian Gulf. Khamenei sees the United States as isolating Iran, strangling it with economic sanctions, sabotaging its nuclear program, and beating the drums of preemptive war. He thinks Washington is pursuing regime change in Tehran by funding his opponents, inciting strife among Iran's ethnic minorities, and supporting separatist organizations such as the Baluchistan-based Sunni insurgent group Jundallah, which has killed scores of Revolutionary Guard members.

Prefer to Deter

Tehran has responded to Washington's policy of containment with a strategy of deterrence. Tehran first developed this strategy against Iraq after Iraq invaded Iran in September 1980 and then, as the 1980s unwound and the menace of Iraq faded, redirected it toward the United States. Today, this approach is the result both of Iran's perception of its vulnerabilities and of the constraints that the international community has imposed on the country.

Iran's deterrence strategy has four components. The first is developing the means to fight an asymmetric, low-intensity war, inside and outside the country. In recent years, particularly after U.S. troops arrived in Afghanistan and Iraq, the Revolutionary Guards have played an increasingly important role in maintaining internal order. They have also improved Iran's retaliatory capability in case of an invasion or surgical strikes against its nuclear facilities or the headquarters of its security forces. Khamenei's recent decision to decentralize the command-and-control structure of the Revolutionary Guards serves this purpose. So do the alleged ability of Iran's troops to transform themselves into nonconventional forces within days and Iran's thousands of small Iranian-made assault boats, which could create havoc for the U.S. Navy, as well as its thousands of motorcycles equipped with light artillery, which could impede the advances of an invading army. Iran's support for terrorist actions against U.S. interests in the Middle East is part and parcel of its strategy of asymmetric warfare. For example, in 1983, during the civil war in Lebanon, a group associated with the Iranian-backed Hezbollah killed 220 U.S. marines.

The modernization of Iran's weapons systems is the second component of its deterrence strategy. Decades of arms embargoes from the West have left Iran with limited access to advanced weapons, and Iran has consequently purchased relatively small arms supplies. Between 2002 and 2006, it spent $31 billion on military purchases, compared with $109 billion for Saudi Arabia and a total of $48 billion for Bahrain, Kuwait, Oman, and the United Arab Emirates—four states with a combined population smaller than that of the city of Tehran. The embargoes have also caused an indigenous military-industrial complex to develop, controlled and financed by the state. It employs thousands of people and is connected to the country's major universities and think tanks. Most important, it is in charge of research and development for Iran's missile and nuclear technologies.

Developing indigenous missile and antimissile systems is the third leg of Iran's deterrence strategy. Tehran began building missiles during the Iran-Iraq War and accelerated its program after the "war of cities," in 1988, when both states showered the other's cities with missiles. Iran has used technical support from China and Russia to develop its missile technology. Now, it manufactures its own missiles and claims that two types, the Shahab and the Ghadr, can reach Israel. These missiles are known for their inaccuracy and limited offensive application. But they give Iran the power to retaliate against attacks, particularly in the Persian Gulf, where it could readily upset international navigation.

The fourth component of Iran's deterrence strategy is its nuclear program. The Iranian government claims that its program is designed for peaceful purposes—using nuclear weapons would violate Islamic law, it says—but Washington (and much of the West) accuses it of having a secret program to build the bomb. So far, the International Atomic Energy Agency has found no smoking gun or any evidence that Iran has diverted its nuclear program toward military purposes. But nor has it been able to confirm Tehran's peaceful intentions, because the Iranian government has refused to answer some major questions. Now that Iran has joined a small club of countries that can enrich uranium to a low level of purity, it seems unlikely to cave in to international pressure and accept zero enrichment in the future.

Why, given all the sanctions imposed by the United Nations, does Iran not cry uncle and stop its nuclear program? For one thing, by insisting that its nuclear project is essential for the country's domestic energy needs and scientific development, Tehran has effectively turned U.S. opposition to its program into a nationalist cause, pointing to it as proof that Washington intends to hold Iran back.

(In an attempt to awaken national pride, the government has had the atom symbol printed on 50,000 rial bills.) For another, the nuclear impasse creates an excellent bargaining chip for Tehran in future negotiations. This maybe the reason that Iran's leaders are cultivating uncertainty about the country's actual capability. It does appear, however, that they have decided to develop the infrastructure to build the bomb but not yet the bomb itself. (Former President Ali Akbar Hashemi Rafsanjani claimed in 2005, "We possess nuclear technology that is not operationalized yet. Any time we decide to weaponize it, we can do so rather quickly") Iran and the United States seem to be engaged in a game of poker, with Tehran not showing its cards about its nuclear capabilities and Washington refusing to exclude the possibility of attacking Iran. Washington has the better hand, but the better hand does not always win.

Countercontainment

For three decades, the United States has sought to contain Iran and has imposed on it a variety of sanctions in an effort to do so. To try to neutralize these measures' effects, Iranian leaders have played major powers off against one another, forged alliances of convenience, and asserted Iran's interests at the regional and global levels.

First, Iran has tried to create a wedge between the United States and the United States' European allies. Iran's leaders believe that increased trade with the European Union will allow them to exploit differences among the organization's 27 members and discourage it from supporting regime change in Tehran, the total containment of Iran, or a military attack. In other words, they see the EU as a potential counterweight to the United States. After Iran restarted its uranium-enrichment activities in 2003, the EU ended its "constructive engagement" policy and imposed limited sanctions on Iran to tame its nuclear ambitions. Although these restrictions have prevented both Iran from gaining access to advanced technologies and European firms from making substantial investments in Iran, they have had a negligible impact on the overall volume of trade. The EU remains Iran's leading trading partner, accounting for about 24 percent of Iran's total international trade: the EU's total imports from Iran (mostly energy) increased from 6.3 billion euros in 2003 to 12.6 billion euros in 2007, and its exports to Iran (mostly machinery) remained the same, at about 11.2 billion euros, during that period. On the other hand, the fact that France, Germany, and the United Kingdom supported the referral of Iran's case from the International Atomic Energy Agency to the UN Security Council in 2005 proved the limits of Iran's wedge policy. The move, which highlighted the determination of the major Western powers to tame Iran's nuclear ambitions, was a major defeat for Tehran and a major victory for Washington.

The second component of Iran's strategy to undermine the United States' containment measures is to move closer to states that could counterbalance the United States. Iran has signed major economic and military agreements with China and Russia. It sees these two countries as natural allies, since they oppose the United States' unilateralism and its efforts to isolate Iran and have only reluctantly backed the sanctions against Iran. But the fact that they have supported the UN sanctions at all has proved to Tehran that when pressed, Beijing and Moscow are more likely to gravitate toward Washington than toward Tehran. Russia has not yet finished building the Bushehr nuclear reactor, which it had committed to completing by 2006, and Moscow may be willing to pressure Tehran to change its nuclear policies if the Obama administration decides not to build antimissile systems in Russia's neighborhood.

But Iran continues its efforts. With little alternative but to rely on China and Russia as counterweights to the United States, it recently asked to upgrade its status in the Shanghai Cooperation Organization, a six-party security organization that includes China and Russia, from observer to full member so that it would receive assistance from other members if it were ever attacked. It has also become much more active in trying to popularize anti-Americanism within the Nonaligned Movement and the Organization of the Islamic Conference, and it has solidified its ties with Washington's most vocal opponents in the United States' backyard: Bolivia, Cuba, Ecuador, Nicaragua, and Venezuela.

The third facet of Iran's countercontainment strategy is to use its energy resources to reward its allies. No country in the region is as well endowed with energy resources as Iran is, not even Saudi Arabia: Iran's oil reserves total about 138.4 billion barrels, and its natural gas reserves total about 26.5 trillion cubic meters. (Although Saudi Arabia's oil reserves, which total approximately 267 billion barrels, are larger than Iran's, its natural gas reserves, which total about 7.2 trillion cubic meters, are much smaller.) Oil diplomacy has long been a strategy of Tehran's, of course. During the Rafsanjani presidency, it briefly served as a means to start normalizing relations with Washington. In that spirit, Iran signed in early 1995 a $1 billion oil deal with the U.S. energy company Conoco, the largest contract of its kind since 1979. But the deal was soon terminated when, under pressure from the U.S. Congress and U.S. interest groups opposed to any opening toward Iran, President Bill Clinton issued an executive order banning U.S. companies from investing in Iran's energy sector. A year later, the IranLibya Sanctions Act was passed, which penalizes foreign companies that invest more than

$20 million in Iran's energy industry. In reaction, in 1997 Tehran signed a $2 billion deal with the French oil and gas company Total.

Meanwhile, many Western companies that have continued to want to do business in Iran have struggled to bid for its huge and untapped natural gas reserves. And to immunize itself against the effects of the sanctions and any potential boycott by the West, Iran has shifted its oil trade from the West to new markets. Before the 1979 revolution, the top five importers of Iranian oil were, in decreasing order, France, West Germany, the United Kingdom, Italy, and Japan. By 2008, they were Japan, China, India, South Korea, and Italy. Iran has also recently helped open up the Persian Gulf to China and Russia, signing multibillion-dollar contracts with the Chinese company Sinopec and granting Russia major concessions and access to the Azadegan oil field. Khamenei has even proposed forming with Russia a natural gas cartel modeled after OPEC.

Despite U.S. opposition, Iran has also made good progress on the construction of a so-called peace pipeline that would carry gas from the Persian Gulf to India through Pakistan, a project that would strengthen Iran's position as a major source of energy for those two countries. Nor should one underestimate the negative long-term implications for U.S. interests of China's and Russia's increasing involvement in the Persian Gulf, which Iran has facilitated, or of Tehran's recent move to use the euro in its international transactions, which has weakened the dollar. On the other hand, the sanctions have hurt Iran badly. Its plan for gas and oil pipelines that would connect the Persian Gulf to the Caspian Sea has stalled because of the restrictions. And its oil industry has been deprived of access to important modern technologies: as a result, Iran's oil production today remains significantly below what it was in 1979. In other words, the sanctions have been a lose-lose economic proposition for both the United States and Iran.

Rising in the Region

After three decades of Washington's containment policies, Iran has nonetheless emerged as a regional power. The collapse of the Soviet Union allowed Tehran to expand its influence in the former Soviet republics, many of which it shares historical ties with. A decade later, the United States accelerated the process by overthrowing the Taliban and Saddam Hussein, Iran's neighboring nemeses. And by failing to reactivate the Arab-Israeli peace process and mismanaging the occupation of Iraq, Washington created enticing opportunities for Iran to expand its power. For the first time in a long while, Iran's influence now radiates west, north, and east. Iran now rightly considers itself an indispensable regional player.

Tehran is trying to neutralize Washington's containment strategy by expanding its own influence in the Middle East.

These ambitions pit Tehran against Washington. As Mohsen Rezai, a former commander of the Revolutionary Guards, stated in 2007, "It is our principal and indisputable right to become a regional power," and the United States "would like to prevent us from playing such a role." According to a March 2007 article in *The New York Times,* a recent UN sanctions package against Iran's nuclear program was passed in order to rein in what U.S. officials saw as "Tehran's ambitions to become the dominant military power in the Persian Gulf and across the broader Middle East."

A pivotal element of Iran's strategy of neutralizing the United States' containment policy is to create spheres of influence in Syria, Lebanon, and among the Palestinians, as well as in Afghanistan and Iraq, by supporting pro-Iranian organizations and networks there. (As Rezai put it, "Iran has no meaning without Iraq, Lebanon, Palestine, and Syria.") An especially controversial part of this strategy is Iran's support for Syria, Hezbollah, Palestinian Islamic Jihad, and Hamas—the rejectionist front in the Arab-Israeli conflict. Iran's three-decade-long alliance with Syria is one of the most enduring alliances between Middle Eastern Muslim countries since the end of World War II. Iran's support of the Shiites of Lebanon and the Palestinians goes back many years. Rafsanjani was incarcerated in the 1960s for translating a pro-Palestinian book into Persian; Khomeini condemned the shah in 1964 for his de facto recognition of Israel; Khomeini also authorized Hassan Nasrallah, the leader of Hezbollah, to collect religious taxes on his behalf in support of the Lebanese Shiites; and many of Iran's current leaders received training in Lebanon in the 1960s and 1970s. At first, Iran's support for Hezbollah and the Palestinians had an ideological basis; now, it has a strategic rationale. It gives Tehran strategic depth in the heart of the Sunni Arab world and in Israel's backyard, which translates into a retaliatory capacity against Israel, as well as bargaining power in any future negotiations with the United States. Moreover, after centuries of using its influence mostly to defend Shiites, Iran is now increasingly trying to transcend the sectarian divide by supporting the Sunni groups Hamas and Palestinian Islamic Jihad. This, in turn, has undermined the regional position of such powerful Sunni countries as Egypt and Saudi Arabia.

That said, Iran's financial and logistical support for Hamas and Islamic Jihad should not be exaggerated. Tehran remains a peripheral player in the Arab-Israeli conflict.

It has no compelling national interest in the dispute and is simply taking advantage of the failure of the peace process between Israel and the Palestinians. What makes Iran an influential player is not its financial support alone—Saudi Arabia and other Arab countries contribute substantially more to the Palestinians—but also the model of resistance it champions. Iran has helped Hezbollah develop an approach that combines Islamic solidarity, populism, some trappings of democracy, strict organizational discipline, extensive economic and social support for the needy masses, and pervasive anticolonial and anti-Western sentiments—all in an effort to mobilize the streets of the Islamic world against Israel and the United States and expand its own power, The effectiveness of that model. and of its asymmetric strategies, was on display during Hezbollah's 34-day war with Israel in 2006. The group's use of anti-tank missiles and portable rockets, which Israel claimed Iran had provided—a charge Iran has denied—inflicted enough damage on Israeli cities to create havoc and mass fear. Hezbollah appeared to have won because Israel could not score a decisive victory against it; the conflict marked the first time that an Arab force was not humiliatingly defeated by Israel. It boosted Hezbollah's popularity in many Sunni countries, gave Iran more credibility in the region, and undermined Washington's traditional allies, such as Egypt and Saudi Arabia, which had not supported Hezbollah. The war, along with the chaos in Afghanistan and Iraq and what the Iran expert Vali Nasr has called "the Shiite revival," has convinced Tehran that a new order is emerging in the Middle East: the United States no longer dominates, and Iran now plays a major role.

Where the Hard Things Are

The complicated nature of the U.S.-Iranian relationship is most evident in Afghanistan and Iraq, where the convergences and divergences of the two sides' interests are the clearest. After the Soviet occupation of Afghanistan in 1979, Tehran became intensely engaged with its neighbor, and Iran subsequently became home to some two million Afghan refugees. Gradually, throughout the 1980s, it built new alliances and new networks with Shiite and Persian- and Dari-speaking minorities. (As the Afghanistan expert Barnett Rubin has put it, during that period, "ironically, the United States was indirectly aligned with 'fundamentalists' while Iran courted the 'moderates.'") Then, in the 1990s, while Pakistan and Saudi Arabia were providing critical support to the Taliban government, which itself backed al Qaeda, Tehran created a sphere of resistance in Afghanistan by supporting the Northern Alliance—a force that cooperated with the invading U.S. troops in 2001 in order to liberate Afghanistan from the Taliban. In helping dismantle the Taliban, in other words, Tehran effectively sided with the U.S. government—even providing Washington with intelligence.

Tehran maintained its policy toward Afghanistan even after U.S. President George W. Bush said Iran belonged to "an axis of evil." Today, still, it entertains close relations with the pro-U.S. government of Afghan President Hamid Karzai. And the convergence between Tehran's interests and Washington's interests in Afghanistan remains substantial. Both want to keep the country stable and prevent the Taliban's resurgence. Both want to control and possibly eliminate drug trafficking, the economic backbone of the region's terrorists and warlords. Both want to defeat al Qaeda (which considers Shiism to be a heresy). And both want to eventually rebuild Afghanistan.

At the same time, Iran's heavy involvement in the reconstruction of Afghanistan has allowed it to create a sphere of economic influence in the region around Herat, one of the most prosperous regions in the country. This, in turn, has helped stabilize the area by preventing al Qaeda and the Taliban from infiltrating it. Iran has also empowered the historically marginalized Afghan Shiites, such as the Hazara and the Qizilbash, who constitute about 20 percent of the Afghan population. At a donors' conference in Tokyo in January 2002, Iran pledged $560 million for Afghanistan's reconstruction, or approximately 12 percent of the total $4.5 billion in international reconstruction assistance that was promised then. During a donors' conference in London in 2006, it pledged an additional $100 million. And unlike many other donors, it has delivered most of its promised assistance. The bulk of the funds are targeted at developing projects for infrastructure, education, agriculture, power generation, and telecommunications. Iran hopes to become a hub for the transit of goods and services between the Persian Gulf and Afghanistan, Central Asia, and possibly also China.

This quest for influence in Afghanistan pits Iran against the United States in some ways. For example, Tehran opposes the establishment of permanent U.S. bases in Afghanistan. And to ensure that Washington will not be able to use Afghanistan as a launching point for an attack on Iran, Tehran is pressuring Kabul to distance itself from Washington. Uncertain about Afghanistan's future and Washington's intentions in the country, Iran is keeping its options open and trying to increase all its possible retaliatory capabilities against the United States. It maintains close ties with the Northern Alliance, as well as with warlords such as Ismail Khan, various Shiite organizations, and the insurgent leader Gulbuddin Hekmatyar and other anti-American fighters. It is turning the region around Herat into a sphere of influence: the bazaars there are loaded with Iranian goods, the area receives the bulk of Iran s investments in the country, and the Revolutionary Guards are reportedly visible and active.

The United States and Iran have tried to strike a fine balance in Iraq as well, but with much less success. If anything, Iraq has become center stage for their rivalry; there they have some common goals but also many more diverging ones. Iran's top strategic priority in Iraq is to establish a friendly, preferably Shiite government that is sufficiently powerful to impose order in the country but not powerful enough to pose a serious security threat to Iran, as Saddam did. Iran was the first country in the region to recognize the post-Saddam government in Baghdad. Since then, it has provided Baghdad with more support than even the staunchest of the United States' allies. It has a close relationship with the two parties that dominate the government of Prime Minister Nouri al-Maliki, as well as with the two major Kurdish parties. Like Washington, Tehran supports Iraq's stability, its new constitution, and its electoral democracy, albeit in the parochial interest of ensuring the dominance of the country's Shiite majority. Like Washington, Tehran opposes Iraq's Balkanization, in its case partly for fear that such fragmentation could incite secessionist movements within Iran's own ethnically rich population. And like Washington, Iran considers al Qaeda in Iraq to be an enemy and seeks to eliminate it.

But as in Afghanistan, Iran is eager to engage in Iraq's reconstruction mainly in order to create an economic sphere of influence in the country, especially in the predominantly Shiite south, where many people of Persian descent live. It has pledged to spend more than $1 billion for Iraq's reconstruction. Tehran seems to believe that with its existing influence in southern Iraq, including close ties to the major Shiite seminaries in Najaf, it can transform the region into a kind of southern Lebanon, creating a ministate within a state.

And then there are some major disagreements between Tehran and Washington. Tehran is determined to keep Washington mired in Iraq and prevent it from scoring a clear victory there. During the sectarian violence in 2004–7, Tehran supplied weapons to Shiite insurgents in Iraq, who then used them against U.S. troops. It supported the Mahdi Army and its founder, Muqtada al-Sadr, the radical Shiite cleric who opposes the U.S. presence in Iraq. Tehran is also vehemently opposed to the establishment of permanent U.S. bases in Iraq, for fear, as with those in Afghanistan, that the United States could use them to attack Iran. The status-of-forces agreement signed by the United States and Iraq in 2008 does seem to have diminished some of Iran's concerns, however. The agreement stipulates that U.S. forces will withdraw from Iraq no later than December 31, 2011, and that "Iraqi land, sea, and air shall not be used as a launching or transit point for attacks against other countries."

Iran's policies toward Iraq in the past few years suggest that when Iran feels threatened and its legitimate security needs and national interests are ignored or undermined, it tends to act more mischievously than when it feels secure. Its Iraq policy, therefore, is directly correlated with its perception of the threat posed by the United States. The security talks between Tehran and Washington launched at the urging of the Iraqi government in 2005 are thus very important. After these meetings began, and after the U.S. government launched its "surge" strategy in Iraq, the level of violence in Iraq subsided. Iran played a role in stabilizing the situation by pressuring its allies, including the Mahdi Army, to refrain from violence against Sunnis or U.S. troops. The simple fact that Baghdad is a close ally of both Tehran and Washington offers a chance for those two governments to build on their interests in Iraq.

Full Engagement

Anti-Americanism is not an insurmountable obstacle to normalizing relations with Iran. For one thing, Iran's elites are heterogeneous; they consist of two rival factions, both of which have come to favor, like a significant portion of the population, normalizing relations with the United States. For another, *maslehat,* or "expediency," is a defining feature of Iranian politics. Even the most ideological of Iran's leaders favor a cost-benefit approach to decision-making. According to the 2007 U.S. National Intelligence Estimate, Iran halted its nuclear weapons program in 2003 based on a cost-benefit calculation. Although the accuracy of that conclusion is debated, there is no question that Tehran has often resorted to that approach. When Iran needed advanced weapons during the Iran-Iraq War, Khomeini approved secret dealings with Israel and the United States, culminating in the Iran-contra fiasco. Despite its general opposition to the presence of U.S. troops in the region, Tehran remained actively neutral during the 1991 Persian Gulf War, seeing it as an opportunity to weaken its archenemy Saddam and improve relations with the West. The Revolutionary Guards, the most ideological group in the Iranian armed forces, rubbed shoulders with U.S. forces when they assisted the Northern Alliance in overthrowing the Taliban in 2001. Far from being a suicidally ideological regime, Tehran seeks to ensure the survival of the Islamic Republic while advancing the country's interests through negotiations.

Iranian policy toward the United States has a logic. It is a logic driven not by a single faction or a single issue but by a stable and institutionalized system of governance with both authoritarian and democratic features, with domestic constituencies and long-standing international alliances. It is a logic that made Iran into a regional power with substantial influence in Afghanistan, Iraq, Lebanon, and the Palestinian territories, and among millions of Muslims around the world. And it is a logic that, despite mounting international pressure, has made it possible for Iran to make advances in asymmetric warfare, nuclear technology, uranium enrichment, and missile and satellite technologies. Now, Iran legitimately demands that Washington recognize these advances and Tehran's new role as a major regional power.

Unless Washington understands that Tehran's U.S. policy has a rationale, it will not be able to develop a reasonable long-term strategy toward Iran. Invading the country is not a viable option. Nor are so-called surgical strikes against Iran's nuclear facilities, which would most likely lead to a protracted retaliation by Iran; a Tehran more defiant and more determined to become a nuclear weapons power; more terrorism; greater instability in Afghanistan, Iraq, Lebanon, and the Persian Gulf; and higher oil prices.

The challenge for the U.S. government is to give Iran incentives to reevaluate its strategy toward the United States. A carrot-and-stick approach designed to stop progress on Iran's nuclear program is unlikely to work. Focusing on a few contentious issues, such as Iran's uranium-enrichment activities, would do little to change the fundamental logic of Iran's U.S. policy. Moreover, the stick part of that approach would only strengthen the anti-American constituencies in Iran while hurting its people. Nor will democracy promotion work. More a feel-good fantasy than a viable strategy, this approach misleadingly assumes that democracy can be exported, like cars, or imposed by force and that a democratic Iran would no longer have any serious conflicts with the United States or pursue nuclear ambitions. Iran was considerably more democratic under Mosaddeq than under the shah, and yet its relations with the United States were much worse then.

A better approach is a strategy of full engagement, one predicated on gradually increasing economic, educational, and cultural exchanges between the two countries; exploiting the commonalities shared by their governments; and establishing concrete institutional mechanisms to manage their remaining differences. Washington must recognize that there is no diplomatic magic wand that can fix its "Iran problem" overnight, normalizing U. S. -Iranian relations will be a long and difficult process. Unless Tehran and Washington make a strategic decision to normalize relations, the many forces that continue to pull them apart are likely to derail the process.

As a first step, the United States should allay Iran's fears about regime change. It can do this by explicitly recognizing that Khamenei is the center of gravity in Iran's decision-making process and establishing a line of communication with his office. Holding direct, comprehensive, and unconditional negotiations with the Iranian government is Washington's least bad option. The two countries' negotiating teams must meet face-to-face to learn firsthand about each other's priorities and interests on all the important issues and break the psychological barriers that have kept the parties apart for three decades. Meanwhile, Washington should provide assurances to Israel and its Arab allies that they should not fear its rapprochement with Tehran and that Iran's nuclear policy will remain the main item on the United States' Iran agenda.

As the Obama administration reviews its options when it comes to Iran, it would do well to examine how, three decades ago, President Richard Nixon brought China back into the community of nations. It took almost eight years after the secret trip by Henry Kissinger, then U.S. national security adviser, to Beijing in 1971 for the United States and China to establish diplomatic relations. Anti-Americanism under Mao Zedong, China's support for North Vietnam, and China's arsenal of nuclear weapons were infinitely more threatening to the United States then than Iran's policies are now. Yet Nixon and Kissinger had

the foresight to map out a new strategic landscape for Beijing. They did not punish it for its policies of the past; they gave it a reason to want something better in the future. And then the two countries built a better relationship on their common recognition of the threat posed by Soviet expansionism. Washington can, and should, do something similar with Tehran today and finally end three decades of hostility by highlighting the two governments' shared interests in defeating al Qaeda and stabilizing Afghanistan and Iraq. Tehran, for its part, must recognize that without some kind of understanding with Washington over the issues that matter to the U.S. government, it will not be able to fully benefit from its recent ascent as a regional power—and could even lose much of what it has gained.

Mohsen M. Milani is Professor of Politics and Chair of the Department of Government and International Affairs at the University of South Florida in Tampa.

Banning the Bomb
A New Approach

WARD WILSON

In July of 1945, U.S. president Harry Truman wrote in his diary, "It is certainly a good thing for the world that Hitler's crowd or Stalin's did not discover this atomic bomb. It seems to be the most terrible thing ever discovered, but it can be made the most useful." Terrible and useful. For sixty years, people have focused on the terrible aspects of nuclear weapons. They have made films about nuclear war, detailed the horrors of Hiroshima and Nagasaki, and imagined the end of life on earth. In those sixty years, on the other hand, people have rarely talked seriously about the usefulness of nuclear weapons. Do they really win wars? Are they effective threats? Fear—engendered by real and imagined cold war dangers—constrained real inquiry. Absorbed by images of destruction, most people didn't ask practical questions. But it turns out that the area that we've explored the most—the terribleness of nuclear weapons—is not the key to understanding them. The key is investigating whether or not they are really useful.

I am not urging the familiar argument that nuclear weapons are too dangerous to be useful; I am suggesting that even if one could use them with impunity, nuclear weapons would still have little practical value. Sixty years of experience, recent reevaluations of the track record of nuclear weapons, and reinterpretations of Hiroshima and Nagasaki based on new research make it possible to argue that there are very few situations in which nuclear weapons are useful. It might, in fact, be possible to demonstrate that nuclear weapons are functionally the equivalent of biological and chemical weapons: powerful and dangerous weapons, but with very few real applications. And therefore it might also be possible to make the case that—as with chemical and biological weapons—there are practical, prudential reasons for banning nuclear weapons.

Current Strategies

To date, two related strategies have been used to oppose the use of nuclear weapons: the horror strategy and the risk strategy. The former relies on moral feelings and tries to persuade people that using nuclear weapons is too immoral to contemplate. The latter relies on calculations of the possibility that a small war could become an all-out nuclear war and tries to persuade people that the danger is too great.

Those who use the horror strategy often make Hiroshima and Nagasaki the centerpiece of their case. They try to drive home the immorality of using nuclear weapons by forcing their listeners to experience vicariously the horror of these cities. Doctors increased the emotional impact of this approach in the 1980s by talking unflinchingly and in detail about the medical consequences of nuclear attacks.

The risk strategy has been more widely embraced than the horror strategy. Vividly given a story line by Nevil Shute in *On the Beach* (a novel later made into a movie in which a nuclear war extinguishes all human life), it has remained a staple of antinuclear argument, used by radicals and sober policymakers alike.

Jonathan Schell updated and expanded the risk strategy in *The Fate of the Earth.* Schell eschewed the normal tack of emphasizing the risks of escalation, arguing instead that an all-out nuclear war might lead to the destruction of all life on earth. So it didn't matter how big or small the risk of escalation was, the consequences were so terrible that no amount of risk was worth running. In 1983, Carl Sagan and four others further buttressed Schell's case with evidence suggesting that severe climatic disruption, dubbed "nuclear winter," could be triggered by a nuclear war.

Sound as their reasoning might be, both these strategies have weaknesses. The horror argument's weakness is that in a crisis necessity almost always trumps morality. People will say, "Yes, it's wrong. But we have to do it. We have no other choice." If the Bomb seems likely to be militarily effective most people will decide to use it, even if they know it is wrong to do so.

The risk strategy has been eroded by the end of the cold war, which led to lowered tensions and significantly reduced the likelihood of nuclear escalation. Another key—but often overlooked—change is the end of "extended deterrence"—the threat by the United States and the Soviet Union to respond to attacks on their client states with nuclear counterattacks. At one time, all of Europe, all of Latin America, some of Asia, and even parts of Africa were covered by extended deterrence. With the collapse of the cold war client-state system, many nations are now out from under the nuclear umbrella. It is now possible for the United States to attack, say, Syria, with nuclear weapons without the threat of a nuclear response from Russia. As the risk of escalation has decreased, the strength of the risk argument has also decreased.

Bigger Is Not Better

It is often said that every weapon that man has invented has been used in war. This statement misses the point. The important issue is not whether this or that weapon has ever been used, it is whether such a weapon—once tried—has become a fixture in the arsenals of warlike nations. Horrible weapons have been imagined and tried. But are they still used?

Consider the Paris Gun. Built by the Germans in World War I, it was more than 90 feet long, weighed 256 tons, and moved on rails. It fired a 210-pound projectile more than 80 miles. Often confused with its smaller cousin, the large mortar called "Big Bertha," in its day it was the largest cannon ever built. It was a terrifying weapon. From March until August of 1918, the Germans used it to rain shells down on Paris without warning. The Parisians were bewildered and terrified. In all, the Paris Gun fired about 360 shells, killing 250 people and wounding 620.

Only a handful of other superguns have since been built (Schwerer Gustav and V3 among them). Their impact on the wars in which they participated was minimal. Today, nations do not race to build their own superguns. African nations, torn by strife, do not try to trade their oil or diamond resources for superguns bought from arms dealers. There are no angry diatribes in liberal papers about the horror of these weapons and the necessity of banning them.

"But of course this is so," someone might say, "because these weapons were not very effective." And that is the point. Decisions about acquiring or banning weapons are not based on their horribleness but on their ability or inability to help win wars.

There are four general ways that nuclear weapons might be used: in a war intended to exterminate an opponent, in a war of coercion, as a threat, and to create terror. For two of these categories—coercion and threats—it is relatively easy to show that nuclear weapons are not ideal weapons and, in some circumstances, are so seriously mismatched to the task at hand as to be useless.

On the other hand, nuclear weapons are admirably suited for wars of extermination. If you have decided on a war in which your goal is to annihilate your opponent, nuclear weapons are your best choice. In this case it is necessary to argue not that the weapons wouldn't be useful, but that such wars are morally wrong. This is not a demanding task. No case can be made that the capability to wage a war of annihilation is valuable or necessary. And this moral judgment is borne out by the practical experience of history: the actual number of wars of extermination is small. (Wars of extermination are distinct from genocide or other murderous actions within a country's own boundaries.) A careful review of human history unearthed only one clear case, the Third Punic War.

The vast majority of wars are wars of coercion. The conventional wisdom has been that nuclear weapons are decisive in this kind of war. After all, they won the war in the Pacific. But when examined closely, the presumption of decisiveness evaporates. Recent reinterpretations of the Japanese surrender call into question the notion that the bombings of Hiroshima and Nagasaki were in any way connected with that decision. The Soviet intervention radically altered the strategic situation and was the decisive event.

The power to destroy cities is not the power to win wars. Freeman Dyson makes this point vividly in an example drawn from the Falklands War. Someone had said loosely about the war that if the British had wanted to they could have "blown Buenos Aires off the map." This was true, but Dyson points out that the British would still have had to send soldiers to re-conquer the Falklands. And destroying Buenos Aires would probably have made the Argentine soldiers defending the islands fight more fiercely. Or the British could have nuked the Falklands themselves, but that would have destroyed the islands. The British abstained from using nuclear weapons not because they have admirable restraint, but because there was no practical application for the weapons.

Sixty years of experience with nuclear weapons does not support the notion that they are singularly useful to their possessors. Despite its nuclear arsenal, the United States was fought to a draw in Korea, lost a war in Vietnam, did not stop genocides in Cambodia or Rwanda, and is currently mired in conflict in Iraq. Despite its sizable nuclear arsenal, the Soviet Union suffered humiliation in its own guerrilla war in Afghanistan. Nuclear nations have fought many wars, but these supposedly powerful weapons have not played a decisive role in any of them.

Nuclear weapons do not appear to be suited to the battlefield. This inutility has already been ratified by two of the most authoritative bodies in a position to make a judgment: the military establishments of the United States and the Soviet Union. If tactical nuclear weapons were really militarily useful, would these two military establishments have allowed almost all tactical weapons to be retired in the 1980s?

Nuclear weapons are also of questionable effectiveness in attacks on economic targets. Most economic targets are roughly building-sized, and with today's precision-guided munitions, conventional weapons are more than adequate. Nuclear weapons, on the other hand, require destruction of an area many times larger than the target. What is the point of destroying a quarter of a city in order to knock out an oil refinery? It is true that a large-scale nuclear attack could effectively shatter a nation's economic infrastructure, but at what point does this become a war of extermination?

Diplomatic Influence

When the United States first got nuclear weapons, there were high hopes that they would provide not just military might, but international influence as well. Truman, when he talked about nuclear weapons being "useful" in the diary entry quoted above, was probably thinking of the upcoming negotiations he faced with the Soviet Union over the shape of the post–World War II world. His secretary of state, James F. Byrnes, told him with a touch of euphoria that nuclear weapons would probably allow the United States to "dictate our own terms after the war." Byrnes returned from the bargaining table a chastened man. The Soviets, he reported ruefully afterward, "are stubborn, obstinate, and they don't scare." Perhaps this is not surprising. Joseph Stalin said in a 1946 interview in *Pravda,* "Atomic bombs are meant to frighten those with weak nerves."

The U.S. nuclear monopoly did not prevent communist domination of Eastern Europe in the years after the Second World War. It did not prevent the Berlin Crisis of 1948. It did not prevent the communist takeover of China in 1949. Of course, any threat will work some percentage of the time—some people scare easily. The question is, are nuclear weapons reliable tools of coercion? Clearly not.

Some people argue that nuclear weapons have kept the United States and other nations safe by deterring nuclear war. This is difficult to prove. Imagine a man who says that the lucky penny he keeps on his dresser has prevented nuclear war. When you ask for proof, he says, "Well, I've kept that penny on the dresser for sixty-two years and there's been no war, so it must be working!" Nuclear weapons may provide crucial safety and security, although it is hard to imagine how dangerous weapons that cannot be defended against are the best means of providing safety. Another—perhaps more certain—way to prevent nuclear war is to ban nuclear weapons.

Of What Use Today?

Another way to assess the usefulness of nuclear weapons is to think about the role they might play in a crisis today. Imagine, for example, that the North Koreans used a nuclear weapon to attack Seoul or Tokyo. The United States, Russia, Great Britain, France, or China would all be in a position to retaliate against Pyongyang. Some might argue that this would be the right way to deter future nuclear attacks against cities. But wouldn't a far more practical deterrent be for the United States, Russia, and China to form an alliance, invade North Korea, and set up a new government? Nuking Pyongyang only punishes the innocent. North Korea's leaders would surely have left the city shortly before the North Korean nuclear strike was launched. Nuking Pyongyang kills North Korean civilians, who, because they live under a dictatorship, have no responsibility for the decision to attack. Rogue states that use nuclear weapons are unlikely to be democratic states, and because what nuclear weapons do best is kill people, nuclear weapons will never be well suited to punishing such a regime.

Many people believe that the most likely use of nuclear weapons in the next few years (barring a war in the Middle East or the Asian subcontinent) is a terrorist attack against a city. Terrorists, whose aim is to coerce political change by irregular attacks on innocents, are the people most likely to imagine that nuclear weapons are useful. On the other hand, it is difficult to imagine nuclear deterrence against terrorists. Imagine that a nuclear bomb hidden in a cargo container is detonated in Baltimore Harbor. What effective nuclear retaliation options are there? It would be very difficult to identify the attackers. But even assuming that a terrorist group takes responsibility—say, al-Qaeda—how can nuclear weapons be used to redress this evil? Would you use a nuclear weapon against a city in Pakistan in which you think Osama bin Laden is hiding? Again, the vast majority of those who die will be innocent, and if faulty intelligence leads you to attack the wrong city you risk punishing *only* the innocent.

A good deal of energy has been devoted to imagining circumstances in which nuclear weapons would be exactly the right weapons to use. But why is it necessary to imagine unlikely or outlandish scenarios in order to justify these weapons?

The current U.S. administration supports research into developing "bunker buster" nuclear weapons that could destroy targets deeply buried or secreted in caves. There are two telling objections to such a weapon. First, as with most applications of nuclear weapons, conventional weapons already provide a fairly extensive bunker buster capability. Nuclear bunker busters would only extend existing capabilities a few hundred meters (to three hundred meters below the surface at most). It is within the capabilities of almost any enemy simply to dig deeper. The second is that the intelligence necessary for such a strike is unimaginable. Even with the sophisticated technology currently available to the U.S. government, for example, we were unable to identify chemical and biological facilities in Iraq, a country with barren, cloud-free, best-case topography. This is an indication of how hard it is to locate secret facilities. And we were looking for facilities on the surface.

The current administration also imagines that mini-nukes would be useful. These are weapons with roughly a third the destructive power of the bomb that destroyed Hiroshima—about the same destructive power that was deployed in the conventional raids against Japanese cities in the summer of 1945. Why build a nuclear weapon with an end result you can already achieve using conventional weapons?

In this connection, the size of nuclear weapons raises a question. Early on in the nuclear age, physicists warned that there was no theoretical limit to the size of hydrogen bombs. The Soviets tested a bomb with a yield of roughly fifty-two megatons in 1962. Larger bombs could have been built. Yet they have not been. In fact, the size of nuclear warheads in the U.S. and Russian arsenals has been shrinking. At one time one megaton (or larger) warheads were common, but today the yield of an average warhead in the U.S. strategic arsenal is only about a third of a megaton. How can nuclear bombs be shrinking if the greater the destructive power the greater the military usefulness? If nuclear weapons are useful, why is it that the trend is toward making them more like conventional weapons?

Benefits of Banning the Bomb

The benefits of a total ban are clear. The chief benefit is that it protects us against the danger that people are currently most concerned with in connection with these weapons: use by a terrorist group against a city. By banning nuclear weapons you substantially decrease the chances that they will fall into the hands of rogue states or terrorist organizations. The only reason that the director of the Pakistani nuclear project was able to sell nuclear technology to the North Koreans is that proliferation had gained such widespread acceptance. The more nations that have nuclear weapons, the more likely someone is to put them into the hands of irresponsible people. (As I write this in

October 2006, North Korea has just tested a nuclear weapon. The international reaction serves as a strong reminder that it is important to keep nuclear weapons out of the hands of unstable leaders.)

Any international ban would have to include careful monitoring of all formerly nuclear nations and inspection of nuclear power reactors. (If nuclear nations are unwilling to give up their weapons entirely, perhaps each could warehouse a small stockpile under UN administration in their own countries. The weapons could be retrieved by their owner, but only by publicly breaking the treaty.) With no military weapons floating around, and access to nuclear power monitored and controlled by international organizations, building a rogue bomb or stealing one becomes almost impossible.

None of the arguments sketched here is the final word on the usefulness of nuclear weapons. There is considerable work still to be done. The Hiroshima argument needs to be more thoroughly researched. The case against city attacks needs to be strengthened with historical examples. And along with work on each of its parts, a systematic treatment of the entire subject is needed. But it should be clear from the limited treatment here that there is enough substance in the approach to merit further work.

In 1775, Edmund Burke rose in Parliament to oppose the use of force against the American colonies. Burke believed strongly that the application of force was not the best way to bind the colonies to the British Empire. Burke said that he opposed force not because it was an "odious" instrument of policy but because it was a "feeble" one. His assertion must have been especially surprising because the British army and navy at that time were the most powerful in the world. Using force, he argued, could intimidate and coerce, but raw power alone would not create obedience in the colonies. In some situations brute force is less effective (or more "feeble") than other means.

It may seem paradoxical to think of them as "feeble," but I want to make something of the same argument about nuclear weapons. The strongest arguments against the use of nuclear weapons are not those that demonstrate that they are horrible or dangerous (although they are certainly both), but those that show that they aren't very useful. Weapons, like tools, are situational: their "power" is measured not by their raw force but by the extent to which their capabilities match the circumstances. A jackhammer is a very powerful tool; it's not much help in repairing a watch. A howitzer is of no use underwater; a shotgun blast doesn't help where stealth is required; a knife has little effect at a thousand yards. It's not the size of the bang, it's the match between the situation at hand and the weapon's capabilities. In most military situations, conventional weapons are better suited to the task at hand than nuclear ones. Only in blowing up cities are nuclear weapons singularly well suited to a task. This is an objective, however, that only terrorists pursue enthusiastically.

If there are hardly any circumstances in which nuclear weapons are militarily useful, and if it seems likely that the more nations that have nuclear arsenals the more likely the weapons are to fall into the hands of terrorists or madmen, then it makes practical sense to ban them.

WARD WILSON is an independent scholar living in Trenton, N.J. He is currently at work on a book about the military usefulness of destroying cities throughout history. He writes regularly at www.rethinking nuclearweapons.org.

UNIT 6

Cooperation

Unit Selections

Key Points to Consider

- Itemize the products you own that were manufactured in another country.

- What recent contacts have you had with people from other countries? How was it possible for you to have these contacts?

- Do you use the Internet to interact with people in other countries?

- How do you use the World Wide Web to learn about other countries and cultures?

- Identify nongovernmental organizations in your community that are involved in international cooperation (e.g., Rotary International).

- What are the prospects for international governance? How do trends in this direction enhance or threaten American values and constitutional rights?

- What new strategies for cooperation can be developed to fight infectious disease, terrorism, international narcotics trafficking, and other threats?

- How can conflict and rivalry be transformed into meaningful cooperation?

Student Website

www.mhhe.com/cls

Internet References

Carnegie Endowment for International Peace
   http://www.ceip.org
OECD/FDI Statistics
   http://www.oecd.org/statistics/
U.S. Institute of Peace
   http://www.usip.org

An individual can write a letter and, assuming it is properly addressed, be relatively certain that it will be delivered to just about any location in the world. This is true even though the sender pays for postage only in the country of origin and not in the country where it is delivered. A similar pattern of international cooperation is true when a traveler boards an airplane and never gives a thought to the issue of potential language and technical barriers, even though the flight's destination is halfway around the world.

Many of the most basic activities of our lives are the direct result of governments cooperating across borders. International organizational structures, for example, have been created to eliminate barriers to trade, monitor, and respond to public health threats, set standards for international telecommunications, arrest and judge war criminals, and monitor changing atmospheric conditions. Individual governments, in other words, have recognized that their self-interest directly benefits from cooperation (in most cases by giving up some of their sovereignty through the creation of international governmental organizations, or IGOs).

Transnational activities are not limited to the governmental level. There are now tens of thousands of international nongovernmental organizations (INGOs). The activities of INGOs range from staging the Olympic Games to organizing scientific meetings to actively discouraging the hunting of seals. The number of INGOs along with their influence has grown tremendously in the past 50 years.

During the same period in which the growth in importance of IGOs and INGOs has taken place, there also has been a parallel expansion of corporate activity across international borders. Most U.S. consumers are as familiar with Japanese or German brand-name products as they are with items made in their own country. The multinational corporation (MNC) is an important non-state actor. The value of goods and services produced by the biggest MNCs is far greater than the gross domestic product (GDP) of many countries. The international structures that make it possible to buy a Swedish automobile in Sacramento or a Korean television in Buenos Aires have been developed over many years. They are the result of governments negotiating treaties that create IGOs to implement the agreements (e.g., the World Trade Organization). As a result, corporations engaged in international trade and manufacturing have created complex transnational networks of sales, distribution, and service that employ millions of people.

To some observers these trends indicate that the era of the nation-state as the dominant player in international politics is passing. Other experts have observed these same trends and have concluded that the state system has a monopoly of

© Ingram Publishing/SuperStock

power and that the diverse variety of transnational organizations depends on the state system and, in significant ways, perpetuates it.

In many of the articles that appear elsewhere in this book, the authors have concluded their analysis by calling for greater international cooperation to solve the world's most pressing problems. The articles in this section provide examples of successful cooperation. In the midst of a lot of bad news, it is easy to overlook the fact that we are surrounded by international cooperation and that basic day-to-day activities in our lives often directly benefit from it.

A Filled Balance

Europe as a Global Player

A Parliamentary Perspective

HANS-GERT POETTERING

In the 28 years since the European Parliament was first elected, it has developed from a largely advisory forum into a full-fledged branch of Europe's legislature. Since the Single European Act of 1986 and the Maastricht Treaty of 1992, the role of the European Parliament in EU decision-making has increasingly changed from one of marginality to one of centrality. Today, members of the European Parliament share law-making powers with the Council of Ministers across many policy areas. The Parliament has truly come of age.

The advent of co-decision between the Parliament and the Council has made the Parliament a major actor in the EU legislative process. The Parliament has become an integral part of a new European political system, in which the vast majority of decisions require explicit approval of the Parliament. Whether it be the liberalization of transport, regulation of financial markets, limits on carbon emissions, or product standards and consumer protection, the decisions of the Parliament are now as important as those of member states in setting EU law.

In recent years, our work as members of the Parliament has shaped and advanced European integration in many fields. We pushed forward the process of EU enlargement when there was reticence in some other quarters. The single market and the single currency would never have occurred without the early and sustained advocacy of Euro-parliamentarians. The political majority in the European Parliament is now critical in determining who is chosen as president of the European Commission. Furthermore, as a result of parliamentary pressure, foreign and security policy has become an integral part of EU activity.

When I first became a member of the European Parliament in 1979, the individual sovereign states guarded their own foreign and security policies, making the policy area something of a taboo subject at the supranational level. This disunity, however, changed in the mid-1980s, when the Single European Act formalized modest arrangements for "European political cooperation." The Maastricht Treaty converted them into a formal Common Foreign and Security Policy, for the first time raising the possibility of a European defense. Today, more than a dozen

EU military and policing missions can be found throughout the world. While deployment of EU troops or police forces outside the European Union was unheard of in 1979, it is a daily reality in 2007.

As the European Union becomes more involved in world affairs and as domestic integration deepens, it becomes more important that the European institutions function as effectively and democratically as possible. These objectives can most effectively be obtained through the ratification of the European constitutional treaty. We need the reforms espoused by the constitution to successfully fulfill our role in EU and world affairs.

European integration has gone through cycles of crisis and self-doubt in the past, but it has usually emerged stronger as a result. When the European Defense Community failed in 1954, it subsequently took less than three years to reach an agreement on the Rome Treaties. When the first effort to establish a common currency failed during the 1970s, the experience of further monetary crises pointed to the continuing necessity for a full economic and monetary union, a logic that led to the adoption of the euro in 2002. While the difficulties in securing ratification of the European constitutional treaty by all member states have been a blow to the development of the European Union, I believe that they can be overcome, just as European integration has cleared previous obstacles that initially seemed insurmountable in its 50-year history.

One clear lesson from the recent ratification crisis is that there is a need to connect more closely European citizens with the project of European integration. Some of the citizens of France and the Netherlands who voted against the constitutional treaty in referenda in the summer of 2005 did so because they regarded the European Union as insufficiently coherent, democratic, or transparent. Yet ironically, the constitutional treaty actually includes many of the changes that are necessary to strengthen democracy, coherence, and transparency in the Union. For example, it extends the mandate of the president of the European Council, gives the European Parliament even greater legislative power, clarifies the competences of the

Union, and simplifies the types of legislative action—all in an effort to improve the overall consistency, clarity, and accountability of EU institutions.

The foreign policy component of the constitutional treaty is especially important. Only an effective and democratic European Union along the lines foreseen in the constitutional treaty can be a credible actor in the world, and furthermore, a reliable partner for the United States. Though commentators like to distinguish between "soft" and "hard" power, I would prefer to distinguish between coherence and incoherence in foreign policy-making. The truth is that even though decision-making at the EU level is now integral to determining the foreign policy of the member states—and the global presence of the European Union is already an important reality in world affairs—the Union as such is not in the position to act coherently in its own right. This limitation stems in varying degrees from the Union's legal status, the institutional division between the Council and the Commission, and the Union's lack of free-standing military resources. The provisions of the constitutional treaty, which establish the post of European foreign minister and create a European external action service, are important for the emergence of a more comprehensive and credible EU foreign policy.

Responsible political leadership in the European Union is rightly committed to putting these provisions into practice. So far, the constitutional treaty has been ratified by two-thirds of the European Union's 27 member states. It is also supported by the vast majority of members of the European Parliament. Our common objective is to implement at least the core propositions enshrined in the treaty—the key substance of the original text—before the next elections to the European Parliament in June 2009.

Europe and Globalization

A constitutional treaty will make it easier for Europe to address the pressing issues of our time, at home and abroad. Globalization poses new challenges to European policymakers in the economic sphere and in many other fields. Europe has been slower in taking full advantage of the opportunities of globalization than the United States, let alone China or India. But the European Union has been fully aware that just as globalization brings new opportunities, as it empowers individuals and expands the global market, creating billions of new consumers, it simultaneously requires changes in European citizens' attitudes toward job security, welfare, and most importantly, investment in human capital through education and life-long learning. The majority of citizens in the European Union would resist any form of globalization that undermined the principles of human dignity, but this outcome need not materialize. The market dynamic can and should continue to be underpinned by a safety net for the weaker members of European society. This is an essential principle of a social market economy.

In a way, European integration has been, and continues to be, an anticipated form of regional globalization. It has been driven, by and large, by political decisions designed to support the freedom and cohesion of European societies, to facilitate the creation of a single European market, and to provide a greater measure

of legal certainty to activities in the European sphere. It is based on supranational law and therefore offers a sort of framework in which a free market can flourish to the benefit of more citizens. Based on this experience, we believe that globalization will progress most smoothly if it goes hand in hand with some legal rules—not ones that undermine the forces of the market, but rules that safeguard the interests of citizens, both as consumers and producers.

Projecting Stability into the World

To date, globalization has too often left out important parts of the world community, notably in the Arab world and sub-Saharan Africa. As both these regions are physically proximate to Europe, we are particularly sensitive to this situation. In fact, it is both a strategic and a moral obligation that we pay more attention to what is taking place in these regions. Poverty, insecurity, and fear can easily produce a dangerous combination of illegal migration, fanaticism, and violence.

The European Union is now the largest donor of development aid in the world. Some critics claim that this assistance is some kind of compensation for the legacy of European colonialism in lesser-developed countries. I think it emphasizes instead Europe's firm desire to be a constructive partner in building a better world.

Europe's political leaders and institutions are determined to fight terrorism and any form of political violence. We are gravely concerned about an ideology of Islamic radicalism that includes the use of violence as a means to succeed in its political and religious goals. We absolutely condemn terror in the name of politics or religion, and we are concerned that the continuation of any form of radical Islamic terror will undermine the chances of a dialogue among cultures that is more vital today than ever.

Europe is an immediate neighbor of the Arab world. The bulk of immigrants into the European Union originate from northern Africa and sub-Saharan Africa, with Spain being the biggest recipient. Muslims have become the second largest religious group in the Union, representing around 3.5 percent of the total population. Mosques are a common sight all over Europe. In our position, a cross-cultural dialogue is crucial. By the nature of our situation and our history, the European Union is absolutely determined to guarantee a peaceful cohabitation of Christians, Muslims, Jews, and all other religious, secular, and atheist people. We can only do this on the basis of mutual respect.

An important component of the emerging foreign policy of the European Union is the effort to project stability into the immediate neighborhood of the Union and into the wider world. The recent enlargement of the European Union was a spectacular example of the success of that policy: the prospect of EU membership played an important part in ensuring the democracy and prosperity of the former Soviet republics and client states which are now safely members of a democratic European family. An enlarged European Union has recently developed a complex web of policies to stabilize its immediate surroundings and to promote peace and affluence beyond its borders. Our partnerships with Russia and other Eastern European countries that are non-EU member states are designed to build a more stable relationship with that part of Europe's neighborhood.

Likewise, the European Union is part of the "Quartet" along with the United States, the United Nations, and Russia that designed the Road Map for Peace in the Middle East. Many obituaries have been written for this Quartet process. But in the end, I believe, a comprehensive solution to the vexing Middle East conundrum will have to follow the main elements of the established Road Map and, in fact, will need the commitment of the Quartet countries. We want a comprehensive, equitable, and lasting peace that recognizes the right of existence of both Israel and a viable Palestinian state. The Euro-Mediterranean Partnership—in which the European Parliament plays a leading role—is an important vehicle for bringing all European countries together with the Arab coastal states of the Mediterranean and with Israel.

Transatlantic Partnership

Rising to the challenge of globalization also requires deeper transatlantic cooperation. Most major global issues we face cannot be resolved solely by the actions of either the European Union or the United States. In general, when we cannot reach agreement across the Atlantic on major global challenges, policy simply fails to be enacted at the international level and the credibility of the Western world decreases. In order to resolve key issues from climate control to global terrorism, the European Union and the United States must be active partners in a common endeavor.

The ties that bind the United States and the European Union are deeply rooted. We are each other's largest economic partners, whether in terms of trade, capital flows, inward investments, or jobs. Ownership of many of our companies is now in effect vested jointly in the hands of both US and EU citizens. Our great universities cooperate actively. There is a regular, intense exchange of ideas, emails, and visitors across the Atlantic. At a political level, however, there is still much to be done. We have the achievements of the NATO Treaty, we have our regular EU-US summits and parliamentary exchanges, but we have no systematic framework within which to organize our overall relations. As early as 1962, President John F. Kennedy proposed a transatlantic treaty broadening the bases for our relationship for this very reason.

In the absence of such a framework, we can still work positively together on a common agenda. The current German presidency of the Council has already declared that strengthening transatlantic relations, particularly in the economic sphere, is one of its major external policy priorities. Chancellor

Angela Merkel has talked of promoting "ever-closer economic cooperation" across the Atlantic, signaling that she particularly wants to see progress toward an EU-US Transatlantic Economic Partnership, based on some variant of a "Transatlantic Market." The latter concept is not a free-trade area or a customs union; rather, it is in effect a single market, in which EU and US technical standards, regulatory régimes, and competition policies would progressively converge. The idea has long been advocated in resolutions of the European Parliament. Indeed, it is a good example of how the Parliament has shifted the policy agenda, in this case, by going out in front of the member-state governments.

The concept of a transatlantic single market has, for the first time, been picked up by the president of the European Commission, José Manuel Barroso, in Brussels, and by the US president and administration in Washington. It is an idea whose time has come. Legislators in the European Parliament, together with senators and congressmen on Capitol Hill, will need to be closely involved. If Parliament and Congress are to approve the result and make all the legislative changes necessary to implement it, it is sensible that we be partners from the start in its design, negotiation, and delivery.

Maintaining the "Atlantic Civilization"

The future of European integration and of a strong transatlantic partnership are important political objectives and key components in maintaining our "Atlantic civilization." The European Union is developing new scenarios to advance both greater unity and stronger Euro-American relations. The German presidency of the Council currently is attempting to identify methods and timelines for achieving each. As a result, there is now a very serious possibility that Europe will overcome the crisis over the ratification of the European constitutional treaty and emerge strengthened by this process. The European Union needs the substance of the reforms enshrined in the treaty, not only to better manage its affairs as a union of 27 or more member states, but also to confront the new and pressing policy challenges posed by globalization and to discharge its responsibilities in the world. Equally, there is an increasing likelihood that we will see significant progress toward a closer transatlantic partnership, at least in the economic sphere, with the concept of a barrier-free single market across the Atlantic firmly on the agenda. These twin achievements would represent major stepping stones toward building a less dangerous and more prosperous world.

HANS-GERT POETTERING, MEP, is President of the European Parliament.

Geneva Conventions

They help protect civilians and soldiers from the atrocities of war. But these hard-won rules of battle are falling by the wayside: Terrorists ignore them, and governments increasingly find them quaint and outdated. With every violation, war only gets deadlier for everyone.

STEVEN R. RATNER

"The Geneva Conventions Are Obsolete"

Only in the minor details. The laws of armed conflict are old; they date back millennia to warrior codes used in ancient Greece. But the modern Geneva Conventions, which govern the treatment of soldiers and civilians in war, can trace their direct origin to 1859, when Swiss businessman Henri Dunant happened upon the bloody aftermath of the Battle of Solferino. His outrage at the suffering of the wounded led him to establish what would become the International Committee of the Red Cross, which later lobbied for rules improving the treatment of injured combatants. Decades later, when the devastation of World War II demonstrated that broader protections were necessary, the modern Geneva Conventions were created, producing a kind of international "bill of rights" that governs the handling of casualties, prisoners of war (POWs), and civilians in war zones. Today, the conventions have been ratified by every nation on the planet.

Of course, the drafters probably never imagined a conflict like the war on terror or combatants like al Qaeda. The conventions were always primarily concerned with wars between states. That can leave some of the protections enshrined in the laws feeling a little old-fashioned today. It seems slightly absurd to worry too much about captured terrorists' tobacco rations or the fate of a prisoner's horse, as the conventions do. So, when then White House Counsel Alberto Gonzales wrote President George W. Bush in 2002 arguing that the "new paradigm" of armed conflict rendered parts of the conventions "obsolete" and "quaint," he had a point. In very specific—and minor—details, the conventions have been superseded by time and technology.

But the core provisions and, more crucially, the spirit of the conventions remain enormously relevant for modern warfare. For one, the world is still home to dozens of wars, for which the conventions have important, unambiguous rules, such as forbidding pillaging and prohibiting the use of child soldiers.

These rules apply to both aggressor and defending nations, and, in civil wars, to governments and insurgent groups.

The conventions won't prevent wars—they were never intended to—but they can and do protect innocent bystanders, shield soldiers from unnecessary harm, limit the physical damage caused by war, and even enhance the chances for cease-fires and peace. The fundamental bedrock of the conventions is to prevent suffering in war, and that gives them a legitimacy for anyone touched by conflict, anywhere and at any time. That is hardly quaint or old-fashioned.

"The Conventions Don't Apply to Al Qaeda"

Wrong. The Bush administration's position since Sept. 11, 2001, has been that the global war on terror is a different kind of war, one in which the Geneva Conventions do not apply. It is true that the laws do not specifically mention wars against nonstate actors such as al Qaeda. But there have always been "irregular" forces that participate in warfare, and the conflicts of the 20th century were no exception. The French Resistance during World War II operated without uniforms. Vietcong guerrillas fighting in South Vietnam were not part of any formal army, but the United States nonetheless treated those they captured as POWs.

So what treatment should al Qaeda get? The conventions contain one section—Article 3—that protects all persons regardless of their status, whether spy, mercenary, or terrorist, and regardless of the type of war in which they are fighting. That same article prohibits torture, cruel treatment, and murder of all detainees, requires the wounded to be cared for, and says that any trials must be conducted by regular courts respecting due process. In a landmark 2006 opinion, the U.S. Supreme Court declared that *at a minimum* Article 3 applies to detained al Qaeda suspects. In other words, the rules apply, even if al Qaeda ignores them.

And it may be that even tougher rules should be used in such a fight. Many other governments, particularly in Europe, believe that a "war" against terror—a war without temporal or geographic limits—is complete folly, insisting instead that the fight against terrorist groups should be a law enforcement, not a military, matter. For decades, Europe has prevented and punished terrorists by treating them as criminals. Courts in Britain and Spain have tried suspects for major bombings in London and Madrid. The prosecutors and investigators there did so while largely complying with obligations enshrined in human rights treaties, which constrain them far more than do the Geneva Conventions.

"The Geneva Conventions Turn Soldiers into War Criminals"

Only if they commit war crimes. For centuries, states have punished their own soldiers for violations of the laws of war, such as the mistreatment of prisoners or murder of civilians. The Geneva Conventions identify certain violations that states must prosecute, including murder outside of battle, causing civilians great suffering, and denying POWs fair trials, and most countries have laws on the books that punish such crimes. The U.S. military, for example, has investigated hundreds of servicemembers for abuses in Iraq and Afghanistan, leading to dozens of prosecutions. Canada prosecuted a group of its peacekeepers for the murder of a young Somali in 1993.

Yet the idea that ordinary soldiers could be prosecuted in a foreign country for being, in effect, soldiers fighting a war is ridiculous. Yes, many countries, including the United States, have laws allowing foreigners to be tried for various abuses of war committed anywhere. Yet the risk of prosecution abroad, particularly of U.S. forces, is minuscule. Those foreign laws only address bona fide war crimes, and it is rarely in the interest of foreign governments to aggravate relations with the United States over spurious prosecutions.

The idea that the International Criminal Court could one day put U.S. commanders on trial is unlikely in the extreme. That court could theoretically prosecute U.S. personnel for crimes committed in, say, Afghanistan, but only if the United States failed to do so first. What's more, the court is by its charter dedicated to trying large-scale, horrendous atrocities like those in Sudan. It is virtually inconceivable that this new institution will want to pick a fight with the United States over a relatively small number of abuses.

"The Conventions Prevent Interrogations of Terrorists"

False. If you've seen a classic war movie such as *The Great Escape,* you know that prisoners of war are only obligated to provide name, rank, date of birth, and military serial number to their captors. But the Geneva Conventions do not ban interrogators from asking for more. In fact, the laws were written with the expectation that states will grill prisoners, and clear rules were created to manage the process. In interstate war, any form of coercion is forbidden, specifically threats, insults, or punish-

ments if prisoners fail to answer; for all other wars, cruel or degrading treatment and torture are prohibited. But questioning detainees is perfectly legal; it simply must be done in a manner that respects human dignity. The conventions thus hardly require rolling out the red carpet for suspected terrorists. Many interrogation tactics are clearly allowed, including good cop-bad cop scenarios, repetitive or rapid questioning, silent periods, and playing to a detainee's ego.

The Bush administration has engaged in legal gymnastics to avoid the conventions' restrictions, arguing that preventing the next attack is sufficient rationale for harsh tactics such as waterboarding, sleep deprivation, painful stress positions, deafening music, and traumatic humiliation. These severe methods have been used despite the protests of a growing chorus of intelligence officials who say that such approaches are actually counterproductive to extracting quality information. Seasoned interrogators consistently say that straightforward questioning is far more successful for getting at the truth. So, by mangling the conventions, the United States has joined the company of a host of unsavory regimes that make regular use of torture. It has abandoned a system that protects U.S. military personnel from terrible treatment for one in which the rules are made on the fly.

"The Geneva Conventions Ban Assassinations"

Actually, no. War is all about killing your enemy, and though the Geneva Conventions place limits on the "unnecessary suffering" of soldiers, they certainly don't seek to outlaw war. Assassinating one's enemy when hostilities have been declared is not only permissible; it is expected. But at the core of the conventions is the "principle of distinction," which bans all deliberate targeting of civilians. The boundless scope of the war on terror makes it difficult to decide who is and is not a civilian. The United States claims that it can target and kill terrorists at any time, just like regular soldiers; but the conventions treat these individuals like quasi-civilians who can be targeted and killed only during "such time as they take a *direct* part in hostilities" [emphasis mine]. The Israeli Supreme Court recently interpreted this phrase to give Israel limited latitude to continue targeted killings, but it insisted on a high standard of proof that the target had lost protected status and that capture was impossible. What standards the United States might be using—such as when the CIA targeted and killed several al Qaeda operatives in Yemen in 2002—are highly classified, so there's no way to know how much proof is insisted upon before the trigger is pulled or the button pushed.

For European countries and others who reject the idea of a "war" against terrorists to begin with, targeted killings are especially abhorrent, as international law prohibits states in peacetime from extrajudicial killings. There are very specific exceptions to this rule, such as when a police officer must defend himself or others against imminent harm. To that end, a suicide bomber heading for a crowd could legally be assassinated as a last resort. By contrast, suspected terrorists—whether planning a new attack or on the lam—are to be captured and tried.

172

"The Conventions Require Closing Guantánamo"

No, but changes must be made. The Geneva Conventions allow countries to detain POWs in camps, and, if someone in enemy hands does not fit the POW category, he or she is automatically accorded civilian status, which has its own protections. But none of the residents of Guantánamo's military prison qualifies as either, according to the Bush administration, thus depriving the roughly 275 detainees who remain there of the rights accorded by the conventions, such as adequate shelter and eventual release.

The possibility that detainees could remain in legal limbo indefinitely at Guantánamo has turned the issue into a foreign-relations disaster for the United States. But let's be clear—the Geneva Conventions don't require the United States to close up shop in Cuba. The rules simply insist that a working legal framework be put in place, instead of the legal vacuum that exists now.

There are several options worth consideration. The prison at Guantánamo could be turned into a pre-trial holding area where detainees are held before they are brought before U.S. courts on formal charges. (The hiccup here is that most of the detainees haven't clearly violated any U.S. law.) Alternatively, the U.S. Congress could pass legislation installing a system of preventive detention for dangerous individuals. The courts could occasionally review detainees' particular circumstances and judge whether continued detention is necessary and lawful. (The problem here is that such a system would run against 200 years of American jurisprudence.) In the end, closing Guantánamo is probably the only option that would realistically restore America's reputation, though it isn't required by any clause in the conventions. It's just the wisest course of action.

"No Nation Flouts the Geneva Conventions More than the United States"

That's absurd. When bullets start flying, rules get broken. The degree to which any army adheres to the Geneva Conventions is typically a product of its professionalism, training, and sense of ethics. On this score, U.S. compliance with the conventions has been admirable, far surpassing many countries and guerrilla armies that routinely ignore even the most basic provisions. The U.S. military takes great pride in teaching its soldiers civilized rules of war: to preserve military honor and discipline, lessen tensions with civilians, and strive to make a final peace more durable. Contrast that training with Eritrea or Ethiopia, states whose ill-trained forces committed numerous war crimes during their recent border war, or Guatemala, whose army and paramilitaries made a policy of killing civilians on an enormous scale during its long civil conflict.

More importantly, the U.S. military cares passionately that other states and nonstate actors follow the same rules to which it adheres, because U.S. forces, who are deployed abroad in far greater numbers than troops from any other nation, are most likely to be harmed if the conventions are discarded. Career U.S. military commanders and lawyers have consistently opposed the various reinterpretations of the conventions by politically appointed lawyers in the Bush White House and Justice Department for precisely this reason.

It is enormously important that the United States reaffirms its commitment to the conventions, for the sake of the country's reputation and that of the conventions. Those who rely on the flawed logic that because al Qaeda does not treat the conventions seriously, neither should the United States fail to see not only the chaos the world will suffer in exchange for these rules; they also miss the fact that the United States will have traded basic rights and protections harshly learned through thousands of years of war for the nitpicking decisions of a small group of partisan lawyers huddled in secret. Rather than advancing U.S. interests by following an established standard of behavior in this new type of war, the United States—and any country that chooses to abandon these hard-won rules—risks basing its policies on narrow legalisms. In losing sight of the crucial protections of the conventions, the United States invites a world of wars in which laws disappear. And the horrors of such wars would far surpass anything the war on terror could ever deliver.

STEVEN R. RATNER is professor of law at the University of Michigan.

Is Bigger Better?

Using market incentives, Fazle Hasan Abed built the largest antipoverty group in the world and helped pull Bangladesh out of the ashes. Now he wants to take on Africa.

DAVID ARMSTRONG

From the large glass window of his modern, well-lit and spacious offices 19 floors above Dhaka, Bangladesh, Fazle Hasan Abed, a former executive for Shell Oil, can keep tabs on nearby Korail, a dense slum of 60,000 people living in single-story mud, aluminum and bamboo shacks, some built on thin stilts over the brackish water of an urban lake. Abed, 72, has more than a little interest in the slum. The organization he founded in 1972, BRAC, the largest antipoverty group in the world, with 110,000 paid employees and a $482 million annual budget, has its hands everywhere in Korail.

Down one muddy lane a teacher trained by BRAC instructs 36 students using a BRAC-designed curriculum of Bengali, math and English. Nearby a group of women in the final month of pregnancy sit shrouded in colorful saris on the floor of a BRAC-built "birthing hut," staffed with BRAC-trained health workers, getting a lesson in prenatal nutrition. Not far away, Mosammat Anwaraan, an energetic woman in her late 50s, runs a mini real estate empire, the fruits of a 3,000 taka ($44) microloan in 1997 from BRAC. She owns 25 rooms in the slum, renting out 18 for 700 to 800 taka a month, making $2,500 a year. "I think rent will go up to 1,000 taka by next year," she says proudly.

Abed has replicated all-in-one programs like these in 1,000 urban slums and 70,000 rural villages across Bangladesh (the group was originally called the Bangladesh Rural Advancement Committee). Its microfinance program has made $4.6 billion in loans versus $6.9 billion from the better-known microlender Grameen. It runs 52,000 preschools and primary schools, with 1.5 million students. Its 68,000 health care volunteers, egged on by financial incentives, cover a population of 80 million. It operates commercial dairies, silkworm-raising centers and department stores to provide markets for the goods its poor beneficiaries produce. Says Abed, "If you want to do significant work, you have to be large. Otherwise we'd be tinkering around on the periphery."

The World Bank credits BRAC in part with what it calls the "Bangladesh paradox": Despite an impotent government (leaders of the two primary political parties are currently in jail on corruption charges), this country of 145 million people has improved significantly. According to the World Bank, the fraction of the population living in poverty (defined as below $2 a day in purchasing power) dropped from 58% in 1992 to 40% in 2005; secondary school enrollment has climbed from 19% in 1990 to 43% today and childhood immunization from 1% in 1980 to 80% today.

In the 1980s a woman had, on average, seven kids. Today it's two.

Thirty years ago a woman had, on average, seven children. Today the fertility rate is two, thanks in large part to widespread delivery of contraceptives to the countryside, a practice pioneered by BRAC. The country's 5% annual average growth in GDP since 1990 (to $2,300 per capita) leads the World Bank to suggest that Bangladesh could join the list of "middle income" countries in ten years. To be sure, trade liberalization, garment exports and remittances from laborers abroad are vital, but the effectiveness of these macroeconomic advances are largely dependent on the kind of ground-level social progress BRAC has made.

"I don't know of any developing-world NGO [nongovernmental organization] that has been more successful," says Dr. Allan Rosenfield, dean of Columbia University's School of Public Health, who serves on the board of BRAC's U.S. arm. "Certainly in terms of the issues they work on, they're more like a minigovernment. If I were giving out Nobel Prizes, there is no doubt I would give it to Abed."

Born to a wealthy landowning family in the Bengal region of British India in 1936, Abed grew up in a household full of servants. His father was a government official. His mother, a religious woman, often brought poor villagers to the Abed home for food. He attended Glasgow University before going to London to study accounting and business. He stayed for 12 years, working as a corporate financial officer and enjoying the life of a professional expatriate: yearly drives through continental Europe, vacations in Italy, reading Western literature. In 1968 he returned to Dhaka with a prestigious job, managing Shell's accounting department.

On Nov. 21, 1970 a cyclone hit the Chittagong area in the southern part of the country, killing perhaps 500,000 people, still the deadliest cyclone on record. Abed and friends volunteered to help. "It really changed the way I look at things," Abed says.

At the time, Bangladesh was the eastern portion of the country of Pakistan, ruled over by an unsympathetic government in Islamabad. A crackdown on the pro-East Pakistan independence movement sent Abed back to London, where he raised funds for the millions of Bangladeshi refugees in India.

After a bloody war Bangladesh won its independence in 1971. Abed sold his London flat for $17,000 and returned to a country that lay in ruins. Hundreds of thousands had been killed and the economy was in tatters—soon after, Henry Kissinger famously called Bangladesh "an international basket case."

Abed and a small group of friends worked on aid projects, but he felt much of the work wasn't benefiting those who needed it most. "Poor people are poor because they are powerless," Abed says. He turned his attention to poverty relief, mapping villages into quartiles based on wealth and focusing his efforts on only those households at the bottom.

Using the proceeds of his London apartment sale, he formed BRAC in 1972. His biggest early success was reducing child mortality. In 1975, 25% of Bangladeshi children wouldn't live to see their fifth birthday; almost half of those deaths were caused by diarrhea. Abed trained groups of women to fan out into the countryside and teach others how to mix a solution of water, salt and sugar that would combat the potentially fatal loss of fluid and electrolytes. Monitors would grade the households based on how well family members did, and that grade would determine the pay of the instructors. This was an incentive-based "social entrepreneurship" program long before that phrase became common. The average worker made $40 a month, with most households scoring in the A or B range.

BRAC researchers estimate that the program, along with a government immunization initiative, has cut the mortality rate of Bangladeshi children ages 1 to 4 from 25% to 7%.

Abed vertically integrates many BRAC programs. A BRAC village organizer will first gather 20 to 30 women and extend microcredit. Many use the loans to set up small shops and grocery stores. If the women buy a cow, for example, BRAC will help them double the price they can get for milk

by collecting it via refrigerated truck and bringing it to one of BRAC's 67 "chilling stations," then to BRAC's commercial dairy production center, which processes 10,000 liters of milk, yogurt and ice cream an hour, and selling it in the cities. It earns BRAC $1.7 million on sales of $13.4 million, all of which goes back into the programs.

Likewise, silkworm raising is the bottom step of another commercial market. Majeda Begum, who lives in a small village a day's drive from Dhaka, used her loan to buy silkworm eggs from BRAC, paying $3 for 50 grams. She hatches them in a tin-roofed shack behind her home. Begum feeds them by spreading mulberry leaves over the top, easy enough to collect, since BRAC has planted 20 million mulberry trees around the area to support the enterprise. She'll sell the cocoons back to BRAC for $5.75 a kilo. She earns, she figures, $370 a year, and no longer needs BRAC's loans. All three of her children, including two daughters, go to school. Without the income? "I'd probably only send my son," she says.

Vertically integrated, BRAC's businesses produce $90 million in revenue.

The silk is eventually woven into clothes and sold to Aarong, a chain of upmarket department stores BRAC owns in Bangladesh's big cities. Aarong netted $4.6 million on $28 million in sales in 2006. In all, BRAC's commercial enterprises account for some $90 million in revenue; it pulls in $116 million from its interest on microloans. BRAC still relies on donor funding for 20% of its budget.

Abed uses incentives for health programs, as well. Community health workers are asked to make home visits to 15 houses a day and can resell at a small markup common medicines, balm and birth control pills that they have bought from BRAC.

Recently health volunteers have been trained to recognize the symptoms of tuberculosis, which kills 70,000 Bangladeshis a year. Volunteers collect a sample of phlegm from suspect people and send it to a BRAC health office for testing. If it's positive, the volunteer gets 200 taka (about $2.50). Patients are given medicine free of charge but must post a $3.50 bond to ensure that they continue the six-month course of medication. "There are market incentives in everything we do," Abed says. Bangladesh has upped its cure rate of known TB cases to 90%.

BRAC has recently started targeting the 14% of women too poor to take advantage of microloans. A day's drive from Dhaka, in an un-air-conditioned BRAC field office swarming with flies, Akhtar Hossain unfurls a large sheet of brown paper on which is drawn a map of a nearby village. His house-by-house survey is meant to find "beggars and those with no land." The government is supposed to give these people a card that entitles the holder to 35 kilos of rice every three months. "But they never get it," he says. "The district official in charge of disbursing the cards gives it to people he knows."

To this group BRAC distributes cows, goats or a small plot of arable land. Haliman Khatun, who once worked as a laborer in others' homes and was paid only with small amounts of rice, shares her small shack in Pakundia with her cow, proudly showing off the space where the cow sleeps next to her own bed. She sells milk from the cow at the market but has bigger ambitions: She might sell it for the end of Eid, a Muslim holiday when livestock is slaughtered; cows can fetch a premium in the marketplace, and with that she could buy a plot of land or more goats, she says.

Abed is now bringing BRAC into Africa. The Gates Foundation has given $15 million in grants and loans to replicate BRAC's microfinance, agriculture and health programs in Tanzania, and the Nike Foundation is giving $1 million to establish designated centers for teenage girls in Tanzania. BRAC has set up organizations in the U.S. and the U.K. to bring in more charitable dollars.

It remains to be seen if BRAC can repeat the success it's had in Bangladesh. But Abed is encouraged by its track record in Afghanistan, where it set up shop in 2002. Some 180,000 women have borrowed $96 million from BRAC, and 4,000 have been trained as community health workers. When Abed sets out to do something, he does it big.

From *Forbes Magazine,* June 2, 2008, pp. 66–70. Reprinted by permission of Forbes Magazine, © 2008 Forbes Media Inc.

A World *Enslaved*

There are now more slaves on the planet than at any time in human history. True abolition will elude us until we admit the massive scope of the problem, attack it in all its forms, and empower slaves to help free themselves.

E. Benjamin Skinner

Standing in New York City, you are five hours away from being able to negotiate the sale, in broad daylight, of a healthy boy or girl. He or she can be used for anything, though sex and domestic labor are most common. Before you go, let's be clear on what you are buying. A slave is a human being forced to work through fraud or threat of violence for no pay beyond subsistence. Agreed? Good.

Most people imagine that slavery died in the 19th century. Since 1817, more than a dozen international conventions have been signed banning the slave trade. Yet, today there are more slaves than at any time in human history.

And if you're going to buy one in five hours, you'd better get a move on. First, hail a taxi to JFK International Airport, and hop on a direct flight to Port-au-Prince, Haiti. The flight takes three hours. After landing at Toussaint L'Ouverture International Airport, you will need 50 cents for the most common form of transport in Port-au-Prince, the tap-tap, a flatbed pickup retrofitted with benches and a canopy. Three quarters of the way up Route de Delmas, the capital's main street, tap the roof and hop out. There, on a side street, you will find a group of men standing in front of Le Réseau (The Network) barbershop. As you approach, a man steps forward: "Are you looking to get a person?"

Meet Benavil Lebhom. He smiles easily. He has a trim mustache and wears a multicolored, striped golf shirt, a gold chain, and Doc Martens knockoffs. Benavil is a courtier, or broker. He holds an official real estate license and calls himself an employment agent. Two thirds of the employees he places are child slaves. The total number of Haitian children in bondage in their own country stands at 300,000. They are the *restavèks*, the "staywiths," as they are euphemistically known in Creole. Forced, unpaid, they work in captivity from before dawn until night. Benavil and thousands of other formal and informal traffickers lure these children from desperately impoverished rural parents, with promises of free schooling and a better life.

The negotiation to buy a child slave might sound a bit like this:

"How quickly do you think it would be possible to bring a child in? Somebody who could clean and cook?" you ask. "I don't have a very big place; I have a small apartment. But I'm wondering how much that would cost? And how quickly?"

"Three days," Benavil responds.

"And you could bring the child here?" you inquire. "Or are there children here already?"

"I don't have any here in Port-au-Prince right now," says Benavil, his eyes widening at the thought of a foreign client. "I would go out to the countryside."

You ask about additional expenses. "Would I have to pay for transportation?"

"*Bon,*" says Benavil. "A hundred U.S."

Smelling a rip-off, you press him, "And that's just for transportation?"

"Transportation would be about 100 Haitian," says Benavil, or around $13, "because you'd have to get out there. Plus [hotel and] food on the trip. Five hundred gourdes."

"Okay, 500 Haitian," you say.

Now you ask the big question: "And what would your fee be?" This is the moment of truth, and Benavil's eyes narrow as he determines how much he can take you for.

"A hundred. American."

"That seems like a lot," you say, with a smile so as not to kill the deal. "How much would you charge a Haitian?"

Benavil's voice rises with feigned indignation. "A hundred dollars. This is a major effort."

You hold firm. "Could you bring down your fee to 50 U.S.?"

Benavil pauses. But only for effect. He knows he's still got you for much more than a Haitian would pay. "*Oui,*" he says with a smile.

But the deal isn't done. Benavil leans in close. "This is a rather delicate question. Is this someone you want as just a worker? Or also someone who will be a 'partner'? You understand what I mean?"

You don't blink at being asked if you want the child for sex. "I mean, is it possible to have someone that could be both?"

"*Oui!*" Benavil responds enthusiastically.

If you're interested in taking your purchase back to the United States, Benavil tells you that he can "arrange" the proper papers to make it look as though you've adopted the child.

He offers you a 13-year-old girl.

"That's a little bit old," you say.

"I know of another girl who's 12. Then ones that are 10, 11," he responds.

The negotiation is finished, and you tell Benavil not to make any moves without further word from you. Here, 600 miles from the United States, and five hours from Manhattan, you have successfully arranged to buy a human being for 50 bucks.

The Cruel Truth

It would be nice if that conversation, like the description of the journey, were fictional. It is not. I recorded it on Oct. 6, 2005, as part of four years of research into slavery on five continents. In the popular consciousness, "slavery" has come to be little more than just a metaphor for undue hardship. Investment bankers routinely refer to themselves as "high-paid wage slaves." Human rights activists may call $1-an-hour sweatshop laborers slaves, regardless of the fact that they are paid and can often walk away from the job. But the reality of slavery is far different. Slavery exists today on an unprecedented scale. In Africa, tens of thousands are chattel slaves, seized in war or tucked away for generations. Across Europe, Asia, and the Americas, traffickers have forced as many as 2 million into prostitution or labor. In South Asia, which has the highest concentration of slaves on the planet, nearly 10 million languish in bondage, unable to leave their captors until they pay off "debts," legal fictions that in many cases are generations old.

Few in the developed world have a grasp of the enormity of modern-day slavery. Fewer still are doing anything to combat it. Beginning in 2001, U.S. President George W. Bush was urged by several of his key advisors to vigorously enforce the Victims of Trafficking and Violence Protection Act, a U.S. law enacted a month earlier that sought to prosecute domestic human traffickers and cajole foreign governments into doing the same. The Bush administration trumpeted the effort—at home via the Christian evangelical media and more broadly via speeches and pronouncements, including in addresses to the U.N. General Assembly in 2003 and 2004. But even the quiet and diligent work of some within the U.S. State Department, which credibly claims to have secured more than 100 antitrafficking laws and more than 10,000 trafficking convictions worldwide, has resulted in no measurable decline in the number of slaves worldwide. Between 2000 and 2006, the U.S. Justice Department increased human trafficking prosecutions from 3 to 32, and convictions from 10 to 98. By 2006, 27 states had passed antitrafficking laws. Yet, during the same period, the United States liberated less than 2 percent of its own modern-day slaves. As many as 17,500 new slaves continue to enter bondage in the United States every year.

The West's efforts have been, from the outset, hamstrung by a warped understanding of slavery. In the United States, a hard-driving coalition of feminist and evangelical activists has forced the Bush administration to focus almost exclusively on the sex trade. The official State Department line is that voluntary prostitution does not exist, and that commercial sex is the main driver of slavery today. In Europe, though Germany and the Netherlands have decriminalized most prostitution, other nations such as Bulgaria have moved in the opposite direction, bowing to U.S. pressure and cracking down on the flesh trade. But, across the Americas, Europe, and Asia, unregulated escort services are exploding with the help of the Internet. Even when enlightened governments have offered clearheaded solutions to deal with this problem, such as granting victims temporary residence, they have had little impact.

Many feel that sex slavery is particularly revolting—and it is. I saw it firsthand. In a Bucharest brothel, for instance, I was offered a mentally handicapped, suicidal girl in exchange for a used car. But for every one woman or child enslaved in commercial sex, there are at least 15 men, women, and children enslaved in other fields, such as domestic work or agricultural labor. Recent studies have shown that locking up pimps and traffickers has had a negligible effect on the aggregate rates of bondage. And though eradicating prostitution may be a just cause, Western policies based on the idea that all prostitutes are slaves and all slaves are prostitutes belittles the suffering of all victims. It's an approach that threatens to put most governments on the wrong side of history.

Indebted for Life

Save for the fact that he is male, Gonoo Lal Kol typifies the average slave of our modern age. (At his request, I have changed his first name.) Like a vast majority of the world's slaves, Gonoo is in debt bondage in South Asia. In his case, in an Indian quarry. Like most slaves, Gonoo is illiterate and unaware of the Indian laws that ban his bondage and provide for sanctions against his master. His story, told to me in more than a dozen conversations inside his 4-foot-high stone and grass hutch, represents the other side of the "Indian Miracle."

Gonoo lives in Lohagara Dhal, a forgotten corner of Uttar Pradesh, a north Indian state that contains 8 percent of the world's poor. I met him one evening in December 2005 as he walked with two dozen other laborers in tattered and filthy clothes. Behind them was the quarry. In that pit, Gonoo, a member of the historically outcast Kol tribe, worked with his family 14 hours a day. His tools were simple, a rough-hewn hammer and an iron pike. His hands were covered in calluses, his fingertips worn away.

Gonoo's master is a tall, stout, surly contractor named Ramesh Garg. Garg is one of the wealthiest men in Shankargarh, the nearest sizable town, founded under the British Raj but now run by nearly 600 quarry contractors. He makes his money by enslaving entire families forced to work for no pay beyond alcohol, grain, and bare subsistence expenses. Their only use for Garg is to turn rock into silica sand, for colored glass, or gravel, for roads or ballast. Slavery scholar Kevin Bales estimates that a slave in the 19th-century American South had to work 20 years to recoup his or her purchase price. Gonoo and the other slaves earn a profit for Garg in two years.

Every single man, woman, and child in Lohagara Dhal is a slave. But, in theory at least, Garg neither bought nor owns them. They are working off debts, which, for many, started at less than $10. But interest accrues at over 100 percent annually here. Most of the debts span at least two generations, though they have no legal standing under modern Indian law. They are a fiction that Garg constructs through fraud and maintains through violence. The seed of Gonoo's slavery, for instance, was a loan of 62 cents. In 1958, his grandfather borrowed that amount from the owner of a farm where he worked. Three generations and three slavemasters later, Gonoo's family remains in bondage.

Bringing Freedom to Millions

Recently, many bold, underfunded groups have taken up the challenge of tearing out the roots of slavery. Some gained fame through dramatic slave rescues. Most learned that freeing slaves is impossible unless the slaves themselves choose to be free. Among the Kol of Uttar Pradesh, for instance, an organization called Pragati Gramodyog Sansthan (Progressive Institute for Village Enterprises, or PGS) has helped hundreds of families break the grip of the quarry contractors. Working methodically since 1985, PGS organizers slowly built up confidence among slaves. With PGS's help, the Kol formed microcredit unions and won leases to quarries so that they could keep the proceeds of their labor. Some bought property for the first time in their lives, a cow or a goat, and their incomes, which had been nil, multiplied quickly. PGS set up primary schools and dug wells. Villages that for generations had known nothing but slavery began to become free. PGS's success demonstrates that emancipation is merely the first step in abolition. Within the developed world, some national law enforcement agencies such as those in the Czech Republic and Sweden have finally begun to pursue the most culpable of human trafficking—slave-trading pimps and unscrupulous labor contractors. But more must be done to educate local police, even in the richest of nations. Too often, these street-level law enforcement personnel do not understand that it's just as likely for a prostitute to be a trafficking victim as it is for a nanny working without proper papers to be a slave. And, after they have been discovered by law enforcement, few rich nations provide slaves with the kind of rehabilitation, retraining, and protection needed to prevent their re-trafficking. The asylum now granted to former slaves in the United States and the Netherlands is a start. But more must be done.

The United Nations, whose founding principles call for it to fight bondage in all its forms, has done almost nothing to combat modern slavery. In January, Antonio Maria Costa, executive director of the U.N. Office on Drugs and Crime, called for the international body to provide better quantification of human trafficking. Such number crunching would be valuable in combating that one particular manifestation of slavery. But there is little to suggest the United Nations, which consistently fails to hold its own member states accountable for widespread slavery, will be an effective tool in defeating the broader phenomenon.

Any lasting solutions to human trafficking must involve prevention programs in at-risk source countries. Absent an effective international body like the United Nations, such an effort will require pressure from the United States. So far, the United States has been willing to criticize some nations' records, but it has resisted doing so where it matters most, particularly in India. India abolished debt bondage in 1976, but with poor enforcement of the law locally, millions remain in bondage. In 2006 and 2007, the U.S. State Department's Office to Monitor and Combat Trafficking in Persons pressed U.S. Secretary of State Condoleezza Rice to repudiate India's intransigence personally. And, in each instance, she did not.

The psychological, social, and economic bonds of slavery run deep, and for governments to be truly effective in eradicating slavery, they must partner with groups that can offer slaves a way to pull themselves up from bondage. One way to do that is to replicate the work of grassroots organizations such as Varanasi, India-based MSEMVS (Society for Human Development and Women's Empowerment). In 1996, the Indian group launched free transitional schools, where children who had been enslaved learned skills and acquired enough literacy to move on to formal schooling. The group also targeted mothers, providing them with training and start-up materials for microenterprises. In Thailand, a nation infamous for sex slavery, a similar group, the Labour Rights Promotion Network, works to keep desperately poor Burmese immigrants from the clutches of traffickers by, among other things, setting up schools and health programs. Even in the remote highlands of southern Haiti, activists with Limyè Lavi ("Light of Life") reach otherwise wholly isolated rural communities to warn them of the dangers of traffickers such as Benavil Lebhom and to help them organize informal schools to keep children near home. In recent years, the United States has shown an increasing willingness to help fund these kinds of organizations, one encouraging sign that the message may be getting through.

For four years, I saw dozens of people enslaved, several of whom traffickers like Benavil actually offered to sell to me. I did not pay for a human life anywhere. And, with one exception, I always withheld action to save any one person, in the hope that my research would later help to save many more. At times, that still feels like an excuse for cowardice. But the hard work of real emancipation can't be the burden of a select few. For thousands of slaves, grassroots groups like PGS and MSEMVS can help bring freedom. But, until governments define slavery in appropriately concise terms, prosecute the crime aggressively in all its forms, and encourage groups that empower slaves to free themselves, millions more will remain in bondage. And our collective promise of abolition will continue to mean nothing at all.

E. Benjamin Skinner is the author of *A Crime So Monstrous: Face-to-Face with Modern-Day Slavery* (New York: Free Press, 2008).

From *Foreign Policy*, March/April 2008. Copyright © 2008 by the Carnegie Endowment for International Peace. Reprinted with permission. www.foreignpolicy.com

Chile Starts Early

JIMMY LANGMAN

Maria estela ortiz, a chilean education specialist, first worked with Michelle Bachelet in the late 1980s, when Bachelet was a doctor treating children whose parents had been tortured or "disappeared" by the Pinochet regime. Today, Bachelet is Chile's president, and since she took office in March 2006, Ortiz has been helping lead one of her administration's defining projects: providing free access to health and education programs for all Chileans under the age of 4. For more than three years now, as part of the effort, Chile has been building new preschools at the astounding rate of 2.5 a day, increasing the country's total from 781 to 4,300. It has also significantly boosted health coverage and nutrition programs for kids. Ortiz, who heads Chile's National Early Education Board, calls it all a vital investment in the country's future that's especially important during the current economic crisis, when more parents are forced to work and fewer have money for school.

President Bachelet leads the way in pushing the advantages of preschool.

Chile, which happens to be led by a pediatrician who's also a single mother and a committed socialist, is a particularly dramatic example of a growing trend throughout Latin America and beyond: as countries grapple with the economic downturn and reconsider spending, more and more are heeding the advice of a coalition of economists, scientists, and experts who argue that the best way to strengthen a society and increase development is to improve health, education, and other services for its youngest citizens.

The trend's most prominent spokesperson is probably Shakira, the Colombian pop singer who is also a founder of a group known as ALAS. This coalition (its name comes from an acronym for "Latin America in Solidarity Action," but also means "wings" in Spanish) has brought together Latino businesspeople, artists, and celebrities such as Jennifer Lopez and Gabriel Garcia Marquez to help end poverty in the Western hemisphere by ensuring that all kids under 6 have access to health care, education, and proper nutrition. Last year, ALAS convinced the Mexican billionaire Carlos Slim and Howard Buffett (the philanthropist son of Warren Buffett) to pledge $185 million for early

related programs in Latin America, and the group has organized huge concerts throughout the region to raise awareness.

ALAS has also sought to affect policy by working with the development economist Jeffrey Sachs and his Earth Institute at Columbia University to persuade Latin American governments to scale up their funding for programs in a region where about 60 percent of all kids still live in poverty. "This is not the time for governments to be cutting back," says Joanna Rubinstein, director of strategic development for the Earth Institute. "No country can afford to put at a risk an entire generation because of the economic crisis."

The advocates have plenty of academic research to back them up. In October 2007, the Inter-American Development Bank brought together a panel of top economists and asked them, if they had $10 billion to solve Latin America's most pressing problems, how would they do it? The group, using cost-benefit analysis, decided that the most effective use of the cash would be to invest it in programs like day care, preschool, parenting and hygiene courses, as well as early childhood health services. Meanwhile, James Heckman, a Nobel Prize-winning economist at the University of Chicago, has found that introducing pre-school education for disadvantaged kids results in at least a 10 percent annual return for society by improving students' intelligence scores and social skills, leading to better school performance and employment prospects in later years as well as reduced crime and teenage-pregnancy rates.

New research also shows how dangerous it is to neglect such programs. Work by Harvard's Jack Shonkoff, for example, has found that depriving poor children of access to good health care, nutrition, and education during their first three years increases the likelihood they'll suffer from disease, learning difficulties, and poverty. Such findings are based in part on studies that show that humans develop 80 percent of their brain in the first three years of life, making nutrition and proper mental stimulation critical during this period. Says Miguel Hoffmann, a Buenos Aires psychiatrist who specializes in early-childhood development, "all the data are showing that proper care and quality education in the first years [ensure that] we learn faster and are emotionally better able to cope with life's challenges."

To provide these goods, in April Colombia announced a new national policy guaranteeing the right to a quality education for all children under 5; as part of the plan, Bogota aims to build 60 new early education centers next year and enroll 400,000 kids in government programs. But the most enthusiastic country has been Chile. In October 2006, Bachelet's government inaugurated a groundbreaking campaign called "Chile Grows With You," which brings together state-supported day care, preschool, family counseling, and health services for all Chileans who participate in the country's public-health system (about 70 percent of the population). The program aims at kids from conception through age 4 and is entirely free for the poorest 40 percent of the population. It also offers subsidies to assist poor families with raising their kids after that.

"Chile has been amazing in its ability to create a national consensus and act on it," says Andrea Rolla, director of A Good Start, a joint early-education program of Harvard University's Graduate School of Education and Chile's Education Opportunity Foundation. Now that the infrastructure is in place, Chilean officials say the next challenge is to boost enrollment and quality. But local preschools are already reporting a dramatic rise in interest. Ortiz even credits the program with a boom in births in the first half of this year, leading to the highest birthrate in the last decade. "Chilean women see the social protections and they are emboldened to have children," she says. If she's right, it's a powerful sign of Chileans' faith in the new campaign—and a show of optimism conspicuously absent in many other parts of the world at the moment.

From *Newsweek*, August 10 & 17, 2009, pp. 48–49. Copyright © 2009 by Jimmy Langman. Used by permission of the author.

UNIT 7

Values and Visions

Unit Selections

Key Points to Consider

- Is it naive to speak of global issues in terms of ethics?

- What roles can governments, international organizations, and individuals play in making high ethical standards more common in political and economic transactions?

- How is the political role of women changing, and what impacts are these changes having on conflict resolution and community building?

- The consumption of resources is the foundation of the modern economic system. What are the values underlying this economic system, and how resistant to change are they?

- What are the characteristics of leadership?

- In addition to the ideas presented here, what other new ideas are being expressed, and how likely are they to be widely accepted?

Student Website

www.mhhe.com/cls

Internet References

Human Rights Web
http://www.hrweb.org
InterAction
http://www.interaction.org

The final unit of this book considers how humanity's view of itself is changing. Values, like all other elements discussed in this anthology, are dynamic. Visionary people with new ideas can have a profound impact on how a society deals with problems and adapts to changing circumstances. Therefore, to understand the forces at work in the world today, values, visions, and new ideas in many ways are every bit as important as new technology or changing demographics.

Novelist Herman Wouk, in his book *War and Remembrance*, observed that many institutions have been so embedded in the social fabric of their time that people assumed that they were part of human nature. Slavery and human sacrifice are two examples. However, forward-thinking people opposed these institutions. Many knew that they would never see the abolition of these social systems within their own lifetimes, but they pressed on in the hope that someday these institutions would be eliminated.

Wouk believes the same is true for warfare. He states, "Either we are finished with war or war will finish us." Aspects of society such as warfare, slavery, racism, and the secondary status of women are creations of the human mind; history suggests that they can be changed by the human spirit.

The articles of this unit have been selected with the previous six units in mind. Each explores some aspect of world affairs from the perspective of values and alternative visions of the future.

New ideas are critical to meeting these challenges. The examination of well-known issues from new perspectives can yield new insights into old problems. It was feminist Susan B. Anthony who once remarked that "social change is never made by the masses, only by educated minorities." The redefinition of human values (which, by necessity, will accompany the successful confrontation of important global issues) is a task that few people take on willingly. Nevertheless, in order to deal with the dangers of nuclear war, overpopulation, and environmental degradation, educated people must take a broad view of history. This is going to require considerable effort and much personal sacrifice.

When people first begin to consider the magnitude of contemporary global problems, many often become disheartened and depressed. Some ask: What can I do? What does it matter? Who cares? There are no easy answers to these questions, but people need only look around to see good news as well as bad. How individuals react to the world is not solely a function of so-called objective reality but a reflection of themselves.

As stated at the beginning of the first unit, the study of global issues is the study of people. The study of people, furthermore, is the study of both values and the level of commitment supporting these values and beliefs.

© Royalty-Free/CORBIS

It is one of the goals of this book to stimulate you, the reader, to react intellectually and emotionally to the discussion and description of various global challenges. In the process of studying these issues, hopefully you have had some new insights into your own values and commitments. In the presentation of the allegory of the balloon, the fourth color added represented the "meta" component, all of those qualities that make human beings unique. It is these qualities that have brought us to this unique moment in time, and it will be these same qualities that will determine the outcome of our historically unique challenges.

Humanity's Common Values

Seeking a Positive Future

Overcoming the discontents of globalization and the clashes of civilizations requires us to reexamine and reemphasize those positive values that all humans share.

WENDELL BELL

Some commentators have insisted that the terrorist attacks of September 11, 2001, and their aftermath demonstrate Samuel P. Huntington's thesis of "the clash of civilizations," articulated in a famous article published in 1993. Huntington, a professor at Harvard University and director of security planning for the National Security Council during the Carter administration, argued that "conflict between groups from differing civilizations" has become "the central and most dangerous dimension of the emerging global politics."

Huntington foresaw a future in which nation-states no longer play a decisive role in world affairs. Instead, he envisioned large alliances of states, drawn together by common culture, cooperating with each other. He warned that such collectivities are likely to be in conflict with other alliances formed of countries united around a different culture.

Cultural differences do indeed separate people between various civilizations, but they also separate groups within a single culture or state. Many countries contain militant peoples of different races, religions, languages, and cultures, and such differences do sometimes provoke incidents that lead to violent conflict—as in Bosnia, Cyprus, Northern Ireland, Rwanda, and elsewhere. Moreover, within many societies today (both Western and non-Western) and within many religions (including Islam, Judaism, and Christianity) the culture war is primarily internal, between fundamentalist orthodox believers on the one hand and universalizing moderates on the other. However, for most people most of the time, peaceful accommodation and cooperation are the norms.

Conflicts between groups often arise and continue not because of the differences between them, but because of their similarities. People everywhere, for example, share the capacities to demonize others, to be loyal to their own group (sometimes even willing to die for it), to believe that they themselves and those they identify with are virtuous while all others are wicked, and to remember past wrongs committed against their group and seek revenge. Sadly, human beings everywhere share the capacity to hate and kill each other, including their own family members and neighbors.

Discontents of Globalization

Huntington is skeptical about the implications of the McDonaldization of the world. He insists that the "essence of Western civilization is the Magna Carta not the Magna Mac." And he says further, "The fact that non-Westerners may bite into the latter has no implications for accepting the former."

His conclusion may be wrong, for if biting into a Big Mac and drinking Coca-Cola, French wine, or Jamaican coffee while watching a Hollywood film on a Japanese TV and stretched out on a Turkish rug means economic development, then demands for public liberties and some form of democratic rule may soon follow where Big Mac leads. We know from dozens of studies that economic development contributes to the conditions necessary for political democracy to flourish.

Globalization, of course, is not producing an all-Western universal culture. Although it contains many Western aspects, what is emerging is a *global* culture, with elements from many cultures of the world, Western and non-Western.

Local cultural groups sometimes do view the emerging global culture as a threat, because they fear their traditional ways will disappear or be corrupted. And they may be right. The social world, after all, is constantly in flux. But, like the clean toilets that McDonald's brought to Hong Kong restaurants, people may benefit from certain changes, even when their fears prevent them from seeing this at once.

And local traditions can still be—and are—preserved by groups participating in a global culture. Tolerance and even the celebration of many local variations, as long as they do not harm others, are hallmarks of a sustainable world community. Chinese food, Spanish art, Asian philosophies, African drumming, Egyptian history, or any major religion's version of the Golden Rule can enrich the lives of everyone. What originated locally can become universally adopted (like Arabic numbers). Most important, perhaps, the emerging global culture is a fabric woven from tens of thousands—possibly hundreds of thousands—of individual networks of communication, influence, and exchange that link people and organizations across civilizational boundaries. Aided by electronic communications systems, these networks are growing stronger and more numerous each day.

Positive shared value: Unity.

Searching for Common, *Positive* Values

Global religious resurgence is a reaction to the loss of personal identity and group stability produced by "the processes of social, economic, and cultural modernization that swept across the world in the second half of the twentieth century," according to Huntington. With traditional systems of authority disrupted, people become separated from their roots in a bewildering maze of new rules and expectations. In his view, such people need "new sources of identity, new forms of stable community, and new sets of moral precepts to provide them with a sense of meaning and purpose." Organized religious groups, both mainstream and fundamentalist, are growing today precisely to meet these needs, he believes.

Positive shared value: Love.

Although uprooted people may need new frameworks of identity and purpose, they will certainly not find them in fundamentalist religious groups, for such groups are *not* "new sources of identity." Instead, they recycle the past. Religious revival movements are reactionary, not progressive. Instead of facing the future, developing new approaches to deal with perceived threats of economic, technological, and social change, the movements attempt to retreat into the past.

Religions will likely remain among the major human belief systems for generations to come, despite—or even because of—the fact that they defy conventional logic and reason with their ultimate reliance upon otherworldly beliefs. However, it is possible that some ecumenical accommodations will be made that will allow humanity to build a generally accepted ethical system based on the many similar and overlapping moralities contained in the major religions. A person does not have to believe in supernatural beings to embrace and practice the principles of a global ethic, as exemplified in the interfaith

declaration, "Towards a Global Ethic," issued by the Parliament of the World's Religions in 1993.

Positive shared value: Compassion.

Interfaith global cooperation is one way that people of different civilizations can find common cause. Another is global environmental cooperation seeking to maintain and enhance the life-sustaining capacities of the earth. Also, people everywhere have a stake in working for the freedom and welfare of future generations, not least because the future of their own children and grandchildren is at stake.

Positive shared value: Welfare of future generations.

Many more examples of cooperation among civilizations in the pursuit of common goals can be found in every area from medicine and science to moral philosophy, music, and art. A truly global commitment to the exploration, colonization, and industrialization of space offers still another way to harness the existing skills and talents of many nations, with the aim of realizing and extending worthy human capacities to their fullest. So, too, does the search for extraterrestrial intelligence. One day, many believe, contact will be made. What, then, becomes of Huntington's "clash of civilizations"? Visitors to Earth will likely find the variations among human cultures and languages insignificant compared with the many common traits all humans share.

Universal human values do exist, and many researchers, using different methodologies and data sets, have independently identified similar values. Typical of many studies into universal values is the global code of ethics compiled by Rushworth M. Kidder in *Shared Values for a Troubled World* (Wiley, 1994). Kidder's list includes love, truthfulness, fairness, freedom, unity (including cooperation, group allegiance, and oneness with others), tolerance, respect for life, and responsibility (which includes taking care of yourself, of other individuals, and showing concern for community interests). Additional values mentioned are courage, knowing right from wrong, wisdom, hospitality, obedience, and stability.

The Origins of Universal Human Values

Human values are not arbitrary or capricious. Their origins and continued existence are based in the facts of biology and in how human minds and bodies interact with their physical and social environments. These realities shape and constrain human behavior. They also shape human beliefs about the world and their evaluations of various aspects of it.

Human beings cannot exist without air, water, food, sleep, and personal security. There are also other needs that, although not absolutely necessary for the bodily survival of individuals, contribute to comfort and happiness. These include clothing, shelter, companionship, affection, and sex. The last, of course, is also necessary for reproduction and, hence, for the continued survival of the human species.

Thus, there are many constraints placed on human behavior, if individuals and groups are to continue to survive and to thrive. These are *not* matters of choice. *How* these needs are met involves some—often considerable—leeway of choice, but, obviously, these needs set limits to the possible.

Much of morality, then, derives from human biological and psychological characteristics and from our higher order capacities of choice and reasoning. If humans were invulnerable and immortal, then injunctions against murder would be unnecessary. If humans did not rely on learning from others, lying would not be a moral issue.

Some needs of human individuals, such as love, approval, and emotional support, are inherently social, because they can only be satisfied adequately by other humans. As infants, individuals are totally dependent on other people. As adults, interaction with others satisfies both emotional and survival needs. The results achieved through cooperation and division of labor within a group are nearly always superior to what can be achieved by individuals each working alone. This holds true for hunting, providing protection from beasts and hostile groups, building shelters, or carrying out large-scale community projects.

Thus, social life itself helps shape human values. As societies have evolved, they have selectively retained only some of the logically possible variations in human values as norms, rights, and obligations. These selected values function to make social life possible, to permit and encourage people to live and work together.

Socially disruptive attitudes and actions, such as greed, dishonesty, cowardice, anger, envy, promiscuity, stubbornness, and disobedience, among others, constantly threaten the survival of society. Sadly, these human traits are as universal as are societal efforts to control them. Perhaps some or all of them once had survival value for individuals. But with the growth of society, they have become obstacles to the cooperation needed to sustain large-scale, complex communities. Other actions and attitudes that individuals and societies ought to avoid are equally well-recognized: abuses of power, intolerance, theft, arrogance, brutality, terrorism, torture, fanaticism, and degradation.

Positive shared value: Honesty.

I believe the path toward a harmonious global society is well marked by widely shared human values, including patience, truthfulness, responsibility, respect for life, granting dignity to all people, empathy for others, kindliness and generosity, compassion, and forgiveness. To be comprehensive, this list must be extended to include equality between men and women, respect for human rights, nonviolence, fair treatment of all groups, encouragement of healthy and nature-friendly lifestyles, and acceptance of freedom as an ideal limited by the need to avoid harming others. These value judgments are not distinctively Islamic, Judeo-Christian, or Hindu, or Asian, Western, or African. They are *human* values that have emerged, often independently, in many different places based on the cumulative life experience of generations.

Human societies and civilizations today differ chiefly in how well they achieve these positive values and suppress negative values. No society, obviously, has fully achieved the positive values, nor fully eliminated the negative ones.

But today's shared human values do not necessarily represent the ultimate expression of human morality. Rather, they provide a current progress report, a basis for critical discourse on a global level. By building understanding and agreement across cultures, such discourse can, eventually, lead to a further evolution of global morality.

In every society, many people, groups, and institutions respect and attempt to live by these positive values, and groups such as the Institute for Global Ethics are exploring how a global ethic can be improved and implemented everywhere.

Principle for global peace: Inclusion.

The Search for Global Peace and Order

Individuals and societies are so complex that it may seem foolhardy even to attempt the ambitious task of increasing human freedom and wellbeing. Yet what alternatives do we have? In the face of violent aggressions, injustice, threats to the environment, corporate corruption, poverty, and other ills of our present world, we can find no satisfactory answers in despair, resignation, and inaction.

Rather, by viewing human society as an experiment, and monitoring the results of our efforts, we humans can gradually refine our plans and actions to bring closer an ethical future world in which every individual can realistically expect a long, peaceful, and satisfactory life.

Given the similarity in human values, I suggest three principles that might contribute to such a future: *inclusion, skepticism*, and *social control*.

1. The Principle of Inclusion

Although many moral values are common to all cultures, people too often limit their ethical treatment of others to members of their own groups. Some, for example, only show respect or concern for other people who are of their own race, religion, nationality, or social class.

Such exclusion can have disastrous effects. It can justify cheating or lying to people who are not members of one's own ingroup. At worst, it can lead to demonizing them and making them targets of aggression and violence, treating them as less than human. Those victimized by this shortsighted and counterproductive mistreatment tend to pay it back or pass it on to others, creating a nasty world in which we all must live.

Today, our individual lives and those of our descendants are so closely tied to the rest of humanity that our identities ought to include a sense of kinship with the whole human race and our circle of caring ought to embrace the welfare of people everywhere. In practical terms, this means that we should devote more effort and resources to raising the quality of life for the worst-off members of the human community; reducing disease, poverty, and illiteracy; and creating equal opportunity for all men and women. Furthermore, our circle of caring ought to include protecting natural resources, because all human life depends on preserving the planet as a livable environment.

2. The Principle of Skepticism

One of the reasons why deadly conflicts continue to occur is what has been called "the delusion of certainty." Too many people refuse to consider any view but their own. And, being sure that they are right, such people can justify doing horrendous things to others.

As I claimed in "Who Is Really Evil?" (*The Futurist*, March–April 2004), we all need a healthy dose of skepticism, especially about our own beliefs. Admitting that we might be wrong can lead to asking questions, searching for better answers, and considering alternative possibilities.

Critical realism is a theory of knowledge I recommend for everyone, because it teaches us to be skeptical. It rests on the assumption that knowledge is never fixed and final, but changes as we learn and grow. Using evidence and reason, we can evaluate our current beliefs and develop new ones in response to new information and changing conditions. Such an approach is essential to futures studies, and indeed to any planning. If your cognitive maps of reality are wrong, then using them to navigate through life will not take you where you want to go.

Critical realism also invites civility among those who disagree, encouraging peaceful resolution of controversies by investigating and discussing facts. It teaches temperance and tolerance, because it recognizes that the discovery of hitherto unsuspected facts may overturn any of our "certainties," even long-cherished and strongly held beliefs.

3. The Principle of Social Control

Obviously, there is a worldwide need for both informal and formal social controls if we hope to achieve global peace and order. For most people most of the time, informal social controls may be sufficient. By the end of childhood, for example, the norms of behavior taught and reinforced by family, peers, school, and religious and other institutions are generally internalized by individuals.

Principle for global peace: Skepticism.

Yet every society must also recognize that informal norms and even formal codes of law are not enough to guarantee ethical behavior and to protect public safety in every instance. Although the threats we most often think of are from criminals, fanatics, and the mentally ill, even "normal" individuals may occasionally lose control and behave irrationally, or choose to ignore or break the law with potentially tragic results. Thus, ideally, police and other public law enforcement, caretaking, and rehabilitation services protect us not only from "others," but also from ourselves.

Likewise, a global society needs global laws, institutions to administer them, and police/peacekeepers to enforce them. Existing international systems of social control should be strengthened and expanded to prevent killing and destruction, while peaceful negotiation and compromise to resolve disputes are encouraged. A global peacekeeping force with a monopoly on the legitimate use of force, sanctioned by democratic institutions and due process of law, and operated competently and fairly, could help prevent the illegal use of force, maintain global order, and promote a climate of civil discourse. The actions of these global peacekeepers should, of course, be bound not only by law, but also by a code of ethics. Peacekeepers should use force as a last resort and only to the degree needed, while making every effort to restrain aggressors without harming innocent people or damaging the infrastructures of society.

Expanding international law, increasing the number and variety of multinational institutions dedicated to controlling armed conflict, and strengthening efforts by the United Nations and other organizations to encourage the spread of democracy, global cooperation, and peace, will help create a win-win world.

Conclusion: Values for a Positive Global Future

The "clash of civilizations" thesis exaggerates both the degree of cultural diversity in the world and how seriously cultural differences contribute to producing violent conflicts.

In fact, many purposes, patterns, and practices are shared by all—or nearly all—peoples of the world. There is an emerging global ethic, a set of shared values that includes:

- Individual responsibility.
- Treating others as we wish them to treat us.
- Respect for life.
- Economic and social justice.
- Nature-friendly ways of life.
- Honesty.
- Moderation.
- Freedom (expressed in ways that do not harm others).
- Tolerance for diversity.

The fact that deadly human conflicts continue in many places throughout the world is due less to the differences that separate societies than to some of these common human traits and values. All humans, for example, tend to feel loyalty to their group, and may easily overreact in the group's defense, leaving excluded

Toward Planetary Citizenship

A global economy that values competition over cooperation is an economy that will inevitably hurt people and destroy the environment. If the world's peoples are to get along better in the future, they need a better economic system, write peace activists Hazel Henderson and Daisaku Ikeda in *Planetary Citizenship*.

Henderson, an independent futurist, is one of the leading voices for a sustainable economic system; she is the author of many books and articles on her economic theories, including most recently *Beyond Globalization*. Ikeda is president of Soka Gakkai International, a peace and humanitarian organization based on Buddhist principles.

"Peace and nonviolence are now widely identified as fundamental to human survival," Henderson writes. "Competition must be balanced by cooperation and sharing. Even economists agree that peace, nonviolence, and human security are global public goods along with clean air and water, health and education—bedrock conditions for human well-being and development."

Along with materialistic values and competitive economics, the growing power of technology threatens a peaceful future, she warns. Humanity needs to find ways to harness these growing, "godlike" powers to lead us to genuine human development and away from destruction.

Henderson eloquently praises Ikeda's work at the United Nations to foster global cooperation on arms control, health, environmental protection, and other crucial issues. At the heart of these initiatives is the work of globally minded grass-root movements, or "planetary citizens," which have the potential to become the next global superpower, Henderson suggests.

One example of how nonmaterial values are starting to change how societies perceive their progress is the new Gross National Happiness indicators developed in Bhutan, which "[reflect] the goals of this Buddhist nation, [and] exemplify the importance of clarifying the goals and values of a society and creating indicators to measure what we treasure: health, happiness, education, human rights, family, country, harmony, peace, and environmental quality and restoration," Henderson writes.

The authors are optimistic that the grassroots movement will grow as more people look beyond their differences and seek common values and responsibilities for the future.

Source: *Planetary Citizenship: Your Values, Beliefs and Actions Can Shape a Sustainable World* by Hazel Henderson and Daisaku Ikeda. Middleway Press, 606 Wilshire Boulevard, Santa Monica, California 90401. 2004. 200 pages. $23.95. Order from the Futurist Bookshelf, www.wfs.org/bkshelf.htm.

"outsiders" feeling marginalized and victimized. Sadly, too, all humans are capable of rage and violent acts against others.

In past eras, the killing and destruction of enemies may have helped individuals and groups to survive. But in today's interconnected world that is no longer clearly the case. Today, violence and aggression too often are blunt and imprecise instruments that fail to achieve their intended purposes, and frequently blow back on the doers of violence.

The long-term trends of history are toward an ever-widening definition of individual identity (with some people already adopting self-identities on the widest scale as "human beings"), and toward the enlargement of individual circles of caring to embrace once distant or despised "outsiders." These trends are likely to continue, because they embody values—learned from millennia of human experience—that have come to be nearly universal: from the love of life itself to the joys of belonging to a community, from the satisfaction of self-fulfillment to the excitement of pursuing knowledge, and from individual happiness to social harmony.

How long will it take for the world to become a community where every human everywhere has a good chance to live a long and satisfying life? I do not know. But people of [goodwill] can do much today to help the process along. For example, we can begin by accepting responsibility for our own life choices: the goals and actions that do much to shape our future. And we can be more generous and understanding of what we perceive as mistakes and failures in the choices and behavior of others. We can include all people in our circle of concern, behave ethically toward everyone we deal with, recognize that every human being deserves to be treated with respect, and work to raise minimum standards of living for the least well-off people in the world.

We can also dare to question our personal views and those of the groups to which we belong, to test them and consider alternatives. Remember that knowledge is not constant, but subject to change in the light of new information and conditions. Be prepared to admit that anyone—even we ourselves—can be misinformed or reach a wrong conclusion from the limited evidence available. Because we can never have all the facts before us, let us admit to ourselves, whenever we take action, that mistakes and failure are possible. And let us be aware that certainty can become the enemy of decency.

In addition, we can control ourselves by exercising self-restraint to minimize mean or violent acts against others. Let us respond to offered friendship with honest gratitude and cooperation; but, when treated badly by another person, let us try, while defending ourselves from harm, to respond not with anger or violence but with verbal disapproval and the withdrawal of our cooperation with that person. So as not to begin a cycle of retaliation, let us not overreact. And let us always be willing to listen and to talk, to negotiate and to compromise.

Finally, we can support international law enforcement, global institutions of civil and criminal justice, international courts and global peacekeeping agencies, to build and strengthen nonviolent means for resolving disputes. Above all, we can work to ensure that global institutions are honest and fair and that they hold all countries—rich and poor, strong and weak—to the same high standards.

If the human community can learn to apply to all people the universal values that I have identified, then future terrorist acts like the events of September 11 may be minimized, because all people are more likely to be treated fairly and with dignity and because all voices will have peaceful ways to be heard, so some of the roots of discontent will be eliminated. When future terrorist acts do occur—and surely some will—they can be treated as the unethical and criminal acts that they are.

There is no clash of civilizations. Most people of the world, whatever society, culture, civilization, or religion they revere or feel a part of, simply want to live—and let others live—in peace and harmony. To achieve this, all of us must realize that the human community is inescapably bound together. More and more, as Martin Luther King Jr. reminded us, whatever affects one, sooner or later affects all.

WENDELL BELL is professor emeritus of sociology and senior research scientist at Yale University's Center for Comparative Research. He is the author of more than 200 articles and nine books, including the two-volume *Foundations of Futures Studies* (Transaction Publishers, now available in paperback 2003, 2004). His address is Department of Sociology, Yale University, P.O. Box 208265, New Haven, Connecticut 06520. E-mail wendell.bell@yale.edu.

This article draws from an essay originally published in the *Journal of Futures Studies 6*.

Life, Religion and Everything

Biologist and author Rupert Sheldrake believes that the world's religions have a crucial role in restoring the earth's ecological balance. Laura Sevier meets the man trying to broker a better relationship between God, man, science and the natural world.

LAURA SEVIER

A long, low drone fills the air. We are all chanting the same sound: OOOOOOOHHHHHHHH. Whistling overtones start to ring out above the group sound and then a lone female voice sings out:

Where I sit is holy

Holy is the ground

Forest mountain river listen to my sound

Great spirit circling all around.

The voice then invites everyone to join in and we sing this verse seven or eight times. Then there is silence.

It's not often you attend a talk given by an eminent scientist that begins with a session of Mongolian overtone chanting followed by a Native American Indian song about the holiness of the earth. It's especially surreal given that we're sitting on neat little rows of chairs in a Unitarian Church in Hampstead, in London.

I was there to listen to renowned English biologist Rupert Sheldrake talk about how the world's religions can learn to live with ecological integrity. The chanting, it appears, is the warm-up act, led by Sheldrake's wife, Jill Purce, a music healer.

So far so extraordinary, but then Sheldrake is no ordinary man. A respected scientist from a largely conventional educational background, he's devoted much of the past 17 years of his life to studying the sort of phenomena that most 'serious' scientists dismiss out of hand, such as telepathy, our 'seventh sense'. But religion? Given the current trend for militant atheism within science, I'm amazed. Besides, isn't religion incompatible with science? Not according to Sheldrake, an Anglican Christian. 'One of my main concerns is the opening up of science. Another is exploring the connections between science and spirituality,' he says.

His take on religion—and science—is refreshingly unorthodox precisely because it factors in a crucial new element:

nature. 'The thrust of my work is trying to break out of the mechanistic view of nature as inanimate, dead and machine-like.' In fact his 1991 book *The Rebirth of Nature: the Greening of Science and God* (Inner Traditions Bear & Company, £11.99) was devoted to showing 'how we can once again think of nature as alive'—and sacred.

The Sacred Earth

Our culture seems to have lost touch with any idea of the land as being alive and sacred and anyone who considers it to be so is often branded a tree-hugging hippie and treated with ridicule or suspicion. Land is mostly valued purely in economic terms. Yet no value is attributed to the irreplaceable benefits derived from the normal functioning of the natural world, which assures the stability of our climate, the fertility of our soil, the replenishment of our water.

Our culture seems to have lost any idea of the land being alive and sacred, and values it only in economic terms.

Religion has, until recently, remained pretty quiet on the issue.

As Edward Goldsmith wrote in the *Ecologist* in 2000, mainstream religions have become increasingly 'otherworldly'. They have 'scarcely any interest' in the natural world at all. Traditionally, religion used to play an integral role in linking people to the natural world, imbuing people with the knowledge and values that make caring for it a priority. 'Mainstream religion' Goldsmith wrote 'has failed the earth. It has lost its way, and needs to return to its roots.'

So if the world's religions are to play a part in saving what remains of the natural world, they not only need to return to their roots but also to confront the threat and scale of the global ecological crisis we now face. This means being open to a dialogue with science. 'No religions, when they were growing up, had to deal with our present situation and ecological crisis,' says Sheldrake. 'People thought they could take the earth more or less for granted. Certainly the idea that human beings could transform the climate through their actions was unheard of. This is a new situation for everybody, for religious people and scientists, for traditional cultures and modern scientific ones. We're all in this together.'

Environmental Sin

'Religion and Ecology' is now a subject of serious academic study. The Forum on Religion and Ecology at Yale University, for example, recently explored the ecological dimension of all the major world religions. The ongoing environmental crisis has sparked a 'bringing together' of the world's religions in a series of interreligious meetings and conferences around the world on the theme of 'Religion, Science and the Environment', exploring the response that religious communities can make. These brought together scientists, bishops, rabbis, marine biologists and philosophers in a way that, according to Sheldrake, 'really worked'.

Within many religions, including all branches of Christianity, there's an attempt to recover that sense of connection with nature. 'There's a lot going on,' says Sheldrake, 'even within the group seen as lagging the furthest behind—the American Evangelicals, who are somewhat retrogressive in relation to the environment.'

Some evangelicals who believe in the Rapture and think the world is soon to end have expressed the view that there's no point in attempting to save the environment because it's all going to be discarded like a used tissue.

But a more environmentally friendly view is held by the Evangelical Environmental Network (EEN), a group of individuals and organisations including World Vision, World Relief and the International Bible Society. An Evangelical Declaration on the Care of Creation, its landmark credo published in 1991, begins: 'We believe that biblical faith is essential to the solution of our ecological problems. . . . Because we worship and honour the Creator we seek to cherish and care for the creation. Because we have sinned, we have failed our stewardship of creation. Therefore we repent of the way we have polluted, distorted or destroyed so much of the Creator's work.'

It then commits to work for reconciliation of people and the healing of suffering creation.

The belief that environmental destruction is a sin isn't a new concept. The spirituality of native American Indians, for instance, is a land-based one. In this culture, the world is animate, natural things are alive and everything is imbued with spirit.

Nature informs us and it is our obligation to read nature as you would a book, to feel it as you would a poem.

In the words of John Mohawk, native American chief: 'The natural world is our Bible. We don't have chapters and verses; we have trees and fish and animals . . . The Indian sense of natural law is that nature informs us and it is our obligation to read nature as you would a book, to feel nature as you would a poem, to touch nature as you would yourself, to be part of that and step into its cycles as much as you can.'

Most importantly, environmental destruction is seen as a sin.

Loss of the Sacred

The question is, how did we lose the sacred connection with the natural world? Where did religion and culture go wrong? According to Sheldrake, the break began in the 16th century. Until then there were pagan festivals, such as May Day, that celebrated the seasons and the fertility of the land; there were nature shrines, holy wells and sacred places.

But with the Protestant Reformation in the 16th century there was an attempt by the reformers, who couldn't find anything about these 'pagan' practices in the Bible, to stamp them out. In the 17th century the Puritans brought a further wave of suppression of these things—banning, for example, Maypole dancing (Maypoles being a symbol of male fertility). 'There was a deliberate attempt to get rid of all the things that connected people to the sacredness of the land and it largely succeeded,' says Sheldrake.

Another factor he believes severed our connection is the view of nature as a machine. 'From the time of our remotest ancestors until the 17th century, it was taken for granted that the world of nature was alive, that the universe was alive and that all animals were not only alive but had souls—the word "animal" comes from the word "anima", meaning soul. This was the standard view, even within the Church. Medieval Christianity was based on an animate form of nature—a kind of Christian animism.'

But this model of a living world was replaced by the idea of the universe as a machine, an idea that stems from the philosophy of Rene Descartes. Nature was no more than dead matter and everything was viewed as mechanical, governed by mathematical principles instead of animating souls.

'This mechanistic view of nature,' Sheldrake says, 'is an extremely limiting and alienating one. It forces the whole of our understanding of nature into a machine metaphor—the universe as a machine, animals and plants as machines, you as a machine, the brain as a machine. It's a very man-centred metaphor, as only people make machines. So looking at nature in this way projects one aspect of human activity onto the whole of nature.'

Hinduism

- The Vedas (ancient Hindu scriptures) describe how the creator god Vishnu made the universe so that every element is interlinked. A disturbance in one part will upset the balance and impact all the other elements.
- Three important principles of Hindu environmentalism are *yajna* (sacrifice), *dhana* (giving) and *tapas* (penance).
- *Yajna* entails that you should sacrifice your needs for the sake of others, for nature, the poor or future generations.
- *Dhana* entails that whatever you consume you must give back.
- *Tapas* commends self-restraint in your lifestyle.
- Mother Earth is personified in the Vedas as the goddess Bhumi, or Prithvi.
- Hindu businessman Balbir Mathur, inspired by his faith, founded Trees for Life (www.treesforlife.org), a non-profit movement that plants fruit trees in developing countries, to provide sustainable and environmentally-friendly livelihoods.

Islam

- Allah has appointed humankind *khalifah* (steward) over the created world.
- This responsibility is called *al-amanah* (the trust) and Man will be held accountable to it at the Day of Judgment.
- The Qur'an warns against disturbing God's natural balance: 'Do no mischief on the earth after it hath been set in order' (7:56).
- Shari'ah (Islamic law) designates *haram* zones, used to contain urban development in protection of natural resources, and *hima,* specific conservation areas.
- The Islamic foundation for ecology and environmental sciences www.ifes.org.uk publishes a newsletter called *Eco Islam* and organised an organic *iftar* (the evening meal during Ramadan) in 2006.
- In 2000, IFEES led an Islamic educational programme on the Muslim-majority island of Misali, in response to the destruction to the aquatic ecosystem by over-fishing and the use of dynamite in coral reefs. The environmental message based on the Qur'an initiated sustainable fishing practices.

Judaism

- The Torah prohibits harming God's earth: 'Do not cut down trees even to prevent ambush, do not foul waters, or burn crops even to cause an enemy's submission' (Devarim 20:19)
- It teaches humility in the face of nature: 'Ask the beasts, and they will teach you; the birds of the sky, and they will tell you; or speak to the earth and it will teach you; the fish of the sea, they will inform you' (Job 12:7-9)
- The Talmudic law *bal tashchit* (do not destroy) was developed by Jewish scholars into a series of specific prohibitions against wasteful actions.
- The Noah Project (www.noahproject.org.uk) is a UK-based Jewish environmental organisation, engaged in hands-on conservation work, and promoting environmental responsibility by emphasising the environmental dimensions of Jewish holidays such as Tu B'Shevat (New Year of the Trees).

Christianity

- Genesis gives a picture of God creating the heavens and earth—and when it was all finished, 'God saw all that he had made, and it was very good.' (1:31) Having made man, he 'put him in the Garden of Eden to work it and take care of it' (2:15).
- Romans 8:19-22 has been interpreted as a message of redemption for the environment, calling on Christians to work towards the time when 'the creation itself will be liberated from its bondage to decay'.
- At the UN Rio Earth Summit in 1992, the World Council of Churches formed a working group on climate change. Their manifesto expresses a concern for justice towards developing countries, who are disproportionately affected by climate change, to future generations and to the world.
- www.christian-ecology.org.uk represents Churches Together in Britain and Ireland. It includes links and a daily prayer guide with references both to the Bible and to scientific and news data. Operation Noah is the climate change campaign.

Buddhism

- Buddhist religious ecology is based on three principles: nature as teacher, as a spiritual force, and as a way of life.
- Buddhists believe that nature can teach us about the interdependence and impermanence of life, and that living near to and in tune with nature gives us spiritual strength.
- Buddha commended frugality, avoiding waste, and non-violence.
- Buddhists believe that man should be in harmonious interaction with nature, not a position of authority.
- Philosopher Dr Simon James, based at Durham University, has studied the Buddhist basis of environmentalism and virtue ethics. A spiritually enlightened individual shows compassion, equanimity and humility—qualities that are intrinsic to an environmentally friendly lifestyle.
- The Zen Environmental Studies Institute (www.mro.org/zesi) in New York runs programmes in nature study and environmental advocacy, informed by Zen Buddhist meditation.

Baha'ism

- Bahá'u'lláh, founder of the Baha'i faith and regarded as a messenger from God, stated 'nature is God's Will and is its expression in and through the contingent world' (the Tablets of Baha'u'llah).
- Baha'is believe that the world reflects God's qualities and attributes and therefore must be cherished.
- The Baha'i Office of the Environment states: 'Baha'u'llah's promise that civilisation will exist on this planet for a minimum of 5,000 centuries makes it unconscionable to ignore the long-term impact of decisions made today. The world community must, therefore, learn to make use of the earth's natural resources . . . in a manner that ensures sustainability into the distant reaches of time.'
- The Barli Rural Development Institute in India was inspired by Baha'i social activism. It has trained hundreds of rural women in conservation strategies such as rainwater harvesting and solar cooking.
- www.onecountry.org is the newsletter of the Bahai international community.

It is this view, he says, that led to our current crisis. 'If you assume that nature is inanimate, then nothing natural has a life, purpose, or value. Natural resources are there to be developed, and the only value placed on them is by market forces and official planners. And if you assume that only humans are conscious, only humans have reason, and therefore only humans have true value, then it's fine to have animals in factory farms and to exploit the world in whatever way you like, and if you do conserve any bit of the earth then you have to conserve it with human ends in mind. Everything is justified in human terms.'

The mechanistic theory has become a kind of religion that is built into the official orthodoxy of economic progress and, through technology's successes, is now triumphant on a global scale. 'So,' says Sheldrake, 'this combination of science, technology, secular humanism and rationalism—all these philosophies that dominate the modern age—open the way for untrammelled exploitation of the earth that is going on everywhere today.'

The Living Universe

It seems like a pretty bleak vision. But there is an alternative: to allow our own experience and intuition to help us see nature and the universe as alive. 'Many people have emotional connections with particular places associated with their childhood, or feel an empathy with animals or plants, or are inspired by the beauty of nature, or experience a mystical sense of unity with the natural world,' Sheldrake says. 'Our private relationship with nature presupposes that nature is alive.'

In other words, we don't need to be told by science, religion or anyone that it is alive, valuable and worthy of respect and reverence. Deep down, we can feel it for ourselves. Many people have urges to get 'back to nature' in some way, to escape the confines of concrete and head for the hills, the sea, a park or even a small patch of grass. These impulses are moving us in the right direction.

Another way forward is through new revolutionary insights within science. 'Science itself is leading us away from this view of nature as a machine towards a much more organic view of living in the world,' says Sheldrake. 'The changes are happening in independent parts of science for different reasons, but all of them are pointing in the same direction: the view of a very organic, creative world.'

The big bang theory gives a new model of the universe that is more like a developing organism, growing spontaneously and forming totally new structures within it. The concept of quantum physics has broken open many of our ideas of the mechanistic universe. The old idea of determinism has given way to indeterminism and chaos theory. The old idea of the earth as dead has given way to Gaia, the living earth. The old idea of the universe as uncreative has given way to the new idea of creative evolution, first in the realm of living things, through Darwin, and now we see that the whole cosmos is in creative evolution. So, if the whole universe is alive, if the universe is like a great organism, then everything within it is best understood as alive.

Encouraging Dialogue

This has opened up new possibilities for a dialogue between science and religion. 'These changing frontiers of science are making it much easier to see that we're all part of, and dependent on, a living earth; and for those of us who follow a religion, to see the living God as the living world,' says Sheldrake. Such insights breathe new meaning into traditional religions, their practices and seasonal festivals.

For example, all religions provide opportunities for giving thanks, both through simple everyday rituals, like saying grace, and also in collective acts of thanksgiving. These expressions of gratitude can help to remind us that we have much to be thankful for. But as Sheldrake points out, 'It's hard to feel a sense of gratitude for an inanimate, mechanical world.'

Helping people see the land as sacred again, Sheldrake maintains, is one of the major roles of religion. 'They all point towards a larger whole: the wholeness of creation and a larger story than our own individual story. All religions tell stories about our place in the world, our relation to other people and to the world in which we live. In that sense all religions relate us to the earth and the heavens.'

Sheldrake thinks we need stories: 'It's part of our nature. Science gives us stories, too—the universe story. So does TV, fiction, books.' And these stories, in his view, unify us in a way that, for instance, some New Age practices (such as personal shrines) don't. While those things have personal value, they don't have the unifying function that a traditional religion does. 'When you go to a Hindu festival or pilgrimage, you see thousands of people coming together, the whole community united by a common story or a celebration of a sacred place.'

The fascinating thing about Rupert Sheldrake is his ability to assimilate ideas from an array of different subjects that are normally kept separate, draw new connections and conclusions and open up new dialogues. He's certainly not afraid to explore new territory or use new metaphors. Thus the big bang is like 'the primal orgasm' or like 'the breaking open of the cosmic egg'.

When talking about the discovery that 95 per cent of the universe is 'dark matter' or unknown, he says, 'it is as if science has discovered the cosmic unconscious'. He embraces the idea of 'Mother Nature'—in fact he believes the old intuition of nature as Mother still affects our personal responses to it and conditions our response to the ecological crisis. 'We feel uncomfortable when we recognise that we are polluting our own Mother; it is easier to rephrase the problem in terms of "inadequate waste management".' He sees the green movement as one aspect of 'Mother Nature reasserting herself, whether we like it or not.'

One of the most significant implications of Sheldrake's worldview is that it connects people to the natural world and 'if people feel more connected to the world around them, they might be less likely to accept its destruction,' he says. Reframing our view to encompass a world that is alive also, effectively, puts humans back in our proper place in the scheme of things.

Sheldrake's scientific and philosophical investigation is fuelled by a passionate concern for all of life, and his vision of life expands to the cosmos. If the earth is alive, if the universe is alive, if solar systems are alive, if galaxies are alive, if planets are alive, then causing harm to any of these systems really is a sin; one that we have committed all too willingly for far too long.

For Further Information

Rupert Sheldrake: www.sheldrake.org

Forum on Religion and Ecology: http://environment.harvard.edu/ religion—the ecological dimension of various religions

The Alliance of Religions and Conservation (ARC): www.arcworld.org

LAURA SEVIER is a freelance journalist and regular contributor to the *Ecologist*.

Don't Blame the Caveman
Why Do We Rape, Kill and Sleep Around?

The fault, dear Darwin, lies not in our ancestors, but in ourselves.

SHARON BEGLEY

Among Scientists at the University of New Mexico that spring, rape was in the air. One of the professors, biologist Randy Thornhill, had just coauthored *A Natural History of Rape: Biological Bases of Sexual Coercion*, which argued that rape is (in the vernacular of evolutionary biology) an adaptation, a trait encoded by genes that confers an advantage on anyone who possesses them. Back in the late Pleistocene epoch 100,000 years ago, the 2000 book contended, men who carried rape genes had a reproductive and evolutionary edge over men who did not: they sired children not only with willing mates, but also with unwilling ones, allowing them to leave more offspring (also carrying rape genes) who were similarly more likely to survive and reproduce, unto the nth generation. That would be us. And that is why we carry rape genes today. The family trees of prehistoric men lacking rape genes petered out.

The argument was well within the bounds of evolutionary psychology. Founded in the late 1980s in the ashes of sociobiology, this field asserts that behaviors that conferred a fitness advantage during the era when modern humans were evolving are the result of hundreds of genetically based cognitive "modules" pre-programmed in the brain. Since they are genetic, these modules and the behaviors they encode are heritable— passed down to future generations—and, together, constitute a universal human nature that describes how people think, feel and act, from the nightclubs of Manhattan to the farms of the Amish, from the huts of New Guinea aborigines to the madrassas of Karachi. Evolutionary psychologists do not have a time machine, of course. So to figure out which traits were adaptive during the Stone Age, and therefore bequeathed to us like a questionable family heirloom, they make logical guesses. Men who were promiscuous back then were more evolutionarily fit, the researchers reasoned, since men who spread their seed widely left more descendants. By similar logic, evolutionary psychologists argued, women who were monogamous were fitter; by being choosy about their mates and picking only those with good genes, they could have healthier children. Men attracted to young, curvaceous babes were fitter because such women were the most fertile; mating with dumpy, barren hags

> ## Rape
>
> ### Old Thinking
> Men who rape produce more offspring, ensuring the survival of their DNA—including the rape gene.
>
> ### New Thinking
> Rapists were often ostracized or killed and their offspring abandoned.

is not a good way to grow a big family tree. Women attracted to high-status, wealthy males were fitter; such men could best provide for the kids, who, spared starvation, would grow up to have many children of their own. Men who neglected or even murdered their stepchildren (and killed their unfaithful wives) were fitter because they did not waste their resources on nonrelatives. And so on, to the fitness-enhancing value of rape. We in the 21st century, asserts evo psych, are operating with Stone Age minds.

Over the years these arguments have attracted legions of critics who thought the science was weak and the message (what philosopher David Buller of Northern Illinois University called "a get-out-of-jail-free card" for heinous behavior) pernicious. But the reaction to the rape book was of a whole different order. Biologist Joan Roughgarden of Stanford University called it "the latest 'evolution made me do it' excuse for criminal behavior from evolutionary psychologists." Feminists, sex-crime prosecutors and social scientists denounced it at rallies, on television, and in the press.

Among those sucked into the rape debate that spring was anthropologist Kim Hill, then Thornhill's colleague at UNM and now at Arizona State University. For decades Hill has studied the Ache, hunter-gatherer tribesmen in Paraguay. "I saw Thornhill all the time," Hill told me at a barbecue at an ASU conference in April. "He kept saying that he thought rape was a special cognitive adaptation, but the arguments for that just seemed like more sloppy thinking by evolutionary psychology." But how to test the claim that rape increased a man's fitness? From its inception, evolutionary psychology had warned that behaviors that were evolutionarily advantageous 100,000 years ago (a sweet tooth, say) might be bad for survival today (causing obesity and thence infertility), so there was no point in measuring whether that trait makes people more evolutionarily fit today. Even if it doesn't, evolutionary psychologists argue, the trait might have been adaptive long ago and therefore still be our genetic legacy. An unfortunate one, perhaps, but still our legacy. Short of a time machine, the hypothesis was impossible to disprove. Game, set, and match to evo psych.

Or so it seemed. But Hill had something almost as good as a time machine. He had the Ache, who live much as humans did 100,000 years ago. He and two colleagues therefore calculated how rape would affect the evolutionary prospects of a 25-year-old Ache. (They didn't observe any rapes, but did a what-if calculation based on measurements of, for instance, the odds that a woman is able to conceive on any given day.) The scientists were generous to the rape-as-adaptation claim, assuming that rapists target only women of reproductive age, for instance, even though in reality girls younger than 10 and women over 60 are often victims. Then they calculated rape's fitness costs and benefits. Rape costs a man fitness points if the victim's husband or other relatives kill him, for instance. He loses fitness points, too, if the mother refuses to raise a child of rape, and if being a known rapist (in a small hunter-gatherer tribe, rape and rapists are public knowledge) makes others less likely to help him find food. Rape increases a man's evolutionary fitness based on the chance that a rape victim is fertile (15 percent), that she will conceive (a 7 percent chance), that she will not miscarry (90 percent) and that she will not let the baby die even though it is the child of rape (90 percent). Hill then ran the numbers on the reproductive costs and benefits of rape. It wasn't even close: the cost exceeds the benefit by a factor of 10. "That makes the likelihood that rape is an evolved adaptation extremely low," says Hill. "It just wouldn't have made sense for men in the Pleistocene to use rape as a reproductive strategy, so the argument that it's preprogrammed into us doesn't hold up."

These have not been easy days for evolutionary psychology. For years the loudest critics have been social scientists, feminists, and liberals offended by the argument that humans are preprogrammed to rape, to kill unfaithful girlfriends and the like. (This was a reprise of the bitter sociobiology debates of the 1970s and 1980s. When Harvard biologist Edward O. Wilson proposed that there exists a biologically based human nature, and that it included such traits as militarism and male domination of women, left-wing activists—including eminent biologists in his own department—assailed it as an attempt "to provide a genetic justification of the status quo and of existing privileges for certain groups according to class, race, or sex" analogous to the scientific justification for Nazi eugenics.) When Thornhill appeared on the *Today* show to talk about his rape book, for instance, he was paired with a sex-crimes prosecutor, leaving the impression that do-gooders might not like his thesis but offering no hint of how scientifically unsound it is.

Lust

Old Thinking
Men desire women with an hourglass figure.

New Thinking
Only in cultures where women are economically dependent does the 36-25-38 ideal prevail.

That is changing. Evo psych took its first big hit in 2005, when NIU's Buller exposed flaw after fatal flaw in key studies underlying its claims, as he laid out in his book *Adapting Minds*. Anthropological studies such as Hill's on the Ache, shooting down the programmed-to-rape idea, have been accumulating. And brain scientists have pointed out that there is no evidence our gray matter is organized the way evo psych claims, with hundreds of specialized, preprogrammed modules. Neuroscientist Roger Bingham of the University of California, San Diego, who describes himself as a once devout "member of the Church of Evolutionary Psychology" (in 1996 he created and hosted a multimillion-dollar PBS series praising the field) has come out foursquare against it, accusing some of its adherents of an "evangelical" fervor. Says evolutionary biologist Massimo Pigliucci of Stony Brook University, "evolutionary stories of human behavior make for a good narrative, but not good science."

Like other critics, he has no doubt that evolution shaped the human brain. How could it be otherwise, when evolution has shaped every other human organ? But evo psych's claims that human behavior is constrained by mental modules that calcified in the Stone Age make sense "only if the environmental challenges remain static enough to sculpt an instinct over evolutionary time," Pigliucci points out. If the environment, including the social environment, is instead dynamic rather than static—which all evidence suggests—then the only kind of mind that makes humans evolutionarily fit is one that is flexible and responsive, able to figure out a way to make trade-offs, survive, thrive, and reproduce in whatever social and physical environment it finds itself in. In some environments it might indeed be adaptive for women to seek sugar daddies. In some, it might be adaptive for stepfathers to kill their stepchildren. In some, it might be adaptive for men to be promiscuous. But not in all. And if that's the case, then there is no universal human nature as evo psych defines it.

That is what a new wave of studies has been discovering, slaying assertions about universals right and left. One evopsych claim that captured the public's imagination—and a 1996 cover story in NEWSWEEK—is that men have a mental module that causes them to prefer women with a waist-to-hip ratio of 0.7 (a 36-25-36 figure, for instance). Reprising the rape debate, social scientists and policymakers who worried that this would send impressionable young women scurrying for a measuring tape and a how-to book on bulimia could only sputter about how pernicious this message was, but not that it was scientifically wrong. To the contrary, proponents of this idea had gobs of data in their favor. Using their favorite guinea pigs—American college students—they found that men, shown pictures of different female body types, picked Ms. 36-25-36 as their sexual ideal. The studies, however, failed to rule out the possibility that the preference was not innate—human nature—but, rather, the product of exposure to mass culture and the messages it sends about what's beautiful. Such basic flaws, notes Bingham, "led to complaints that many of these experiments seemed a little less than rigorous to be underpinning an entire new field."

Later studies, which got almost no attention, indeed found that in isolated populations in Peru and Tanzania, men consider hourglass women sickly looking. They prefer 0.9s—heavier women. And last December, anthropologist Elizabeth Cashdan of the University of Utah reported in the journal *Current Anthropology* that men now prefer this non-hourglass shape in countries where women tend to be economically independent (Britain and Denmark) and in some non-Western societies where women bear the responsibility for finding food. Only in countries where women are economically dependent on men (such as Japan, Greece, and Portugal) do men have a strong preference for Barbie. (The United States is in the middle.) Cashdan puts it this way: which body type men prefer "should *depend on* [italics added] the degree to which they want their mates to be strong, tough, economically successful and politically competitive."

Depend on? The very phrase is anathema to the dogma of a universal human nature. But it is the essence of an emerging, competing field. Called behavioral ecology, it starts from the premise that social and environmental forces select for various behaviors that optimize people's fitness in a given environment. Different environment, different behaviors—and different human "natures." That's why men prefer Ms. 36-25-36 in some cultures (where women are, to exaggerate only a bit, decorative objects) but not others (where women bring home salaries or food they've gathered in the jungle).

And it's why the evo-psych tenet that men have an inherited mental module that causes them to prefer young, beautiful women while women have one that causes them to prefer older, wealthy men also falls apart. As 21st-century Western women achieve professional success and gain financial independence, their mate preference changes, scientists led by Fhionna Moore at Scotland's University of St Andrews reported in 2006 in the journal *Evolution and Human Behaviour*. The more financially independent a woman is, the more likely she is to choose a partner based on looks more than bank balance—kind of like (some) men. (Yes, growing sexual equality in the economic realm means that women, too, are free to choose partners based on how hot they are, as the cougar phenomenon suggests.) Although that finding undercuts evo psych, it supports the "it depends" school of behavioral ecology, which holds that natural selection chose general intelligence and flexibility, not mental modules preprogrammed with preferences and behaviors. "Evolutionary psychology ridicules the notion that the brain could have evolved to be an all-purpose fitness-maximizing mechanism," says Hill. "But that's exactly what we keep finding."

One of the uglier claims of evo psych is that men have a mental module to neglect and even kill their stepchildren. Such

Infanticide

Old Thinking
Men are predisposed to kill their stepchildren rather than waste precious resources on another man's DNA.

New Thinking
A man who supports his stepchildren improves his chances of mating with their mother, and the kids themselves can become valuable source of labor.

behavior was adaptive back when humans were evolving, goes the popular version of this argument, because men who invested in stepchildren wasted resources they could expend on their biological children. Such kindly stepfathers would, over time, leave fewer of their own descendents, causing "support your stepchildren" genes to die out. Men with genes that sculpted the "abandon stepchildren" mental module were evolutionarily fitter, so their descendants—us—also have that preprogrammed module. The key evidence for this claim comes from studies showing that stepchildren under the age of 5 are 40 times more likely to be abused than biological children.

Those studies have come under fire, however, for a long list of reasons. For instance, many child-welfare records do not indicate who the abuser was; at least some abused stepchildren are victims of their mother, not the stepfather, the National Incidence Study of Child Abuse and Neglect reported in 2005. That suggests that records inflate the number of instances of abuse by stepfathers. Also, authorities are suspicious of stepfathers; if a child living in a stepfamily dies of maltreatment, they are nine times more likely to record it as such than if the death occurs in a home with only biological parents, found a 2002 study led by Buller examining the records of every child who died in Colorado from 1990 to 1998. That suggests that child-abuse data undercount instances of abuse by biological fathers. Finally, a 2008 study in Sweden found that many men who kill stepchildren are (surprise) mentally ill. It's safe to assume that single mothers do not exactly get their pick of the field when it comes to remarrying. If the men they wed are therefore more likely to be junkies, drunks, and psychotic, then any additional risk to stepchildren reflects that fact, and not a universal mental module that tells men to abuse their new mate's existing kids. Martin Daly and Margo Wilson of Canada's McMaster University, whose work led to the idea that men have a mental module for neglecting stepchildren, now disavow the claim that such abuse was ever adaptive. But, says Daly, "attempts to deny that [being a stepfather] is a risk factor for maltreatment are simply preposterous and occasionally, as in the writings of David Buller, dishonest."

If the data on child abuse by stepfathers seem inconsistent, that's exactly the point. In some circumstances, it may indeed be adaptive to get rid of the other guy's children. In other circumstances, it is more adaptive to love and support them. Again, it depends. New research in places as different as American cities and the villages of African hunter-gatherers shows that it's common for men to care and provide for their stepchildren. What seems to characterize these situations, says Hill, is marital instability: men and women pair off, have children, then break up. In such a setting, the flexible human mind finds ways "to attract or maintain mating access to the mother," Hill explains. Or, more crudely, be nice to a woman's kids and she'll sleep with you, which maximizes a man's fitness. Kill her kids and she's likely to take it badly, cutting you off and leaving your sperm unable to fulfill their Darwinian mission. And in societies that rely on relatives to help raise kids, "it doesn't make sense to destroy a 10-year-old stepkid since he could be a helper," Hill points out. "The fitness cost of raising a stepchild until he is old enough to help is much, much less than evolutionary biologists have claimed. Biology is more complicated than these simplistic scenarios saying that killing stepchildren is an adaptation that enhances a man's fitness."

Even the notion that being a brave warrior helps a man get the girls and leave many offspring has been toppled. Until missionaries moved in in 1958, the Waorani tribe of the Ecuadoran Amazon had the highest rates of homicide known to science: 39 percent of women and 54 percent of men were killed by other Waorani, often in blood feuds that lasted generations. "The conventional wisdom had been that the more raids a man participated in, the more wives he would have and the more descendants he would leave," says anthropologist Stephen Beckerman of Pennsylvania State University. But after painstakingly constructing family histories and the raiding and killing records of 95 warriors, he and his colleagues reported last month in *Proceedings of the National Academy of Sciences,* they turned that belief on its head. "The badass guys make terrible husband material," says Beckerman. "Women don't prefer them as husbands and they become the targets of counterraids, which tend to kill their wives and children, too." As a result, the über-warriors leave fewer descendants—the currency of evolutionary fitness—than less aggressive men. Tough-guy behavior may have conferred fitness in some environments, but not in others. It depends. "The message for the evolutionary-psychology guys," says Beckerman, "is that there was no single environment in which humans evolved" and therefore no single human nature.

I can't end the list of evo-psych claims that fall apart under scientific scrutiny without mentioning jealousy. Evo psych argues that jealousy, too, is an adaptation with a mental module all its own, designed to detect and thwart threats to reproductive success. But men's and women's jealousy modules supposedly differ. A man's is designed to detect sexual infidelity: a woman who allows another man to impregnate her takes her womb out of service for at least nine months, depriving her mate of reproductive opportunities. A woman's jealousy module is tuned to emotional infidelity, but she doesn't much care if her mate is unfaithful; a man, being a promiscuous cad, will probably stick with wife No. 1 and their kids even if he is sexually unfaithful, but may well abandon them if he actually falls in love with another woman.

Let's not speculate on the motives that (mostly male) evolutionary psychologists might have in asserting that their wives are programmed to not really care if they sleep around, and

---

Lust

Old Thinking
Women are attracted to alpha males.

New Thinking
Warring types make terrible mates: they leave behind widows and orphans who are often the target of rivals' counterattacks.

---

turn instead to the evidence. In questionnaires, more men than women say they'd be upset more by sexual infidelity than emotional infidelity, by a margin of more than 2-to-1, David Buss of the University of Texas found in an early study of American college students. But men are evenly split on which kind of infidelity upsets them more: half find it more upsetting to think of their mate falling in love with someone else; half find it more upsetting to think of her sleeping with someone else. Not very strong evidence for the claim that men, as a species, care more about sexual infidelity. And in some countries, notably Germany and the Netherlands, the percentage of men who say they find sexual infidelity more upsetting than the emotional kind is only 28 percent and 23 percent. Which suggests that, once again, it depends: in cultures with a relaxed view of female sexuality, men do not get all that upset if a woman has a brief, meaningless fling. It does not portend that she will leave him. It is much more likely that both men and women are wired to detect behavior that threatens their bond, but what that behavior is depends on culture. In a society where an illicit affair portends the end of a relationship, men should indeed be wired to care about that. In a society where that's no big deal, they shouldn't—and, it seems, don't. New data on what triggers jealousy in women also undercut the simplistic evo-psych story. Asked which upsets them more—imagining their partner having acrobatic sex with another woman or falling in love with her—only 13 percent of U.S. women, 12 percent of Dutch women and 8 percent of German women chose door No. 2. So much for the handy "she's wired to not really care if I sleep around" excuse.

Critics of evo psych do not doubt that men and women are wired to become jealous. A radar for infidelity would indeed be adaptive. But the evidence points toward something gender-neutral. Men and women have both evolved the ability to distinguish between behavior that portends abandonment and behavior that does not, and to get upset only at the former. Which behavior is which depends on the society.

Evolutionary psychology is not going quietly. It has had the field to itself, especially in the media, for almost two decades. In large part that was because early critics, led by the late evolutionary biologist Stephen Jay Gould, attacked it with arguments that went over the heads of everyone but about 19 experts in evolutionary theory. It isn't about to give up that hegemony. Thornhill is adamant that rape is an adaptation, despite Hill's results from his Ache study. "If a particular trait or behavior is organized to do something," as he believes rape is, "then it is an

Infidelity

Old Thinking
Men prize sexual fidelity, while women prefer emotional constancy.

New Thinking
Both men and women are concerned with threats to their bond, which vary greatly by culture: one country's harmless tryst is another's irreconcilable differences.

adaptation and so was selected for by evolution," he told me. And in the new book *Spent,* evolutionary psychologist Geoffrey Miller of the University of New Mexico reasserts the party line, arguing that "males have much more to gain from many acts of intercourse with multiple partners than do females," and there is a "universal sex difference in human mate choice criteria, with men favoring younger, fertile women, and women favoring older, higher-status, richer men."

On that point, the evidence instead suggests that both sexes prefer mates around their own age, adjusted for the fact that men mature later than women. If the male mind were adapted to prefer the most fertile women, then AARP-eligible men should marry 23-year-olds, which—Anna Nicole Smith and J. Howard Marshall not-withstanding—they do not, instead preferring women well past their peak fertility. And, interestingly, when Miller focuses on the science rather than tries to sell books, he allows that "human mate choice is much more than men just liking youth and beauty, and women liking status and wealth," as he told me by e-mail.

Yet evo psych remains hugely popular in the media and on college campuses, for obvious reasons. It addresses "these very sexy topics," says Hill. "It's all about sex and violence," and has what he calls "an obsession with Pleistocene just-so stories." And few people—few scientists—know about the empirical data and theoretical arguments that undercut it. "Most scientists are too busy to read studies outside their own narrow field," he says.

Far from ceding anything, evolutionary psychologists have moved the battle from science, where they are on shaky ground, to ideology, where bluster and name-calling can be quite successful. UNM's Miller, for instance, complains that critics "have convinced a substantial portion of the educated public that evolutionary psychology is a pernicious right-wing conspiracy," and complains that believing in evolutionary psychology is seen "as an indicator of conservatism, disagreeableness and selfishness." That, sadly, is how much too much of the debate has gone. "Critics have been told that they're just Marxists motivated by a hatred of evolutionary psychology," says Buller. "That's one reason I'm not following the field anymore: the way science is being conducted is more like a political campaign."

Where, then, does the fall of evolutionary psychology leave the idea of human nature? Behavioral ecology replaces it with "it depends"—that is, the core of human nature is variability and flexibility, the capacity to mold behavior to the social and physical demands of the environment. As Buller says, human variation is not noise in the system; it *is* the system. To be sure, traits such as symbolic language, culture, tool use, emotions, and emotional expression do indeed seem to be human universals. It's the behaviors that capture the public imagination—promiscuous men and monogamous women, stepchild-killing men, and the like—that turn out not to be. And for a final nail in the coffin, geneticists have discovered that human genes evolve much more quickly than anyone imagined when evolutionary psychology was invented, when everyone assumed that "modern" humans had DNA almost identical to that of people 50,000 years ago. Some genes seem to be only 10,000 years old, and some may be even younger.

That has caught the attention of even the most ardent proponents of evo psych, because when the environment is changing rapidly—as when agriculture was invented or city-states arose—is also when natural selection produces the most dramatic changes in a gene pool. Yet most of the field's leaders, admits UNM's Miller, "have not kept up with the last decade's astounding progress in human evolutionary genetics." The discovery of genes as young as agriculture and city-states, rather than as old as cavemen, means "we have to rethink to foundational assumptions" of evo psych, says Miller, starting with the claim that there are human universals and that they are the result of a Stone Age brain. Evolution indeed sculpted the human brain. But it worked in malleable plastic, not stone, bequeathing us flexible minds that can take stock of the world and adapt to it.

With Jeneen Interlandi.

Test-Your-Knowledge Form

We encourage you to photocopy and use this page as a tool to assess how the articles in *Annual Editions* expand on the information in your textbook. By reflecting on the articles you will gain enhanced text information. You can also access this useful form on a product's book support website at *http://www.mhhe.com/cls*.

NAME:

DATE:

TITLE AND NUMBER OF ARTICLE:

BRIEFLY STATE THE MAIN IDEA OF THIS ARTICLE:

LIST THREE IMPORTANT FACTS THAT THE AUTHOR USES TO SUPPORT THE MAIN IDEA:

WHAT INFORMATION OR IDEAS DISCUSSED IN THIS ARTICLE ARE ALSO DISCUSSED IN YOUR TEXTBOOK OR OTHER READINGS THAT YOU HAVE DONE? LIST THE TEXTBOOK CHAPTERS AND PAGE NUMBERS:

LIST ANY EXAMPLES OF BIAS OR FAULTY REASONING THAT YOU FOUND IN THE ARTICLE:

LIST ANY NEW TERMS/CONCEPTS THAT WERE DISCUSSED IN THE ARTICLE, AND WRITE A SHORT DEFINITION:

We Want Your Advice

ANNUAL EDITIONS revisions depend on two major opinion sources: one is our Advisory Board, listed in the front of this volume, which works with us in scanning the thousands of articles published in the public press each year; the other is you—the person actually using the book. Please help us and the users of the next edition by completing the prepaid article rating form on this page and returning it to us. Thank you for your help!

ANNUAL EDITIONS: Global Issues 10/11

ARTICLE RATING FORM

Here is an opportunity for you to have direct input into the next revision of this volume.
We would like you to rate each of the articles listed below, using the following scale:

1. **Excellent: should definitely be retained**
2. **Above average: should probably be retained**
3. **Below average: should probably be deleted**
4. **Poor: should definitely be deleted**

Your ratings will play a vital part in the next revision.
Please mail this prepaid form to us as soon as possible.
Thanks for your help!

RATING	ARTICLE
	1. Global Trends 2025: A Transformed World: Executive Summary
	2. Could Food Shortages Bring Down Civilization?
	3. Navigating the Energy Transition
	4. The Rise of the Rest
	5. Feminists and Fundamentalists
	6. Get Smart
	7. The Century Ahead
	8. Population & Sustainability
	9. Why Migration Matters
	10. Pandemic Pandemonium
	11. The Next Breadbasket?: How Africa Could Save the World—and Itself
	12. Climate Change
	13. The Other Climate Changers
	14. Water of Life in Peril
	15. Troubled Waters
	16. Acacia Avenue: How to Save Indonesia's Dwindling Rainforests
	17. Cry of the Wild
	18. Globalization and Its Contents
	19. It's a Flat World, after All
	20. Why the World Isn't Flat
	21. Can Extreme Poverty Be Eliminated?
	22. The Ideology of Development
	23. The Quiet Coup
	24. The Case against the West: America and Europe in the Asian Century

RATING	ARTICLE
	25. "Chimerica" Is Headed for a Divorce
	26. Promises and Poverty
	27. Not Your Father's Latin America
	28. It's Still the One
	29. Seven Myths about Alternative Energy
	30. The Revenge of Geography
	31. The Real War in Mexico: How Democracy Can Defeat the Drug Cartels
	32. The Long March to Be a Superpower
	33. What Russia Wants
	34. Lifting the Veil: Understanding the Roots of Islamic Militancy
	35. Tehran's Take: Understanding Iran's U.S. Policy
	36. Banning the Bomb: A New Approach
	37. Europe as a Global Player: A Parliamentary Perspective
	38. Geneva Conventions
	39. Is Bigger Better?
	40. A World Enslaved
	41. Chile Starts Early
	42. Humanity's Common Values: Seeking a Positive Future
	43. Life, Religion and Everything
	44. Don't Blame the Caveman: Why Do We Rape, Kill and Sleep Around?

ABOUT YOU

Name   Date

Are you a teacher? ❏ A student? ❏
Your school's name

Department

Address   City   State   Zip

School telephone #

YOUR COMMENTS ARE IMPORTANT TO US!

Please fill in the following information:
For which course did you use this book?

Did you use a text with this ANNUAL EDITION? ❏ yes ❏ no
What was the title of the text?

What are your general reactions to the Annual Editions concept?

Have you read any pertinent articles recently that you think should be included in the next edition? Explain.

Are there any articles that you feel should be replaced in the next edition? Why?

Are there any World Wide Websites that you feel should be included in the next edition? Please annotate.

May we contact you for editorial input? ❏ yes ❏ no
May we quote your comments? ❏ yes ❏ no